European Society

International Studies in Sociology and Social Anthropology

Series Editor

Alberto Martinelli (*University of Milan*)

Editorial Board

Vincenzo Cicchelli (*Ceped, Université Paris Descartes/IRD*)
Vittorio Cotesta (*Università degli Studi Roma Tre*)
Benjamin Gregg (*University of Texas at Austin*)
Leo Penta (*Katholische Hochschule für Sozialwesen Berlin*)
Elisa Reis (*Universidade Federal do Rio de Janeiro*)
Madalina Vartejanu-Joubert (*Institut National des Langues et Civilisations Orientales, Paris*)

VOLUME 133

The titles published in this series are listed at *brill.com/issa*

European Society

By

Alberto Martinelli
Alessandro Cavalli

BRILL

LEIDEN | BOSTON

Cover illustration: background: political map of Europe, Wikimedia Commons, https://commons.wikimedia.org/wiki/File:Europe_map.png; foreground: European flag by 3D Animation Production Company (QuinceCreative), via Pixabay, https://pixabay.com/images/id-2891828/.

The Library of Congress Cataloging-in-Publication Data is available online at http://catalog.loc.gov
LC record available at http://lccn.loc.gov/2020941045

Typeface for the Latin, Greek, and Cyrillic scripts: "Brill". See and download: brill.com/brill-typeface.

ISSN 0074-8684
ISBN 978-90-04-43515-5 (hardback)
ISBN 978-90-04-35177-6 (e-book)

Copyright 2020 by Koninklijke Brill NV, Leiden, The Netherlands.
Koninklijke Brill NV incorporates the imprints Brill, Brill Hes & De Graaf, Brill Nijhoff, Brill Rodopi, Brill Sense, Hotei Publishing, mentis Verlag, Verlag Ferdinand Schöningh and Wilhelm Fink Verlag.
All rights reserved. No part of this publication may be reproduced, translated, stored in a retrieval system, or transmitted in any form or by any means, electronic, mechanical, photocopying, recording or otherwise, without prior written permission from the publisher.
Authorization to photocopy items for internal or personal use is granted by Koninklijke Brill NV provided that the appropriate fees are paid directly to The Copyright Clearance Center, 222 Rosewood Drive, Suite 910, Danvers, MA 01923, USA. Fees are subject to change.

This book is printed on acid-free paper and produced in a sustainable manner.

Contents

List of Tables and Figures   ix

Introduction   1

1 The European Identity   15
   1 Preface: Identity and Identification   15
   2 One or Many European Identities?   19
   3 Rationalism and Individualism/Subjectivity   21
   4 University and Scientific Research, Market Capitalism and Industrial Enterprise, Nation State and Representative Democracy   25
   5 An Unusual and Controversial Identity   29
   6 Changes in the Content of European Identity and the Perception of their Meaning   31
   7 How European Citizens' Identification with Europe has Changed   34
   8 Identity Techniques   37
   9 The Renewed Relevance of the European Project   40

2 Nationalism   41
   1 Nationalism as the Ideology of the Modern State   41
   2 The Double Matrix of European Nationalism and Its Relationship with Democracy   44
   3 Main Alternatives to the Modernist Approach   49
   4 Nationalism in the First Decades of the 21st Century   52
   5 Nationalism and the Contradictions of European Integration   54
   6 Main Causes of the National/Populist Upsurge in Contemporary Europe   58

3 Languages   67
   1 The Distant Past   67
   2 The Recent Past   69
   3 Multilingualism and Plurilingualism: Europe's Inevitable Future   72
   4 The Linguistic Policies of the EU   75
   5 English as Lingua Franca   77
   6 Languages and the Culture Industry   80

4 Religion and Religions   87
1. A Look at the Past   87
2. Rationalization, Modernization, and Secularization   91
3. Europe and America – A Comparison   94
4. The Return of Religiousness in New Forms   97
5. Contemporary Fundamentalism   99
6. Migration and Religious Pluralism   102
7. Religious Pluralism and Cosmopolitanism   104

5 The Universities   106
1. Introduction   106
2. *Studium Generale* in the Middle Ages   106
3. The Universities on the Threshold of the Modern Age   108
4. The Birth of the Scientific Societies   109
5. University Models in the Age of the Nation States   111
6. From University for the Elites to University for the Masses   113
7. The Changing Relationship between Teaching and Research   117
8. Current Tendencies: Where Are European Universities Going?   119

6 The Cities   124
1. From the Ancient City to the Medieval City   124
2. State and Industry during the Formation of the Modern City   127
3. The Contemporary European City   129

7 Population and Family Structures   141
1. How Many Europeans Are There and How Many Will There Be?   141
2. Household Units and Family Structures   143
3. Declining Birth Rates   146
4. Couples, Families, and Reproductive Decisions   148
5. Fewer People Die and Live Longer   155
6. Social Policies for the Family   159

8 Internal and External Migrations   163
1. A Challenge (Also) to the Sense of Identity   163
2. The Europe as an Area of Emigration and of Immigration   164
3. Internal and External Migrations to the EU   166
4. The Reasons and Causes of Migration   169

	5	The Migration Emergency of 2015 and Subsequent Years 171
	6	Models and Ways of Integration 177
	7	Stages and Obstacles in the Admissions/Integration Process 178
	8	Xenophobic Movements and Welcoming Culture 180
	9	Necessity of and Obstacles to a European Migration Policy 182
9	**The Dimensions of Inequality** 185	
	1	Rich and Poor People in Rich and Poor Countries 185
	2	Dualism and Territorial Inequalities 189
	3	Beyond Economic Inequalities in the EU 192
	4	Conclusion 204
10	**The Political-Institutional Architecture of the European Union** 207	
	1	The EU as an Example of Bold Institutional Innovation 207
	2	The Main Phases of European Integration 213
	3	The Basic Institutions of the European Union 216
	4	EU Decision-making 227
11	**Parties, Elections, Pressure Groups** 233	
	1	Transnational Party Federations and European Parliament Party Groups 233
	2	National Parties, Europarties and EP Party Groups 238
	3	The 2019 Elections of the European Parliament: Voter Turnout 243
	4	The 2019 Elections of the European Parliament: Results and Recognized Party Groups 245
	5	EP Elections Results in the Largest EU Member Countries 250
	6	President Ursula von der Leyen's Programme Priorities and the Composition of the 2019–2024 Commission 256
	7	Interest Groups and Pressure Politics 262
12	**The European Welfare State** 267	
	1	Welfare and the European Social Model 267
	2	Welfare State Models 268
	3	Challenges Confronting the European Welfare State 271
	4	The European Social Model as Common Core of European Welfare Systems 273
	5	The Three Phases of European Welfare 275
	6	The Effects of the Global Financial Crisis and the Reaction of European Welfare Regimes 278

	7	The Critics from Opposite Sides 283
	8	The Reformers: The Social Investment Approach 285
	9	The Open Method of Coordination 287
	10	Conclusion 290

13 **The European Economy**   294
   1. Unity and Diversity of the European Economy   294
   2. European Economic Development since the Start of the Integration Process   299
   3. The 1970s Regime Change in the World Economy   303
   4. The EU in the Global Market   307
   5. The Choice of the Euro   310

14 **The Global Financial Crisis**   316
   1. An Interpretation of the Global Financial Crisis   316
   2. The Financial-Economic Crisis in the EU and the Predominance of the Intergovernmental Regime of Decision-making   318
   3. The Stages of the EU Exit Strategy   322
   4. The Crucial Role of the European Central Bank   327
   5. Fiscal Stringency and a Difficult Return to Economic Growth   329

Conclusion   335
   1. External Constraints, Internal Cleavages, and Reform of the European Union   335
   2. Amending the Treaties   338
   3. Reform Proposals under Existing Treaties   341
   4. Key Decisions for Moving Forward a Greater Union   346

Afterword   352
Bibliography   357
Index   370

Tables and Figures

Tables

3.1 Use of languages in the EU (%)   78
5.1 Long-term development of the enrolment rate at institutions of higher or tertiary learning   114
5.2 Enrolment rate at university-type institutions of tertiary learning (% of the age group at the beginning of the studies)   115
6.1 European metropoles in Global Cities Index   134
7.1 Mean household size in some countries   144
7.2 Fertility rates (2017)   147
7.3 Marriage and divorce rates (per 1,000 population) in some countries of the EU   149
7.4 Percentage of live births outside marriage of total births   152
7.5 Age at which young people leave their parents' home, start living with a partner, and become parents (2013)   153
7.6 Infant mortality rate in Western Europe (deaths in the first year of life per 1,000 births)   157
7.7 Infant mortality rate in Eastern Europe (deaths in the first year of life per 1,000 births)   158
8.1 People born abroad and percentage of the total population of some European countries as of 1/01/2018   167
8.2 Origin of the population born outside of the United Kingdom, Spain, and Italy   169
8.3 Annual percentage of asylum seekers in some European countries   172
8.4 Countries of origin of asylum seekers in 2016   175
8.5 First time asylum applicants in EU countries 2016–2019   176
9.1 European states by GDP (PPP) per capita   187
9.2 Gini coefficient of equivalized disposable income (2017) × 100   188
9.3 Wealth per capita and its distribution   190
9.4 Main indicators for public expenditure on education (excluding early-childhood educational development), 2012   198
9.5 Absolute mobility statistics by cohort and sex (24 EU member states)   202
9.6 EU Social Justice Index   205
11.1 Distribution of seats in the 2019–2024 European Parliament   246

11.2 Number of MEPs for each member state by year of joining the EU, population in 2014 and 2019, and sequence of legislatures   254

Figures

7.1 Average household size, 2008 and 2018 (average number of persons in private households)   145
7.2 Estimated average age of young people leaving the parental household, 2018   154
7.3 The demographic situation in the European Union (total period fertility rate)   156
8.1 Asylum applications (non-EU) in the EU-27 Member States, 2008–2019   173
9.1 Top 10 per cent national income share, 2016   186
12.1 Total general government expenditure on social protection, 2017 (% of GDP)   269
13.1 Growth rate of the world economy, 2012–2018   295
13.2 EU GDP in billion US dollars at current prices   295
13.3 GDP in Purchasing Power Standard (PPS) per inhabitant by NUTS 2 region (% of the EU-28 average, 2004 and 2014)   298
13.4 US vs. EU: GDP PPP per capita comparison 1980–2018   310
14.1 Real economic growth since Q3 2006   320

Introduction

We want first to explain the reasons that led us to write this book and, subsequently, to identify its audience. It is not only an 'academic' book that is written for professionals, European Studies experts. We do not intend just to add yet another title to the long list of specialized legal-economic-political-sociological literature of the last half-century that has examined all the possible implications of the European integration process. Our book is 'academic' in the sense that, in writing it, we always had in mind our students (or ex-students), whom we wanted to invite to explore European society in a way that would not make them feel to be 'foreigners'. Our intent is to contribute to the formation of what is usually called the 'Erasmus generation' and to invite more and more young people to be part of it, in the belief that there is no real 'European citizenship' without mutual knowledge, without recognition of similarities and differences, without the awareness of sharing a memory, but above all without a common destiny.

We started with a realistic, even bitter, observation. The realization of the project of European unification started more than 70 years ago. It has been marked by a number of significant successes and sometimes a few steps back, and today clearly seems to be at an impasse. In June 2016, a slight but definite majority of British voters decided that their country should leave the European Union (EU), and Brexit is now taking place. In 2017 Emanuel Macron won the French Presidential election against the nationalist anti-European Front National of Marine Le Pen. New member states formed the so-called Visegrád Group (Poland, Hungary, Czech Republic and Slovakia), challenging Commission's proposals like that of receiving a share of the refugees who had arrived in Greece and Italy. Early in 2018, 11 North European member countries expressed their unwillingness to support a set of proposals intended to strengthen the EU's ability to respond to a serious financial crisis together. In almost every country the forces opposing any step forward toward a closer union are receiving increasing popular support. In Italy, after the elections of March 2018, a centre-right government was formed that challenged all directives coming from Brussels (but it was followed in August 2019 by a centre-left pro-EU government).

For the first time, the EU is facing risks that threaten its very existence. The outcome of this crisis, in the short term, will depend on the decisions that political leaders are able to take under the pressure of this emergency; in the long run, however, it will depend on the support of public opinion and of European society as a whole as it evolves. This book is intended to strengthen this second aspect, to look at it in depth and with the long term in mind. To this end, it stresses the originality of the European project, sums up the roots and major steps of the integration process, analyses the complexity of its institutions, discusses current difficulties, and puts forward some proposals to overcome them and resume the journey toward an authentic political union.

The story started when Europe was still a wasteland caught in one of the most terrible wars in the history of humankind. In 1942, Eugenio Colorni, Ernesto Rossi, and Altiero Spinelli, imprisoned on the island of Ventotene by Italy's fascist regime, had written a 'manifesto', or rather, a 'draft manifesto', which they entitled: "For a Free and United Europe" (Spinelli & Rossi, 2016). It is a document that is still worth reading more than three-quarters of a century later, but here it suffices to recall a central passage:

> The dividing line between progressive and reactionary parties no longer follows the formal line of greater or lesser democracy, or of more or less socialism to be instituted; rather the division falls along the line, very new and substantial, that separates the party members into two groups. The first is made up of those who conceive the essential purpose and goal of struggle as the ancient one, that is, the conquest of national political power – and ... those who see the creation of a solid international State as the main purpose; they will direct popular forces toward this goal ...

It is significant that, once the power that aimed at unifying Europe as a German empire was defeated, the goal of European unity was first clearly formulated in a famous speech delivered in 1946 to the students of the University of Zurich by none other than Winston Churchill, the leader of a country that had emerged victorious, but exhausted, from the war (Churchill, 1946). It is worthwhile to reread a passage:

> Yet all the while there is a remedy which, if it were generally and spontaneously adopted by the great majority of people in many lands, would as by a miracle transform the whole scene and would in a few years make all Europe, or the greater part of it, as free and happy as Switzerland is today. What is this sovereign remedy? It is to recreate the European fabric, or as much of it as we can, and to provide it with a structure under which it can dwell in peace, safety and freedom. We must build a kind of United States of Europe.

At the beginning, therefore, there was the war or, more precisely, the desire to put a definitive end to a history of intra-European wars that had lasted for centuries, if not millennia. Yet the two world wars have taken on a new meaning:

they are no longer just world wars, in the sense of having involved all great global powers in European affairs; they are also, from the point of view of a future European citizenship, seen as European civil wars.

But the times were evidently not yet ripe for this. The war and its immediate aftermath were the first missed opportunity for the great leap toward a united Europe. The reconstruction of the nation states was inevitable in order to re-establish a viable political order. Europe, split in two by the Iron Curtain along which two great extra-European powers confronted each other in the Cold War, faced the urgent task of reconstruction and somehow had to restore a political order that was capable of leaving behind the conflicts that had characterized the first half of the century and that had required the mobilization of the rest of the world to extinguish the blaze. At least in the western part, this new order had to be founded on nation states that were all finally democratic, but it also had to aim for a more distant but already clearly outlined purpose.

A few years after national sovereignty had been restored to Western Germany, the dilemma arose of whether or not to allow the reconstruction of the German coal and steel industry, which was still decisive for the military strategies of the time. It was decided to take control of these strategic resources away from the individual countries and entrust it to an institution of supranational authority. The foundation of the European Coal and Steel Community (ECSC) in April 1951 was the true beginning of the institutional journey of European integration. Even before the Treaty of Paris concerning the iron and steel industry came into force, in 1952 the governments signed a second treaty to establish the European Defence Community (EDC or CED), practically a European army, and thus a political community. The failure in 1954 of the law establishing the EDC to gain approval by the French parliament – the proposal had not even been submitted to the Italian Parliament for approval yet – marked the end of the attempt to unify Europe based on the needs of foreign and military policy, during the climate of the Cold War and the division of the world into two blocs and the oppressive memory of the great bloodbath of the Second World War.

A few years later, in 1957, an attempt was also made to regulate nuclear energy – a strategic resource for both war and peace – across Europe (by establishing Euratom). However, this did not prevent individual countries from proceeding to develop nuclear energy on their own, above all as an energy source. More important than Euratom, the European Economic Community (EEC) was founded, also in 1957, laying the foundation for the gradual construction of a common market through the removal of customs barriers between member countries (six at the time: France, Germany, Italy, Belgium, the Netherlands, and Luxembourg), the creation of an external common customs tariff, and the establishment of a common policy to subsidize agriculture. Compared to the

ECSC, the EEC has a much more intergovernmental and much less supranational structure. This also explains why in the next 20 years no new institutional breakthroughs were made in the integration process, except for the community's enlargement by admitting new member states: first the United Kingdom (UK), Ireland and Denmark, then Greece, Spain and Portugal – the last three being countries that had recently emerged from authoritarian, antidemocratic regimes.

In 1979, the European Parliament was elected for the first time by universal suffrage. The significance of this step is ambiguous: on the one hand, a popular vote certainly increases a parliament's democratic legitimacy, yet on the other hand, electing a parliament without the power to produce an actual government and decide fiscal policy does not exactly serve democracy well. The initiative to advance this effort was resumed in the mid-1980s with the 1986 Single European Act in preparation for a treaty on the free movement of persons (the Schengen Agreement) and the establishment of a monetary union with the signing of the Maastricht Treaty in 1992. Meanwhile the Berlin Wall had fallen and Germany had enlarged its borders. In order to tie the increased German power to Europe, it was decided to proceed with the establishment of a single currency (the euro) which went formally into circulation in 1999 and as a real currency in 2002, and which, as several politicians thought at the time, would pave the way toward a political union. Some member countries (with the UK in the lead, followed by Sweden and Denmark) decided not to adopt the new currency. Thus began the differentiation process within the Union between countries that have proceeded at variable speeds. Some have chosen 'enhanced cooperation', while others prefer to wait. A convention made up of government representatives, the Commission, the European Parliament and national parliaments, drafted a Constitutional Treaty between 2001 and 2003 which was signed in Rome and which required parliamentary ratification in some countries and the ratification by popular referendum in others. In 2005 the referendums held in France and the Netherlands rejected the treaty, and in the UK it did not even take place after these rejections. To overcome the crisis produced by the failure of the Constitutional Treaty, in 2007 the Treaty of Lisbon was signed, which introduced some not very substantial changes in the institutional framework of the EU. All this happened just before the outbreak in 2008 of the most serious financial and then also economic and social crisis to hit the West since 1933 (which, let us not forget, had opened the door to National Socialism). Since then, the history of integration in the EU has been one of attempts to curb the crisis and temper its impact. Several proposals have been made to strengthen the EU's ability to face what have been called the 'asymmetrical effects' of financial disturbances on member states.

The debates over the establishment of a banking union were intended to move in this direction.

With this very quick summary, we arrive at today. As we have seen, the history of the EU has been a story of accelerations and slowdowns, of successes but also of heavy defeats. It may not be an idle undertaking to imagine a different scenario and ask ourselves where we would be today if, for example, the European army and the political union had been established in 1954, or – to jump ahead half a century – if the Constitutional Treaty had been approved in 2005. Perhaps we would not find ourselves at the current dead end. During that period, two approaches and two trends were at odds with one another: on the one hand we have an intergovernmental logic that aims to strengthen collaboration between countries which, however, maintain their full or almost full sovereignty; on the other there is the community or federal method, which aims at the transfer, if only gradual, of powers from the governments and the parliaments of the nation states to European institutions, with the ultimate goal of creating a European federal union.

In fact, however, a number of reform projects were supported or opposed by economic and political elites without the effective participation of the peoples and with little consideration of public opinion. On the few occasions (the various referendums that have been held: in Norway, Ireland, Denmark, Spain, France, and the Netherlands) where citizens have been called upon to express their consent to or disagreement with their country's EU membership or the ratification of some treaty, the result was often negative, and participation was rather modest. Voter turnout in elections for the European Parliament is scarce and has declined over time from 62 per cent in 1979 to 42.5 per cent in 2014 (but increasing again in 2019 to 50.9 per cent). The periodic surveys conducted by the EU Statistical Office, the Eurobarometer data, have indicated for some years a constant erosion of the favourable opinion of and support for the EU institutions. Eurobarometer surveys after 2017 show a slight reversal of this trend; some segments of public opinion seem to perceive a threat to the health of the Union and have decided to oppose the dwindling support.

The initial momentum was fuelled by the memory of the war. Memories that are based on direct experience, or on the stories of parents and grandparents who experienced these events as protagonists or spectators, are inevitably destined to fade. Today, the younger generations in most of Europe (but certainly not those living in the Balkans or in Ukraine) are fortunately growing up infinitely removed from the direct experience of war. Europe has never lived through such a long period of peace in its history. Today, only those aged over 80 can tell us what the war meant, because they have seen it with their own eyes.

In the consciousness of its citizens, Europe has gradually lost its original meaning of guarantor of peace, essentially for two reasons. First, it has become unthinkable that war may break out again among the states that are now members of the Union. However serious the conflicts of interest may be between Greece and Germany, or between the creditor states of the North and the debtor states of the South, it is frankly beyond any imagination that they might be resolved through arms. Secondly, external threats, albeit serious (post-Soviet Russia pushing toward its neighbours in the west and the penetration of Islamic extremism on the eastern and southern borders), are not currently felt with the same urgency that characterized the Cold War in the era of Stalin.

However, the unification process was not accomplished or accompanied by great enthusiasm, by the mobilization of collective feelings or with perfect momentum. If there was a sense of mobilization concerning European unification, it was directed against rather than in favour of it. There were no crowds to fill the squares, no mass rallies to march through the streets of our cities to the cry of "Europe, Europe!" Rather, we have seen groups of farmers and rows of tractors heading for the places of power, sometimes going as far as Brussels to protest against the Community's agricultural policies. European federalists have always been an active minority, and they have never been involved in mass participation.

In a century that has seen masses forcefully enter the scene (not only democracies, but above all totalitarian regimes have all been marked by the presence of mass movements), European unification happened as the result of a process promoted and conducted by elite groups with basically rational motivations and strategies, without these elites having felt the need to call for the participation and appeal to the feelings of the masses.

The European ideal, therefore, is a 'cold' one which appeals to reason rather than emotions, to the point that among those who express scepticism toward its feasibility there are some who speak of a utopia to suggest that it is difficult to achieve and that this goal cannot be attained by involving and mobilizing the deep feelings of the peoples of Europe.

Some believe that if European unity is really to be achieved, a process of nation-building must be put in motion, of building a European nation, not unlike the one European nations underwent in the 19th and other parts of the world in the 20th century. The concept of nation and institutional structure in which it has been realized (the nation state) is certainly a product of European culture, a product that in 20th-century Europe could be exported to almost all continents, even where the idea of nation and nation state had no roots in native cultural traditions. The extraordinary success of the concept of nation is certainly connected to the need for collective identification in an age when political regimes, for the most part with weaker roots in religious beliefs, felt the need for finding consensus in and secular legitimization by the masses. Let us not forget that nation states, like religious faiths, have often asked their citizens to make the greatest conceivable sacrifice – that of giving one's life – and therefore had to develop the most profound sense of identification, loyalty, and even devotion to the collective.

If this extraordinary product of European culture, in all the variations that have historically emerged over the last two centuries, has been so successful, why should it not become the foundation on which to build the edifice of the EU? Is it possible, one wonders, to achieve the unification of a plurality of states – especially if this is designed to lead to a strong and stable union with a federal structure – without giving rise to an equally strong European identity? One wonders if there exists a common foundation beyond the national variants and tradition, and if yes, what it is; if there is a common denominator of European culture on which to build the collective identity of Europe and to differentiate it from other large continental cultures and civilizations. A not insignificant corollary of this debate is the definition of the geographical boundaries of the area occupied by European culture both in the West and in the East. The very fact that the idea of Europe is somehow connected with the idea of the West poses a series of questions whose answers are not a foregone conclusion with regard to the definition of a distinct European identity. How to think about relations with those parts of the West that are not Europe? And above all, where does Europe end in the east? Do Russia and Turkey belong to Europe or not?

If in the future the EU were to consolidate and could wield instruments of a common foreign and military policy toward the rest of the world – which is not about to happen at this point – it might be necessary to accept the challenge of Europe as a new nation. History as taught at school would then need to be rewritten from a European point of view, and it would be necessary to unify the symbols of identity (from the hymns to the flags) so as to strengthen the sense of loyalty toward the new political community and consolidate the legitimacy of its institutions.

However, we may ask ourselves whether Europe will really have to follow the same path of the 'nationalization of the masses' that the nation states took in the 19th and 20th centuries. Do we really need something that looks like the idea of a European nation and some form of European nationalism to give a collective soul to a union that would otherwise only seem a stage for the pursuit of economic interests, often by way of conflict? Perhaps situations may arise which would kindle the need to refer to unity, traditions, and common myths. There are those who fear a clash of civilizations, who feel the risk of colonization by Islam or by China. If it becomes a real state, Europe will not be able to escape from the iron laws of the *raison d'état*, in the sense that it cannot help but worry about strengthening the loyalty of its citizens. And yet there are reasons to believe that European nationalism will be 'weak' even if Europe is 'strong'.

Europe is the realm of differences. We can endlessly discuss whether national cultures are merely variants of a common European culture (where the common traits tend to prevail over the specific traits of each nation), or whether it is its specific characteristics, its distinctive traits, that dominate in each national culture. Differences in fact do exist and are visible even to the most superficial observer; just as, on the other hand, common values are evident. It can also be argued that the differences within each individual nation are very pronounced and sometimes appear even greater than the differences between different nations. However, ever since the existence of nation states, European societies have been subjected to a massive process of cultural nationalization that has created unprecedented homogeneity, suppressing minor nationalities and overshadowing regional cultures rooted in ancient traditions.

First state schools, then radio and television have, for example, strongly homogenized spoken languages, reducing the importance of regional languages/dialects and thus facilitating communication between all inhabitants of the various regions of a country – communication that was once restricted to the educated elites. Even in countries where the process of forming a nation state has been delayed, such as Italy or Germany, while more than a century and a half of nationalization policies may not have succeeded in cancelling regional differences, but they have nevertheless left a profound mark. There are contrasting interpretations of the relationship between the nation and the state: some think that it was the nation state that produced, in a certain sense, the nations, while others believe that nations preceded states. The fact is that nations exist, and, however weakened the sense of national belonging may be in the face of the opposing forces of localism and globalization, the sense of national belonging tends to prevail almost everywhere. The ongoing sovereignty crisis of the nation state will certainly have the effect of further increasing cultural heterogeneity within individual nations, but some effects of the process of nationalization (especially as regards the spread of the national language to a country's entire population) are for the most part irreversible and destined to persist.

The resulting cultural differences are a great wealth that Europe possesses, a heritage that the process of unification will fortunately not be able to erase. European unification, if it is ever completed, will not eliminate the differences that history has produced. The United States of America (USA) can undoubtedly serve as a model for Europe in terms of its constitution, but the historical narrative from which American society and culture have emerged has gone in the opposite direction.

At this point, a reflection on the example of America is very illuminating. The society of the USA (and in some ways also Canadian or Australian society) is the result of one of the most extraordinary social experiments human history has witnessed. There is no continent that has not contributed to making up the population of North America. What we normally call Americans are nothing but a mixture of various migratory waves from every corner of Europe, Africa, Asia, and Latin America, not to forget the descendants of the indigenous people exterminated by colonization – a case certainly not unique, but no less terrible, of de facto genocide. The integration of such heterogeneous populations has not been easy. The obstacles to integration have not even been removed to this day: the Afro-American and the Hispano-American populations have shown subjective and objective resistance to integration. This integration was successful only for elite groups, while the majority of these minorities are still marginalized. The melting pot where races and nationalities blend together has not produced a homogeneous amalgam; it is rather a salad bowl in which all the 'ingredients' coexist but are still distinct from one another. On the whole, it cannot be said that the experiment to populate an entire continent with the 'surplus' of all the others has failed. This experiment was based on a deep conviction, if only implicit, of the substantial plasticity of human beings, on the belief in the possibility of transforming anyone, whatever his or her origin, into an 'American'. So, if not the first generation, the second unlearned the language of the parents, left behind a large part of its cultural heritage, adopted a new language, new customs and traditions, new values and attitudes, learned to love a new homeland, to greet a new flag, to feel part of a different narrative that of the New World. We can say that Americans are not born but *become*, even if this is less and less true for the current generations, where the proportion of new immigrants has greatly declined.

The American case certainly represents a model of integration. In fact, in spite of its frequent inner conflicts and tensions, there is no other place on earth where people of different racial and ethnic origins coexist relatively peacefully – although occasionally with bitter and violent conflicts – and work together to make their nation 'successful'. There is no doubt that the USA has evolved into a nation, if by nation we mean a collective unity with a sufficient degree of internal cohesion and self-awareness. Even though in the USA there are today those who speak of the decline of the traditional civic virtues that de Tocqueville had called the foundation of democracy in the 19th century, the sense of belonging to a political community remains firmly established (Martinelli, 2007).

However, the American model of the integration of differences is not applicable to Europe. Americans have become the way they are because they left their old homelands behind; at their origin there was therefore a rupture, an abandonment, voluntary or forced, a turning point, one of those moments of crisis that allow us to question our old collective identities and acquire new ones. Europe's problem is that it must achieve integration by keeping all the differences without having to go into the melting pot. The model is that of Switzerland rather than that of the USA. Integration in Europe cannot mean the cancellation of cultural differences, or even just their attenuation.

The task is by no means easy. Just think of the great expenditure of energy and resources needed to make institutions work in which the number of official languages is almost equal to that of the member countries. The task at hand is this: Europe must demonstrate to the world that it is possible to unify populations that have cultures that are, and are destined to remain, different; what is more, that coexistence and collaboration is possible among populations that fought each other fiercely until very recently. The European model of integration must therefore rest on the basic principle of recognition of diversity and otherness and not on their denial. It is a very broad principle that goes well beyond the political integration of large territorial areas and heterogeneous populations; Jürgen Habermas calls it the *Einbeziehung des Anderen* (the inclusion of the other). The guiding value is the recognition of otherness.

If Europe succeeds in generating unity from diversity without erasing diversity (the European model of integration), its example will contain a message of universal significance that can contribute to global understanding and, hopefully, global governance. That territorially differentiated cultures are destined to continue and reproduce themselves in tomorrow's Europe is perhaps the greatest antidote to the risk of 'European nationalism'. The Europe of the future (if it succeeds in becoming united) will be able to develop a sort of federal pride, the pride of having overcome an idea that has always been ingrained in humankind: that the different is a potential adversary and enemy. If what is different is no longer perceived as a threat because an order has been established in which the different has its place, this will mean that humankind will have taken a huge step in its long and tortuous journey toward unity, toward emancipating itself from the violent parts of its nature.

That this is a universal message is not only due to the fact that the ongoing globalization processes entail the problem of coexistence and collaboration among populations of different cultures for everyone on the planet, but also because the number of migrations of individuals and groups is probably destined to grow exponentially. Unlike in the past, the experience of migration will no longer lead to a sharp break with one's past and one's own traditions, which is necessary if the imperative is to integrate as quickly as possible into a new culture so that one's own children are no longer distinguished from the children of those who belong to previous waves of immigrants. Europe will be a multinational society, that is to say a society where integration does not mean that migrants have to abandon their own culture in order to adopt the indigenous culture, but where different cultures are able to live side by side, mutually influencing each other, changing over time, without the sense of threat caused by the presence of the other. The application of the principle of recognition of otherness definitely has its limits; for example, it is not possible to recognize differences when they involve the violation of the law and the fundamental rights of the individual, as in the case of practices that are harmful to other persons' physical integrity, such as infibulation (female circumcision). The scope of recognizable differences as 'legitimate' remains, however, broad enough to allow for respect for the principle of recognizing otherness.

This book was written for the audience of a European society in the making. It was conceived especially for today's young people in training who are beginning to look beyond the boundaries of their own 'back yard', be it their own municipality, province, region, or nation state. It is necessary to increase mutual knowledge, to break down prejudices toward their neighbours that are transmitted from generation to generation, to attenuate the contrast between 'us' and 'them', to widen the boundaries of 'us' so that when you arrive in Paris or Berlin, in London or Madrid, in Lisbon or in Warsaw, you do not feel completely 'abroad'. The world in which the younger generations will have to live will always be more cosmopolitan, and they must equip themselves to make this world a familiar place.

When different cultures meet, the outcomes can be manifold: one can absorb the other or others and eliminate them (this happened to a large extent in the USA, but also, albeit in different ways, in France), or the culture that feels threatened with extinction can implement survival strategies that crystallize some or all of its fundamental traits, or the contact can produce reciprocal effects, where the different traditions intertwine and change without disappearing in the process. What is important is not to cling to traditions as to sacred objects whose loss is perceived as a threat of extinction of one's collective identity, but rather to let traditions compete with other cultures with which they are in contact, from which they can emerge strengthened or weakened, intact or modified. The latter is the form of integration that we have called the 'European model'. Do not congeal the differences as if they were immutable, coming from eternity and destined to remain forever, but make them interact on the basis of a relationship of mutual recognition.

In order for this to happen, it is necessary to create a European multinational public space, a space for the aggregation of interests and the formation of opinion that crosses national boundaries. Currently, the 'public space' (a concept that is close to that of civil society) still remains largely limited to the national dimension. The political arena in which the democratic game takes place is that of the nation states. Public attention – if we can call it attention – is still to a large extent focused on national governments and parliaments. The European Parliament is still too distant and weak; the European parties still form only tenuous organizational ties between different and highly autonomous political bodies. Confidence in the parties, and in the state and its institutions, has declined dramatically in all European countries (and this undoubtedly constitutes a danger to democracy), but the organization of the political struggle is still in fact concentrated around the power of nation states. Political communication takes place almost exclusively in the national sphere. The media operate in a national dimension. It is true that we can easily access the satellite networks of television communication and that radio networks have no borders, that there are transnational programs like ARTE, the German-French TV channel, and it is also true that there are people who habitually listen to the BBC, France 24, Deutsche Welle or teleSUR newscasts even if they do not live (respectively) in the UK, France, Germany, or Latin America. But these are small, if professionally qualified, minorities. Capital and goods (and in part ideas too) are now circulating (almost) freely across Europe, but language barriers are still a serious obstacle to the formation of a European public sphere.

The formation of a single European civil society is certainly not at the year zero. However, it is still only embryonic. For example, within the institutions of the Union in Brussels, a rather sizable bureaucratic class has formed which undoubtedly has a vested interest in ensuring that the integration process is expanded, deepened, and consolidated. Public opinion accuses Brussels of having a bloated bureaucracy, but the European Commission has only about 33,000 employees, about 17.000 are employed by the Parliament, the Council and the Court of Justice, which taken together makes half the size of those working at the local government of a regional capital like Berlin. Moreover, numerous lobby organizations have been created around this bureaucracy, representing interests that are not always exclusively national. European associations of various types, as well as supranational professional communities, have been spreading for quite some time. And, most importantly, let us not forget the scientific communities for which national boundaries are no longer a constraint on the mobility of people, projects, and research results.

However, the fact that the knowledge of at least one foreign language has become widespread encourages not only trade and communication, but also people gathering together. Collective movements (for example, ecological and consumer protection movements, youth movements) sometimes take on European perspectives and dimensions, as they are organized in the form of networks that are not exclusively confined to national territories. Yet the difficulties of organizing on a supranational scale are still great. This is widely demonstrated by workers' unions that have rarely managed to coordinate demands even within the same multinational companies.

But despite all this, slowly a European civil society, a European public space, is forming. The 3 million young people who have participated in the Erasmus programme and who already occupy senior positions in their respective fields, and the 12 million Europeans living in a country other than the one in which they were born, are the avant-garde of European civil society. If it is not swept away by some ruinous crisis (unfortunately, this possibility is never excluded), the process of building a European civil society will go hand in hand with the institutional process that sees governments as main protagonists, and the two processes will together eventually achieve what we have called the 'European model of integration'.

We had to make choices that took into account possible users as well as our fields of competence. We have chosen to focus on a number of topics that, for different reasons, nevertheless seemed central to us. The chapters start with a look at European identity and nationalism, as briefly mentioned in this introduction; we then move on to discuss languages, religious traditions, universities, and cities – issues that require us to go back in time: they cannot be addressed without examining history, because the present is opaque without the past. Subsequent topics also involve references to the past but must mainly focus on current developments: demographic trends, migrations, social and territorial inequalities, political and institutional arrangements, economic processes, the reform of the welfare state, and the management of the euro crisis. These problems are still not resolved, and their future outcome is particularly uncertain.

It goes without saying that we could have added several other chapters on different issues and problems, especially those that cannot be addressed without adopting a European perspective and requiring institutions that take responsibility at European level. Take, for instance, energy, environmental protection, territorial imbalances between North and South, international relations, or security. Being exhaustive was clearly not our intention (or within our abilities). However, in the Conclusion which focuses on the reform of the Union, we did not want to avoid the responsibility, of making reasonable and realistic proposals on what we consider to be necessary actions to take and matters of urgency to deal with in the short- and medium term – in the belief that if something is not done, and soon, Europe will risk falling into a crisis from which it would be difficult, if not impossible, to recover.

Alberto Martinelli has written Chapters 1,2,10,11,12,13 and 14. Alessandro Cavalli has written Chapters 3,4,5,6,7,8 and 9. We have jointly written the Introduction, Conclusion and Afterword.

CHAPTER 1

The European Identity

1   Preface: Identity and Identification

Does a supranational economic and political entity such as the European Union possess a recognizable identity? And if this identity indeed does exist, what are its distinctive features? Has it changed over time? How does it differentiate itself from the national identities of European citizens? These complex and controversial questions are not only scientifically interesting, but also politically relevant, because today, sixty-three years after the signing of the Treaty of Rome, the European Union finds itself for the first time facing risks that threaten its own existence. There is a strong need for Europeans to recognize themselves within a set of shared values, institutions, and common living standards that legitimize common institutions.

First of all, let's clarify the difference between collective identity and identification. The concept of identification defines a set of individual attitudes of a cognitive, emotional and evaluative nature – having to do with belonging to a community, the sharing of a common destiny and of consequent behaviours of loyalty, trust and solidarity. On the contrary, the concept of identity refers to an aggregating and motivating nucleus of values, symbols and meanings that translate into norms of coexistence, political and social institutions as well as life practices (Smith 1991). Identification consists of subjective dispositions and people's behaviours; collective identity is a social fact connected to institutional realities. The identity of a group of people is the result of a genetic process of shared values that become symbolic-cultural factors of aggregation (*mitopoiesis*).

The two concepts are linked in the way that the contents of identity are at the basis of the process of identification. They delineate the borders between those who belong and those who do not belong to the community, influencing others' perception, while the way and degree in which the members of a community recognize themselves as such modifies the content itself. Another way to define the two concepts is to distinguish between the subjects (who identifies with whom) and the objects or content of the identification (values, meanings, symbols, norms, institutions) that permit us to define who we are. Most empirical research on the European collective identity is of the first type and examines whether, to what extent and for what reasons European citizens identify themselves with the European Union as a community or with Europeans in general. But there are also contributions that, like this one, examine the substance of European collective identity, deducing it from philosophical arguments (the legacy of the Enlightenment), historical and sociological studies (on modernization), normative principles of constitutions, but also content analysis of the speeches of political and intellectual leaders, the products of popular culture and of traditional and digital mass media. In this chapter we will first concentrate on the concept of identity as we have defined it, that is, on the nucleus of common values and institutions, and we will then discuss how European identity and citizens identification with the EU have changed over time (also in relation to national identities) and what are the mechanisms that may favour its taking root in the current situation.

The study of the European identity has become one of the most widespread fields of research, since the Fifth Framework Program for Research and Technological Development in the EU, promoting a growing body of studies on vastly differing topics, from cultural heritage to cultural conflict and linguistic diversity, from national museums and artistic festivals to the European public sphere, from the relationship between media and citizenship to the interaction between national identity and European identity. This research has produced a multiplicity of publications, policy reviews, conferences and has provoked interesting debates of theoretical and methodological nature in the context of different disciplines (sociology, political science, social psychology, contemporary history, political philosophy, comparative law), improving our knowledge of the phenomenon but leaving a series of questions unresolved.

The question of the European identity is scientifically interesting and controversial, it raises three fundamental objections: first of all, it is more appropriate to speak of European identities in the plural, since through the centuries Europe has been an open and multiform world with several cultural identities, which has constantly put into question its common beliefs and unifying ties. Second, one cannot really speak of a European identity, because, also as a result of this diversity, only some of the constituent elements of a people's collective identity are present: neither a European *demos* nor a unique historical memory exists (it is not possible to transform the mythical and celebratory epic into an experience of shared events, the military victories of one are the defeats of another, Austerlitz is celebrated in Paris, Trafalgar is celebrated in London), nor a common language transfigured in value (as in the case of Greek *koinè*), nor a network of relationships of kinship, lineage and race (mixed marriages are still a minority, even though growing, and only a small percentage of European families are related across national borders). Third, it is difficult, or even impossible, to identify a European specificity because European culture has become an integral part of the culture of modernity, progressively permeating the whole world and producing, although in a multiplicity of different forms, a global modern condition.

Concerning the first objection, one can remark that the variety of cultural codes and the plurality of paths towards and through the modernity of European peoples does not prevent recognition of the existence of a core of specific cultural values and attitudes (distinctly European from a distant past) that are crystallized into a specific normative setting with the advent of modernity, producing profound structural transformations and bold institutional innovations. This recognition of distinctive traits and common roots does not, however, mean that they constitute an almost unchanging primeval nucleus, and that the development of European culture has been a homogeneous and continuous process, without fractures and critical junctions.

With regard to the second objection, it must be remembered that citizens of member countries of the European Union share a common, not only divisive, historical memory– in the sense of belonging to the same civilization, characterized by the same historical processes and events – even if it is true that the epic transformation of most of these is not possible. The absence of a single common language means the absence of a symbolic element of great aggregate value, but it does not prevent the formation of a European cultural *koinè* and does not constitute an insurmountable obstacle to the interplay of daily interaction and communication between the inhabitants of various European states. The conscious renunciation of linguistic homogeneity is in fact justified as the price to pay if we want to affirm cultural diversity and the conservation of the extraordinary mosaic of languages and culture of the European continent as European Union's founding values. Comparative social-historical research shows that the collective identity of a people can be very strong even in the absence of ethnic-cultural homogeneity historically acquired, as in the case of the United States of America. What does not exist, and cannot exist, is a centralized European nation state; but what can exist is a European federation of different peoples and states.

Concerning the third objection, I note that recognizing that a set of modern institutions of European origin have been diffused across the globe and modernity has become a common global condition (Wittrock, 2000) does not imply at all that every process of modernization must inevitably proceed towards a unique cognitive structure (scientific rationalism, instrumental pragmatism, secularism) and identical institutional structures (popular government, bureaucratic administration, market-driven industrial economy). What we really see is the development of multiple modernities (or varieties of modernity), i.e. changing cultural and institutional forms that are influenced by the variety of specific contexts in which the modern project is constantly interpreted, reinterpreted and transformed (Eisenstadt, 2001), also in response to challenges, threats and opportunities deriving from the distinctive features of Western modernity (Martinelli 2005).

European identity is not only a scientifically interesting question, but also a politically important issue. The European Union is a limited and incomplete project because Europe's economic integration has not been accompanied by a genuine supranational political union and a greater cultural integration. The deficit of democratic representation and integration is due to the fact that the community process is based only on economic rationality and not on a feeling of common belonging. It is therefore necessary to complement the policy of interests with a policy of identity, in the current situation in which the Union faces difficult challenges that can undermine the future.

In this chapter we will argue the following theses:

a) The diverse identities of the European peoples coexist with a common European identity that is the result of a long historical legacy of common cultural roots (Greek philosophy, Roman law, Jewish and Christian religious traditions, Renaissance civilization) and consists of a nucleus of specific cultural attitudes organized around the dialectical relationship between rationality and individualism/subjectivity. These common roots are long-lasting European features but crystallized in the specific historical context of modernity and the culture of the Enlightenment, producing fundamental institutional innovations: market economy and industrial capitalism, representative liberal democracy, nation-states, research universities. In this perspective, the European Union's project is still a modern project. Far from being completed, it is an expression of radical modernity, which imagines modernity as a future-oriented, better than the present and the past (Habermas 1985). The development of European identity and culture has not been a homogeneous and continuous process, without fractures and critical junctures, but a constantly changing process that has evolved into heterogeneous manifestations in the various national and local contexts, in a dialectical relationship with the different national identities.

b) A common European identity, while referring to a shared memory, is not the passive preservation of past ideals, but is the active implementation of an open, dynamic project, powered daily by "spontaneous" integration processes "from below" even more than by the deliberate action of the institutions from above. The European project came from the decision to put an end to European civil wars and the perception of common economic interests, but to achieve it requires the strengthening of values, cultural attitudes, specific institutions: political and economic freedom, constitutional democracy, rule of law, scientific rationality, and a welfare state.

c) The core values and institutions of identity have persisted over time, but both the significance attributed to them in the process of political integration by the countries joining the Union at different times and the intensity of identification of European citizens have changed.

d) The European project is an ambitious project because it proposes to build unity through diversity, confuting solid beliefs that what is different is intrinsically hostile and that identity can only be built on the contrast between "us" and "them". European identity is not exclusive, it may seem weaker than traditional national identities, but is certainly more suited to the characteristics of democratic governance in a globalized world: mutual understanding and respect, multilateral cooperation and peaceful international relations.

e) The difficulties encountered by the development of a European identity are witnessed by the impetuous rise of nationalism, fuelled by the intertwining of the economic financial crisis, the refugee emergency and terrorism and are due to two contradictions in the integration process: the project of building a supranational union using national states as constituent elements with the illusion of ending connected nationalisms, and the transfer of increasing portions of national sovereignty from the state to the supranational level without a corresponding transfer of commitment and loyalty from the citizens of different member countries to the institutions of an evolving supranational community.

f) The widespread insecurity arising from the entanglement of crises makes it all the more necessary to reaffirm the reasons for cooperation between the peoples and states of Europe and to consolidate the values and institutions of a European identity as a complement to the multiple identities of European citizens. To this end, the multifaceted experiences of interdependence and coexistence must be accompanied by reforms that improve the quality of European democracy and by effective identity techniques.

2   One or Many European Identities?

Apparently, there is *no* European identity, but rather *many* different European identities. Throughout the course of the millenary history of European peoples, many different collective identities developed which were fuelled and codified in the process of nation-building, interacting with a wide range of other identities: sub-national, transnational, ethnic, religious and class. The multiplicity of cultures which characterized European history has been the source of deep cleavages, violent conflicts, idiosyncratic controversies, and even many errors and crimes, but it has also proved to be highly capable of assimilation and integration, as well as of creating extraordinary opportunities of scientific and technical development, economic growth and social and cultural innovation. The values and attitudes of European culture have nourished and have been fed by a relatively open and autonomous social structure characterized by a multiplicity of elites, classes, ethnic, religious and political entities with defined boundaries and constant redefinition, frequent interactions between centres and peripheries, a high degree of social mobility, a legal system relatively independent from politics and religion as well as highly autonomous cities.

European civilization has been characterized by the intersection and intertwining of different cultural attitudes and institutional arrangements, but also by a strong orientation towards common goals and beliefs, including the fundamental autonomy and responsibility of the individual and the tension between worldly and transcendent order (Eisenstadt, 1987). Europe has traditionally been an open and multiple world, a kind of great social laboratory where unity and multiplicity have interacted in a continuous tension. As Johannes Weiss states, "the culture of Europe ... cannot be regarded as a unified culture, as homogeneous, but at best as a kind of 'stabilized tension' between deep, indeed antinomian contrasts" (translated from Mongardini 2001:17).

Recognizing this European peculiarity allows us to avoid two opposing and equally unsatisfactory positions: on the one hand, the precise definition of a list of exclusively European consolidated cultural elements that would distinguish us from all other peoples; on the other hand, the denial of any common cultural trait and the connotation of a European identity only in negative terms, as a permanent conflict and a confused crossroads of ethnic, local and national identities.

The attempt to identify what European identity is today can only take place through the critical reappraisal of the great historical processes which resulted in the formation of modern Europe; through the analysis of the dialectics between change and persistence, and of the alternation of Europe's openings toward other cultural worlds and closures within its own geographic and ethnic borders; through the study of the sequence of struggles, at first between supranational entities such as the Pope and the Emperor and national and regional political entities such as the city republics and the emerging sovereign states, and, later, among the various nation-states for the economic and political hegemony of the continent; through the appraisal of the great cleavages between centre and periphery, state and church, land and cities, bourgeois and workers, in the path toward and through modernity, as they are portrayed in Rokkan's 'geo-political map of Europe' (1970,1975). Key features of European identity are the constant dialectic among different and often conflicting *Weltanschaungen* and the development of the critical mind-that continuously puts into question temporarily hegemonic beliefs and conceptions and that forms the basis of European scientific thought.

From this kind of historical appraisal it clearly emerges that contemporary Europe is a Europe of difference and diversity and that a primary feature of European identity is the extraordinary complexity of the cultural heritage, where different realities co-exist in both cooperative and conflictual forms (trade and war) without losing their specificity.The great political wager of the new Europe is that the plurality of identity cultures, which for centuries fostered a semi-permanent state of local or generalized wars, can now be reconsidered as a common good and a basic resource for the development of a free and prosperous community, harmoniously diversified inside and peacefully open to the outside world.

Recognizing the extraordinary diversity of the European cultural heritage does not, however, imply denying the existence of common constitutive elements, a kind of genetic cultural code which, although constantly modified and very differently declined in historical contingencies and geo-political particularisms, identifies a 'European specific'. These basic elements can be found in varying degrees and forms in the different parts of a Europe which sometimes goes beyond the geographical borders of Europe and at other times stops at the boundary of the so-called 'Western Europe' which more or less coincides with what was Charlemagne's empire. They are of an institutional nature but are rooted in- and at the same time foster- closely related values, norms, attitudes and languages, which can be identified in the constant tension between rationalism and individualism/subjectivity. I analysed them in depth in *Transatlantic Divide* (Martinelli, 2007) and will briefly summarise them in the following pages.

3 Rationalism and Individualism/Subjectivity

The fundamental value of European and Western identity can be identified in the constant tension between rationalism and individualism/subjectivity, considered as opposing and complementary principles at the same time. These two principles have characterized the whole of European history but have coagulated in a specific set of cultural orientations and institutional arrangements only with the advent of modernity. They express the tension between individual freedom and social organization, desire for autonomy and a need for security, and have created the specific modern attitude of the European identity that consists of the constant effort to free itself from constraints and to overcome its internal and external boundaries (D'Andrea 2001). We can generally define rationalism as the ability of the human mind to know, control and transform nature (according to a conception of the world as an environment that can be shaped to meet human needs and desires) and individualism as a legitimate aspiration to self-realization, responsible autonomy, and reflexivity, such as the confidence of humans in their ability to pursue their own ends and ultimately to be the creators of their own destiny.

Rationalism manifested itself in Europe in a variety of different forms: from Romanesque architecture to Renaissance painting, from Descartes' philosophy to the music of Bach, from the concept of the democratic citizen of the Enlightenment to the postulate of *homo oeconomicus* of classical economic theory. With its confidence in the power of reason to control and transform nature, European and Western rationalism has been the terrain for cultivating scientific and geographic discoveries as well as technological and entrepreneurial innovations. Confidence in reason is closely linked to the perception of the absence of limits, to that particular restlessness of the Europeans, symbolized by the paradigmatic figures of the Dantesque Ulysses and the Goethian Faust, and is exemplified by so many events in European and Western history, from transoceanic travels to colonial adventures, to the "American spirit of the frontier".

The value of knowledge, present in both ancient and modern civilizations of the various regions of the world, has received a special impetus from European modernity, where knowledge has been freed from its subordination to a given religious truth or for a specific political goal. The incessant search for the unknown is the product of the critical mind, which originates from ancient Greek philosophy and has developed into modern philosophical criticism, in particular that of the Enlightenment.The development of science is linked to the enthralling force of technology and capitalism which is in turn linked to the belief in progress. European modernity was the era of Shelley's *Prometheus Unbound*, which expresses the absence of political and religious limits in the technical dominion of nature. Capitalism is a mode of production based on technical instrumentation and economic rationality which are both necessary to compete successfully in the market.

Reason, on the other hand, was also conceived as a system of shared rules that makes coexistence possible in society. Kant did not write an apology of reason, but an investigation of its limits. The rational mind is strong only if it is aware of its limits, if it does not pretend to know the absolute truth, but paves the way for relentless pursuit. In this sense reason is intrinsically anti-totalitarian and directly related to the individual's freedom.

Rationalism is closely connected, complementary and altogether opposed to the other fundamental characteristic of European and Western identity: individualism/ subjectivity. Individualism and subjectivity are closely related, but not synonymous concepts, in the sense that they tend to be preferred by different groups of sholars.. There is a tendency to use preferably the first by scholars who have a positive view of modernity, of which the consciousness of their individuality is considered a distinctive trait, along with the confidence in scientific knowledge, the development of a secular vision, the doctrine of progress and the contractual conception of society. The concept of subjectivity tends instead to be preferred by those who associate individualism to negative aspects of modern culture that they criticize, such as the tendency to pragmatic calculation of utility, arid search for enrichment and a lack of moral passion; to these they oppose alternative values of subjectivity such as self-care, spontaneous expression and the authenticity of experience. In fact, economic and political individualism as well as moral and aesthetic subjectivity are both dimensions of the same principle; and this principle, in turn, interacts dialectically with the principle of rationality. These may foster two different visions of modernity (one more praiseworthy, the other more critical, one more attentive to structural processes, the other more concerned with cultural aspects), but are actually elements of the same cultural and institutional syndrome (Martinelli 2005). The world of the capitalist entrepreneur is a world of relentless change and creative innovation that also offers a favourable environment for the aesthetics of the self. Imagination and reason are not enemies but are rather allied in the work of the scientist or the artist. Each of them tries to explore and experience everything without limiting themselves. Therefore, even when the only term of individualism is used here, it should be understood in the twofold style that has been specified.

In time and space, even individualism has taken on many differing forms of expression: the evangelical personalism of Christians, the individualism of free inhabitants of autonomous medieval republics, the rational economic subject in the market, the free citizen of modern liberal democracies, the reflective subjectivity of contemporary Europeans. Like rationalism, individualism has developed within the cultural heritage of European history, but it has emerged only with the advent of modernity. Its affirmation was not only the symptom of the dissolving primacy of the community in its traditional religious significance, but also the necessary condition for the discovery of society in a strictly secular sense. As long as the ideological primacy of individual interests and passions had not been postulated, the constraints imposed on such interests and passions by an autonomous social and political order, subject to its own laws, were not defined (Polanyi, 1944).

Individualism is at the root of the principles of freedom and equality affirmed by Natural Law Theory (which asserts that all human beings are the same in that they are endowed with reason), Anglo-Saxon political thought as well as French and German Enlightenment. The principles of liberty and equality were recognized in the prerogatives of the English Parliament after the "glorious revolution" of 1688–89 and solemnly proclaimed by the American Constitution of 1776 and by the French *Declaration de Droits de l'Homme et du Citoyen* of 1789. These principles affirm the inviolable rights of individuals to life, freedom and full realization of their potentialities. Freedom is expressed both as a negative freedom – the protection of human rights against abuse of power, or as a positive freedom– the right of citizens to participate in the formation of the common will. Equality was initially defined as equality of rights and duties of citizenship and equal treatment by law but soon became also equality of opportunity and of chances for life, thus opening the way for progressive liberalism, social democracy and welfare policies, inspired by the third principle of modern revolutions – fraternity or solidarity – and constituted an essential component of the European political culture of the twentieth century. The struggle to achieve satisfactory and effective compromises between freedom, equality and solidarity has been a leitmotif in the history of European political thought. Being European should also mean engaging in the realization of the "1789 sacred principles" of freedom, equality and fraternity. The increase in socioeconomic inequalities between and within EU member states as well as the refusal of some governments to share the duties of common citizenship and solidarity policies pertaining to refugees are today alarming signs of a crisis of the common European identity.

The dialectical relationship between the principle of rationality and the principle of individualism/ subjectivity also manifests itself in the double matrix of change and routine in which the modern self lives. "Each of those unforgettable figures of modernity – Marx's revolutionary, Baudelaire's dandy, Nietzsche superman, Weber's vocational scientist, Simmel's foreigner, Musil's *Mann ohne Eigenschaften*, Benjamin's flaneur- is grabbed and dragged away by the rushing intoxication of an epochal change, yet it is determined and framed within a system of social roles and functions" (Gaonkar 2001). It is worthnoting that this list of characters (to which I would add Schumpeter's entrepreneur) is strictly European, proving that the culture of modernity is closely linked to European identity (including in it the peoples of "Europe outside of Europe"), although it should be pointed out that in the contemporary world there are multiple modernities or different paths towards and through modernity.

Rationalism, individualism/subjectivity, the incessant quest for knowledge, innovation and discovery, the constitution of the self as an autonomous subject, the refusal of limits, the principles of liberty and equality of rights and opportunities, represent the core values of the civilization of modernity, which developed first in Western Europe, then spred to the rest of this continent, the Americas and throughout the world, giving rise to continuously changing cultural and institutional patterns which constituted different responses to the challenges, threats and opportunities inherent in the core characteristics of Western modernity (Eisenstadt, 2001, Martinelli, 2005).

4 University and Scientific Research, Market Capitalism and Industrial Enterprise, Nation State and Representative Democracy

These values, attitudes, interpretations of reality and the related cultural programs, combine in modern civilization with a set of new institutional forms (mostly experimented first in Europe and later spread in America and the rest of the world), giving life to the university and scientific research, market capitalism and industrial enterprise, the nation state and representative democracy.

European and Western science and technology define a particular approach to the knowledge of physical and human reality capable of transforming nature in order to meet individual and collective needs. The depth of Indian and Chinese religion and philosophy, the richness of Islam's scientific and religious thinking, the development of astronomical knowledge in Mesopotamia or pre-Columbian America, are only a few examples of the fact that Western knowledge is not at all exceptional. What is characteristic in this is the greater propensity to combine scientific discoveries, inventions and technological innovations under the constant pressure of both war and commercial competition. Specifically, it is also the greater capacity to design institutions that are particularly suited to the formation and dissemination of knowledge: the Italian, French and Spanish universities of the medieval era, the British and French scientific academies of the seventeenth century, German research universities of the nineteenth century, and the large research laboratories of contemporary America. European modernity was not only a package of technological and organizational developments; it was closely linked to a political revolution and to an equally important transformation of the practices and institutions of scientific research (Wittrock 2000). Europe invented and refined a mode of understanding in science that has developed since the Renaissance, and has become a global model. Its main features are the recognition of the role of mathematics as a measure of scientific accuracy, the union between freedom of inquiry and freedom of criticism as well as the dependence of empirical knowledge on conceptual reflection (Cerutti & Rudolph 2001).

European modernity is also characterized by the development of industrial market capitalism. Its guiding principle is constant rational research to maximize utility in order to successfully compete in the market. The efficient combination of production factors in the industrial enterprise and the exchange of goods and services in the self-regulated market are the two fundamental institutions of capitalist development. The industrial revolution of the latter half of the eighteenth century (a powerful process of innovation, accumulation of capital, exploitation of labour and market expansion) was also due to the availability of iron and coal and surpluses deriving from agriculture and long-distance trade but was first generated by the special bond with the scientific-technical revolution of modernity. Commerce and markets also developed in the ancient empires and in much of the non-European world, but the particular combination of technological innovation, industrial revolution and self-regulated market represented a European specificity that gave capitalist growth a force and dynamism without precedent. Capitalism was radically criticized, in particular by Marx and Marxist scholars, but proved to be a more effective model of economic relations than the alternative model of state planning, was transformed through endemic crises, became increasingly globalized and created varieties of capitalism with different political and institutional structures (the market-driven Anglo-Saxon variant, the European-continental variant of the social market economy, the Scandinavian variant and the Asian authoritarian variant).

The third fundamental institutional component of European identity is the nation state. From the late Middle Ages, Europe, or at least its western part, came to be increasingly made up of societies of peasants, lords who recognized the authority of a king, traders and craftsmen, joined together in common ties of language and religious faith (Mendras 1997). The nation state, characterized by the unity of a people, a territory and a distinctive culture, slowly took shape in opposition to multiethnic empires and the supranational church.The nation- state is another typically European innovation that has been successfully exported to the rest of the world.It is a peculiar institution that arises from the encounter between a sovereign, autonomous and centralized political organization, endowed with a civil bureaucracy, armed forces, diplomacy, and a community based on real or imaginary ties of blood, language as well as shared traditions and collective memory. We develop the analysis of nation and nationalism and their relations with the European Union in the following chapter.

The nation-state is more controversially related to the values of rationalism and individualism than either science and technology or capitalist market and industry: one of the two components, the nation, is rooted in primordial ties, appeals to passions and emotions, and places emphasis on collective ends, while the other component, the state, is a rational organization that has evolved through a relationship with the law and the development of an efficient public administration. The advent of representative democracy that "civilizes" state power is favoured by the congruence of the values of individualism and rationalism with the institutions of the national state.

Representative democracy (a political system composed of elected officials representing the interests and opinions of citizens in the context of the rule of law, based on popular sovereignty and citizen consensus) is in fact a fourth aspect of European and Western identity. The Greek *polis*, the Roman *res publica*, the free cities of Italy, Germany and the Flanders in the late Middle Ages, were all precedents of this European specificity. The various forms of modern democracy (majority government and minority rights protection, free and periodic elections, separation of constitutional powers, freedom of the press and association) are innovations born and grown in European culture, and developed in Europe and in the United States of America (the first "new nation" built by European emigrants), during the three major modern democratic revolutions: English, American and French. The significance of the values and institutions of representative democracy in European identity is evidenced by the fact that, along with free market ones, they are considered necessary, scrupulously established requirements for joining the Union.

The "catalogue" of the distinctive features of European identity would not be complete without reference to the relationship between the principles of individualism/subjectivity and rationalism and the Christian religion. In the debates on the failed 2004 Constitutional Treaty, the relationship between the Christian religion and European identity was a particularly sensitive issue. Christianity is a transcendent monotheism that postulates the direct relationship of every creature with its Creator, but has since its origins been a strong element of communion that manifested itself in the early Christian communities, in the transformation of the hermits into monastic orders starting from the ones founded by Martin of Tours and Benedict of Norcia, and in the mediation between the believer and God exercised by religious ceremonies and clergy. It gave rise to the most ancient and long-standing institution existing today: the Roman Catholic Church. Two aspects, the subjective one, which originates from the individualism of the Gospel message and re-emerges periodically in various forms of mysticism and asceticism, and the collective/institutional one, which finds expression in the hierarchical organization of the church and in liturgical rites and ceremonies, have dialectically interacted, causing violent conflicts such as those between Rome and Byzantium and between the Reformation and the Counter-Reformation, struggles against heretical movements and religious wars.

The relation of the Christian religion to individualism/subjectivity and to rationalism is ambivalent. On the one hand, along with Greek philosophy and Roman law, it contributed to the development of European and Western individualism. According to the well-known Weberian thesis, the great rational prophecies of the Bible, the rational life plan of monastic orders, and the theory of predestination have all contributed to the growth of rational mentality. Christianity has profoundly influenced European culture and institutions sometimes as a source of inspiration, sometimes as a dialectical counterpart. Our highest values and the rules associated with them, such as the dignity and inviolability of the person, human rights, conscience and individual responsibility, cannot be extrapolated from the historical experience of Jewish-Christian religious tradition, but are rather defined and articulated through it. On the other hand, the notion of the absence of the limit and the belief of human beings as the creators of their own destiny (distinctive features of the modern mentality) were strongly opposed by the anti-modernist positions of the Church – from the trial of Galileo Galilei to the struggle against the theory of Charles Darwin. It is only through secular struggles that the division between temporal power and spiritual power (which originates from the famous "Give to Caesar what is Caesar's, and to God what is God's.") has become a consolidated principle of modern Western democracies.

Although born in Palestine and spreading to various regions of the world, Christianity strongly identified itself with European civilization; but the religious factor has not been translated into either a monopoly or an undifferentiated unity in the culture of Europe, due to other religions (such as Islam) that have had a significant presence, and to the great religious diversity of Christianity itself with its many heretic movements – the schism between the Orthodox Church and the Catholic Church and the Protestant Reformation. In many ways, European life is secularized, but religion continues to play an important role: a sizeable minority of European citizens claim to belong to a church, institutions, religious leaders have a significant influence on the political and cultural life of EU member countries, and there are deep convergences between Christian doctrine and lay ethics on many issues. The continuing presence of the Christian religion in the contemporary life of Europeans is also based principally on the fact that most great expressions of architecture, painting, music, literature and even philosophy and science are not interpretable without taking into account the role – inspiration or critical, benevolent or repressive – carried out by Christian doctrine and ecclesiastical authority.

5 An Unusual and Controversial Identity

The necessarily succinct picture of the European identity we have outlined risks to propose an uncritical and ethnocentric image. Some clarifications are therefore needed to avoid misunderstandings. First, it should be noted that the characteristics identified are defined as fundamental aspects because they have played a significant role in building a European identity but are not present in a uniform and pervasive way in contemporary Europe, as the case of religion shows. Fundamental values and institutions are also not necessarily positive or unambiguous. As already noted, European history has been the source of deep fractures, violent conflicts, idiosyncratic disputes, as well as many crimes and errors. The values of rationalism and individualism and the institutions of market capitalism and nation state have produced contradictions, violations, deformations such as the contradictions between capital and wage labour and between economic growth and environmental protection due to the commodification of human labour and nature, the conflict between colonial (and neo-colonial) exploitation and the individual and collective freedom of non-European peoples, not to mention wars, mass murders, and genocide.

From each of the basic elements of European culture one can derive dialectical polarities and give contrasting images: the universal faith of Christian love has been in certain historical phases in strident contrast with the wars of religion and the intolerant repression of the infidels. The free market constantly produces monopolistic rent and financial crises; the struggle for political independence degenerates into aggressive nationalism. In the heart of the 20th century, the European political order collapsed due to devastating totalitarianism. Jaspers (1947) argues that it is not possible to isolate substantial values that characterize European culture in a non-ambiguous way, because for every valued orientation, Europe has also produced its opposites: faith and reason, tolerance and religious war, democracy and totalitarianism.

Nevertheless, those who criticize inclusion among the constituent elements of European identity of aspects that also had morally reprehensible effects forget that the European project shows that history can be the object of reflective reconsideration through a learning process, that is, to draw lessons from mistakes and crimes of the past. Rooted in the contradictory identities of religious fundamentalism and belligerent nationalism, the religious wars of the sixteenth and seventeenth centuries and the national conflicts of the 19th and 20th centuries were subsequently rejected establishing the principle of religious pluralism and making the European integration the antidote against the repetition of the multi-century "European civil wars". The conception of history underlying the efforts to establish an ever closer political union is not formulated in terms of any "manifest destiny" of the continent or Europeans as an elected people, it is the conception of the disciples of history, not of its masters. The cultural foundations of the new European institutions are a collection of lessons from the recent history of European modernity, the lessons of nationalism and other dangerous "isms" that need to be regulated (Therborn 1995).

Furthermore, the fundamental aspects of European identity are not exclusive to the contemporary world. The reason for this non-exclusivity does not lie so much in the fact that these elements are shared from the origins with other peoples as that they are "exported" and assimilated/reinterpreted in other regions of the world. The thesis that European culture is intrinsically de-territorialized since it spread throughout the world and can therefore no longer define the specificity of a single part of the world (D'Andrea 2001) does not convince; it forgets that any transition to modernity does not imply the mere spread of a single type of mentality (scientific rationalism, instrumental pragmatism, secularism) from so-called "developed" countries to so-called "emerging" countries, but processes of creative adaptation, contamination or hybridization (such as the coexistence between modern technology and traditional culture in post-restoration Meji Japan or the combination of market economy and single party regime in contemporary China). The encounter/confrontation between modern European civilization and other civilizations deeply changes the identities of both.

The thesis of the Europeanization of the world, unduly generalizes the experience of countries which were culturally closer to Europe. If, in fact, European identity is not easily distinguishable from the "Western" countries of the so-called "Europe outside Europe" and if, indeed, fundamental features such as individualism and scientific-technical rationality are even more frequent among Americans that among Europeans (Martinelli 2007), cultural differences are far more profound with the inhabitants of the nonwestern regions of the world, where they unequally affect the various aspects of the culture of modernity. Scientific rationalism, technological innovation and market capitalism have become more popular because they are perceived as more efficient cognitive and institutional tools and as means to a certain extent indifferent to the ends. Individual rights, cultural and political pluralism, the rule of law, separation of powers and representative democracy face greater difficulties because they collide with alternative models of the relationship between the individual and society. Comparative research on the "varieties of capitalism", welfare state models and political regimes shows how there are widely different responses to common problems such as those of the economic and financial crisis, the relationship between competitiveness and social cohesion, sustainable development and political order.

6   Changes in the Content of European Identity and the Perception of their Meaning

We have argued that within the historical legacy of the European peoples, alongside different national and local identities, exist the common cultural roots that, with the advent of modernity, have transformed and crystallized into a specific nucleus of boldly innovative values, meanings and institutions, constituting a collective European identity. And we have pointed out that this content is constantly evolving and is prone to exceptions in different national contexts. In order to appreciate whether and how the nucleus of European identity has developed, we will briefly discuss the foundations of the reconstruction of Europe after the end of World War II and, in particular, Jaspers' thesis (1947), which identifies in freedom, history and science the three factors that make up the essence of Europe. The desire for freedom is in fact universal, but developed to the highest degree in Europe, where was to defeat despotism by transforming itself into concrete institutions and by fuelling the feeling of justice and the constant sense of restlessness and turbulence felt by Europeans. Freedom nourished the second factor, the need to understand historical time and to play an active role as humans within the *polis*. True freedom lies in the pursuit of political freedom within the community and in the development of the individual together with that of the social world that surrounds it. The third factor: science, or the constant effort to penetrate into the heart of all that can be penetrated, is also linked to freedom because it is knowledge and love for knowledge that liberates humans by attributing them not only the external freedom acquired through the knowledge of nature, but also and above all the inner freedom that flows from the knowledge of oneself and of others.

Freedom, that is closely linked to individualism/subjectivity, remains as the fundamental value today, further strengthening over time, extending from the defence of peace, liberal political democracy and economic freedom (opposed to the authoritarianism and self-planned economy of Eastern European Communist regimes) to the protection of human rights codified in the Charter of Fundamental Rights of the EU (Nice, 2000). Articles 6–19 are dedicated to freedom, Articles 1–5 are dedicated to dignity, Articles 20–26 to equality, Articles 27–38 to solidarity, Articles 39–46 to citizenship and Articles 47–50 to justice). The promotion of science, that is closely linked to rationality, continues to be another founding value, constantly reaffirmed in the documents of the European Union as the one outlining the "Lisbon Strategy" aimed at transforming the European economyinto a knowledge-based economy: the most competitive and dynamic in the world. Lacking, however, is the other factor identified by Jaspers: the full, historically conscious exercise of political freedom which did not make significant progress due to the European Union's long-suffered crisis of democratic representation This democratic deficit also makes more difficult to implement policies against the growing inequalities that run against the principle of solidarity (Martinelli, 2016).

What has changed significantly during the seventy years of the history of European integration is the role attributed to European identity by European leadership classes and the intensity of European citizens' identification with Europe vs their own nationhood. Regarding the first aspect, in the post-war decade, a sense of patriotism and common citizenship of peoples belonging to the "European family" was wished by many European leaders, beginning with Winston Churchill in his famous speech to the students of the University of Zurich in 1946. The defence of peace was the fundamental value, which subsequently became increasingly linked to the protection of human rights which, although not included in the original project of European communities (but in the Council of Europe), was progressively appropriated and claimed as originals until their solemn formulation in the Charter of Fundamental Rights of the EU. In the post-war era, European identity was regarded as an antidote to the disastrous nationalisms that had caused the World War II catastrophe, a prerequisite for the continent's moral and economic reconstruction and the most effective alternative to the resurgence of separate national identities and opposing nationalisms. It was believed that the stronger the sense of belonging to Europe, the more it weakened nationalist ideology. This antagonistic conception of the two types of identities, and the related interest in the issue of European identity, gradually faded as the integration process progressed, for two orders of reason. Firstly, because the national states were the foundations on which the supranational union was built and perpetuated by it along with related national identities and sovereign views. Secondly, because of the 1957 Treaty of Rome, the process was developed mainly in its economic dimension of the integrated single market rather than in the political and cultural dimension.

At the beginning of the 1970s, there was a renewal of interest in the issue of European identity in order to manage the growing diversity and disparities resulting from the enlargement from six to nine member states. In 1973, with the signing of the Declaration on European Identity in Copenhagen, a change of perspective was sanctioned in the explicit expression of the compatibility of the European identity and national identities. This concept was reaffirmed in subsequent documents, in particular in the 1992 Maastricht Treaty, which states that respect for national and regional diversity and the flourishing of different national cultures are an integral part of the appreciation of the common identity and legacy of European culture. The thesis of "unity in diversity" formulated at the beginning of the 1990s became a central aspect of the European project and summarizes the EU's strategy of placing itself in an intermediate position between an almost national concept of European identity (which is unrealistic for the reasons we discussed earlier) and a universalistic concept (which would negate its specificity). It involves self-limitation both of unity, in the sense that separate identities are constituent elements of the common identity (which does not claim any priority over them) and of diversity, in the sense that none of the separate identities question the existence of the common identity.

The most advanced version of the European project requires, however, a subsequent step: achieving unity through diversity. The memory of a common past is not enough to create a strong sense of belonging to Europe unless it is accompanied by a sincere and active sharing of the political project of a federal union in which unity is strengthened through the enhancement of diversity. It is the sharing of this project that distinguishes the EU from the other half of Europe made up of Russia and the countries that are not a part of the Union, while sharing the same historical past.

The European project of political integration cannot be acheved by applying the nation-state model- in the sense of a univocal collective identity that legitimizes the unification of Europe as a single political entity- because there is a lack of centralized power as well as a standardized culture that is articulated through a common language. Nor should this model be applied, because building a European identity cannot be based on opposition between ourselves and others. Lessons in history: religious fundamentalism, political dogmatism, and aggressive nationalism should have taught us that this negative and arrogant way of defining one's identity merely in opposition to someone else's -from time to time, the infidel, ideological foe, alien (Fontana, 1994)- threatens peace and is therefore not a road to travel in the contemporary world.

For the first time in the history of Europe, political authority does not rely on military structures to integrate such a large and economically developed territory, but rather relies upon a legal and economic community while not endeavouring to deprive its members of their cultural specificities. The European Union is a multicultural entity with a strong core of shared principles (democratic citizenship, scientific freedom, competitive market, human rights, social cohesion and solidarity, respect for different cultural heritages, peaceful relationswith all peoples of the earth), which in turn establishes common institutions. Already in ancient Greek philosophy we find the notion of harmony that emerges from contradictory elements. If one postulates unity at the outset, it results in an eternal tendency to return to the original lost design. If, on the contrary, diversity is postulated, unity is conceived as the constant effort fed by conflict and competition, never predetermined. European culture can only be differentiated and plural, united in its diversity, forged and continuously renewed by it (Eliot, 1948). Unity calls for the redefinition of identities, both of the different European peoples and also those of immigrants from other regions of the world: the redefinition of identity does not require their abolition. European citizens can get used to having multiple identities: urban, regional, national and supranational.

The formation of a united Europe can build itself around a concept of unity that derives from diversity and multiple citizenship. And yet, one must be aware of the difficulty of this path, because recognizing multiple identities within a single supranational political entity can be a destabilizing factor, as it alters the delicate relationship between *ethnos* and *demos*. For this reason, while reaffirming that European peoples and governments must build unity through diversity and that European identity and citizenship must be multifaceted, we must realistically enhance those traditional attributes of nationality, of a cultural-symbolic nature, which result as being compatible with the supranational and multicultural project and which can integrate and strengthen the civil-political identity of Europeans, even with appropriate identity techniques.

7   How European Citizens' Identification with Europe has Changed

Along with the significance attributed to European identity by community institutions, the kind and degree of European citizens' identification with Europe and their nation of has also changed over the years. The two aspects of the issue are linked to the fact that the self-image and self-definition of the European Union influences the reasons for Europeans to identify with their fellow citizens and with the Union. We have defined identification as the set of cognitive orientations (recognizing oneself as European, member of a European cultural family defined by values, norms and institutions, considering this fact as a constituent element of personal identity together with other collective identities), emotional and evaluative (sympathy, common sense, the reasons for and pride of a common belonging, the perception of sharing meaningful and to some extent exclusive experiences, the development of identity values, institutional expressions and common memory, the adoption of a *Wir-Perspective*) as well as related and coherent behaviours of mutual trust, solidarity, and the willingness to make personal or group sacrifices for common goals.

Periodic surveys of attitudes and views of statistically representative samples of European citizens such as the Eurobarometer (not without methodological weaknesses, but they still providing us with interesting indication of the changes), have signalled for some years after 2007 a decline in the identification with Europe and support for EU institutions. But support has risen in the last years and consolidated recently: the first Standard Eurobarometer survey conducted after the European elections in June 2019 (in all at the time 28 EU countries and five candidate countries) shows a strong increase in citizens' positive perception of the European Union, from the economy to the state of democracy (at its highest level since the June 2014 Eurobarometer survey conducted before the Juncker Commission took office), with a record-high support for the euro and climate change turning into the second top concern at EU level, after immigration (European Commission, Press release, 5 August 2019). Among the findings: trust in the EU has increased in 20 Member States and remains higher than trust in national governments or parliaments; 61 per cent on average of Europeans are optimistic about the future of the EU and 55 per cent are satisfied with the way democracy works in the EU; 76 per cent of respondents in the eurozone are in favour of the single currency (a record high support); 73 per cent feel that they are citizens of the EU, more than half in all Member States; 81 per cent support the free movement of EU citizens who can live, work, study and do business anywhere in the EU; among the most important concerns at EU level immigration remains the main one (with 34 per cent of mentions), despite a strong decrease, but climate change is now the second, with a strong increase, and the economic situation is unchanged in third place, while unemployment remains the main concern at national level.

Survey data should however be supplemented with other data on the variety of forms of social interaction, (work, study, economic and cultural cooperation) as well as political participation and the percentage of European citizens who have experienced them. An attitude of identification ("measured", for example, from the affirmative answer to the question "do you feel like European citizens") is in fact not a sufficient enough condition to ensure consequential behaviour, whereas a negative response can be given by citizens who actually live as members of the same supranational community.

The development of a genuine identification process starts from the awareness of a common membership, but is in fact completed only with consistent practices and behaviours. In this regard, the intensity of the sentiment of identification with Europe leaves something to be desired. In the various referendums that have taken place over time (Norwegian, Irish, Danish, Spanish,

French, Dutch) where citizens were asked to express their consent or dissent for the accession or ratification of a treaty, the response was rather negative and almost always fairly modest. Participation rates in the European Parliament elections are lower compared to national elections, and have been declining over time, but signficantly increased in 2019, when the EU future seemed at stake. Decisions and concrete actions, which involve sharing the problems and the costs to be paid for their solution, show the cleavages among citizens of different member states. For example, German citizens (from the western part of the country) showed a great deal of willingness to accept their government's decision to devote very substantial resources to east lander development, expressing a high level of identification with those who are considered as nationals of their own nation, while not being willing to (at least in part) subsidize the sovereign debt of countries such as Greece. This shows an inadequate degree of identification with those who should be considered a European fellow. Such behaviours are more eloquent than the answers to Eurobarometer questions.

What are the main factors influencing the change of type and degree of identification with Europe? There are three in particular: generational culture; the legacy of the recent past that precedes the entry of a country into the European Union; the changing interests and economic conveniences and the distribution of costs and benefits amongst various social groups. Each of these factors outlines significant cleavages within the EU between social groups favoured or threatened by the monetary union, between northern countries with strong economies and southern countries with weak economies, between Western older member countries and eastern countries of more recent entry, between governments with a pro-EU community orientation and governments with a sovereign orientation, between advocates of a market Europe conception and supporters of a social Europe. These cleavages contribute to nourishing the most important alternative identities with respects to the common European identity: namely generational, national, and class.

The generational factor matters; the younger and the elderly show higher degrees of identification than the intermediate generations. The generation that had a direct or close experience of World War II feels a common identity with greater intensity and awareness, but its importance is declining; memories based on direct experience or on the tales of fathers and grandparents who lived through those events as protagonists or spectators, are destined to fade away irretrievably. Younger generations are growing up today in a Europe that has never experienced such a long period of peace in its history and fortunately, they have not had a direct experience of war. There have been and there are still conflicts in eastern Europe (ex-Yugoslavia, Chechnya, Ukraine); and the consequences of war in the Middle East are evident in the form of the millions of refugees fleeing to Europe and the attacks of fundamentalist Islamic terrorism. But these are challenges and threats that do not have such an intensity that, at least for the moment, they provoke a strong emotional reaction convincing the majority of European citizens to mobilize themselves to seek greater co-operation in foreign policy and greater supranational solidarity. Young people from the "Erasmus generation" who have a personal experience of a transnational European society feel themselves Italian-European, French-European, German-European, Spanish-European, Polish-European, etc., but as many of their peers, they take for granted the benefits coming from the European Union, while those who support sovereignist parties utterly forget those benefits and blame the EU for the problems and difficulties they face in their daily lives, like unemployment and under-employment, social spending cuts and increased insecurity and violence.

The historical past is the second important influencing factor mainly for two reasons. States that belonged to the Soviet sphere of influence in the decades of the Cold War came out of a state of limited sovereignty and are now reluctant to surrender spontaneously to supranational institutions portions of that sovereign power that they only recently regained. Furthermore, ancient cleavages as well as ethnic, national and religious tensions that were reabsorbed and anesthetized in the bipolar context of the antagonism between the USA and the USSR were then re-invented, favouring the overwhelming resumption of alternative identities and in particular of national-populist ideology. The rise of national- populism is, however, not limited to the former communist countries, but extends to many other countries in Europe; it shows the difficulties encountered by the development of a common European identity and threatens the EU project.

A third factor, which adversely affects the sentiment of identification with Europe, is represented by the 2008 financial crisis and the long economic downturn that deepened the inequalities between strong and weak economies and the sharp contrasts already produced by globalization among those who benefited and those who were harmed. The economic and financial crisis has further deteriorated the condition of the 'globalization losers', increasing unemployment and precariousness and cutting welfare spending, so that many of them tend to identify the European Union with the neoliberal set-up of the global economy and involve them both in a single judgment of rejection and condemnation.

8   Identity Techniques

Today, the development of European identity is at a point of crisis. Different but intertwined crises of the economic recession, the reception and integration of millions of refugees as well as terrorism fuel aggressive neo-nationalism that adopts a populist rhetoric and proclaims the necessity to re-nationalize political choices, recover national sovereignty and dismantle the common European house. What is needed is an overhaul of the EU; the institutions of European democracy must be reformed and the opportunities for participation and cooperation among citizens should be enhanced, but a shared European identity should also be developed, putting in place appropriate "identity techniques" (Kaina and Karolewski 2013).

Such techniques can refer to only some of the symbolic categories that contribute to form the identity of a people (Tullio Altan, 1999); we can neither refer to the relationships of kinship, lineage and race (*genos*), since they tend to produce closure, exclusion and discrimination, in a clear contrast to the founding values of the Union; nor to a common language (a basic aspect of *logos*), because the defence of multilingualism is a fundamental requirement of the policy of respect and protection of different cultural identities in the EU, but other elements of a cultural *koinè* can be valued, such as ways of thinking, communicating and actions (that are actually becoming increasingly similar to citizens from different European countries). Even the transfiguration of the space in which Europeans live (*topos*) can be of help. To a certain extent, cities, buildings, squares, parks, other European public and private spaces have common and distinctive features compared to other regions of the world, although cultural globalization with its global-local dialectics tends to mitigate this specificity. Where we can and must invest more is in the *ethos* (namely basic values, conceptions of the world and ethical principles of knowledge and action) which define the new European identity and the rights and duties of the European citizenship; and in the *epos* (the celebration of significant events and the memory of great historical figures that testify to the achievements of European civilization in science, art and culture).

Both *ethos* and *epos* should inform the contents of the educational programs of young Europeans and the activities of the mass media in order to build a public space and a shared culture that orient the views of European citizens about important collective choices. Common values can be reaffirmed by means of authentically European *lieux de memoire* such as monuments, museums, pilgrimages, celebrations, anniversaries, myths, heroes, feasts, flags, hymns, which today continue to have mostly strong nationalistic expressions. Symbolic content of this kind is to be enhanced despite the difficulties encountered by the creation of a Museum of Europe and the tormented work of the commission of historians responsible for drawing up the textbooks of European history. For example, it would be desirable to have an increasing number of streets and squares in the cities of Europe to bear the names of great artists, scientists, builders of peace, solidarity and European unity as a counterweight to all those who remember dates and places of battles won by some and lost by others. A flag (the 12 stars in the blue field) and a hymn (the hymn to the joy of the Beethoven's Ninth Symphony) already exist today (although not formally included in the current Treaty of Lisbon) just as each year Europe Day is celebrated on May 9th and a European Capital of Culture is nominated. These symbolic events do not need to replace similar initiatives of member states, but should complement them.

The process of identity construction is not limited to these aspects. Strategic political decisions such as the creation of the common currency have a strong symbolic significance too. The euro has established a tangible link between the Union's institutions and the daily lives of its citizens; its iconography has achieved an effective compromise between the commonality of values expressed in coins and banknotes and respect for cultural diversity that is expressed with different iconographic features (Risse, 2003).

Finally, the significance of the foundation myths that lie at the intersection of *ethos* and *epos* should be emphasized, similar to those which play a key role into the building of national identities. They, in fact, represent the glorious past of a political community to be conveyed in posterity, fuelling a sense of continuity between the old and new generations. Examples of such myths are the celebrations of "founding" acts and documents both of an intellectual nature such as the "Ventotene Manifesto", and of a political nature such as the Treaties of Rome, Maastricht and Lisbon as well as the Charter of Fundamental Rights of the European Union.

However, symbolic identity techniques are likely to be perceived as mere manipulation mechanisms by the elite if they are not accompanied by real experiences of sharing and policy reforms aimed at reducing the deficit of democratic representation and forming a genuine European *demos* that exercises its own sovereignty within the limits and forms established bythe European Union's treaties. To this end, we must increase the density of EU's economic and social life by multiplying the opportunities for meeting and collaborating. The sentiment of a common membership is favoured by the set of practices and symbols operating predominantly at the subconscious level, fuelled by the abolition of borders, the use of the same currency, easier and more frequent opportunities to study, work, travel and visit nearby countries. It is also necessary to strengthen the institutions that can feed supranational commitment and loyalty, i.e. create a European space for schools and universities, preserve multilingualism, develop pan-European mass media and establish a civil service for all young Europeans. We must strengthen the participation of a democratically informed and active European citizenship through the formation of truly European parties, the election of European parliamentarians by common rules and unified nominations, citizens' greater involvement in policymaking and greater accountability of MEPs and EU governance top officials, the adoption of a referendum on relevant issues of the political agenda.

9   The Renewed Relevance of the European Project

The whole of Europe is going through a decisive moment in its history, in which it is called to affirm its common identity. This requires rediscovering its roots in order to shape its future. In the face of break-up efforts, it is urgently necessary to update the idea of Europe," to give light to a new humanism based on the ability to integrate, to dialogue and to generate that which has made the so-called Old Continent great" (Pope Francis, 2016). In a Europe that faces the challenges of the financial crisis, refugees from violence and hunger, fundamentalist terrorism, there is a risk of closure within national boundaries, disseminating national-populist rhetoric, affirming separate and diffident identities, by resigning or even abandoning the European project of political integration. To counteract these trends, the current European project of political unification needs to be re- emphasized, finding the way to a European collective identity, not contrasting but complementing the different national identities, which fosters loyalty and shared commitment to the whole of cultural values, social norms and political institutions we have outlined: fundamental human rights, civil liberties, democratic political institutions, rule of law, freedom of movement of people, goods and capital, social justice and non-violent resolution of conflicts. This regulatory body has been codified in the Nice Charter, was incorporated into the Lisbon European Treaties 2007, lies at the basis of Community documents and defines the unavoidable requirements of access to the European Union. But these identity values must above all be practiced in the everyday behaviour of European citizens and respected in the decision-making process of European institutions. The European identity, made possible by the common cultural heritage which innervates in various forms and degrees different European *ethnoi*, can only be developed through the growth of a European *demos* defined in terms of a set of shared rights and duties, capable of consolidating citizenship ties within democratically elected institutions. If this happens, if a sense of community with shared rights and duties is strengthened among Europeans, and if European governance institutions become more legitimate and effective, the EU can play a key actor in the multipolar context of global politics.

We can finally answer the question "who are we Europeans?": we are those who feel that they belong to a common space of civilization and intend to face together the challenges of our time.

CHAPTER 2

Nationalism

1 Nationalism as the Ideology of the Modern State

Nationalism is a key concept in the political lexicon of modernity. Although polysemic, ambiguous, and changing in time and space, the concept connotes a defined and well-structured ideology with a strong emotional appeal that has been a powerful factor in the political struggles of the last two centuries by shaping mass political behaviour. Nationalism can be defined as the ideology – or discourse – of the nation. It fosters specific collective movements and policies promoting the sovereignty, unity, and autonomy of the people gathered in a single territory, united by a distinctive political culture and sharing a set of collective goals. Nationalism is the political principle that affirms the necessary congruence between political unity and national unity and helps to achieve the political project of the fusion of state and nation.

Nationalism is historically specific, closely related to the modern nation state and modern politics, and to the formation of mass industrial society; it provides an answer to the specific modern problem of how to create solidarity in an atomistic society by evoking a strong collective sentiment: all citizens come to experience a shared collective identity and to embrace a common national purpose.

Antony Smith (1991) remarks that the term 'nationalism' has been used in five different ways: the whole process of forming and maintaining nations; a consciousness of belonging to the nation; a language and symbolism of the nation; an ideology (including a cultural doctrine) of nations; and a social and political movement to achieve the goals of nations and realize the national will. Since the first way can be better referred to as 'nation-building', and the second and third are components of the latter two, the most appropriate meanings are the fourth and the fifth: nationalism can be defined, *lato sensu*, as the ideology of a specific political entity, the nation state, and as a social and political movement aimed at exercising state power that is justified by a nationalist doctrine. According to this doctrine, nations with an explicit and peculiar character do exist, nation-related values and interests have priority over all others, and nations must be independent and politically sovereign (Breuilly, 1982). There is also a *stricto sensu* definition of nationalism, which applies to those collective movements that subordinate any political value to the national one, pretend to be the only legitimate interpreter of the national principle and the only effective defender of the national interest, and consider social conflicts and democratic party competition as divisive phenomena that must be substituted by national solidarity (such as Maurras' Action française, Hugenberg's Pangermanik League, Corradini's Associazione nazionalista italiana in the early 20th century, and various radical right parties and xenophobic movements nowadays). Here we will define nationalism in its broader sense: not just as a political doctrine and a political activity, but also as a more basic way of thinking and acting.

In this broader definition, the concepts of nationalism, nation, and nation state are strictly related, since nation states are the context in which nationalism develops and, in turn, the nationalist discourse helps to make nations. For Haas (1997: 23), "a nation is a socially mobilized body of individuals who believe themselves united by some set of characteristics that differentiate them (in their own minds) from outsiders and who strive to create or maintain their own state". Their collective consciousness is based on a sentiment of difference or even uniqueness that is fostered by shared core symbols. Their wish is self-determination. "Nationalism is a belief held by a group of people that they ought to constitute a nation or that they are already one. It is a doctrine of social solidarity based on the characteristics and symbols of nationhood. A nation state is a political entity whose inhabitants consider themselves a single nation and wish to remain one" (Haas, 1997: 23).

The nation state is the institutional embodiment of political authority in modern society, an impersonal and sovereign political entity with supreme jurisdiction over a clearly delimited territory and population that claims monopoly over coercive power and enjoys legitimacy as a result of its citizens' support. It is a particular institution resulting from the encounter between a sovereign, autonomous, centralized political organization on the one hand, and a community (real and imagined at the same time) based on common citizens' rights and/or founded on ties of blood, language, shared tradition, and collective memory on the other.

Nation states – characterized by the unity of a people, a territory, and a distinctive culture – slowly took shape in opposition to the multiethnic empires and/or the supranational Church; they developed historically through the growth of a civil bureaucracy, an army, and a diplomacy, and through the formation of a nation as an imagined community (Anderson, 1991), resulting from the action of nationalist elites in the modernization process (Gellner, 1983), and capable of evoking primordial ethno-symbolic roots (Smith, 1991).

Nation-building and the growth of nationalism are interconnected since, on the one hand, the centralization of power in a sovereign state allows national ideology to prevail over the many regional/local and social/cultural autonomies of pre-modern societies, thus contributing to attaining the political project of fusing state and nation, through the unification of territory, language, culture, and tradition; and, on the other hand, nationalism legitimizes the formation of an independent state based on people's sovereignty, and coordinates and mobilizes collective action in nation-building through a sense of belonging to the nation as a primary identity. Gellner's paradoxical argument (1983: 55) that "it is nationalism which engenders nations" – since nations can be defined only in terms of the age of nationalism, rather than, as you might expect, the other way around – contains some truth; but it is more appropriate to consider nation-building and nationalism as complementary processes.

From the vast literature on nationalism (thoroughly analysed in recent works such as those of Hutchinson and Smith 2000, Motyl 2001, Lawrence 2005, Delanty and Kumar 2006, Ozkirimli 2010), we select a few key aspects – or critical areas of agreement (Cerulo, 2001) – that shape the modernist perspective, still the most influential approach to the study of nationalism. We will adopt this perspective, adequately updated, in our analysis of contemporary European society.

Nationalism is a basic aspect of the culture and institutions of modernity, although, both as an ideology and a political movement, it uses and re-elaborates pre-modern symbolic materials such as ethnicity with the aim of forming a new collective identity and a new base of solidarity in a modern society of individuals. Nationalism is a response to the central sociological question: what are the bases of solidarity in a modern society of individuals? Performing the three key functions of coordination, mobilization, and legitimacy, nationalism has played a key role in both major forms of response to the crucial question of how modern societies can establish an effective state–society connection and reconcile the public interests of citizens and the private interests of selfish individuals. The first response is political and rests on the idea of citizenship: the nation is simply the body of citizens who participate in liberal-democratic institutions. The second response is cultural, and stresses the idea of collective identity: the nation is made up of all those who feel they belong to the same cultural community, an idea that is upheld by political elites confronting the problem of securing the support of the masses, since the idea can provide a common national identity for members of different social groups (Breuilly, 1996).

Nationalism is a modern phenomenon because it is closely related to the interconnected set of economic, political, and sociocultural transformations that characterize the various roads towards and through modernity (industrialization, bureaucratization, democratization, mass communication). The role of nationalism varies in the different routes to modernity (Greenfeld, 1992), but there are common processes and recurrent features (Martinelli, 2005, 2012). Modern industrial societies require the free movement of labour, capital, and goods throughout the national community, universal schooling and a standardized national language, and intensified social and geographical mobility.

Nationalism is a successful example of those 'invented traditions' that occur at times of rapid social change; it is developed in order to secure cohesion in the face of the fragmentation and disintegration caused by rapid industrialization (Hobsbawm and Ranger, 1983). It responds to the emergence of mass politics, when the insertion of hitherto excluded social groups into this sphere creates unprecedented problems for the ruling elites, who find it increasingly difficult to maintain the loyalty, obedience, and cooperation of their subjects. It contributes to the development of a national culture by destroying both the exclusiveness of elite high cultures and the parochialism of local cultures (Gellner, 1983). And it grows through the development of primary education, the invention of public ceremonies, and the mass production of public monuments, to the point of becoming a new secular religion.

2 The Double Matrix of European Nationalism and Its Relationship with Democracy

The national principle and the democratic principle are historically linked, but their relationship is ambivalent and controversial. Modern nations are formed when large masses of people start to make political demands on the basis of a sense of cultural distinctiveness. National movements, in other words collective movements embracing the nationalist ideology, aim to make people conscious of their equal rights as members of a single political entity and to foster the political independence of their own country. The *Declaration des droits de l'homme et du citoyen* states: "the principle of sovereignty essentially lies in the nation; no political body, no individual can exercise any authority that does not emanate directly from it". The word *Fraternité* – which replaced the previous formula *Unité indivisible de la republique ou la mort* as the third 'immortal principle' of the French revolution – is the most complex of the three; it tries to transfer at state level the sentiments of belonging that people feel for their natural communities, and for this reason it needs – and tries to impose – a common language and a unique culture; but here it finds its limit, or even its impossibility. Popper (1963), for instance, affirms that the absolute absurdity of the principle of self-determination should be evident to anybody, since it implies that every state is a national state, limited by natural borders and the natural place of an ethnic group, the nation, with the consequence that it should be the ethnic group to determine and protect the natural borders of the state.

And yet, in spite of this type of criticism, nationalism matters and makes people think that the nation really exists. Democratic ideology was insufficient to guarantee the unity of the state against the divisive forces of class antagonisms and conflicts among nations. It required the ideology of nationalism as a key means of political integration. Nationalism may be an absurd doctrine, but, as Breuilly remarks (1982: 343), "as far as it is successful, it proves to be true"; and it is effective. National interests, values, and identities are indeed stronger than all other, as the defeat of Socialist and Christian internationalists at the outbreak of the First World War made clear.

European nationalism has two basic sources. It was Kohn (1948) who introduced first the widely known distinction between the political concept of the nation (French revolutionary doctrine) and the cultural notion of the nation (German Romanticism). The first root of European nationalism is the French Revolution, from Rousseau's political philosophy to the *Déclaration des droits de l'homme et du citoyen* to the radical nationalism of the Jacobins. The battle of Valmy on 20 September 1792, when a ragged people's army defeated the better trained and equipped Prussian infantry at the revolutionary cry 'Long live the nation!' inspired Goethe to comment that the day marked the beginning of a new epoch in human history. Sieyes in *Qu'est-ce que le Tiers Etat?* (1789) identifies the national community with the third estate without either privileged or oppressed people. This concept of nationalism is synthesized in Renan's famous expression: *l'existence d'une nation est un plebiscite quotidian* (1887). A nation is a large scale solidarity that presupposes a common heroic past, great leaders, true glory, and also implies collective forgetting of previous divisive identities, but it is summarized in the present by consent, by the clearly expressed desire to continue a common life and willingness to live together as members of the same community. Renan's view leaves, however, unsolved the question of how this specific type of community differs from others.

The second main source of European nationalism is German romanticism (that of Herder, Fichte), which stresses the cultural and linguistic meaning of the nation and is also related to some extent to *Blut und Boden* (blood and territory). For Herder (1791), the concepts of nation, people, and national culture are closely related; every nation is an objective reality with its own inexpressible individuality; the nation's cultural unity, based on history, language, art, and science, shapes the people as a single entity possessing its own authentic spirit. The strong ties of spiritual cohesion of the middle ages are revalued, as are Romanticism's 'sentiment' versus Enlightenment's 'reason', and the rooting into a specific culture versus cosmopolitanism and cultural assimilation. In Fichte's *Reden an die deutsche Nation* (1807–8), the distinctive character of the German national spirit is not ethnicity or language but the spiritual freedom that Germans defended in the ancient wars against Roman rule, developed in the statutes and customs of free medieval cities (which were later suffocated by princes' tyranny), and affirmed through the defence of religious freedom in the Protestant reformation; spiritual freedom is the historical mission of the German people in the world, since striving for their national progress contributes to the moral progress of humanity.

These different historical sources risk giving rise to a polarized view of nationalism and national identities: civic and ethnic, political and cultural, liberal-associational and organic-integral, Western rationalist – democratic and Eastern mythical-reactionary. This polarization is due to the different national histories of French republicanism and German totalitarianism, which in their turn are responsible for the dichotomy between good democratic patriotism and bad undemocratic nationalism. For instance, Simone Weil in *Enracinement* (1943) sees patriotism – based on compassion and freedom of expression – as a human need of spiritual rooting, opposed to nationalism's blind attachment and arrogant pride. Carlo Rosselli in *Socialismo liberale* (1929) makes a clear-cut distinction between reactionary nationalism (Italian fascism being an example) and democratic patriotism that is respectful of other people's rights. Actually, the national principle and the democratic principle can be compatible, as in the case of the United States (USA). Already Tocqueville (1835–40) remarked that American patriotism is based on the rule of law, citizenship rights, democratic participation, and republican pride. And Walzer (1992) argues that American patriotism cannot be rooted in blood, religion or territorial ancestry, but can only be political, based on the principles of the Declaration of Independence, since this is the only possible form of collective engagement and loyalty in a multicultural society.

The civic/ethnic or political/cultural polarized view of nationalism and national identities has been persuasively criticized by scholars such as Huntington and Yuval-Davis. The former defines these pairings as "a false dichotomy" since "the ethnic category is a catch-all for all forms of nationalism that are not clearly contractual, civic and liberal. In particular, it combines two very different conceptions of national identity: the ethnic-genealogical (or ancestral), on the one hand, and the cultural, on the other" (2004: 30). While ascriptive elements such as ethnicity and ancestry are relatively permanent, cultural ones (i.e. language, religious beliefs, social and political values, assumptions about what is right and wrong, appropriate and inappropriate, and the objective institutions and behavioural patterns that reflect these subjective elements) are much more open to change. Besides, the relative importance of the elements of national identity varies with the historical experience of the people. In a similar vein, Yuval-Davis (1997) differentiates between three key dimensions of nationalist projects: the genealogical dimension that is constructed around the specific origin of the people (*Volknation*), the cultural dimension in which the symbolic heritage provided by language, religion, and other customs and traditions is constructed as the essence of the nation (*Kulturnation*), and the civic dimension, which focuses on citizenship, state sovereignty, and territoriality as determining the boundaries of the nation (*Staatnation*).

The analytical distinction of these three dimensions is important; it can be used to analyse how different mixes of the three components can foster different political arrangements. Whenever the three components are not well balanced problems arise: if the national identity is too heavily based on the civic dimension, the associated collective sentiment can be weaker than other subnational identities (ethnic, religious, local, regional) to the point of breaking the nation apart; if, on the other hand, the national identity is too heavily based on ethnic/genealogical and cultural aspects, it can become the ideology of a non-democratic state and foster xenophobic attitudes.

A shared collective identity and a common sense of national purpose are not necessarily democratic. The belief that the fight for national independence is intrinsically democratic and the prerequisite for the establishment of a peaceful community of nations (Mazzini, 1847) has been falsified by several historical cases. In spite of the historical linkage between national identity and democracy, nation states can be totalitarian as well, as Nazi Germany or the Stalinist Soviet Union (USSR); in both countries the nationalization of the masses was a key component of totalitarian consensus formation (Mosse, 1973). In many new nations, doctrines of self-determination turned into doctrines of aggressive nationalism that denied for others the same claims to independence. The independence of nations – even if achieved through a principle of self-determination – did not imply the end of the unequal distribution of power in world politics and, indeed, contributed to violent conflicts. Cattaneo's vision (1860) of the formation of a federal Italian republic as a basic step towards a federal Europe did not prevail in the process of Italian nation-building (*Risorgimento*), and it is still unaccomplished in today's European Union (EU).

The ambivalent nature of nationalism can be better understood by focusing on the basic claims of nationalist ideology. Ozkirimli (2010) identifies three sets of interrelated claims in the nationalist discourse: (a) identity claims: the world is divided into 'us' and 'them', friends and foes, positing a homogeneous and fixed identity on either side and stressing the characteristics that differentiate 'us' from 'them'; (b) temporal claims: the nationalist discourse is obsessed with the propagation of the 'authentic' version of the historical past and with establishing meaningful links to the past (also promoting social amnesia of problematic aspects that are not congruent with the official narration; and c) spatial claims: nationalists presume an inextricable link between the nation and the physical and built environment of a territory that is often seen as formative of the national character and bearing the indelible marks of the nation's presence. As a result of the previous claims, at the core of the nationalist discourse lies the affirmation of three priority claims: the values of the nation must have absolute priority; the loyalty to the nation overrides all other forms of loyalty, individual and collective (family, class, ethnicity, religion, etc.); the nation is the ultimate source of sovereignty. These ideological claims respond to the individuals' need to overcome the feelings of insecurity and perceived endangerment that result from uprootedness and the dissolution of old securities and old faiths (Hroch, 1985; Giesen, 1991).

But why is the nationalist ideology so powerful in convincing people that loyalty to the nation is supreme? If one focuses only on the ethnic/ancestral component, why this type of loyalty overrides others is not explained; the cultural and/or the political components of national identities must be also taken into account. Three specific answers can be given: the first is Anderson's well-known answer (1991): the nation is an imagined political community, since although no single member personally knows all other members of the nation, in their minds they all live in a community; it is a sovereign, limited, and particular community, imagined as creating a deep, horizontal comradeship. Anderson even speaks of the need to overcome the fear of an individual death by identifying with an immortal nation. A second type of response is more political and stresses the linkage with the nation state: nationalism is first on the scale of group values because it reflects a situation in which the most important actions of human beings are linked to the maximum locus of political power, that of the state (Albertini, 1981). A third response is sociopolitical: nationalist ideology, or discourse, has a powerful appeal because by affirming that it can abolish the distinctions between culture and politics, society and state, and private and public, it can mobilize the elites and the masses through the appeal to a shared historical destiny. In this respect, nationalism has an instrumental nature (Brass, 1991): ethnic and national identities are convenient tools in the hands of competing elites for generating mass support in their struggle for power, wealth, and prestige. The existence of objective cultural markers of ethnic differences, elite competition for leadership and the control of resources, and the communication of selected symbols of identity to a mobilized population (through growth in literacy rates, mass communication media, standardization of local languages) are the necessary conditions for successful ethnic identity formation and its transformation into nationalism; but the success of a national movement in its bid to control state power differs from time to time and from place to place, since it also depends on its political organization, the nature of government response, and the general political context. We developed our discussion so far within the modernist perspective, that is shared by most studies and by us as well. However, we will not neglect its main alternatives.

3 Main Alternatives to the Modernist Approach

A major alternative to the dominant modernist approach is the ethno-symbolist approach, which emphasizes the role of myths, symbols, memories, values, and traditions in the formation, persistence and change of ethnicity and nationalism, and argues that, although nationalist ideology and movement are modern, nations exist throughout history. Armstrong (1998) develops a century-long study of the formation of ethnic identities, focusing on the shifting significance of boundaries and on the long-term influence of 'myth-symbol complexes' on the emergence of modern national identities. Tullio-Altan (1995) considers *ethnos* as one of the five basic components of nationhood, together with *logos*, *topos*, *ethos*, and *epos*. Smith develops a complex and articulated theory of nation formation based on the interplay between *ethnie*, nationalism, and the modern state, where the *ethnie* is the core concept, defined in terms of six attributes (a collective proper name, a myth of common ancestry, shared historical memories, one or more differentiating elements of a common culture, an association with a specific homeland, and a sense of solidarity for significant sectors of the population). The nation is defined accordingly as "a named and self-defined community whose members cultivate common myths, memories, symbols and values, possess and disseminate a distinctive public culture, reside in and identify with a historic homeland, and create and disseminate common laws and shared customs" (2005: 98). Smith argues that the identities and legacies of earlier ethnic communities are the foundations of contemporary nations, and reconstructs the main trajectories of different ethnicities (lateral/aristocratic and vertical/demotic) in the process of nation-building through dynamic processes of ethnic self-renewal. The 'ethnic imperialism' of this view (Goio, 1993) is tempered by the distinction of two types of nationalism – territorial and ethnic – that give rise to different types of pre-independence and post-independence movements. Certain events, such as war and conquest, exile and enslavement, the influx of immigrants and religious conversion, generate profound changes in the cultural contents of ethnic identities; but even the most radical changes cannot destroy the sense of continuity and common ethnicity, partly owing to external forces that help crystallize ethnic identities and ensure their persistence over long periods, such as state-making, military mobilization, and organized religion.

This view of nations as solid and long-living social realities, changing but enduring, is shared by Hutchinson (2005), who argues that conflict is endemic to all nations, and that all nations contain plural ethnic repertoires that give birth to competing cultural and political projects in the modern period. Hence the formation of nations is an unfinished and evolving process, and "the preservation of persisting differences and rival cultural repertoires is one of the important reasons for the adaptability of the nation throughout two centuries of tumultuous change" (Hutchinson, 2005: 5). The ethno-symbolic critique of modernism is not ideological and does not prevent an integration of the two approaches.

The critique of the modernist approach waged by non-Western post-colonial leaders is more radical. Nationalism was a successful export of European modernity; it emerged in the late 18th century and exploded in the 19th, first in Europe and then in the Americas; in the 20th century it spread to Asian and African post-colonial nations, where it took new, autonomous forms, in the context of multiple modernities (Martinelli, 2005). The modern idea of popular sovereignty as an identity of people and nation state contributed to legitimizes the rise of anti-colonial movements; recognizing this fact does not imply affirming that the nationalist experiences in Asia and Africa are moulded on the modular forms of national society propagated by the modern West (Chattergie, 1993). But the most radical Asian and African nationalist leaders and intellectuals reject any link between nationalism and Western modernity, arguing that nationality is an inherent attribute of the human condition and praising the ancient (even eternal) character of their nation, the memories of a superior golden age, and the awakening of the nation after a period of decadence (Kedourie, 1971).

The view of these leaders is close to the most radical alternative to the modernist approach, the so-called perennialist/primordialist approach (Hastings, 1997; Grosby, 2001), which provides a quite different answer to the question "when is the nation?" by arguing that nations can be found in all historical epochs and are timeless, and that nationalism existed as a powerful reality in some places long before the 19th century. According to the sociobiological version of this approach (van den Berghe, 2001), nations are politically conscious ethnies, and ethnic groups have always existed, coalesced and broken up, appeared and disappeared in history. The sociological and anthropological studies that have inspired this approach (those of Shils and Geertz) are more sophisticated. The objects of primordial attachments such as blood, language, religion, and particular social practices are not given, but are assumed to be given by individuals. In *Primordial, Personal, Sacred and Civil Ties*, Edward Shils argues that family attachment can only be described as primordial because it is not just a function of interaction, but "because a certain ineffable significance is attributed to the tie of blood" (1957: 142). In *The Interpretation of Cultures*, Clifford Geertz writes:

> by a primordial attachment is meant one that stems from the 'givens' of social existence: immediate contiguity and kin connection mainly, but beyond them the givenness that stems from being born into a particular religious community, speaking a particular language, or even a dialect of a language, and following particular social practices ... One is bound to one's kinsman, one's neighbour, one's fellow believer, ipso facto; as the result not merely of personal affection, practical necessity, common interest or incurred obligation, but at least in great part by virtue of some unaccountable absolute import attributed to the tie itself. (1993: 259–260)

This perspective maintains that characteristics generally associated with nationalism exist in different ways and to different degrees throughout history, but it does not explain how nationalism differs from other types of primordial bonds, nor why it becomes the dominant type in given historical epochs. Several convincing critiques of this approach have been developed; we will mention three. Horowitz (2002) remarks that a lot is left unexplained in primordialist formulations; first of all why some affiliations become primordial while others lose out, and why ethnic boundaries include some subgroups and exclude others. Balibar (1990) criticizes the double illusion of nationalist narratives, that is the belief that the generations that succeeded one another over centuries on an approximately stable territory, under an approximately univocal designation, have handed down to each other an invariant substance, and that the process of national formation was the only one possible and represented a destiny. But the most sweeping critique is that of Hobsbawm, who considers primordialism dangerous for both historians and sociologists, because:

> it confuses socio-cultural analysis by failing to distinguish between the essentially state-aspiring 19th-to 20th-century 'nation' from ensembles of

communities politically dispersed by their structure, such as the ancient Ellenes ... it confuses socio-political analysis by failing to distinguish, as 19th-century politicians did so clearly, between achieved national reality (with or without recognized group history) and indeterminate national potential (2005: 81–82).

Although there is some truth in all three approaches (modernist, ethnosymbolic, and primordialist), the modernist is the most convincing: and can be usefully integrated with the other two. Nationalism is a modern phenomenon, closely related to the formation of modern nation states and to the other major economic and cultural transformations of modernity, but makes use of materials that antedate the modern era (primordial ties as elements of its emotional appeal), while the relationship between ethnicity, culture, and politics is a key analytical focus in the study of nationalism.

4   Nationalism in the First Decades of the 21st Century

In the first decades of the 21st century the legacy of nationalism is a mixed and contested one. The affirmation of the national principle can be seen as a fundamental step in modern history, insofar as it allows individuals to experience a shared collective identity and to embrace a common national purpose and contributes to make peoples key actors in world politics. But the nation state can also be (it was and still is) an instrument of authoritarian rule and violent international relations. Nation-building has historically been linked to war. Although the picture of nationalism drawn by scholars such as Carr (1945) and Kedourie (1960) who, shocked by the tremendous experience of the Second World War, saw nationalism as a dangerous legacy of the past, one that was invented by irresponsible intellectuals and spread by equally irresponsible demagogues, is too negative, one has to admit that nationalism continues to be a source of prejudice, tensions, and conflicts. Given the different timing and sequence of the path towards and through modernity and the unequal distribution of power in world politics, aggressive nationalism – with its the appeal to national interests and identities – can lead to protectionism and trade wars, regional conflicts, and hegemonic confrontation.

In today's world both nationalism and the nation state are facing new challenges in their relationship with the new global order and the fragmentation of ethnic, religious, class, and gender identities. Nation states are subject to the twofold pressure applied by the growing global interconnectedness of social relations from above and by the reaffirmation of regional and local identities and the emergence of new claims of autonomy from below. The process of globalization and the reaction to it brought some scholars to argue for the demise or the withering away of the nation state and given its close ties with nationalism, of nationalist ideologies as well. This was, however, a too hasty *de profundis*. In the post-bipolar world of the 21st century, the nation state is still the institutional embodiment of legitimate political authority, the key actor in international relations, and the taken-for-granted context of everyday life in most societies. No surprise, then, that its related ideology, nationalism, is alive and well; it is a powerful discourse that claims to produce collective identity, mobilize people for collective projects, and evaluate people's deeds. As Calhoun observes (2007: 1), "even when we are deeply critical of the nationalism we see, we should recognize the continued importance of national solidarities". The idea of the nation maintains a strong appeal to an inclusive collective identity and solidarity; it is a reaction to globalization, global interdependence, and cultural homogenization. The sovereign state does not wither away but transforms and adapts itself. The traditional ethnically and culturally homogeneous nation state is less fit for the new global context than the multiethnic and multicultural unions of the USA, Russia, India, Brazil, Canada, Australia, Germany, and the EU. The real alternative to the upsurge in nationalism is not a vague cosmopolitanism, but fully fledged federalism.

The 19th century and the first half of the 20th century were the age of the irresistible rise of nationalism. This nationalist fever did not decline among the peoples of Europe after the useless slaughter of the First World War; on the contrary, it reached a new level with the advent of totalitarian regimes and the global conflagration of the Second World War. Only the death of tens of millions, the shame and horror of the concentration camps, and the enormous destruction perpetrated by the war induced peoples that had fought against each other for centuries to put an end to the 'European civil wars', to establish peaceful relations, and to outline the supranational regime of the EU.

After the end of the Second World War, nationalism did not disappear but took other forms, first of all in the anti-colonial independence movements of Africa and Asia. At the end of the 20th century, it strongly re-emerged in Europe, where the collapse of the USSR caused the explosion of ethnic, religious, and national conflicts and tensions that had been latent and to a great extent absorbed into the Cold War confrontation between the two superpowers. The surfacing of these old conflicts was linked with the new conflicts that stemmed from the economic and political changes taking place in the post-Soviet world.

The nationalist parties and movements of Eastern Europe are not, however, the only instance of resurgent contemporary nationalism, since in many other European countries national populism is growing as a reaction to the threat of deterritorialization and uprooting caused by globalization and as a response to the problems raised by the economic financial crisis and the poor functioning of representative democracy both at EU and member state level.

Nationalism and nation have once again become a key yet controversial research topic in social sciences. There is a new awareness that nations and nationalism still matter. Although a key theme in the history of political thought, they were only a peripheral concern for political and sociological research until the last decades of the 20th century. This is no surprise: sociology and political science have developed as disciplines of the modern world, and the nation state has been the basic unit of analysis and frame of reference for most research. Besides, the fact that the world is divided into nations, and every person is born into a nationality, was seen as a feature of ordinary common sense and made nationalism a fact that was taken for granted. In recent decades, on the one hand, economic and cultural globalization has been eroding national sovereignty, while, on the other, with the end of bipolarism in world politics, old national and ethnic conflicts have re-emerged and new ones have appeared. In the following paragraphs we will discuss nationalism in the EU.

5   Nationalism and the Contradictions of European Integration

The birth of the European community at the end of the Second World War was rooted in the desire to put an end to the 'civil wars' of modern European history and to avoid the disastrous impact of aggressive nationalism. The EU is a specific and novel political construction, both institutionally and culturally. It does not reproduce the European model of nation state building, since it lacks fundamental characteristics such as a strong centralized power and a standardized culture articulated through a common language, and it seeks to preserve cultural diversities and different identities. For the first time in European history the state is relying not on military structures for the integration of such a huge and economically potent body, but rather on a legal and economic community, and does not aim to deprive its members of their cultural specificities. The memory of the tragedies stemming from competing nationalisms runs against the political construction of the EU as a nation state. The EU is a multinational union with a core of shared values (democratic institutions, basic human rights, free competition, preservation of different cultures and languages, peaceful coexistence in international relations) that are at the foundations of common institutions.

The question of nationalism is at the centre of two main contradictions in European integration. The first is the formation of a supranational union that uses nations as basic building blocks but pretends to get rid of the related nationalistic ideologies. The second is the contradiction between the transfer of growing portions of national sovereignty from nation state level to the supranational level (first the common management of the coal and steel industry and agricultural policy, and subsequently the measures designed to create an open European space for the free movement of people, goods, services, and capital, the establishment of a court of justice, the introduction of a single currency), and the still insufficient transfer of commitment and loyalty from member states' citizens to the evolving supranational community and European institutions.

The two contradictions are closely interconnected, since policy decisions at EU level unevenly distribute costs and benefits not only among social groups but also among member countries. This unequal distribution has contributed to the revival of what Emmanuel Macron in his 27 September 2017 speech at the Sorbonne defined as "les passions tristes de l'Europe: nationalisme, identitarisme, protectionisme, souvereinisme de repli", ideas that were thought to be defeated, after they had risked destroying Europe forever, but are now returning, clad in new clothes, because they cynically exploit the fear of the European peoples. These ideas foster a renationalization of conflict that must be countered by a commitment to the shared project and the development of a common identity by European citizens (as we argue in Chapter 1).

This is all the more required given the nature of European democracy. Most decision-making in the EU is still top-down, although efforts have been made to move towards a multilevel and multi-stakeholder governance. The national interests of the member states are predominant, something that is also caused by the 'democratic deficit' of the EU. The members of the European Council of heads of government – which is the body that holds the ultimate decision-making power in the tripartite structure of governance – are not chosen by a European-wide constituency of all citizens but derive their legitimacy from the respective national constituencies, and therefore tend to put national interests above common European interests. The attitudes of many citizens of member states do not differ from those of their leaders and are sometimes even more nationalistic. Bonds of affinity and shared values are still stronger at that national level, also as a consequence of the decline of the grand narratives. Idiosyncratic beliefs and stereotyped pictures of other peoples ('stingy Germans' and 'lazy Greeks') are hard to destroy. Europeans are inadequately aware of their common citizenship alongside national ties, do not identify enough with European institutions, and often oppose communitarian policies on the basis of national interests and identities. Charles De Gaulle's 'Europe des patries' is also, at least potentially, a Europe of nationalisms. Neo-nationalism in combination with populism blocks the road towards a stronger political community, which in its turn could provide legitimacy for a more encompassing supranational governance ("an ever greater union").

The intention of Europe's founding fathers, both political and intellectual, was that European institutions would gradually extend beyond nation states until they replaced them, but that this process should take place under the control of those nation states. It is somehow ironic that European integration, which intended to provide a substitute for national sovereignty, *de facto* ensured their survival and resilience in an increasingly complex world (Badie, 1995). Constructing a supranational union with nation states as building blocks was an effective compromise, but with risky implications. It was a compromise because it allowed the 'functional shift' (spillover) of increasing quotas of national sovereignty to the supranational level in spite of the resistance of nation states to any attempt to move into a federal direction. But it guaranteed the survival and to some extent the strengthening of nationalism. Also for this reason European integration was a stop-and-go process, with slowing down phases as in the 1970s and accelerating ones as from the mid-1980s to the mid-1990s. In to-day globalizing world it is more and more clear that no member country, no matter how economically powerful or politically ambitious, could face by itself the challenges of globalization, but member nation states must be persuaded that the EU is the best way to enable them to compete in the new global context, safeguarding some basic sovereign prerogatives.

The EU does not substitute for the nation states of member countries, since these have been simultaneously strengthened and weakened by European integration. To a certain extent, the EU can be seen as an instance of Lijphart's well known ideal-type of "consensual democracy"(1999), insofar as the different sociocultural components of European society are recomposed at political level by democratic elites that are open to cooperation and agreement.But nationalism at country level often makes cooperation and agreement difficult. The role of member nation states in European decision-making has been tempered by multilevel governance, that is a system of governance that relies on action taken at a whole series of levels (local, regional, national, supranational) by a variety of state and non-state actors who exist in an integrated hierarchy of decision-making (Rumford, 2002). Multilevel governance rather than government, and regulation rather than rule, are more appropriate expressions of European institutions and policies (Majone, 1996; Stone and Sandholz, 1998). But insofar as nations remain the building blocks of the supranational union (and actually have strengthened their role after the increasing power granted to the Council by the Maastricht and Amsterdam treaties), nationalism at the state level continues be a major obstacle, especially when it is used instrumentally by populist leaders as a main consensus strategy, and continues to obstruct the path towards an ever greater union. The response to anti-EU nationalism should not be to persecute the patriotic sentiments that support the national democracies of member countries, but to respect them while at the same time developing a European patriotism.

The second contradiction lies in the fact that there are limits to the extent to which a supranational government can advance the development of transnational economic, administrative, and legal integration with little community-building. European integration has advanced significantly within these limits through several sociopolitical mechanisms. First, there are the spontaneous and incremental processes resulting from the internal logic of integration (the spillover effect). Functional spillover occurs when the integration of a given sector implies the incorporation of other sectors because of economic interdependence. Political spillover is the result of a the consequent shift in political decision-making; as decisions are now taken at the European level, powerful interest groups shift their lobbying there in order to influence the decision-making process, and pressure their national governments into transferring ever more political functions to the supranational level. Second, European integration has advanced mostly as negative integration, through removing barriers to free circulation within the common market. Consensus has often been easily reached because the abolition of obstacles against the free circulation of people, capital, goods, and services has been a positive sum game. Third, innovative governance has been introduced, such as the Open Method of Coordination, which is based on participation and transparency as general principles and on guidelines and timetables, indicators and benchmarking, regional and national targets and measures, periodic monitoring, evaluation, peer review, and feedback as key steps. Finally, the EU has contented itself with member states respecting basic standards on the basis of minimum compliance, and has tolerated frequent violations of its rules and policies.

Economic globalization and the birth of the euro have changed the situation. Competition in the global market requires more positive integration, with greater coordination and further regulation, and this carries the risk of arousing strong reactions by national governments and by key actors in civil society. A single monetary policy increases the interdependence of the national economies of the eurozone, but the European Central Bank does not yet have the same powers that other central banks have, and there is not yet a EU Treasury that can issue Eurobonds. A single monetary policy requires a single fiscal and public expenditure policy, with strict controls on national governments by European institutions that are resented by citizens. Conflicts of interests increase among the member countries of the eurozone, between the more successful economies and those plagued by high state debt and unemployment, between the citizens of the former who do not want to repay the debts of others, and the citizens of the latter who protest against the sacrifices imposed by EU authorities and the loss of national sovereignty. In the post-reunification decade West Germans accepted with little protest their leaders' decision to grant about 700 billion euro to East Germans, because they were considered fellow Germans. But the same German citizens (who are also European citizens) are unwilling to give much smaller amounts to Greece and other member countries affected by the sovereign debt. As long as national politics is more important than European politics, political leaders will subordinate their decisions at the supranational level to the electoral competition at home. Functional spillover and the political mechanisms of the past are no longer enough. A greater normative consensus and a stronger commitment to a shared project are needed.

Moreover, the question of nationalism in contemporary Europe is not limited to member nations, but also involves the growing immigrant population that increases social heterogeneity. Immigration is not a question of national sovereignty but of cultural cleavages and involves both the cultural/ethnic dimension of nationalism and the political/legal one. The different member states' policies can be located on a continuum between the pole of assimilation (every individual enjoys the same rights and duties of citizenship, disregarding ethnic, religious, gender, and other differences) and that of multiculturalism (every member of a community has the right to keep its own distinctive values and practices). It is necessary to reduce the fragmentation and diversity of member states' policies, since they contribute to foster nationalistic prejudices and xenophobic closures. A single European immigration policy is needed, but it does not yet exist.

6   Main Causes of the National/Populist Upsurge in Contemporary Europe

Nationalism in contemporary Europe is often associated with populism, which is like nationalism, both an ideology and a strategy of consensus organization, but has a thin and less elaborated core (Mudde, 2007). A populist rhetoric is present in the language of almost all political leaders, but in some cases populism acquires the distinctive features of a specific ideology, thin but very strong. The populist ideology is organized around the two concepts of people (as the legitimate source of power) and community (as the legitimate criterion for defining the people), and emphasizes the antagonistic relationship between two homogeneous groups: *We* (the pure, virtuous people) and *Them* (the corrupt, inefficient, and negligent elite or establishment). It also upholds the right of the majority against the minority. Populism is a controversial, slippery, polisemic concept: it can refer to the sovereign *demos* (the legitimate foundation of the political order) or to the people-mass (the common people), or to the people-nation, with its ethnic roots (Meny and Surel, 2000). Populists differ on who should be included in or excluded from the people and which elites or minorities, besides established party leaders, should be blamed (Eurocrats, global finance, transnational elites, asylum seekers, specific immigrant groups). Common ideological elements are the mistrust of any elite, first of all the political elite, and the emphasis on the people as the true legitimate actor of public decision-making, the antagonism against international finance, the affirmation of the social bonds within organic communities which goes together with diffidence towards and refusal of others-immigrants, strangers, ethnic minorities, members of other religions (Martinelli, 2016).

The vagueness and plasticity of populism's ideological core, thin and strong at the same time, allows to combine it with a variety of 'thick' ideologies, such as nationalism or leftist radicalism, which add more specific content to it. In other words, conceiving populism as a 'thin' ideology allows us to account for the variety of political content and orientation of populist movements (on the right and the left), while simultaneously stressing a set of common features; it also illustrates the dependent relationship of populism on more comprehensive ideologies that provide a detailed set of answers to key political questions (Stanley and Ucen, 2008).

The link with nationalism is dangerous since it can imply violent conflicts and a non-democratic drift. Although not present in all forms of contemporary European populism, the link with nationalism reinforces and organizes populist ideology around the key questions of inclusion in/exclusion from the community and of the reaffirmation of national sovereignty against the EU 'super-state', in opposition to the project of an ever closer union. There is the widespread belief that some immigrant groups (as a whole, not single members) are culturally incompatible with the native community and are threatening national identities; and EU institutions are blamed for fostering the threat by upholding the free movement of people. Nationalism and populism have a lot in common (the demonization of political opponents, a conspiratorial mindset, the search for scapegoats, the fascination for more or less charismatic leaders), but, first and foremost, an anti-European stance. The hostility towards the European project of an ever greater union and opposition to the euro represent the connecting link between populism and nationalism.

The main causal factors of the rise of national populism in contemporary Europe are only partially common to this kind of political phenomenon in other regions of the world. European national populist leaders have been encouraged by Donald Trump's presidency, from Marine Le Pen of Front National to Nigel Farage of the United Kingdom Independence Party (UKIP), from Geert Wilders of the Partij voor de Vrijheid (Party for Freedom) in the Netherlands to Matteo Salvini of the Lega (League) in Italy, from Jörg Meuthen of Alternative für Deutschland to the leaders of the government parties of Hungary (Viktor Orbán) and Poland (Jarosław Kaczyński). Many of them welcomed Donald Trump's victory as the sign of new times and new opportunities for the majority that has been betrayed by globalization, and they have agreed with Trump's protectionism and demagoguery ("produce American", "buy American", "today power returns to the people"). However, they exaggerate the similarities between European and American politics, since European populism also has specific features that combine in different ways in the various EU member states.

In contemporary Europe, various interrelated causes contribute to the national populist upsurge (Martinelli, 2018). First, the post-Cold War scenario has brought to light old cleavages and old nationalisms and has created difficult problems of regime change, thus fostering the political career and access to power of populist leaders in Eastern Europe. Second, there is the double crisis of legitimacy and efficiency in representative democracies: on the one hand, mainstream political parties are less and less able to mobilize voters and to structure political conflict; on the other, global trends erode national sovereignty and limit the capacity of national governments to implement effective policies. In addition, the EU governance system does not yet have the legitimacy and scope of action necessary to deal with problems that are too big to be resolved at national level. Third, there is the impact of the long economic crisis, which interacts with the implications of the political Middle Eastern and African crises (asylum seekers and terrorist attacks against European cities), with the result that uncertainty, resentment, and fear for the future have been fed, creating favourable ground for anti-establishment parties. Let's see these causal factors in more detail.

The first set of causes – and opportunity structures – specifically concern the family of national populist parties of Central and Eastern Europe that in the 45 years after the Second World War experienced limited sovereignty, authoritarian regimes, and planned economies. The implosion of the USSR has awakened cleavages and conflicts that during the long Cold War had been absorbed into the bipolar confrontation between the USA and the USSR. The end of the struggle between two alternative *Weltanschauungen* helps explain the resurgence of national, ethnic, and religious identities and the related geopolitical conflicts that had been anaesthetized and hidden behind the rhetoric of the competing universalistic ideologies of free society and communism.

Old cleavages inherited from the past intersect, and partly overlap, with the new conflicts stemming from the political, economic, and cultural transformations of the present and the new global processes. With the collapse of the old regime, when the planned economy and the social security system are breaking down and when traditional social relations are in flux and a sentiment of general insecurity is growing, ethnic groups are forced to rely on their cultural and linguistic communities. Where society fails, the nation seems the only guarantee, and national populism prospers. Moreover, the Eurosceptic attitude of many leaders and citizens of countries such as those of the Visegrád Group (Czech Republic, Hungary, Poland and Slovakia) can be traced to the reluctance to give up (though partially) their recently regained national sovereignty to supranational institutions. The Visegrád Group countries share a notion of the EU *'à la carte'*: they gladly accept the financing of the social cohesion policy, but refuse to accept the agreed quotas of asylum seekers within their national borders.

The second group of causes that favour the rise of national populism concerns the pathologies of representative democracy and the crisis of its main actors – political parties. A representative democracy works well when a government, legitimized by the free vote of the majority and accountable to all citizens, can effectively handle complex issues. Today, both legitimacy and efficiency are in crisis.Traditional mass parties have been losing consensus and influence as a result of different yet interrelated processes of change: first, the declining appeal of the great ideological narratives owing to the failure of communism and the USSR's collapse, but also the helplessness of social democracy in the face of growing inequalities, and the boiling down of liberalism to a self-regulating market doctrine. The great cleavages – both of a political and cultural nature (state versus church, centre versus periphery) and of a socio-economic nature (land versus industry, capital owner versus worker) – that marked the formation of modern European society and gave birth to traditional parties were weakened by the combined impact of secularization, growth of the service economy, feminization of the workforce, and the extension of welfare. Together these processes lessened class and religious conflicts and undermined the traditional bases of mass parties. The economic and cultural processes of globalization deepened this transformation.

Contemporary globalization is characterized by the contradiction between growing economic interdependence at global level on the one hand and persistent political fragmentation in sovereign nation states on the other. This creates new technological and economic opportunities but also growing inequalities;

by distributing costs and benefits unequally, it fosters new cleavages in society between those social groups that are (or are deemed to be) favoured by the global economy and a multiethnic society and those that are (or are deemed to be) harmed; and these new cleavages exacerbate a misalignment between traditional parties and their voters. Until the 2008 global financial crisis, opportunities seemed to outweigh costs not only for the large emerging economies of Asia and the USA, but also for the EU; but after 2008 the balance has reversed, with economic stagnation, unemployment, and sovereign debt severely affecting several EU countries, which have only partially recovered.Traditional parties seem less and less capable of channelling, filtering, and processing the increasingly fluid and heterogeneous demands coming from civil society, with the result that their integration into coherent government programmes becomes more and more difficult.

Globalization has created problems not only for representative democracy but also for performing democracy. More than three decades of globalized economy have eroded the sovereignty of the nation state (which has been the context in which modern democracy has developed), reduced the range of government policy options and their effectiveness, thus further enlarging the gap between what is promised by leaders and what is delivered, implied a shrinking and redefinition of the welfare state, jeopardized the traditional intermediary role of parties, unions, business organizations, and professional associations, and fostered citizens' disaffection with and distrust of leaders' skills and democratic governments. In the EU, the erosion of national sovereignty of member states could be compensated for by supranational governance, but this has happened only to a limited extent because the EU is still unaccomplished, and also suffers from a democratic deficit.

The third main root cause is the global financial crisis and economic stagnation. These have amplified globalization's negative impact on some social groups (low-skill workers in traditional industries with diminishing wages, unemployed and underemployed women and youth finding only precarious jobs, and other globalization losers) and have furthered the opposition to migrants, who compete for jobs with the natives, and to transnational corporations, who cut jobs at home through offshoring (a major propaganda item in Trump's and European nationalist leaders' electoral campaigns). The prolonged economic and financial crisis and growing unemployment and underemployment have fostered a climate of psychological uncertainty, fragmentation, and precariousness with consequences for the political system of EU countries, specifically the rise of national populist movements.

Mainstream government parties, already under stress, have become the target of national populist propaganda that portrays them as the docile instruments of supranational technocratic and financial elites. For Marine Le Pen's

Front National, for instance, "le mondialisme" is the new contemporary slavery, and the vagrant, anonymous bosses of international finance are the new slave traders, who in the sacred name of profit want to destroy everything that tries to oppose their tyranny – first of all, the identity and sovereignty of the nation. The euro is involved in this condemnation and is defined as not only treason of France but of Europe at large, since it means the forced integration of the European economies into a US-dominated world market.

Together with global elites, the EU superstate, and the euro, immigrants are easy scapegoats: the long crisis has revived the denunciation of migrants stealing jobs and welfare subsidies from the indigenous population. National populist parties in many European countries – such as France's Front National, UKIP, Italy's Lega, the Perussuomalaiset (Finns Party, previously known in English as the True Finns), the Volkspartij voor Vrijheid en Democratie (People's Party for Freedom and Democracy) in the Netherlands, the Flemish Vlaams Belang (Flemish Interest), Fidesz (the Hungarian Civic Alliance), the Freiheitliche Partei Österreichs (Austrian Freedom Party) – uphold policies of welfare state chauvinism that restrict social protection only to natives (Kitschelt and McGann, 2000). The anxiety related to the economic crisis intersects with the fear caused by the consequences of Middle Eastern wars and African failed states; the terrorist attacks of Islamic fundamentalism against European cities and the pressure of asylum seekers who escape from war, political instability, and the social disintegration of many territories foster a diffuse sense of insecurity, resentment, and fear, and create favourable ground for the growth of parties and movements that name and shame the political and economic establishment.

The rise of national populism can also be traced, last but not least, to the cultural dimension of globalization – namely, to the explosion of digital communication, which has amplified the role of mass media in the political space. Traditional media, and commercial television in particular, have exerted for a long time a significant influence in politics, insofar as they contribute to the increase in costs of electoral campaigns and the connected influence of political lobbies, to the personalization of leadership, to the weakening of internal party dialectic, and to the depoliticization of mass protest. Communication specialists have replaced party cadres and foster the personalization of leadership. The marketization of mass media dictates its own logic, to which political actors have to adapt. Televised talk shows treat politics as any other message, fulfilling the need of drawing viewer attention by turning everything into something spectacular, oversimplifying and overdramatizing every issue, stereotyping and demonizing rivals, and reiterating scandals and personal accusations. Commercial TV appears coherent with the populist rhetoric of glorifying the common sense of the man in the street, even when it equals prejudice, disinformation, and false messages.

The new digital media turned out to be even more influential than television (Kriesi and Pappas, 2015) since they have further weakened political parties' capacity to mediate and intermediate and have undermined the authority of scientists, academics and intellectuals. Authority based on knowledge and experience is challenged daily by millions of web users who pretend to be experts in everything and are perennially indignant. The refusal to listen to the opinion of an expert or to verify the reliability of a presumed scandal is part and parcel with the populist distrust of and hostility towards any type of elite, including the intellectual elite, with the consequence that many people are victims of false news, concealed manipulations, conspiracy theories, 'post-truths' (2016 neologism of the year, according to the Oxford Dictionaries). This is an alarming picture: while the digital revolution offers many opportunities, it also raises worries when it comes to public democratic discourse. Blogs and social networks are seldom used in order to better the knowledge of reality, to develop the critical mind, to experiment with forms of deliberative democracy, to educate citizens to respect different opinions and be open to dialogue, debate, and compromise. The Internet is, on the contrary, more often used for naming and shaming, making up scapegoats, expressing frustrations and prejudices, and complaining, while putting the blame on others for misdoings and failures in a game of collective lack of responsibility. The field is thus open for the diffusion of messages with a strong and immediate emotional impact, such as those of nationalism, populism, and anti-Europeanism.

We argue that the hostility towards the European project and the opposition to the euro is the connecting link between populism and nationalism. As we discuss in Chapter 11, the 2019 European Parliament (EP) elections were a key confrontation between pro-EU and anti-EU parties. The latter, although increasing their consensus in several countries, achieved less than they expected and are marginalized in the EP. They hold more influence in the European Council, since Eurosceptic parties are in government in several EU countries: the four of the Visegrád Group (Poland, Hungary, the Czech Republic, and Slovakia), Austria, Bulgaria, Latvia, but no longer Italy (where Lega has gone into opposition). But does the attitude toward the EU change or remain the same when eurosceptic or europhobic populist parties are no longer in opposition?

What actually happens when national populist parties get to power? Do they show a clear discontinuity from their electoral/opposition past? Do they emphasize core populist topics (polarization of people/elites, scapegoating, conspiratorial beliefs, simplistic notions), or do they strengthen their nationalistic component, compensating for their weak populist one? The empirical evidence is contradictory. When in government some populist parties, such as the Italian Lega, remained strongly anti-EU, blaming the technocratic elite in Brussels for the poor performance of the Italian economy and even threatening to leave the monetary union, while other parties, such as those of the Visegrád Group, have been more cautious in their relations with European governance. Some common traits can be however detached.

Having become the new elite, national populist (or sovereignist) parties tend to underplay the core 'people versus elite' ideological item and shift the blame for their unfulfilled promises to previous governments and traditional elites. Populist parties display a strong ethics of conviction but a weak ethics of responsibility (in Max Weber's sense); that is, they underestimate the consequences of their ideological claims and policy choices. This attitude can help to win elections insofar as it allows them to promise ambitious reforms, knowing that they can hardly be implemented, but, together with the complementary attitude in which everything is simplified, makes policy delivery very difficult when these parties are in power. For leaders who proclaim that the key problems of the country are not complex and difficult to manage but just require simple, univocal solutions, that experts are useless since the wisdom of the people is enough, that for problems to be solved voting for the 'right' people is enough, it is hard to explain to voters, once elected, that their promises have to be watered down, delayed, or utterly forgotten, proclaimed party values no longer apply, external constraints (such as the reaction of financial markets or criticism by the European Commission) must be taken into account, and technocrats have to be recruited.

A frequent way out of these contradictions is blame shifting; national populist parties, when in power, try to persuade supporters that goals cannot be achieved because of the negative legacy of previous governments, narrow-minded Eurocrats, selfish international investors, and envious foreign countries; to this purpose conspiracy theories of various kinds are often developed. The link with nationalism plays an important role in this respect, since potential scapegoats are often foreigners, and the appeal to close ranks against aliens reinforces the consensus that is beginning to falter because of unfulfilled promises.

Another way to cope with the problems of difficult delivery of electoral promises by national populist parties in government is the attempt, made both by Fidesz in Hungary and Prawo i Sprawiedliwość (Law and Justice) in Poland, to implement constitutional reforms that reinforce executive power and 'direct' democracy at the expense of parliaments and the judiciary. In contemporary Europe, national populist parties are not anti-democratic; they are the permanent shadow of representative politics (Muller, 2016), and sometimes even claim to be the true interpreters of democracy – but they are against political pluralism, since they proclaim that the interests of the people and nation must have absolute priority. Populist leaders have an illiberal conception of democracy that stresses the democratic component ("government of the people, by the people, and for the people", the absolute power of the majority) at the expense of the liberal component (division of powers, constitutional guarantees, institutional checks and balances, minority rights) (Urbinati, 1998). In Italy Lega's leader Matteo Salvini criticizes verdicts by judges, affirming that they are not elected and therefore should be secondary to the will of the people, and the Movimento 5 Stelle (the Five Star Movement) extols the true democratic practice of the so-called Rousseau platform for supporters' online approval of party decisions. Victor Orbán's government introduced constitutional changes in Hungary aimed at reducing the power of the constitutional court, the independence of the judiciary, the freedom of the press, and religious pluralism, and Jarosław Kaczyński's government made similar attempts but run against a strong opposition in Polish civil society.

The challenge of national populism must be faced quickly and forcefully. The critiques directed at economic and cultural globalization (deepening inequalities, the fomenting of intercultural conflicts) and at representative democracy (legitimacy deficit, scarce effectiveness, mismanagement and corruption) must be taken seriously as a stimulus to implement reforms aimed both at bettering the quality of democracy, but avoiding the illiberal and anti-EU drift that populism implies. The strategy of restoring full national sovereignty and of renationalizing policy-making cannot respond effectively to the challenges of globalization, the digital age, climate change, immigration. The effective response is the construction of a great political union.

CHAPTER 3

Languages

1   The Distant Past

As Europe is an area of such diversity, one encounters a large number and great variety of languages in a very limited space. By whatever modern means of transportation you travel across Europe, you are very likely to find that in the course of a single day you must communicate with people in two or more different languages. The metaphor of the Tower of Babel applies to Europe more than ever. Its linguistic fragmentation is remarkable. From the Atlantic to the Urals, Europe's 730 million inhabitants speak 40 national languages, and another 13 recognized languages (such as Catalan, Ladino, and Provencal) – a unique variety that is comparable only to India, which has 23 official languages and a large number of minor languages. Moreover, many languages have such great and numerous variants that communication between persons speaking what purports to be the same language can sometimes be difficult. Yet these figures must all be regarded with caution, as they are based on different criteria. De Mauro, ironically alluding to the amorous conquests of Mozart's Don Giovanni, holds that there are "103 in Europe alone" (De Mauro, 2014).

It is estimated that between 6,000 and 7,000 languages are spoken in the world. In 98 per cent of cases, these are languages without, or almost without, written records, hence being expressions of exclusively oral cultures, and in total, they are spoken by no more than 10 per cent of the world population. At the beginning of the 21st century, there no longer exist any communities, and therefore no languages, that are completely isolated. Every linguistic community, however small, has its 'intermediaries', who know at least one other language and are thus able to communicate with the outside world. Consequently, next to thousands of 'peripheral' languages, about a hundred more restricted 'central' languages have evolved: these are the backbone of the global linguistic system, with the vast majority of European languages part of this core (De Swaan, 2001). With few exceptions, as we shall see, the European languages all pertain to the Indo-European language family; that is, they derive from a single language that no population speaks any more but linguists have reconstructed based on existent languages. This origin language is similar to Sanskrit, a holy language of the Brahmin caste in India. That it belongs to the same linguistic family indicates its remote origin and the earliest mix of populations in Europe, who came from the Middle East and Central Asia, probably Siberia.

The origin and formation of languages is a fascinating subject. They contain the history of different populations and indicate the migrations that have taken place over the millennia. Genetics, demography, and linguistics converge in the study of the formation and spread of languages. For instance, two of the languages that do not belong to the Indo-European family – in some ways opposites – are Basque and Maltese. Basque is a language with ancient origins that is spoken by a population that lives shielded from the world in the Pyrenees mountains. The Basque people have been isolated for thousands of years, and today claim autonomy from the countries between which their territory is divided: Spain and France. By contrast, Maltese is a Semitic language, hence belonging to the Arabic and Hebrew family, but over time it has been contaminated by Greek, Latin, Sicilian, Italian, and English influences for the simple fact that an island in the middle of the Mediterranean cannot possibly remain isolated.

Then there are the languages of the Finno-Ugric family (Hungarian, Finnish, and Estonian). These derive from the populations from Central Asia that settled partly in the Baltic region and partly in ancient Pannonia around the first millennium A.D. Today, even though their languages belong to the same linguistic family, a Hungarian and a Finn cannot understand one another: unless there is a modicum of constant contact, languages tend to develop in different directions under the influence of the historical experience of the populations that speak them. Turkish also belongs to the category of non-Indo-European languages. It is true that geographically the Anatolian peninsula is part of Asia, but the Bosporus divides Istanbul into two parts that physically belong to two continents. Taking into account Turkey's possible, albeit unlikely, membership of the European Union (EU) and the presence of strong Turkish minorities in various European countries, we must include their language among those that are spoken in this part of the world.

The pioneering research of Colin Renfrew (1996) seems to have confirmed the theory that the Indo-European language family followed the spread of agriculture from the Orient to the Occident, even though more recent research into the history of population genetics (Cavalli-Sforza, 1996) suggests that Indo-European populations settled in Europe in the Palaeolithic, several thousand years previously. We will probably never know with certainty where and when Indo-European populations established themselves in Europe. What we do know is that lexical and grammatical similarities confirm the theory that today's languages are the result of the differentiation of a single linguistic family, a process that lasted thousands of years.

We have a fairly cohesive picture of the Indo-European languages that were spoken in Europe from the first millennium A.D. onwards. Apart from languages that are extinct or spoken by tiny minorities, they can be divided into a few major subfamilies: Romance or Neo-Latin, Germanic, and Slavic. In addition to these three subfamilies, there are the Celtic (Gaelic, Scottish, Breton), Baltic

(Latvian and Lithuanian), Greek, and Albanian languages. Latin and Greek, the two ancient languages, have left considerable traces in the languages of Europe, in particular in scientific jargon. The split of the Roman Empire in A.D. 476 and the schism between the Roman and the Orthodox Churches have resulted in the influence of Latin in the West and of Greek in the East. We have a clear sign of this in the alphabets used: all Western languages have adopted the Latin alphabet, whereas the Greek alphabet and its variant, Cyrillic, have become established not only in Greece but also in part of the Slavic world, in Russia, Serbia, and Bulgaria.

Latin would probably have become extinct after the fall of the Roman Empire if it had not already been adopted by the Church. A second factor, after the 13th century, was its use by the emerging universities and in particular by the professional class of lawyers and other legal experts who linguistically followed the tradition of Roman law. Even though vernacular languages established themselves on an intellectual and literary level, Latin remained, until relatively recently, a learned language that was used almost as a second tongue by clerics, literati, lawyers, philosophers, and scientists. As late as the 17th and 18th centuries, people such as Copernicus, Kepler, Newton, Descartes, Spinoza, and Leibniz used their native language in everyday communication but resorted to Latin in scholarly work. Even today, in order to overcome the difficulties of what is considered excessive linguistic fragmentation, there are voices – though finding little support – that are suggesting a return to Latin. However, historic, and hence also linguistic, processes are irreversible.

It is quite unlikely that European languages will undergo a process of Creolization and pidginization (in which mixed languages develop through the interplay between two languages, the local one and that of the colonial conquerors) or that they will fuse into one language that is capable of merging various components. As we shall see, however, what is bound to happen is plurilingualism, or a stabilized diglossia, which combines the respective national language and English.

2 The Recent Past

The spread of vernacular languages that have established themselves through everyday use has received a powerful boost from a number of factors that have had either a synergistic or an isolating impact. These are the creation of language academies, the formation of the absolutist state and its connected bureaucratic organizations, the invention of the printing press, the Protestant Reformation, and, from the 19th century onwards, mass literacy.

The language academies that were established between the 17th and 18th centuries, to an extent modelled on the Accademia della Crusca (La Crusca) in

Florence (founded in 1603), were the prime contributors to the lexical and grammatical standardization of languages. This standardization met the demands of the emerging fiscal and military bureaucracies of the absolutist state. The invention of the printing press contributed to the spread of written language, which formerly had been the prerogative of clerics and scholars, among broader social classes. This occurred mainly, and initially, in countries through which the Reformation swept, where religious practice directed the faithful to read and interpret biblical texts without the mediation of the Church. In the 19th century – in different ways and at different times in individual countries – the state, by establishing mandatory elementary education, assumed the task of language instruction from childhood onwards for all those who would be called upon to serve the nation. The establishment of a national language in a specific territory was a process in which the state took on a leading role. It had to deal with two obstacles on different levels: Latin as the language of the educated and the various dialects as the language of the people.

The nations did in fact unify their territories from a linguistic point of view (see Chapter 2, on nationalism). The tool of this unification was compulsory education. France, for instance, has many peripheral languages: Breton, Flemish, Alsatian, Occitan, Corsican, Catalan, Ligurian (Nizza), and Basque; The United Kingdom (UK) has the Celtic languages (Scottish, Welsh, Irish, Cornish, and Manx). The official national language is the language in which every law, regulation, and administrative act is written, and in which instruction is held in school. It is the language that must be used for every report in the public administration system. It is the language of the rich and educated, of people with prestige; it is the language of newspapers, of radio and television. In addition, it is the language of those who are put in charge of the language's preservation (linguists, academics, etc.) and the establishment of standards for its correct use. When a state is strong, so is its language, to the point where language and the country's population tend to become synonymous. Many countries, for instance, consider adequate language skills to be one of the requirements that allows immigrants to obtain citizenship, indicating their integration into society and, especially, the labour market and community in which they live.

Moreover, since the end of the 19th century, mass communication, that is to say the publishing industry, daily newspapers, films, and, most importantly, radio and television, has effectively unified countries linguistically. This process has taken place – albeit with marked differences from country to country – relatively recently. Merely a century ago, for example, the vast majority of the population of the Italian peninsula was unable to effectively communicate among each other as dialects still constituted serious linguistic barriers.

Dialects merit a closer look. In Italy, in fact, a little over 45 per cent only use Italian within their families, while no more than 16 per cent speak dialect; the remaining 39 per cent speak both. We can say – as suggested by De Mauro (2010) – that a century and a half after the country's unification half of all Italians are practically bilingual. In effect, many of the so-called dialects are actually languages (often with a substantial and remarkable body of literature). Even so, with dialects, just as with languages, it is difficult to determine where one ends and the other begins. Languages are like nebulae; they blend into each other. Generally speaking, two languages are different from each another if those who speak one do not understand those who speak the other, and vice versa. To this day – using an extreme example – when a Sicilian and a Friulian speak dialect, they do not understand each other. If they want to communicate, both can learn Italian, the Sicilian must learn Friulian, or the Friulian must learn Sicilian.

What applies to the relationship between language and dialects on a national level also applies to the relationship between languages at a European level. It is easier to learn a language that belongs to the same linguistic family as one's own. For Italians, it is easier to learn Spanish (or, to be precise, Castilian or Catalan) or French than German. All Indo-European languages belong to the same extended family. Learning them is not an impossible task. For one thing, all European languages are based on an alphabetic, as opposed to an ideographic, writing system, which is a major advantage, even though not only the Latin but also the Greek and Cyrillic alphabets are used. The tendency in other respects is for similarities to be reinforced (Banfi & Grandi, 2003). All the linguistic features that are involved in this process of convergence are referred to as Standard Average European (SAE). The Standing Committee for Humanities of the European Science Foundation has identified the ten most representative features of SAE. First, there are the lexical similarities (many words are derived from Greek or Latin and, today, from English). Yet the similarities are not confined to lexical features; they also comprise aspects of syntax. For example, the common word order is subject–verb–direct object, the use of prepositions (rather than postpositions) is common, the use of auxiliary verbs (mainly to be and to have) is widespread, there are both definite and indefinite articles, and there is a tendency not to omit the personal pronoun (e.g. English, French, and German always require that the subject be indicated: I, you, he, we, etc.), the agent does not necessarily have to be the subject of the sentence, ("Anthony has broken the window with the ball" as opposed to "The ball has broken the window"), and the existence of the passive voice, which allows the identification of the agent ("The glass was broken by the ball"). However, there are also some morphological characteristics: agreement of the infinitive form of the verb and the subject (English is an exception here, as opposed to, say, Italian or German; the verb form is the same in such sentences as "I purchase a book" and "We purchase a book"). Finally, a reduction in the number of cases in the declination of nouns has taken place, with, for example, limits on the dative, accusative, and genitive cases (here Hungarian is an exception).

The European languages can be arranged according to how many of the ten features of SAE they possess, and their frequency. The list begins with the completely European languages (German, French, Dutch), followed by the medium European tongues (English, Italian, Spanish, Portuguese, the Slavic languages, etc.), and finally the barely European languages (such as the Ural languages, Basque, Turkish, and Kalmyk). If we look at the geographic distribution of the converging features, we can make out a correspondence with a certain area: this encompasses Flanders and includes the Rhine valley, Lorraine, Alsace-Lorraine, Switzerland, and Northern Italy. This is basically the Europe of Charlemagne, the area that, owing to the frequency of contact, communication, and commerce, has experienced more intense linguistic contamination during the past millennium.

3 Multilingualism and Plurilingualism: Europe's Inevitable Future

Europe is destined to be a society in which different languages live side by side. Multilingualism is an obligatory and also a desirable path. Even though the processes of convergence that have led to SAE will continue, there is no way in which a common language will ever replace current languages, not even in the very long run. Thanks to their lexical, grammatical, and syntactic similarities, European languages can at least be partly understood even by those who lack good language skills, and, most importantly, learning languages that differ from one's mother tongue does not present insurmountable difficulties for the majority of normally gifted men and women. In future, Europe will not only be multilingual but also plurilingual, meaning that an increasing percentage of its population will master a foreign language, or more than one. The increase in potential communication that this will bring about will no doubt accelerate the process of contamination between the various linguistic communities, and the percentage of those who can only express themselves in their native tongue will drop considerably.

The European languages are also for the most part destined to survive because they are actively protected through the policies either of individual countries or of the EU. Linguistic communities, which are usually organized in the form of nation states, can adopt one of two strategies: local protection or cosmopolitan opening up. In the former instance, they will appeal to the sense of remaining faithful to one's own – sometimes mythical – origin and in the latter case to the free circulation of ideas. Obviously, the size of the respective linguistic community is an important factor in defining linguistic policies. Estonia, with nearly 1.5 million people who speak Estonian, does not have the same problems as neighbouring Russia, with its population of a hundred times that size.

The opening up strategy on the one hand favours plurilingualism and on the other stimulates the translation of texts from and into the language. Learning one or more languages or making translations both require the public to shoulder economic costs; but there are other costs as well. As an example, let us take an author of literary texts for a linguistic community of limited size. He or she can settle for a potential audience of readers who only read in their mother tongue, learn to write in a more widespread language (at considerable effort), or else put himself or herself in the care of translators, activating channels that agree to access international publishing. An author of scientific texts will not have this dilemma: he or she will doubtless tend to write in the most widespread language in his or her particular scientific community, which is almost invariably English. These are more or less costly and risky strategies, with the risks being small or great. Since they are more expensive, the strategies that involve being open obviously also contain greater risks. It is simply not worth translating, or having translated, your text if you lack access channels to the publishing market of the language into which the text is being translated.

The relationship between learning languages and translations is complex. If I know a language and other conditions are the same (for instance, the obstacles regarding the circulation of texts, such as forms of censorship) it is not necessary to translate the texts that are written in that language. On the other hand, the possibility of gaining access, via translations, to the cultural heritage of another country can be a stimulus to learning that language, to the extent that one can at least translate from it. However, knowing a language that is not studied widely and from which only a few translations have been made gives those who master it what may be called an income monopoly, as all communications between the two communities are compelled to pass through the channel of those who function as mediators. A particular aspect of the relationship between learning languages and translating them is that of the dubbing industry, which prospers where foreign language skills are scarce. Conversely, and in a vicious circle, a lack of dubbed films constitutes an incentive to learn foreign languages. It would not make much sense to dub English-language films for a Swedish audience or that of any other Scandinavian country.

Where there are no obstacles of a political nature, such as censorship, to create protectionist barriers, the flow of translations from and into a specific language is left for the publishing industry to evaluate from the viewpoint of free trade. In some cases, states intervene in order to facilitate – for example, through subsidies – the translation of texts from the national tongue into other languages, thus adopting a policy of promotion with protectionist effects. If we look at the *Index Translationum*, a database of statistics on books translated throughout the world that the United Nations Educational, Scientific and Cultural Organization (UNESCO) has been entirely computerized in 1979 (the League of Nations having established it in 1932), we note that the language from which most texts are translated is English – as expected – followed by French, German, Russian, Italian, Spanish, and Swedish. The first non-European language that appears on the list is Japanese.

We must also take into account the great technical progress in automated, digital translations (using tools such as Google Translator) that has been made during the past decades. Even though it is likely that there are insurmountable limits to computerized translation work, the great speed and acceptable degree of accuracy that have been achieved permit us to predict more interesting progress in this direction.

In summary, it is safe to say that more is being done in Europe than anywhere else to overcome the challenge (or curse) of the Tower of Babel. To preserve one's own language and avoid the danger of becoming extinct, linguistic policies around language learning can include:

1. promoting the learning of one or more foreign languages by supporting public education;
2. promoting the learning of the national language among immigrants;
3. promoting the teaching of the national language outside the language borders.

In some countries (the Netherlands, Denmark, Sweden, and Norway), 80 per cent of the population is already diglossic. The risk here is that the dominant language is used when natives communicate with one another, putting the local language at risk of being supplanted –no longer being passed on to the next generations. This is the process that has begun with the (partial) disappearance of dialects, and may continue with the minor languages that are only spoken by a few tens of thousands. The collective cultural capital that these languages have accumulated is at risk of being lost. This also happens in areas with numerous local languages, where there is resistance to learning one as the common language. India is a case in point: English – already the means of communication among the elite – is turning into the language for communication between the various local linguistic groups that prefer to use English than to learn Hindi, the most widespread language on the subcontinent (spoken by nearly half a billion people).

The European languages are almost all strong enough not to have to fear extinction, even though the increasing frequency of relations between them will no doubt generate further contamination. A few very small linguistic communities run some risk of isolation, and will find it more difficult to maintain intensive and frequent relations of any kind with other populations. European languages that are widespread in other parts of the world certainly do not have this problem. The colonial expansion of European powers in other continents in the 18th and 19th centuries led to their languages being spread outside Europe. The fact that tens of millions of people in the world use English, French, Spanish, and Portuguese is a consequence of the colonial past of the European powers, whereas the scarcity of Italian and German speakers outside their countries' national borders can be explained by the brief duration of their colonial empires, these being too short to impose their own languages onto the colonial populations.

4 The Linguistic Policies of the EU

In the EU in 2020, about 12 million European citizens live in a country other than the one in which they were born. Many companies have established offices in various countries within and outside the EU, and even more maintain almost daily relations with partner companies that operate in other countries. The flow of international tourists is intense, while thousands of students participate in exchange programmes, attending classes at universities in different countries for differing periods of time. The free circulation of persons as defined in the Schengen Agreement of 1985 has facilitated an increased frequency and volume of communication (Recchi, 2013). Enabling and augmenting these flows of communication obviously requires knowledge of languages other than one's mother tongue. From the beginning, the European Commission has set itself the goal of increasing the number of citizens who are able to interact with people outside their own community. Even though the EU has no actual say in matters of education and instruction, which remain the domain of member countries, it has nonetheless repeatedly urged the Parliament, the Council, and individual states to launch policies that promote plurilingualism, making clear its objective that every European citizen should know two languages other than her or his own. The objective is doubtless realistic – even though rather long term – for every country, but especially so for some of them.

A 2011 study by Eurostat (see http://ec.europa.eu/eurostat/statistics-explained/index.php/Foreign_language_skills_statistics) has painted a picture of the plurilingualism among the European population that is both positive and negative. On average, 34.3 per cent of EU citizens do not master any language other than their own, 35.6 per cent master only one, 21 per cent two, and 8.8 per cent three languages. Yet plurilingualism is distributed quite unevenly among different countries, as well as among different generations and social classes.

Some countries have a high degree of competence and an acceptable level of plurilingualism has already been achieved, with three out of four people being able to sustain a conversation in a language other than their mother tongue (Estonia, Latvia, Lithuania, Luxembourg, Malta, Holland, Germany, Slovenia, Slovakia, Denmark, Sweden, and Finland). As we can see, apart from Holland, Austria, Germany, Denmark, Finland, and Sweden, these are very small linguistic communities, where it is essential for people to speak at least one foreign language as soon as they leave their house. Then there is a group of countries that are halfway to the goal, with more than two-thirds of the population already speaking at least one language other than their own (in descending order: Cyprus, Belgium, Czech Republic, and Poland). At the tail end are the countries that still have a great distance to cover in order to reach an acceptable level of plurilingualism (in descending order: Greece, France, Ireland, Spain, Italy, Portugal, the United Kingdom, and Hungary). In this not very laudable company, we can make out different situations. In some countries, such as the United Kingdom and Ireland, there is less of a need to communicate in a language other than one's own, for obvious reasons; the same applies, albeit to a lesser degree and in a different way, to France, Spain, and Portugal, which have considerable communities of people who can speak their language within their country, and especially beyond the confines of Europe. Then there are also two eastern countries (Poland and Hungary) and two countries in the Mediterranean (Greece and Italy). That one of them is considered the eighth greatest industrial power in the world is certainly not very encouraging in terms of building a European citizenship.

Apart from the political effort to increase the knowledge of languages other than people's mother tongues, an area in which the EU can only attempt to guide the actions of member countries, it is also important to consider the reverse, in other words how member states influence how the institutions of the Union operate in terms of languages. Currently there are 24 official EU languages among the 28 member countries. Even in the future, it is quite impossible that the principle of equality of these different official languages will be abandoned in the EU's formal circles. Identity is a stronger rationale than efficiency and economy and will continue to be so in the future. The proposal to adopt a single language (e.g. English) or to reduce the number of official languages will never gain a majority among the member states of the European Parliament. In fact, though, within the Brussels bureaucracy English and French remain the working languages used for everyday communication. Initially, when there were only six member states, French was the prevalent language. Later, English became more established, especially after the United Kingdom joined the group. This situation is probably not going to change drastically following the 2016 referendum that initiated the exit of the United Kingdom from the Union, even though the percentage of representatives in the Brussels bureaucracy whose mother tongue is English will certainly dwindle.

By now, EU officials are used to thinking in a language other than their mother tongue and to be constantly switching from one language to the other in everyday interactions. In addition, multilingualism is dictated by the fact that European laws are integrated into national laws. Hence, all directives must be translated into all 24 languages, while other official documents are only issued in French, English, and German, with other languages being used at the discretion of the Directorate-General for Translations or upon request. Since every deputy has the right to speak in his or her own language, up to 800 interpreters are hired during parliamentary sessions, a number that could be even higher if every discourse in the official languages was simultaneously translated into all the other languages. The principal argument against multilingualism is obviously the expense of translation and interpretation services. In the EU budget, administrative expenses amount to about 6 per cent (of €142 billion), and the language costs make up nearly 30 per cent of administrative expenses, a figure that exceeds the €300 million that it costs to remunerate about 2,500 translators and 570 permanent interpreters.

5   English as Lingua Franca

For thousands of years, languages have spread through migration, wars, conquests (the language of the victor is typically imposed on that of the defeated), commerce, and more or less coerced religious conversion. European languages have spread as a result of (English, French, Spanish, and Portuguese) colonialism. German and Japanese (but also Russian) disappeared as 'imperial' languages with the fall of the respective empires. The spreading of languages therefore depends on many factors of a political nature. Politics and culture tend to mutually reinforce one another, but it is politics that ultimately exerts the primary influence.

TABLE 3.1 Use of languages in the EU (%)

	As mother tongue	As foreign language	Total
English	13	34	47
German	18	12	30
French	12	11	23
Italian	13	2	15
Spanish	9	5	14
Polish	9	1	10
Dutch	5	1	6
Russian	1	5	6
Other	2	3	5

SOURCE: EUROBAROMETER, 2006

Today, the chief instrument for acquiring a language is educational institutions, but, indubitably, the fact that English has become ever more established as the lingua franca during the last half-century has coincided with an extended period of hegemony on the part of the United States (USA), not only in international politics but also in the fields of cultural production and scientific research. To understand this privileged position of English, it is helpful to look at the data concerning the size of the community of those who speak English, either as their mother tongue or as a foreign language, within the EU (until the day of UK membership).

The number of those who use English is much larger than that of English native speakers. German has a greater ratio of native speakers and also a larger number of non-natives (primarily because of the immigrants from Italy, Spain, and Greece in the 1960s who now speak the language of the country that has given them jobs). As for French, for every native speaker there is almost one who speaks it as a foreign language, and the same applies to a lesser degree to Spanish (whose potential for growth lies mainly outside Europe). The other languages – including Italian – are not used much outside the circle of 'natives', while within the EU, Russian is spoken only by a small minority in the Baltic states – as they were once part of the Soviet Union.

English has now practically won the competition against all other languages that might have had a shot at becoming the lingua franca of international relations. French resisted the longest, but in the end had to succumb. It is an unequal competition, and Europe cannot but adapt to the conditions that are becoming established around the globe. Today, almost 1 billion people are able to communicate in English – geographically, it is the most widespread language (from Australia to New Zealand, from India to South Africa, from North America to Europe). It has become the language of digital communication, and hence of globalization. From a linguistic point of view, its richness is related to its expansion, in that every experience of expansion signifies enrichment. A fact that may have contributed to this is that English is a language that developed through a process of hybridization. Historically, English followed its singular course because of factors that have nothing to do with the structure of the language. It is derived from Old Saxon, the language of the conquerors who arrived on the island from what today is Germany and Denmark, but even before the Norman Conquest (1066) expansion of the Roman Empire during the age of Caesar subjected it to the influence of Latin. After 1066, Norman French added to the influences. English developed as a mixed language, a product of the hybridization of Anglo-Saxon, Norman French, and Latin. Modern English is therefore a hybrid, a sort of linguistic hodgepodge. English owes its extraordinary lexical richness to the fact that the same object often has several synonyms, which are derived from different components. Global English (Globish) is a language that exhibits remarkable flexibility, this being manifested in its capacity to create neologisms and to adapt itself to innovations in every field. Yet there are also those who caution against the impoverishment and flattening of national languages that the spreading of Globish (known in German as *Globalesisch*) may entail (Trabant, 2014). Those who consider the dominant position that English has acquired to be excessive may be pleased about the possible, albeit unlikely, outcome that English will diminish in importance in the wake of Brexit.

From a strictly linguistic point of view, an artificial language such as Esperanto might have been able to become a lingua franca more efficiently, and at a lower cost (Eco, 1993). From a lexical, grammatical, syntactic, and phonetic point of view, English is not a particularly easy language to learn. Yet even though linguistic phenomena are influenced by economic and political factors, they are not the result of 'rational' political decisions. The language system that today sees English in a dominant position has not been designed for purposes of efficiency. It simply happened owing to the convergence of many factors and as an unintended consequence of a number of decisions, non-decisions, relinquishments, and adaptations whose cumulative effects were altogether ignored. "In the long run", writes Abram de Swaan, "it turned out to be a process of continuous integration that greatly increased the coherence of the human species in its entirety" (De Swaan, 2001: 186).

6   Languages and the Culture Industry

The development of culture is marked by a series of epochal transformations. The first of these was no doubt the transition from oral communication to writing (Ong, 1986). The second was the invention and spreading of the printing press. However, for hundreds and even thousands of years, cultural production remained the prerogative of a rather small elite. As we have seen, the situation changed drastically with the advent of mass education, which spread linguistic faculties among ever larger groups of the population. Until the digital revolution of our age, which has seen the centres of innovation shift across oceans (the Atlantic and also the Pacific), the cradle of these changes was always Europe.

The quantity of print products (books and periodicals) is a good indicator of the significance of various linguistic communities, even though we must keep in mind that the size of linguistic communities does not correspond exactly to nations and their populations. This is partly because some countries are multilingual and partly because there are languages that are spoken (written and read) in a large number of countries. The potential market for published material is obviously related to the size of the speech community toward which it is directed, but also to its spending power and its propensity to consume books and periodicals. Economic obstacles to their consumption have shrunk over time not only because incomes have gone up, but also and above all because of the considerable reduction in the cost of individual books: nowadays, there are affordable editions available in every language that has a certain level of importance, at least for works with a large circulation, and they are available to everyone who can read. However, there are still cultural barriers owing to reading (or non-reading) habits that have been acquired over time, and turn out to be very difficult to change.

With regard to these reading habits, there are marked differences exhibited across Europe. Unfortunately, Italy does not shine in terms of the consumption of printed material, owing to an old cultural discrepancy between a small educated elite and a large majority of people who have hardly any education, a discrepancy that has shrunk over time but is still considerable. Data published by Italy's National Institute for Statistics tell us that 10 per cent of families own no books at all, 63.7 per cent own fewer than 100, 11.8 per cent between 101 and 200, and only 14.5 per cent more than 200. In the last 12 months, only 45 per cent of Italians have read a book, a little lower than Spaniards (52 per cent) and Flemings (57 per cent), much lower than the Dutch (70 per cent), and especially the Finns (83 per cent). Women and young people read the most, while only 27 per cent of Italians over 65 have read a book in the last year. The data concerning the use of public libraries show the same tendency: while cost may be a factor that prevents people from buying books, this does not apply to visiting a public library. If one considers the number of titles published every year, differences between individual countries are not particularly pronounced, appearing to depend mostly on market size and different reading habits, and hence indirectly on differences in levels of education.

However, the publishing industry does not just publish books that were written in the language of its consumers. Translations constitute a prominent part of book production, especially in Europe. UNESCO's *Index Translationum* indicates that nowadays currently about 90,000 books are translated every year from all the world's major languages. Europe is a 'translation factory' – about 80 per cent of all translated books are published in Europe, and in the field of fiction the percentage is even higher (85 per cent). The novel is a literary genre that originated in Europe, while readers of novels also participate in a European culture that sustains translators' work. It comes as no surprise that English is the language from which most works are translated: out of ten translated books, typically six were originally written in English, followed by French, German, Spanish, Italian, Swedish, and Russian. As noted earlier, the first non-European language from which books are translated is Japanese, and this s followed by Arabic and Chinese. Yet the differences are quite pronounced: while every year about 25,000 titles are translated from English, the number of translations from French and German is no more than 3,000, while Italian and Spanish barely amount to 1,000 and Russian to 600; for other languages (Dutch, Danish, Norwegian, Portuguese, Polish), the figures are even smaller. It is curious to note, for example, that in France, apart from English, more books are translated from German, Japanese, and Spanish than from Italian, partly perhaps because a number of French people are able to read Italian. In Germany, after English and French comes Italian, from which more books are translated than from Spanish (or more specifically Castilian), Dutch, Swedish, or Russian. In Italy, the languages other than English from which books are translated are, in descending order, French, German, and Spanish.

In Europe, the country with the fewest translations from other languages is, understandably, the United Kingdom, but France does not show an impressive number of translated books either. This is an aspect of countries that profit (especially the United Kingdom) from having a lingua franca that is disseminated outside their national borders, but also of countries that cultivate what we may call a certain cultural narcissism: in Sweden, 60 per cent of published books are translations from other languages; in Italy, Holland, Spain, and Germany the figure is more than 20 per cent; in France it is 15 per cent; and in the United Kingdom it is only 2.5 per cent.

The minority languages (Catalan, Gaelic, Breton, Friulian, etc.) that are spoken in some regions, and whose presence in European culture depends heavily on translations, deserve a separate discussion. It is interesting to note, for instance, that more than 20 per cent of translated books from Catalan and Breton are found outside Spain and France respectively, signalling the vitality, or at least the capacity to survive, of these minority cultures and languages.

Shakespeare is one of the most translated classic authors. This is partly because he wrote in English and partly because he wrote for the theatre (and hence his works have been available for cinema and opera). Most importantly, though, he dealt with universal traits of the human spirit, such as envy, jealousy, ambition, power, pleasure, and hate, which do not belong to any one specific culture. Mysteries also know no borders: Agatha Christie and Georges Simenon are always found at the top of lists of authors who have been translated into other languages. Generally speaking, translations reduce the isolation of national literary cultures (although literary awards are almost exclusively given to authors who write in the national language of the country where the prize has been established). Readers of literary works display preferences and reading habits that are influenced from outside the confines of their country. Some best-selling non-Anglophone authors, for instance, have spread throughout the world, including English-speaking countries (take, for example, the books of Thomas Mann, Antoine de Saint-Exupéry, or Paulo Coelho, to name just a few), while in Germany as well as Italy, authors who write in English have the most bestsellers. This is even the case if the recent success of books by such authors as Ken Follett or J.K. Rowling is disregarded. For example, the five-volume *Harry Potter* series has sold over 270 million copies worldwide, a global phenomenon, more so than the fairy tales of the Brothers Grimm and of Hans Christian Andersen, to which millions of children have been lulled to sleep for more than a century. Movies often repopularize books (e.g. *The Lord of the Rings*), and sometimes the success of a book anticipates that of the film (such as the Harry Potter series).

Every autumn, the Frankfurt Book Fair takes place, at which publishers negotiate contracts for translation rights. This is one of the more significant European cultural events, symbolizing the scope of the flow of ideas that push the boundaries of that cultural object par excellence: the book.

While culture crosses borders by way of translations, the publishing industry is still very much nationally based from an economic point of view, as the majority of publishers and editors work within their respective linguistic community. There are, however, some indications that things might be changing in the not too distant future, or are already changing, in the direction of globalization: the German Bertelsmann publishing group has acquired Penguin

Random House, which operates in England, North America, Spain, and Latin America, as does Springer. Australian financier Rupert Murdoch acquired the publishing house William HarperCollins. The scientific publishing sector is very much globalized, but essentially has a European mould. The story of such publishing houses as Brill, Elsevier and Kluwer goes back to the Netherlands of the 16th and 17th centuries; today they are global giants.

In the daily newspaper segment, the publishing branch of Rupert Murdoch's News Corporation, in 2013 split from the media branch (renamed 21st Century Fox and in 2019 Fox Corporation), and gave rise to a publicly traded company that publishes 175 newspapers worldwide, including *The Times*, the *Sunday Times,* and *The Sun* in the United Kingdom, the *New York Post* and the *Weekly Standard* in the USA; 40 million copies are sold per week on all continents. Yet the daily newspaper sector is in more or less slow decline, depending on the country. In United Kingdom 14 million copies were sold in 1975, but today this figure is less than 8 million copies, and the same phenomenon can be observed in nearly all countries. Young people in particular do not read the daily press; their main source of information, apart from television, is certainly the Internet. Dailies typically have a local or national circulation, and it is difficult for them to cross the borders of their respective language community. The only newspapers with a worldwide circulation are English-language publications. The *Financial Times* is currently printed in Frankfurt, New York, Paris, Tokyo, Stockholm, Madrid, Los Angeles, Hong Kong, Milan, and Chicago, while the *International New York Times* (heir of the historic *Herald Tribune*) is printed at 35 different locations and sold to a sophisticated readership throughout the world, with the *Wall Street Journal* in a distant second place. Attempts to launch a daily European newspaper have all failed so far. There are, however, collaboration agreements among various newspapers, and on occasion they publish the same articles simultaneously in different languages.

Television broadcasts also have an essentially national audience. At irregular intervals, though, the Eurovision network broadcasts sports and cultural events of special interest. With a few exceptions, the collaboration arrangements have no significant influence on the programming of national and local television networks. One exception is the Franco-German ARTE channel, although it has a rather limited audience as it focuses on cultural programming. The absence of information agencies that address a large audience throughout Europe is doubtless one of the factors that is impeding the formation of public opinion on a European scale: the European *demos* is still in an embryonic state.

Movie production often crosses linguistic barriers, either because there is an audience with plurilinguistic skills or via subtitles and dubbing. The film market has transnational dimensions as far as the audience is concerned, in terms of demand (the award-winning films at the large festivals in Cannes, Venice, Berlin, and Los Angeles with the Oscars, are distributed throughout the world), whereas production, or supply, is still essentially a national affair. Some other media have a transnational market, essentially global in scope, such as TV series, animated cartoons, and video games, whose production industry is, however, again a national affair.

As far as theatre productions are concerned, local and national dimensions have certainly acquired much more clout. Leaving dialect theatre enclaves aside, if we look at the programmes of the major European theatres, we may note that the authors of the works performed are very often from foreign countries and, with a few important exceptions, are for the most part European. Classical theatre is a specifically European tradition. Even so, we can make out considerable differences in the frequency of theatrical performances between Northern and Southern Europe: the further south you go, the less often do people go to the theatre.

For segments of the culture industry that are less language-based, it is obviously easier to take on a transnational dimension. Music in all its forms is a much more international cultural segment, at least in higher-brow circles. In classical music, including opera, the majority of performers appear in concert halls and on opera stages throughout the world once they are famous. Classical concerts are attended by an elite minority everywhere. In Italy, only 10 per cent of the population goes to a concert at least once a year; the percentage is slightly higher in Finland (11 per cent) and in Holland (16 per cent), while almost one-third (31 per cent) of Flemings in Belgium show an interest in classical music. Pop music concerts attract mainly young people, without major differences across all European countries, and the great stars are all in a thoroughly cosmopolitan firmament. The star system is characteristically international, but next to the Beatles, the Rolling Stones, and rock celebrities such as Mick Jagger and David Bowie, there are also national idols who have leaped across their borders. Examples are French chansonniers such as Edith Piaf, Charles Trenet, and Yves Montand, who were famous in the first decades after the Second World War, and also Italian singers of recent years such as Gianna Nannini, Laura Pausini, and Eros Ramazzotti.

The music reproduction industry is also highly international (more than 3 billion compact discs were produced and sold in the world in 1995). The European market is one of the largest, and record labels are almost all multinational (American – RCA, Japanese – Sony, but also European – Philips). Today popular music tends to be sold online rather than on discs. On the one hand, consumers can download either whole albums or individual songs, onto their MP3 player or, rather, smartphone. On the other end there are digital streaming services, such as Spotify. However, production is often geared to the specific musical culture of individual countries. The role of the radio in the promotion of pop music has certainly been enormous, but the overwhelming majority of radio stations provide local broadcasting, very often also available on the Internet.

Overall, music is global, but there are also breeding grounds of resistance in every country that defend local and national traditions. Folk music, including its various politicized variations, tends to be tied to specific regional contexts (to remain in Italy, examples are Jannacci, Gaber, and De André).

We can also consider other aspects of the culture industry. It is interesting to note that major museums are also part of collaboration and distribution networks and belong to international groups. It is not rare for major cultural events (e.g. exhibitions of the works of famous artists) to travel from city to city across different countries. Almost all great museums were established between the 18th and 19th centuries to celebrate first the monarchy and secondly national identity. National heritage for the English, *patrimoine* for the French, and *Kulturgut* for the Germans are terms that summarize the totality of cultural goods in which a nation recognizes its own traditions. Today, the functions of celebrating and educating the public about the cultural heritage of the nation has been taken to the next level: museums have become a primary means of cultural tourism that rarely remains within national borders. The initiative of the EU and the European Council to designate two cities as European Capitals of Culture every other year is important in this context. Since this idea was born in 1985, about 50 European cities have been Capitals of Culture and, even though this has been for the most part a tourism marketing initiative, it has always triggered great interest among the great many cities that have been presented as candidates.

If the city, as we shall see in greater detail in Chapter 6, is clearly an undisputed part of European culture, so is rural culture. There is practically no region, province, or district in Europe that has failed to establish a museum of farming culture in the past 50 years to document the centuries, or even millennia, that preceded the Industrial Revolution. Territories, cultures, climates, property, and bonds between people and the Earth are extremely varied across Europe, so it is surprising to learn how great the similarities in farming cultures still are.

There are marked differences in museum attendance. According to most recent data, in Greece, nearly 90 per cent of people have not entered a museum in a year, in Spain the figure is 71 per cent, Italy 70 per cent, in Holland 68 per cent, and in Denmark 64 per cent, whereas museum-goers make up almost half of the population of Belgian Flemings and Finns.

The electronic toy industry (especially in America, Japan, and the UK) also merits a glance: it has sold more than 2 million products in the past 20 years. This market has reached considerable dimensions and has become one of the factors that impact the skills, and also the behaviour, of younger generations.

This last area is an aspect of the digital revolution that has changed and will continue to change the everyday culture and life of men and women throughout the world. Its expansion is unstoppable. Within a few decades, practically the entire world population (except marginal fringes) will have access to the Internet. There is no doubt that the so-called dot com revolution is part of the globalization process, nor is there any doubt that English is the language that dominates the Internet. The messages that circulate, however, consist of pictures, sounds, and also words that reflect a linguistic Babylon. Is there a 'global village' in the making? Will it be dominated by American culture, or will fragmentation and diversity increase? What will become of European identity online? Will it be watered down in the undifferentiated space of globalization or will the Internet become one of the vehicles through various territorial identities, and hence also the identity of Europe, can be expressed?

CHAPTER 4

Religion and Religions

1   A Look at the Past

The range of religions in contemporary Europe has developed over the centuries in the course of a long and often tormented history. The faiths and cults that preceded the advent of the three great monotheistic religions are a subject of interest for historians and anthropologists. The culture of current European populations contains only vestiges of rituals, which have been syncretically incorporated in subsequent religious practices and in memories that have been recorded in literary texts. Some popular holidays in honour of patron saints preserve traces of pagan festivals. They are almost always connected to important moments in the cycle of the seasons and of farming activities, but they are residues that are disappearing more or less quickly. The principal characteristic of pagan religions was polytheism; that is to say, the presence of a large number of cult objects or divinities that were endowed with sacred qualities and were mostly derived from natural elements. Even though, as we shall see, we are experiencing a renaissance in forms of neopaganism, religious history of the last two millennia – at least as far as Europe and America are concerned – is marked by the clear supremacy of monotheistic religions.

The first monotheistic religion in Europe was Judaism. The first Jewish community lived in Rome in the pre-Christian era and, according to the Bible, the Jewish Diaspora began many centuries before Christ with the exodus of the Jewish people from Babylonia and Egypt. This was followed by the destruction of the Temple in Jerusalem by the Roman Empire in AD 70 and the expulsion of the Jews from the land they had inhabited until then. Whether the entire Jewish population was expelled, or only part of it, is a matter of debate. The fact remains that throughout the Middle Ages, and up to the Modern Age, there was no city and region in Europe that did not have a Jewish community, towards which it sometimes had a welcoming and sometimes a hostile attitude. Calle Judios, Giudecca, Cartier Juif, and Judenstrasse, for example, are urban place names that indicate the areas where a Jewish community resided.

Until the beginning of the 19th century, 90 per cent of Jews lived in Europe. Today, the majority of those who consider themselves Jewish in one way or another live outside Europe, for the most part in America and the state of

Israel. In the 19th and 20th centuries, Europe became particularly unwelcoming to Jews, but anti-Semitism does not seem to have disappeared even in the 21st century. The beginning of Jewish emigration from Europe coincided with the advent of nationalism. While the Jews were first persecuted essentially for religious reasons, the advent of the 'holy nation' rendered their presence especially suspect for political reasons as well. Many believed that a population whose primary bonds of solidarity were with fellow believers could not fully understand the concept of loyalty to a nation. Yet even though today the presence of a population in Europe that adheres to the Jewish religion is much reduced, relations with Judaism are a continuous element in European religious history, just as Jewish culture constitutes an essential component of European culture.

More recently, however, the relationship with Islam and Islamic culture has been another constant in European history. From the 7th century, and for several centuries (until the fall of Granada in 1492), significant parts of the European continent (from the Iberian Peninsula to Sicily) were under Arab rule and the influence of Arabian culture in the fields of science, philosophy, and religion. Moreover, the complex events concerning the Crusades marked lines of conflict, but also relationships, between the European world and the Islamic world. Subsequently the conquests of the Turkish-Ottoman Empire in the Balkans and Hungary, which extended to the gates of Vienna and Poland, once again led to links that lasted centuries and were marked by conflict, but at the same time also by change and mutual influence. Today, as we shall see, we are witnessing the renewed presence of the Islamic religion as a consequence of migration from the shores of the Mediterranean and from Islamic countries in the Near East, Sub-Saharan Africa, and Central Asia, with all the problems this entails, not only in the field of religion.

At the beginning of the third millennium, there was a moment of heated debate about the Jewish and Islamic presence in European history when the wording of the preamble to the agreement that was to be implemented in the European Constitution was discussed. At the conference, the so-called Convention for Europe, which had been given the task of revising this text, made proposals to explicitly include a reference to Europe's "Judeo-Christian roots", which collided with the views of those who considered this to be inappropriate, either in light of the notion that Church and state should be separated, the presence of an Islamic population in many member states of the European Union (EU), or the (in 2020 rather remote) possibility that Islamic countries such as Turkey would join the Union. In the end, the European Parliament adopted generic wording that mentioned "cultural, religious, and humanistic roots" without specifically referring to Christianity.

The failure to ratify the treaty after the referendums in France and the Netherlands in 2005 shifted the problem to the next level in the public debate. Yet what remains is the question about Europe's religious identity, an issue that raises a number of open questions that are of extraordinary and perpetual interest. There can obviously be no doubt that Christianity is the predominant religion in Europe. There is, however, doubt about whether it is possible to speak of a single Christianity, given the large number of denominations, practices, and organizations that invoke the teachings of Jesus of Nazareth and his apostles. The history of Christianity in Europe is dotted with schisms, splits, conflicts, and religious wars. This began with the separation between the Church of Rome and that of Constantinople, which dates back to the Schism of 1054 and led to the split between the Catholic and the Orthodox Church, and between Western and Eastern Christianity – a split that has not only recurred but has also heralded wars, the most recent being that between Serbs, Croats, and Bosnians in the early 1990s.

From theological disputes to fighting on the battlefield, elements of division prevailed for centuries over the unifying elements that existed among the various Christian currents in Europe. From the 16th century onwards, the split between North and South compounded the continuing division between East and West as a result of Reformation and Counter-Reformation. The religious wars between Protestants and Catholics, the brutal persecution to which Protestants were subjected in territories governed by Catholic kings and princes (and also sometimes the other way around), continued through the centuries following the Reformation, until the 18th century and even beyond. Within the Protestant camp, however, there have been many variations: Calvinism is quite distinct from Lutheranism in a number of aspects, as are Anabaptists from Methodists. The forms of Protestantism are extremely diversified, and, as we shall see, these differences can become more marked under the influence of migration and the religious experiences that developed in the former colonies of Africa and Latin America.

Eastern Christianity is also anything but homogeneous. The Orthodox churches are independent from one another and have an essentially national basis. Some recognize the primacy of the ecumenical patriarchate of Constantinople (e.g. the Estonian and Finnish churches) and others the patriarchate of Moscow (e.g. the Bulgarian, Georgian, Serbian, Romanian, and Ukrainian churches), while still others are completely autocephalous (e.g. the Greek, Albanian, and Cypriot churches).

The tendency toward division and often to fights without quarter between members of different faiths, however, does not specifically pertain to Christianity but rather to all monotheistic religions. In the Islamic world, the contrast between Sunnis and Shiites goes back to Mohammed's first successors, and is perpetuated to this day. In the Jewish world, the divisions as a consequence of the Diaspora (e.g. between North African Sephardic and East European Ashkenazi Jews) are linked to the theological divisions between Orthodox and Reformed Jews. Together they form a community in which living together is often difficult, as evidenced in Israel.

As Max Weber and Sigmund Freud maintain, the monotheistic religions postulate the concept of a single and absolute truth as revealed by God. Those who do not accept this truth remain irredeemably in error, believe in a false revelation and in a false divinity, and are infidels and idolaters who must be fought so that the only true faith can triumph. This explains not only the implacability of the conflicts between the three great monotheistic religions, but also the brutality of the internal conflicts within each of them. When there is only one truth, people's reasoning is applied to the interpretation of the truth, so that there can also only be a single interpretation – one that is incompatible with all others. Since there cannot be several truths that are all valid, there cannot be several interpretations of one truth. Hence, the monotheistic religions often exhibit an intrinsic tendency towards what was later called 'religious fundamentalism'. This thesis was recently convincingly posited again by Jan Assmann, who traced the idea of a single god back to Moses, who is recognized as a prophet in Judaism, Christianity, and Islam, which holds him as a precursor of Mohammed (Assmann, 2009).

During its history, Europe has seen the most sublime manifestations, but also the most horrible potential consequences, of faith on the part of those who are convinced they are in possession of the absolute truth. Dissent about fundamental tenets, or dogmas, is inevitably branded as heresy and is fiercely combated. A famous example is the crusade that was organized in 1209–29 by Innocent III against the Albigensians to fight the heresy of Catharism.

The hypothesis that the monotheistic religions provide a battlefield that is conducive to the development of radical and violent conflict rests on convincing arguments and a wealth of compelling historical evidence. Even so, it would be reductionist to maintain that these conflicts can only be explained by religious motives. Very often, religion is used to mask interests and conflicts of a different nature, be they political or economic. It has been used as an ideological weapon to justify other conflicts whose real issue was not the revealed truth or the salvation of the soul but the acquisition or preservation of power. The Crusades blatantly had objectives other than the desire to liberate the sepulchre of Christ from the infidels. Ferdinand and Isabella of Castile, the 'Catholic kings', certainly combated the heirs of Al-Andalus in order to expel the Moors from Spain, not only to affirm their faith. In the same vein, the historic rivalry between Austria and Prussia – the cause of many wars in the 17th and 18th centuries – only had little to do with the fact that the Habsburgs were Catholic while the Hohenzollern were Protestant. Or, to take a more recent example, the conflict between Serbs, Croats, and Bosnians during the last decade of the 20th century was doubtless not just a consequence of the fact that the Serbs were Orthodox, the Croats Catholic, and the Bosnians partly Muslim.

However, it would also be reductionist to regard theological conflicts strictly as reflections of conflicts of a different nature, as certain scholars do who dogmatically follow Marx's concept of religion as a mere superstructure. Religious motives are often inextricably intertwined with political, economic, or ethno-cultural motives. As Max Weber has taught us, any monocausal and unilateral explanation becomes reductive. The religious sphere, in any event, always maintains an autonomy of its own, if only within the social context in which it happens to operate. Furthermore, there are historic epochs in which religions and their organizations profoundly penetrate the life of society and the individual, whose behaviour they shape, while in others religions seem to recede into the background. Religions not only confront, and crash into, one another, but also often encounter indifference and sometimes hostility within the societies to which their messages are addressed. Agnosticism and atheism are phenomena which run in parallel with religious faiths.

2   Rationalization, Modernization, and Secularization

The great authors in the classic sociological tradition who have studied religious phenomena, including initially Durkheim and Weber, among others, agree on the notion that modern life has reduced the influence of religion in society as well as in the life of individuals. In other words, they agree that the processes of rationalization and modernization have also entailed a process of increasing secularization.

This is a controversial hypothesis that has been debated at length. Its most controversial aspects concern the date, the extent, and the importance as well as the concept of secularization itself. When it comes to dating this process, some place it at the beginning of the Italian Renaissance, some in the 15th century at the birth of modern science, and some in the 18th century, during the Age of Enlightenment. As for the geographic range and scope of the process, everyone agrees that it started out in Europe, and it is an incontrovertible fact that it involved, in different ways and extents, various countries such as England and France, Germany and Italy, Spain and Russia, as well as the

African, Asian, and American orbits. Moreover, the concept has clearly had several levels of meaning. One approach is to focus on believers' practices, another is to examine religious organizations' impact and social power, and yet another is to examine the degree to which religious faiths shape other spheres of life within society, from art to law and from the economy to education.

Apart from these controversies, the debates have indicated a few points where a certain degree of consensus can be ascertained. The first goes directly back to Max Weber, for whom the process of rationalization is rooted in religion itself, and specifically in those forms of Protestantism that, postulating the absolute transcendence of God, have eliminated all traces of magic from religious beliefs and practices. According to this argument, once the rationalization process had been set in motion, it spilled into other spheres of behaviour, specifically the economy, creating the basis for the increasing marginalization of religion. It is an exemplary case of the heterogenesis of purposes (Weber, 1929).

The second point indicates another process that is deeply rooted in European history: the relationship between the institution of the Church and that of the state; from Jesus Christ's famous phrase as reported in the Gospels, "Render to Caesar the things that are Caesar's; and to God the things that are God's", to many modern constitutions that stipulate, in one way or another, the separation of Church and state. They are two powers that are independent of each other, but also interdependent in the sense that they have confronted each other throughout history, sometimes mutually supporting one another and sometimes using one to serve the needs of the other. In any event, the two powers have always maintained a tense and sometimes unstable relationship, ranging from open conflict to negotiation and concord. Institutional arrangements and cultural traditions have assumed many different forms throughout history, but the principle of separation of Church and state has marked Western societies, and hence European society above all (Paolo Prodi, 2012).

The third point concerns the relationship between religion and science. If religion deals with what is beyond – beyond the Earth or in fact the known universe – and with the salvation of the soul through eternal life, it should in principle not collide with science on earthly matters, as science deals with everything that is in this life; that is to say, in reality as can be perceived and understood through empirical observation. In fact, even though atheism is especially widespread among scientists – more so than among any other professional group – there are clearly also scientists whose values are rooted in a profound religious faith and do not in the least find their profession to be incompatible with their faith. Yet history tells us that things have been quite different. Scientific progress has enabled us to answer questions that once solely belonged to the religious sphere. We can understand, for example, that our ancestors explained storms, lighting and thunder as manifestations of the wrath of the gods, while today we can come up with more credible explanations of these phenomena, based on science. To give another example, before the achievement of modern science, earthquakes were seen as a punishment meted out by God for sins committed. Today we understand a little, though not much, more about the dynamics that lead to earthquakes, and we no longer need to refer to the obscure workings of a divine will.

Religious organizations have often reacted negatively to science's shattering of beliefs that were rooted in a mysterious truth as revealed by a divine power. The trial the church hierarchies brought against Galileo for having endorsed with convincing proof Copernicus's theory of the universe is the most spectacular historical example. Yet the theory of evolution by another great scientist, Charles Darwin, has also met with great resistance among the religions that follow the Bible, as it challenges the Biblical version of the history of creation. Even today, there's still a clear and vocal divison between 'evolutionists' and 'creationists'in the US, and in the UK, the land where Darwin was born, there is still a small minority of creationists, although the majority Christian view sees no incompatibility between scientifc evoilutionary theories and the creation myths of Genesis.

On the other hand, there are strictly ethical issues, such as abortion or euthanasia, on which science as such does not have the last word without entering a field that is traditionally and legitimately suffused with religious ideas. Furthermore, there are applications of scientific progress in the field of biomedicine that pose new problems of an ethical nature that cannot be resolved by science but only by a debate between different ethical positions, which can be rooted in religious faiths to a greater or lesser degree.

The rationalization of religion, tension between Church and state, and tension between science and the religious sphere: these are the major themes in which reflections on the process of secularization will develop (Wilson, 1982).

Contemporary sociology has picked up the subject in the context of a comparative analysis, in which the question has been asked if secularization is a phenomenon that is tied to the process of modernization (but how come that in the United States (USA), doubtless a modern country, religion seems to be in much less of a decline than it is in Europe?), or if it is a specifically European experience that cannot be generally applied to other historical and social contexts. Is the exception in the first instance the USA and in the second Europe?

3 Europe and America – A Comparison

As often happens, there are good arguments for either thesis. As far as Europe is concerned, it is difficult to contest the claim that a secularization process has taken place on an empirical level if we take the behaviour pertaining to adherence to a religious organization as an indicator. For example, if we enter a church on holiday, we typically find it deserted unless it contains certain works of historical, artistic, or architectural value, and nowadays it is much more likely that we will encounter almost exclusively tourists. If we take Catholicism as an example, and look at the number of people attending Sunday Mass, the ratio between religious and secular wedding ceremonies, the number of people who partake in the sacrament of baptism, of confirmation, or first communion, at the number of men entering priesthood, or the membership of religious orders, we note that practically everywhere in Europe the indicators all point in the same direction, while this does not hold true for the USA. Based on data from the World Value Survey, Inglehart and Norris maintain that the tendency toward secularization affects all advanced industrialized societies, including Australia, New Zealand, Canada, and Japan (Inglehart & Norris, 2004). This makes the USA an anomaly. In fact, in Europe – albeit with different degrees of intensity – all churches are in trouble, more so those in Protestant regions than those in traditionally Catholic areas, whereas the tendency is even quite pronounced in the Christian Orthodox zone.

Explaining the mystery of the two societies – both of them modern – that find themselves on opposite sides in terms of the place that religion takes in them is no easy task. There is a substantial consensus in pinpointing the differences. The first of these concerns the pluralism of religious expression in America since colonial times and the absence of this in Europe where, with few exceptions, different religious denominations until recently enjoyed a near monopoly in their respective regions or greater territories. In the USA, in a sense, Churches are in competition with one another, and individuals are free to join one or another, while their credibility would be compromised if they did not to belong to any. The USA speaks of the 'diversification' of religious beliefs, using a metaphor taken from marketing speak, and it is in fact by no means infrequent for someone to switch from one denomination to another during his or her lifetime. According to some studies, 40 per cent of Americans change their religious affiliation, choosing a denomination that is different from the family into which they were born (Aldridge, 2000: 67).

Pluralism also marks the relationship between the state and religious denominations. In America, the principle of separation was in place from the beginning, whereas in Europe, as we have seen, the intermingling of state and

Church – if only in the form of tension – is inscribed in a secular history that has lasted to this day. Education, and specifically religious education, is a perfect example of this relationship. In the USA, there is no religious instruction in public schools, even though private religious schools are cofunded by the government. In Europe, the situation is quite different. In some countries, there is no religion at all in public schools. In France, for instance, the secular state has taken on the task of protecting new generations from indoctrination by the Church. The same is true for Hungary and Slovenia. In other countries (Latvia, Lithuania, Poland, and Portugal), ethics is a school subject, which may be replaced by religion. In the German states of Berlin and Brandenburg, a recent referendum has rejected the proposal to introduce religion as a compulsory subject. In other states, as well as other countries, religion is a compulsory subject (which can be dropped or replaced by an alternative subject) or it is an optional subject, typically an alternative to ethics. When there is a specific arrangement between the state and the Church, as is the case in Italy, religion is an optional subject matter in the sense that it is possible to request exemption from it and choose an alternative subject instead. Instruction is handed to teachers who are appointed by the Church authority, but they are paid by the state.

The problem arises anew in light of the presence of a growing population of students from families that adhere to the Islamic faith. Currently the size of Islamic population in the EU 28 (plus Norway and Switzerland) as of mid-2016, is estimated at 25.8 million (4.9% of the overall population), up from 19.5 million (3.8%) in 2010. Will the state have to provide instruction in the Quran, or hand over the subject to local mosques, or will a specifically non-spiritual subject of ethics or religious history be introduced for everyone? The issue of religion and education policies remains an open one: how should religion be treated in school in the context of increasing secularization and the growth of religious minorities?

According to Berger and Davie (2008), there are other characteristics that distinguish the religious situation in America from the one in Europe. One of these is the different influence of the Enlightenment. In Europe, especially in France, this developed in fierce opposition to the Catholic Church, which was considered to be the stronghold of obscurantism and against whose dogmas freedom of thought was demanded. In America – continuing the tradition of Enlightenment in the British mould – the accent was placed on tolerance and the demand for freedom of conscience; that is to say, the freedom of choosing one's own religious practices.

A further distinctive feature is the relationship between religion and social classes. In the USA, members of various religious denominations belong to specific social classes: they attend the church where they are likely or able to meet their peers; whereas in Europe, different classes can have the same religious affiliation, with the middle class representing the majority while the upper classes, in particular intellectuals, and the working classes making up a disproportionate percentage of atheists and agnostics.

Another sphere that involves religion is the different role of the welfare state. In the USA, welfare services are for the most part provided by hundreds, even thousands, of charitable, often religious, organizations, while in Europe these tasks tend to be carried out by the state. However, Europe is anything but homogeneous, especially when we look how different countries are responding to the welfare state crisis, which could reinforce the tendency to hand health, education, and social services to organizations of the so-called 'third sector', which are often of a religious nature.

Among those who have emphasized that the European picture is highly differentiated, Inglehart and Norris have studied two variables from the European Value Survey participation in rituals and frequency of prayer. This has resulted in a map that distinguishes three groups with respect to the distribution of these behaviours across different countries. In the first group (low participation in rituals and low prayer frequency), we find all the Scandinavian countries, France, the United Kingdom (UK), the Netherlands, the former East Germany, as well as various ex-Communist countries in Eastern Europe (Russia, Hungary, Estonia, Belarus, Bulgaria). In the second group, which shows higher but still moderate figures for both indicators, we find traditionally Catholic countries (Bavaria and the German Rhineland states, Spain, Italy, Portugal, Austria, Slovakia, and Lithuania) and an orthodox country (Romania). The third group of countries, with high religious participation, includes only two European countries: Ireland and Poland.

Therefore, it does not suffice to explain the differences between Europe and the USA; one must also explain the differences within Europe and why Ireland and Poland (based on the above indicators) are more similar to the USA than they are to France or the UK.

Generally speaking, those countries with a Catholic tradition certainly exhibit a greater attachment to religion than countries with a Protestant tradition (Garelli, 1996). However, it is very likely that in order to explain these differences we must consider a complex combination of factors. Inglehart and Norris, for example, maintain that the variable best explaining the strength of religions is existential insecurity due to precarious living conditions, exposure to diseases, risks, unexpected events, and disaster. Where these conditions prevail, and where there is tremendous social inequality, recourse to religion as a fount of hope and comfort tends to increase. And so poor countries, and the poorer segment of the population in rich countries, exhibit stronger religious convictions, practices, and behaviour.

The assumption that modernization generates higher levels of security is debatable. There is no doubt, though, that death is no longer a daily occurrence as it was in pre-modern societies (leaving aside road accidents), and where the welfare state is solidly established, security is widespread and enjoyed by large portions of the population. This would explain, at least in part, the secularization of Scandinavian countries as well as the strong persistence of religious practices and beliefs in the USA, where economic inequality is enormous and there is a consistent ratio of the population that has no social protection. But other insecurities have appeared, in connection with environmental risks, the military and civil use of nuclear energy, and the globalization of markets. As we shall see, these can explain some of the phenomena of the religious revival. It is no coincidence that Ulrich Beck, the theoretician of the risk society, was also quite interested in an examination of the new forms of religiousness (Beck, 2010).

4 The Return of Religiousness in New Forms

There are many signs to indicate that empty churches and the scarcity of 'callings' do not signify the disappearance of religion even in a society that is highly secularized, such as Europe's. On the contrary, we are witnessing a return of religiousness, albeit often in new forms and in different and even contradictory directions.

The first direction indicates a process of slow and gradual transformation from collective religiousness within the framework of church organizations toward a more individual religiousness as manifested in the search for an intimate exchange with the divine and in the cultivation of the spiritual sphere. There is a part of human nature that continues to ask what the meaning of life is, of injustice, of suffering, of death; and this does not find satisfactory answers in science or political faiths. In our day and age, institutionalized religions as well as all the political ideologies that pretend to provide answers have lost much of their ability to provide assurance. The need for faith remains as a mostly individual quest and consists of cultivating one's own spirituality. As Beck (2009, 2010) emphasizes, searching for faith means renouncing its claim to be true. After all, there are ever fewer people who maintain that their own religion is the only 'true' one.

Inglehardt and Norris advance the hypothesis that in the absence of safety nets, a situation caused by crises in welfare institutions and the inability of the state to deal with personal and social emergencies, conditions of precariousness, of social marginality, of problems brought about by economic crisis or adversity that befalls individuals or families, conditions are conducive to the development of protest movements, which often have a religious component. Where protection against risk and the promise of security (and of salvation) are not provided by earthly institutions, even today, as in the past, those who feel great insecurity turn to religions that promise salvation and redemption in the beyond. This is what explains the success on a global scale (hence also in Europe) of movements as diverse as Scientology, the Jehovah's Witnesses, and the Church of Jesus Christ of Latter-Day Saints.

More generally speaking, however, there is a criterion that has begun to attract the attention of those who study religious phenomena: the frequency with which people interviewed in sample polls state that they turn to prayer. Various studies – including the International Social Survey Programme and the European Value Survey – indicate that there is an increasing percentage of Europeans who pray with a certain amount of regularity. Altogether, 37 per cent do so, if not every day at least several times during the week, and another 30 per cent pray irregularly. This figure obviously varies from country to country, but it applies to all, albeit with different degrees of intensity. We must therefore acknowledge that prayer is a much more frequent practice than participation in the rituals of an organized Church. This only confirms the tendency toward a more personal religiousness that is not mediated by traditional affiliations, as noted by researchers from Hervieu-Léger to Ulrich Beck, and others.

Yet it is not easy to determine what this data signifies. What do people mean when they state that they pray outside specific places and times of worship? This is clearly not prayer as a collective practice, in concert with other believers, as it does not take place in the locations intended for it (temple, church, mosque, synagogue) and during worship. And it is not even the collective recital of the rosary, which used to be carried out during the evening prayers, perhaps next to or around the fireplace and mostly by women. Prayer is certainly what the priest does when he reads his breviary, and prayer is also what individual people whisper or recite in their mind before going to bed or upon waking up, or during the course of the day when the occasion presents itself and the situation allows it. However, those moments of concentration, meditation, and reflection on the meaning of certain events or of life in general, on moral dilemmas, on good and evil, on the ultimate values that guide, or should guide, one's existence, on suffering and death, and on the existence of a transcendental sphere are probably prayers too. Perhaps it is possible to pray even without truly believing personally, but as a way of entering the spiritual realm.

This broader meaning of the practice of prayer applies to a large number of religions, faiths, and rituals of very different kinds that together have led to the formation of religious groups that are certainly minorities but combined constitute a phenomenon that is not negligible in terms of size. Consider, for example, the numerous followers of various Eastern religious movements within, or even outside, Buddhism and Hinduism that have prospered to a degree in the Western world, including in Europe. Or think of the forms of modern paganism, nature cults, or the invocation of ancient deities that belong to religions that preceded the Judeo-Christian tradition and have also gained moderate currency on both sides of the Atlantic in recent times. In these instances, we are looking at phenomena that combine individual choice and the need to belong to a group, to a community with which one can share religious experiences, and also the spheres of everyday life.

Religious groups can exhibit different degrees of openness and enclosure. When they are enclosed, they approach the status of sects and can, in times of declining political participation, operate a collective identity, something that was once done by political groups, especially those with a distinct and pronounced ideology and faith. By contrast, the more open groups are, the more blurred are their borders and the more multifaceted the identity of their members. Groups of this type frequently show a process of hybridization in which beliefs and practices from various traditions are mixed and fused with one another in a sort of patchwork or religious do-it-yourself mosaic, where practices of, say, Eastern meditation are combined with snippets of Christian ethics and rituals that belong to esoteric cults.

5 Contemporary Fundamentalism

One function of the revival of religion – a response and reaction to ever greater modernization and secularization, which are seen as a loss of values and the triumph of selfish materialism – is also carried out by movements of a fundamentalist mould that exist within the orbits of the three monotheistic religions. We can observe a conservative revival in the three monotheistic religions (Judaism, Christianity, and Islam) in the mid-1970s, which "took place against the backdrop of a crisis of modernity which has seen the fall of communism and growing discomfort with the problems generated by scientific and technological progress" (Aldridge, 2003: 177). This neo-fundamentalism preaches the prevalence of divine law over secular law and hence conflicts with the principle that the sacred and the political sphere should be separated, calling the secular character of the state into question. Subjects that have instigated bitter debates and created strong tension mainly concern the field of bioethics (assisted reproduction, abortion, end-of-life care, euthanasia, etc.), but also manifest in the influence of Church organizations and hierarchies on the education system. We may, for instance, recall the conflict in Italy about the legitimacy of displaying the crucifix in school halls and in public places in general, or the question whether Islamic girls should be allowed to wear veils in French schools.

Discussing the revival of fundamentalism, Giddens maintains that fundamentalists (whether Jews, Christians, or Muslims) reject the universal values embraced by the rationalist Western Enlightenment, as their faith provides "precise answers on what to do in an age in which the great, definitive authorities have been abandoned". In other words, the individual cannot do without a degree of certainty, and he or she looks for it in religion or in forms that do not appear to be contaminated by modernity (Giddens, 1994: 191–192).

In the Catholic world we have witnessed the birth and development of two movements that are very different from one another but are joined by their need to return to origins, to defend traditions, and to hold on to a more authentic form of religiousness: on the one hand there is the so-called Lefebvre movement (of the followers of Bishop Marcel Lefebvre), which developed in response to the renewal initiated by the Second Vatican Council (1962–5), and on the other the Communion and Liberation movement. The Catholic Church, alongside other variations of Christianity, has faced great challenges in the past; just think of the acceptance and rejection of slavery. Today, modernity poses other crucial challenges: divorce, abortion, birth control, euthanasia, gay rights, and the emancipation of women. With respect to these challenges, conflicts are developing that inevitably pit innovators and reformers against conservators and traditionalists. The Second Vatican Council, which was convened by Pope John XXIII, certainly made much room for transformation, but also provoked more or less open counter-reactions: take, for instance, the opposition to ending the use of Latin in the celebration of Mass, which was one of the key points of the Lefebvre movement. Within Catholicism, the defence of mandatory celibacy for priests and the opposition to women's ordination to the priesthood remain strong. The cult of the Virgin Mary certainly plays an important role in the liturgy of the Catholic Church, and the figure of Mary possesses extreme significance that is inferior only to the Trinity. Even so, the symbolic subordination of women remains a deeply rooted element in the tradition that is fiercely defended. The Protestant churches, and recently the Anglican churches in the UK, have granted women access to the priesthood, an important step in the direction of modernity.

The Communion and Liberation movement, which was founded in the mid-1950s by Father Luigi Giussani, a teacher of religion at a secondary school in

Milan, cannot be equated with Lefebvrian fundamentalism. Rather, the fundamentalists consider it to be a movement that is infected by modernism, whereas reformers accuse it of traditionalism and integralism. Sometimes encouraged, sometimes mistrusted, and sometimes even opposed by the Church hierarchy over the course of its history, it has demonstrated an extraordinary capacity to grow, especially among young people. Having spread quickly in approximately 80 countries on all continents, it has proven its ability to respond to profound needs of the community of believers and, at the same time, adapt to different historical or social situations. In the words of its founder, Communion and Liberation merges the need for religious experience, which has faded in everyday life, and a sense of the great estrangement from values in the modern world, against which one must take a defensive stand:

> I am deeply convinced that a faith that cannot be detected and found in present experience, that cannot be confirmed by this experience and be useful in answering its needs, would be a faith that is unable to stand firm in a world where absolutely everything has proclaimed and still proclaims the opposite. So much so that even theology has succumbed to this process of crumbling.
>
> translated from GIUSSANI, 2005: 20–21

The desire for an authentic faith, combined with resistance to modernity, has demonstrated a remarkable capacity for mobilizing large groups of Catholics, mostly young people, for whom the annual Rimini Meetings are occasions for intensive collective participation. The other components of Catholicism also seem to moving in that direction on a global level. Another important experience is that of Opus Dei, an organization that was founded in Spain in 1928 and today is spread over 68 countries, currently with about 90,000 members, almost all of them laypeople with professional training who bear witness in the real world to a solidarity that is rooted in the spiritual realm. We have seen that it is one characteristic of the contemporary religious scene that it is the affirmation of an individualized and personal sense of religiousness, which stresses spirituality rather than participation in rituals and faithfulness to tradition: "believing without belonging", according to Hervieu-Léger (2003). The Catholic world – obviously not only in Europe – responds to this tendency, which is perceived as a faith, by organizing large collective mass events in which the individuals (Catholics speak of 'persons') do not disappear but merge together in a communal sense that unites people and groups of different provenance. Examples are the week-long World Youth Days, which are held every two to three years in different cities around the world and in which millions of believers participate. Aside from – obviously – Rome, other European cities that have staged these encounters include: Santiago de Compostela, Czestochowa, Paris, Cologne, and Madrid. In an age of global digital communication, this aspect is bound to prevail, especially given the new approach by Jorge Bergoglio (as Pope Francis), who succeeded Joseph Ratzinger (Pope Benedict XVI) as head of the Holy See in 2013, a succession that is certainly a sign of the vitality of the different spirits that are living together in a dialectical relationship within the Catholic Church.

6   Migration and Religious Pluralism

The growing pluralism as a result of immigration is also related to the religious revival that marked Europe in various forms in the decades around the turn of the 21st century. In fact, one could even say that the new religious pluralism is one of the factors that triggered this process. As we see in Chapter 8, since the second half of the last century we have witnessed an increase in the mobility of populations throughout the world. If in around 1960 the number of people who were living in a country other than the one in which they were born was about 80 million, 50 years later that figure had risen to 214 million, which equals approximately 3 per cent of the world population. These movements have affected all continents. While the country with the largest percentage of the population living outside their native country – apart from Israel – remains the USA (13 per cent), many European countries (including Germany, Switzerland, France, the UK, and Spain) have come very close to this figure in recent years.

If we exclude internal migration among the countries of the EU, the majority of immigrants come from 'Christian' countries (Russia, Ukraine, Serbia, Albania, and also Latin America and the Philippines), while the second, larger, group consists of migrants from Muslim countries in North Africa, Turkey, the Middle East, and Palestine, as well as Pakistan. The Buddhists, on the other hand, come for the most part from Vietnam, Thailand, and Sri Lanka. It appears that the migration experience is connected to a reinforcement of religious ties, in that they help to lessen the break with people's original community and foster the cohesion that is needed to cope with the difficulties that come with assimilation to a new reality. Religious organizations therefore find an audience among migrants that is particularly receptive to the spreading of their message, quite apart from the assistance services they can provide. This aspect becomes very clear when we look at migration to North America. The religious organizations that are tied to their members' ethnic identity assume an important role in the integration of immigrants in American society by helping the newly arrived to overcome the difficulties of their initial integration and reinforce bonds with a community of people from the same area. The first colonies that settled in Massachusetts on the North American East Coast in the 17th century were founded by religious members of Puritan sects who had been persecuted in their country of origin.

Nonetheless, on a religious plane, migration has diverse effects depending on the discrepancy between the religion of the native country and the one that is dominant in the country of destination. From Latin American countries (e.g. Brazil, Ecuador, Colombia) there arrives in Europe a population with a mostly Catholic background (the same as in Poland), whereas Christian Orthodox believers come from the rest of Eastern Europe and Muslim groups come from North Africa, Turkey, and Pakistan, but also from Palestine, Bosnia, and Albania, to name only the major migration flows in terms of number. In addition, it is estimated that Europe has 1 million Buddhists – only some of them, however, as the result of migration, the others being converts.

In migration processes, religious factors become intertwined with ethnic and national factors of the native country. Excluding Bosnia, where 40 per cent of the native population is of the Islamic faith, the more than 16 million other Muslims who are currently living in Europe have immigrated from over 50 different countries. Therefore, it is quite a heterogeneous group, also in terms of religion. Not only do Shiites and Sunnis belong to two different religious traditions, which are often hostile to one another, but also, because of the lack of a church organization for the entire Islamic world, the religious beliefs of the various ethnic or national elements are highly heterogeneous. Thanks to migrations and conversions, even relatively minor groups, such as the radical Islamic Baha'i movement, which developed in the mid-19th century and today has 7 million followers throughout the world, is also present in Europe, specifically in the UK, France, and Germany.

Places for Muslim rituals can be found all over Europe. They number more than 10,000, even though mosques proper with classic minarets are relatively rare. Italy has only three (in Catania, Rom, and Milan/Segrate), with others being in the project and realization phase. France has over 100, and in Germany, the UK, and the Netherlands there are also several dozen. The rest are places of prayer that are somewhat haphazardly located in shops, garages, and shacks where the faithful gather to pray facing in the direction of Mecca. Often the construction of mosques is met with fierce opposition from xenophobic groups who mobilize residents in a district where the building is to be erected. In Switzerland, a popular referendum even blocked the construction of new mosques on the territory of the Confederation. In France and the UK, which have a longer history of Islamic presence, freedom of religion is a widely accepted value, even though various models have been adopted vis-à-vis the immigrant population. In other countries, such as Italy and Germany, whose history of religious pluralism and Islamic immigration is more recent, the construction of mosques often meets with considerable resistance. The fact that there is no single spokesperson can sometimes constitute an obstacle. The 'concordatary' model (i.e. the agreement signed by the two single top authorities of two religious communities) that often regulates relations between the state and religious denominations cannot be applied in the case of Islam. In Sunni Islam, the imam is a figure who oversees a community of believers and belongs to one of several theological and legal schools of Quran interpretation, but is not part of a uniform church organization as whose representative he could serve. The relationship between the Islamic community and the civil authorities therefore greatly depends on the local situation as well as the personal qualities of the imam, who may be influenced by fundamentalist movements to a greater or lesser degree (Pace, 2004).

The presence and spread of the Pentecostal movement in Europe is also essentially a consequence of migration. The movement, which originated in the last century within the Methodist and Baptist denominations of Protestantism, has had an extraordinary development throughout the world, particularly so in Latin America (Brazil), Asia (South Korea and China), and Africa (Nigeria). The immigrants brought their religion to Europe, which has led to the appearance of dozens of Pentecostal churches in Italy, Germany, and other European countries. Pentecost is an ancient Jewish festival that takes place in the seventh week (i.e. 50 days – hence its name) after Easter. Transferred to Christianity, it celebrates the descent of the Holy Spirit, and in the meaning it has assumed in Pentecostalism it glorifies the emotional and ecstatic moment of the communion between the faithful and the Holy Spirit. This makes it a religious movement of a profoundly charismatic nature (Pace, 2010).

Perhaps Europe, under the influence of charismatic movements brought by immigrant groups, will experience a return to Christianity; or perhaps immigrants, to the degree in which they find ways to become integrated in their host societies and of which they sooner or later become citizens, will tend to broaden a religious pluralism within a profoundly secularized environment. It is likely that these two hypotheses do not suggest alternative paths but indicate tendencies that are both contained in the religious panorama of contemporary Europe.

7   Religious Pluralism and Cosmopolitanism

We have seen that religious pluralism has also been established where until recently a single religion dominated. Pluralism is chiefly the consequence of the spread of Islam and other internal and external movements that in Europe bring different religious faiths into close proximity with one another, together with individuals and groups who do not subscribe to any religion. Differently from the USA, Europe does not have a tradition of religious pluralism, neither in Catholic nor in Protestant regions, and to this day has distrusted religious diversity; but even so, pluralism is becoming a reality in every corner of the continent. Islam, too, is changing through its contact with other religions, even though these changes can go in the opposite direction: they can either foster fundamentalism or promote individualized tendencies. Islamic fundamentalism seems to exert a strong attraction on the fringes of the younger generation in many European countries, but it also seems that the attraction is more based on the extremism of the movements than on the religious conviction they purport to endorse. In any event, pluralism greatly weakens the connection between religion and a respective state in the sense that it is increasingly more difficult to claim the existence of a state religion, even if it is established in the country's constitution. These are, however, very slow and not necessarily irreversible processes.

It is wise not to delude oneself. The coexistence of different religions on the same territory probably enhances tolerance and dialogue in a civil debate, but it is not impossible that ancient conflicts will erupt again from time to time, even the violence that marked the history of religion in Europe for centuries. The examples of Ireland and the Balkans remind us that this risk has not vanished. On the other hand, however, ecumenical tendencies have established themselves, albeit very slowly, within the Christian churches, and the dialogue between the great monotheistic religions has also made a few careful steps forward. Pope Francis's visit to Egypt in 2017, where he met the imam of Al-Azhar, was a very important signal.

As Ulrich Beck writes, "religion can either civilize or barbarize individuals", and seen from that angle, the European context seems to be the "crossroads of the contradictory dynamics of the religious phenomenon" (Beck, 2009: 81).

CHAPTER 5

The Universities

1   Introduction

It is that after the Catholic Church, the universities are the oldest and most enduring institutions in European history. At least some of them can boast a continuous history of nearly a thousand years, and others of several hundred years. Countries, or better states, cannot claim such distant origins. We can leave this issue to the historians, though. It is clear that the history of institutions always includes moments of discontinuity as well as continuity, and it is certain that today's universities – disregarding the dates when they were founded – are very different from those of a thousand or even just a hundred years ago. Nonetheless, aside from the term itself, something of the 'idea' of the university must have remained, and not only to allow the oldest academies to bask in their heritage. Remembering what the university was in the past not only satisfies our curiosity but also sheds light on how they have evolved and on what they are today.

2   *Studium Generale* in the Middle Ages

Among the characteristics of medieval society are two that are particularly relevant for the context in which the universities were born: on the one hand, flourishing urban life, specifically in the age of city states, and on the other, the dialectic between the temporal power of the state and the spiritual power of the Church. The university is a typical institution that was born and evolved within an urban environment. Medieval cities are the first location in which forms of autonomy from feudal authorities began to develop, where professional associations organized as autonomous guilds, where spaces of freedom were created and defended. It is clear that it was in the cities where favourable conditions were created for groups of scholars and students to meet and promote their common interests in some areas of knowledge, draw up contracts, and seal them with oaths (Prodi, 2013: 71). This ritual is repeated to this day on some ceremonial occasions, testifying to the corporate origin of the medieval university. Let us imagine a group of students of different ages who agree to meet a professor to be taught by him, a professor who, at least in part, is paid from their contributions, called *collectio*. Often it was the pope or the emperor, or both, who officially acknowledged and granted the instructor the authority to teach other *studia*. Sometimes it was territorial rulers themselves – an example being Frederick II of Swabia in Naples in 1224 – who wanted to institute an academy within their own territory. But even where the initiative to found such an institution came from on high, it was always about giving a group of professors and students privileges and liberty that were not granted to others.

In this way, a network of relationships among the community of scholars was created. This established a culture of dialogue and also provoked competition for attracting teachers as well as recruiting students. This is how the first three great European universities, Bologna in 1088, Paris in 1090, and Oxford in 1096, came into being: they are not only still in existence today but are also flourishing and highly prestigious. Many others followed in the 12th, 13th, and 14th centuries. In the order in which they were founded, these were Cambridge, Salamanca, Padua, Naples, Montpellier, Coimbra, Rome, Perugia, Florence, Camerino, Pisa, Prague, Pavia, Kraków, Vienna, Pécs, and Heidelberg. This list is certainly incomplete and imprecise, as often historians have difficulty providing precise dates if there are no official documents or they have been lost. One thing is certain, however: the universities were a European phenomenon, established at centres that experienced a strong urban renaissance.

To recognize the needs to which these new institutions responded, it is necessary to understand some basic characteristics of the society of the time. First, there was the always problematical relationship between two powers, the pope and the empire, which contended for prerogatives and privileges, allegiance and loyalty, thereby posing sensitive problems on a legal as well as a theological plane (giving rise to the so-called 'investiture struggle'). Secondly, in the cities, the revival of commerce and the development of local government posed sensitive problems that required legal and administrative competence and a recourse to the great traditions of Roman law. It was certainly not by chance that the costs for the establishment and operation of the universities were in large part the responsibility of the cities. Moreover, within the Church, there was recognition of the need to provide places of theological study and teaching that were not directly dependent on the Church hierarchy or involved with temporal powers.

We need to be cautious about offering strictly functional explanations for the emergence of universities. It was the ferment permeating feudal society in the first two centuries of the millennium that generated conditions for a general awakening of intellectual life. While it was initially Bologna from which the legal culture of the day spread, while Paris was the centre of theological reflection, subsequently every university taught most of, if not all, the disciplines of the trivium (grammar, rhetoric, and philosophy) and the quadrivium (arithmetic, geometry, astronomy, and music); these were soon joined by medicine.

3 The Universities on the Threshold of the Modern Age

With the formation of territorial states from the 13th and 14th centuries, we witness the autonomy of the city taking on a new dimension. Alongside this development, the universities were reshaped as institutions that were autonomous from the cities. Autonomy – if only on a limited scale – was continually attacked and defended, but it remained a characteristic trait of the universities that, as we shall see, never disappeared. It was chiefly nation states that encouraged the establishment of new universities, exercising various forms of control but at the same time protecting them from demands made by other powers, especially the Church. Universities continued to spring up. There were not many more than about ten before 1300, almost all of them in Southern Europe (especially in Italy), but in the course of the 14th and 15th centuries their number multiplied rapidly, so that by 1500, there were no fewer than 66, many of them in Central and Northern Europe.

Universities were not just relatively protected places in which knowledge could be cultivated, but they were also places where special skills could be formed and, most importantly, codified. This was required for the expansion of economic activities and to meet the needs of a public administration that was growing in size and complexity, as well as for the development of free professions. At this time, the state did not provide schooling for its population, which for the most part remained illiterate, or health services, but needed officials who were able to administer justice and could ensure it had revenue and services to allow the armed forces to serve on land and at sea; this absorbed a large part of public funds.

In the other great power of the time, the Church, strong tensions began to manifest themselves in the 14th century. This led to the Western Schism (1378–1417), a symptom of the general weakening of the pope's power as a leader as well as in relation to the empire; this had implications for the universities. Eventually, in the early 16th century, this led to the great split brought about by the Protestant Reformation, which divided Europe along confessional and at the same time political lines. The universities became one of the places where the religious wars were waged in doctrinaire terms. Martin Luther was an Augustine monk who had studied law in his youth at the University of Erfurt and was later appointed to teach theology at the University of Wittenberg, which had been founded shortly before by the Elector of Saxony. Not only the

Reformation, but also the Counter-Reformation used the universities to develop and defend their own doctrines. In 1551, Ignatius of Loyola founded the Collegio Romano, which soon became the Gregorian University, the oldest and most important education institution of the Jesuit Order – which later established similar institutions and today is spread across many countries on all continents. In the Catholic world, universities became a sphere in which theology was studied with relative autonomy, to the point that the Church, at the time of the Council of Trent (1545–63), felt compelled to establish seminaries that were separate from universities in order to maintain direct control over the training of bishops.

4   The Birth of the Scientific Societies

One sign that the university was subject to political and ecclesiastic powers is the fact that some of the most revolutionary and innovative minds of the 16th and 17th centuries were educated in prestigious institutions, but developed their ideas in opposition to the teachings they had received that were for the most part moulded by the Aristotelian and scholastic traditions, not becoming university teachers. Examples are Bacon, Hobbes, Locke, Descartes, and Leibniz, but not Galileo and Newton – the former taught in Pisa and Padua, and the latter in Cambridge. The university monopoly on the production and distribution of knowledge was gradually lost, a fact that is confirmed by the foundation of academies and scientific societies in the course of the 17th century. These scientific academies sometimes developed in relation to, but often also in competition or downright conflict with, universities, and became centres where research was conducted and debates took place on subjects and with methods that were different from those traditionally cultivated in the more traditional institutions. The Accademia dei Lincei was the first scientific academy in Europe. It was established in Rome in 1602 by natural science students whose interests arose from true scientific passion and the conviction that the secrets of the univerwse could be unveiled through science. It is certainly no coincidence that in 1611 Galileo was welcomed there: the academy actively promoted his theses, which, it was noted, were in contradiction to the orthodox views of the Church hierarchy. Later, though, the centre of gravity for scientific development shifted elsewhere, first to the British Isles, then to France, and gradually also to Germany (Ben-David, 1975). But let us not forget that Poland gave birth to no less a mind than Copernicus.

A few decades later, toward the mid-17th century, a group of natural philosophers, today we would call them scientists, gathered in London to discuss how to promote knowledge that was based on observation and the experimental method. In 1660, this group, in which astronomers, mathematicians, physicists, and chemists participated (among them personages of the stature of Robert Boyle), decided to found a college. Having obtained the king's approval, this was consequently called the Royal Society of London for Improving Natural Knowledge, which may still be the most prestigious scientific society in the world. Almost simultaneously, in 1666, Colbert convened a gathering of astronomers, mathematicians, physicists, chemists, physicians, botanists, and zoologists in Paris, and founded the Academie des sciences, which 30 years later became the Academie Royale des Sciences, whose statutes were approved by and received the support of the crown. In 1700, the Kurfürstlich-Brandenburgische was established by Leibniz; it later became the Königliche Akademie der Wissenschaften and today is the Berlin-Brandenburgische Akademie der Wissenschaften. This bloomed during the reign of Frederick II of Prussia (1740–86), a great patron of the arts and of knowledge. Always inspired and advised by Leibniz, Peter the Great founded an Academy of Sciences in St Petersburg in 1724; this later became the Russian and then the Soviet Academy, ultimately dissolved by Vladimir Putin in 2013. During the Napoleonic Age, the Koninklijk-Nederlandsch Instituut van Wetenschappen, Letteren en Schoone Kunsten was established in the Netherlands, and later the Kaiserliche Akademie der Wissenschaften was founded in Vienna in 1847.

Regardless of the royal seal that was almost always received, these scientific societies, or academies, came into being as brotherhoods, as places that were equipped with instruments and laboratories where scientific experiments could be conducted in public and procedures and results discussed. The public character of research that was conducted under the supervision and control of the scientific community had its origin in these institutions. During this period, one aspect of the scientific academies deserves to be singled out: their distinctly international character. Among the very first members of the Accademia dei Lincei were two German physicians, Johann Faber and Johann Schreck, together with the Dutch physician Jan van Eck. Leibniz himself was a member of the Royal Society, and not only Euler, Lessing, and Kant, but also the authors of the great *Encyclopedie*, d'Alambert and Diderot, and such eminent minds as Voltaire and Montesquieu, belonged to the Prussian Academy. Members of the Savoy Academy – today the Accademia delle Scienze di Torino – which was founded later, in 1757 – were d'Alambert and Condorcet, as well as Euler and Linnaeus. The same holds true for the Istituto Lombardo Accademia di Scienze e Lettere, which was founded by Napoleon. On the whole, even though they were born under the patronage of ruling dynasties, the academies of the 17th and 18th centuries reflected the decidedly cosmopolitan qualities of the culture of the Enlightenment. Nationalization of these scientific organizations did not take place until the 19th century.

5 University Models in the Age of the Nation States

At the end of the 18th century, at the time of the French Revolution, Europe had about 140 universities. Most of them were on German territory (34) and the Italian peninsula (26), where their development was stimulated by political fragmentation, which induced every state to have its own university. There were also 25 in France, 23 in Spain, 12 in the Habsburgs' Austro-Hungarian Empire, and more in the Netherlands, Scotland, and the kingdoms of Scandinavia, Portugal, and Ireland, and in Switzerland. Russia and England each had only two. In the centuries of the scientific revolution and the Enlightenment, the universities experienced a partial loss of their privileged position as the only places where new ideas were developed and new knowledge was acquired. This does not apply to England, where Oxford and Cambridge held an incomparable position of absolute predominance, at least until the University College London was founded in 1826, following the example of Scotland.

In France, on the other hand, the university declined. It comes as no surprise that the Revolution made a clean sweep of the universities, replacing them with institutions that had already existed in pre-revolutionary times: the *grandes écoles*. These institutions took shape during the Napoleonic Empire and have been subjected to numerous transformations over time, but they have nonetheless remained a characteristic feature of the French education system to this day. There are schools that prepare their students for the professions that require specialist knowledge in a technical field (such as the École Polytechnique, the École des mines, the École des ponts et chaussées, and the École de médecine), and there are others that train managers and prepare students to become high-ranking officials in public administrations (such as the École Normale Superieure or the École Normale d'Administration). These are schools (the latter two especially) with rigorous entrance exams, still reinforcing their elitist function that ensures the reproduction of what the sociologist Bourdieu calls the *noblesse d'état* (Bourdieu, 1989). It was not until the late 19th and the beginning of the 20th century that the universities, for decades confined to a secondary position behind the *grandes écoles,* regained their significance.

In the 19th century, innovations in university institutions did not come from the large countries, specifically France and England, which had seen the flourishing of science and the philosophy of the Enlightenment, but from an almost marginal country that had the ambition to become a great power: Prussia, after its sudden defeat by the hands of Napoleon in 1806. It was at the court of the Prussian sovereign that the idea of a new university in Berlin was born, and the task of conceiving and founding it was entrusted to Wilhelm von Humboldt, who united the figure of a scholar – he was a linguist and philosopher of language – and of a statesman. Humboldt designed the concept of a university that was to carry his name and was mainly inspired by the experiences he had gathered during a sojourn in Paris. The philosopher Johann Gottlieb Fichte became the university's first rector in 1810. Humboldt's idea of a university was based on a few simple and clear principles: the unity of research and teaching, the freedom of teaching and research, the idea that a university must be in the service of 'pure science', disinterested, without the immediate goal of professional training, the belief that science can in effect also be the principal ethical guide, and that it should be the task of philosophy to ensure the synthesis and hence unity of all sciences. These ideas are expressed in the concept of *Bildung*, a term not found in other languages that envisions the formation of an ideal human being as a synthesis of culture, science, and ethics.

The Humboldtian ideal, born under specific historical conditions and the context of a specific form of enlightened absolutism, had a great impact and spread throughout many countries, even though it has never been fully realized in any university institution, not even the one in Berlin. It did, however, certainly help the academic class – specifically its humanist component – to reaffirm its tradition of autonomy from political power as well as dominant social concerns. Yet the idea of a 'pure science' that is not compromised by interests that are extraneous to science, and not even by the potential practical consequences of scientific discoveries, was a factor that delayed the establishment of experimental and applied research at German universities. This explains why there was a need for other institutions that were more geared toward applied science, and in the first decades of the 19th century, polytechnic schools were founded to fulfil this requirement. Towards the end of the century, they were transformed into *Technische Hochschulen*, which obtained the status of institutes of higher learning at university level. It was also at the end of the 19th century that institutions exclusively dedicated to research without any teaching obligations were founded, an example being the Kaiser Wilhelm Gesellschaft, which we will consider later.

In Italy, some universities managed to maintain, more or less successfully, their privileges as centres of excellence of teaching and research: towards the end of the 16th century, figures such as Luigi Galvani, Lazzaro Spallanzani, and Alessandro Volta taught and conducted research in the laboratories of the universities of Bologna and Pavia. Still, the delayed unification of the nation and the launch – likewise belated – of the development of industry did not allow Italian universities to quickly adapt to the changes that were under way in the countries that were in the vanguard during the 19th century. At the time of its unification (1870), Italy had about 20 universities, but fewer than half of them could match what was happening across the Alps – although the new initiatives that were being advanced by the beginning of industrial development were a partial exception. Immediately after the unification, higher institutes of engineering were founded in Milan and Turin. These went on to become polytechnics that were modelled on the corresponding German and Swiss institutions.

6 From University for the Elites to University for the Masses

When society changes, sooner or later universities, or rather the systems of higher education and research, are destined to change as well, with more or less resistance and more or less effectively. For centuries, it had been universities' main function to teach the skills required for the administration of the state and the exercise of traditional professions (including ecclesiastical ones), and perhaps to provide an environment for the development of philosophy and science. With the Industrial Revolution, though, and the transformations that it set in motion, new functions and demands arose and the old ones changed. New professions connected to science, technology, and the creation of complex organizations developed, so it became necessary to form the pertinent skills. When 99 out of 100 people in society were farmers or workers, there was no great need for a large percentage of educated men (and even less of women). Until the mid-19th century, throughout Europe less than one in 200 people attended an institution of higher learning. Between the middle of the century and the beginning of the 20th century, this proportion doubled, growing to 1 per cent of the population in the relevant age class. This increase partly took place because women began to be admitted to higher education (in Italy this was the case from 1874 onwards). The first industrialization also doubtless increased the demand for employees with better qualifications, and public administration became more structured. Above all, the development of schooling required a growing number of individuals who were devoted to teaching. Yet these developments were only moderately reflected in higher education. In the first half of the 20th century, the percentage of students enrolled in universities doubled almost everywhere in Europe, but even so, at the outbreak of the Second World War it reached or just barely topped 2 per cent of the population groups in question.

TABLE 5.1 Long-term development of the enrolment rate at institutions of higher or tertiary learning

Year	Germany	Italy	France	USA
1861	0.47	0.35	–	–
1870	0.45	0.53	–	1.25
1880	0.70	0.50	0.33	1.27
1890	0.84	0.79	0.50	1.25
1900	1.02	1.02	0.91	1.87
1910	1.26	0.95	1.32	2.02
1920	2.17	1.65	1.51	2.62
1925	1.45	1.40	1.60	4.58
1930	2.11	1.25	2.18	5.63
1935	1.41	1.66	2.70	6.29
1938	1.63	2.15	2.81	7.24
1946	–	6.36	3.76	6.73
1950	3.93	5.78	5.30	18.60
1955	4.40	5.23	6.07	13.28
1960	5.85	6.48	8.83	17.60
1965	8.10	10.75	17.66	19.49
1970	13.45	16.20	18.29	24.06
1975	18.60	24.34	22.42	26.41
1980	21.00	25.49	24.58	23.45
1985	23.87	24.00	28.57	24.92
1990	28.43	23.96	37.64	28.27
1992	32.49	26.99	42.83	37.25

SOURCE: PAUL WINDOLF, *DIE EXPANSION DER UNIVERSITÄTEN 1870–1985: EIN INTERNATIONALER VERGLEICH*, STUTTGART: ENKE VERLAG, 2ND ED., 2004

From 1945 onwards, the university population exploded. The intensity of this process and when it took place differed somewhat from country to country, but the trend was substantially the same everywhere. Compare the European data with those from the United States (USA), and we may note that in the USA the process happened first and with greater force. The figures (see Table 5.1) must be taken with caution, as they are not always homogeneous in that survey criteria may vary; however, the trend is unequivocal: in the mid-century the rate of young people (females and males) who attended university

TABLE 5.2   Enrolment rate at university-type institutions of tertiary learning (% of the age group at the beginning of the studies)

	Germany	Italy	France	UK	Spain	Sweden	USA
1995	26	–	–	–	–	57	57
2000	30	39	–	47	47	67	58
2005	36	56	–	51	43	76	64
2010	42	49	39	63	52	76	74
2012	52	47	41	67	52	60	71
2015	64	44	–	61	72	62	–
2017	63	48	52	66	74	56	–

SOURCE: *EDUCATION AT A GLANCE*, 2016

multiplied by five, and the trend has been rising (see Table 5.2) until today, even though at declining, and in some cases slightly negative, growth increments. Moreover, we must add that in certain instances the enrolment rates do not adequately reflect the percentage of the population that actually completed university studies by earning a degree. In some countries, for instance Italy, and in some fields more than in others, it is simply impossible to determine the dropout rate.

How to explain such a major change within such a relatively short time? There can be no doubt that industrialization, the drastic shrinking of the agricultural population, the development of the service sector for businesses and families, the growth of the public sector, the mass availability of primary and to a large degree also secondary education to a growing percentage of the population, and, finally, the advent of what is called the 'knowledge economy', are all processes that help to increase the need for the skills that only higher education and training can satisfy. However, an explanation that considers only the needs of an advanced technological society – a demand side explanation, as economists would say – seems insufficient; supply side factors are certainly also at work. If we want to know why so many young people enrol at universities, we must no doubt think at individual utilitarian motives. A university degree – assuming the student earns it and does not drop out before achieving this goal – is almost always, and regardless of the skill that has been acquired, an advantage when presenting oneself on the labour market in terms of job opportunities, job quality, and salary. Yet even this strictly utilitarian angle is not entirely convincing. Besides, in the post-2008 period which in many countries have been marked by economic/financial crises, the tendency to enter higher education seems to have halted, if not gone into reverse. Is this a temporary phenomenon or will it last? Are there other factors that may help us to explain the general increase in education level of the population, an increase that manifests itself, for example, in university studies becoming accessible to social strata which used to be excluded from them?

Pierre Bourdieu (2002) has suggested another explanation. Individuals and their families, he argues, do not invest in education solely for future benefits in terms of job and career, but also to consolidate or improve their own social position and the prestige this brings. In other words, education is considered as a means for realizing social mobility aspirations for members of the lower middle class, or for consolidating the position achieved by one's parents for members of the upper middle and upper class. Education is therefore a legitimate channel of social mobility. This explains why it often happens that these aspirations are not realized: there are fewer top positions available than people who want to attain them. The – at first glance paradoxical – result is that the more the education system expands, the more the degrees obtained lose their worth in terms of opportunity for social advancement. There are positions that in the past were accessible to people with a medium education level but today require an advanced academic degree. While it used to be true that the few who obtained a post-graduate degree were guaranteed access to a higher professional and social position, this is no longer true. The expansion of universities is driven by a demand that reflects the aspiration for mobility, which is bound to be at least partly disappointed. This is especially true in the case of a society, such as Italy's, where the expansion of the higher education system has not been accompanied by an equally substantial transformation in productive structures and public administration.

Does this mean there are too many young people who study too long? This is one opinion that is voiced in debates. Though not naïve, it reveals a shortsighted and backward view. That ever more young people study longer should be considered valuable in itself. There should be no doubt that a society where the average education level is rising, where the percentage of the uneducated is declining, and that of educated people is climbing is preferable to a society in which a limited elite that has been carefully selected and formed rules over crude and uneducated masses. Behind this opinion of excessive education hides the failure to recognize a profound transformation in higher education from universities for the elite to universities for the masses. As Martin Trow states in a famous article (Trow, 1973), in which he compared USA and Canada, a university attended by half the population is an institution that is radically different from one in which a maximum of 10 per cent of young people are enrolled, as was the case for centuries and until the mid-20th century. Besides its traditional function of educating the ruling classes and highly specialized professions, in all their expressions, higher education also has the function of ensuring that the maximum number of people can enjoy all the goods that culture has to offer. This latter function no longer concerns only young people, but also the adult population, partly because of the necessity to adjust to the needs of a world in which professional skills are changing all the time and also in order to raise competent citizens and to feed cultural consumption at a high level. The opportunities for lifelong learning as a function or independently of professional needs are bound to create a new social need for higher education. Aside from basic instruction and research, universities are therefore said to have a third mission. In a nutshell, they cease to be places exclusively assigned to the formation and reproduction of the ruling classes; their functions and structures are becoming ever more diverse and complex.

7 The Changing Relationship between Teaching and Research

The great expansion in the student population, the growing need for both theoretical and practical knowledge, as well as the strengthening of activities that fall into the third mission category, have forcefully driven the internal differentiation of the various systems of higher education. This has led to a crisis for the traditional Humboldtian model, which is based on the connection between teaching and research. One kind of differentiation concerns the names of study programmes. In almost all of Europe, as well as many other countries, three levels of academic titles have become established: the first level, often called BA (Bachelor of Arts), can typically be obtained after three years; the second level, called MA (Master), after another two years; and the third level, the doctorate (in the Anglo-Saxon world PhD, or Doctor of Philosophy), which takes no less than another three years. Not all institutions are able or plan to offer courses at all three levels and/or in all fields. Specifically, they can only offer doctoral courses if they have developed significant lines of research in particular fields. A doctorate consists by definition of training in how to conduct research, and where research cannot be conducted, a doctorate cannot (or must not) be conferred. In various sectors, typically in the pure and applied experimental sciences, research often requires equipment that only a few institutions are able to provide, as well as rare competencies. These limits are much less compelling in the humanities and social sciences, but to conduct research these branches also require a degree of excellence that is not readily available.

The tendency to distinguish between research universities on the one hand and academic institutions that pursue almost exclusively an educational function (teaching universities) has prevailed in the USA, which today has the largest and best-structured higher education system in existence. This tendency is also under way in Europe. In addition to Oxford and Cambridge, the United Kingdom (UK) has at least a dozen or so other universities at the forefront of advanced research; in Germany, the federal government has passed a programme that allocates considerable resources to a few leading institutions; France has favoured the fusion of academies and the building of networks to promote excellence in research; Sweden, Switzerland, and the Netherlands also have centres that offer state-of-the-art university research. Even so, there are relatively few European universities that are among the top in the rankings of universities on the basis of their performance indicators, which almost always put more weight on the quality of their research. From a competition point of view, the North American universities (in particular those in the USA) far surpass the European institutions, and specifically those in Continental Europe.

There are many reasons for this. First, the rankings place great weight on bibliographic indicators, and hence on publications in English. Secondly, in Europe there is greater resistance to privileging a limited number of institutions as research universities. Thirdly, many European universities achieve a level of excellence in one or a few fields, and it is rare for an institution to recruit the best that are available in all disciplines on the international research market, in the way Oxford and Cambridge do. Fourthly, and finally, in Europe, more so than in the USA, advanced research is not only conducted at universities but very often at institutions that are exclusively devoted to scientific purposes. France has the Conseil Nationale de la Recherche Scientifique with its more than 1,000 institutes, research centres, and laboratories – some of which collaborate with universities while others are entirely independent – in almost all research disciplines of the sciences and humanities. In Italy, the Consiglio Nazionale delle Ricerche, which is roughly based on the French model, has 115 institutes and numerous research centres together with other affiliated public research institutions, such as the Istituto Nazionale di Fisica Nucleare, the Istituto Superiore di Sanità, and the Agenzia Spaziale Italiana. In Germany, there are various research institution networks, such as that of the 90 institutes of the Max Planck Society, the members of the Helmholtz Association, or of the Fraunhofer Society, which mainly deal with applied science on an industrial level. In addition, there are some large supranational research institutions that are supported and funded on an international or European scale, such as CERN in Geneva, where thousands of researchers from many different countries work.

Moreover, the countries of Eastern Europe that from the Second World War followed the Soviet model have maintained a distinction between university and academy of science, with the latter's internal structure being subdivided into several disciplines. In a sense, the Academies of Sciences fulfil the tacit ideal of a number of academics: creating a university without students, except those who must be trained in conducting research. In fact, this separation confirms a characteristic – perhaps undesirable for some, but inevitable – of modern systems of higher education: that a considerable part of the institutions in that sector must remain connected to developments in scientific research and cease being active centres of production (Moscati, 2012).

Still, there is no need to confuse the academies of sciences based on the Soviet model and the organizations inherited from the scientific societies of the 16th and 17th centuries that were discussed in Section 5.4, even though these often define themselves with the term 'academy'. They are not, and often have never been, places where research is actually carried out. The Accademia dei Lincei, to take the oldest scientific society in Europe as an example, does not have its own laboratories in which groups of researchers can work on new scientific discoveries day after day. Rather, it is a place where scientists in various disciplines can meet periodically to discuss the developments and implications of research that is conducted elsewhere. Even so, they have an important function in that they promote dialogue among scientific disciplines, thus increasing the likelihood that the results of research in one area will generate new questions in related, or sometimes even remote, fields. In other words, they constitute a place where an exchange takes place that can also stimulate forms of interdisciplinary collaboration, thus counteracting the tendency toward overspecialization and closure of single disciplines.

8   Current Tendencies: Where Are European Universities Going?

The various higher education systems work differently according to their historical and cultural context and the traditions and organizations of pertinent interests. Burton Clark, an American scholar who extensively analysed higher education systems, created a typology based on whether the centralizing logic of the state, the decentralizing logic of the market, or the self-referential logical of the academy prevailed. Thus there are models that heavily depend on decisions taken centrally by the political authorities (such as in Russia, Sweden, and France), models strongly influenced by the configuration of interests of those who use services provided by the system (such as in the UK), and models that are characterized by the influence of an internal academic oligarchy (Italy and Germany). In actuality, these are ideal models that are not implemented in their pure form in any higher education system, as each changes over time, generating mixed systems. In France, for example, the recent tendency has been to reduce centralization and to expand the autonomy of individual institutions, whereas in England, by contrast, the evaluation mechanisms have had the effect of strengthening central control, and in Italy phases in which autonomy is strengthened and recentralization takes place alternate. At this point, it is necessary to ask whether the distinctions between the various systems are shrinking or growing.

We can say that the hundred years that passed between the mid-19th century and the Second World War were the years that put a national mark on European education systems, including higher education. During the post-war period, what had been destroyed was essentially restored, but the continuity with the past was not actually broken in a profound way in any country. As diverse as they were, the traditional models held up until the late 1960s, when the student movement happened almost everywhere and nearly simultaneously. This demanded profound changes in the way the university institutions worked, especially to create universities that were aligned to the needs and interests of the students. The transformation into universities of the masses was under way. From this point on, driven by various external and internal factors, and not only by student demands, processes of change were activated that have transformed the nature of the higher education system in Europe. One may claim that these processes have reduced the differences between the systems, that a certain convergence has taken place, but that they have at the same time increased the internal heterogeneity of the individual systems.

One of these impulses came from the European Union (EU), initially with the launch of the Erasmus programme and then with the so-called Bologna Process. Launched in 1987, by 2016 the Erasmus programme allowed more than 3.5 million young Europeans to study at a university institution in a country other than the one in which they were enrolled. In relation to a student population that over the course of 30 years has amounted to some 70 million, this is still a modest number, but it is nonetheless significant – as in every single instance it caused both students and the universities to compare their respective courses of study and to adopt measures to make syllabi and exam results comparable. The widely known European Credit Transfer System, which today has been adopted almost everywhere, is the logical consequence of the Erasmus programme. The Bologna Process, which was set in motion by the ministers of education of the members of the EU and has been adopted by over 40 countries – many more than the initial countries – has helped generate some kind of homogeneity, leading to a general model that is essentially derived from the English model and to which we referred in Section 5.7 (Regini, 2011; Triventi, 2012).

Suggestions that have been made since the 1950s, namely to institute truly European universities (or at least one such university to start with), have run aground in the face of opposition from more influential countries and the resistance of the academic world itself. Years of discussions and compromises finally led to the foundation of a European University Institute (EUI) in 1976. It was decided to establish this in Florence, and only doctoral courses can be studied there, at the highest level. There can be no doubt that for years the best scholars in the world dealing with European integration have graduated from the Abbey of Fiesole – the home of the EUI – and that it has become a point of reference for historians, economists, law professors, sociologists, and political scientists conducting research on European society.

Yet these are not the only factors that have led to a certain convergence of Europe's higher education systems. At least four other factors must be pointed out: the students and their families, the users of the 'products' (specialist skills and research results), financial status, and the ranking agencies. Students and families think most of all about what happens afterwards, when they have to measure up to the demands of the market. A higher education system that does more than guaranteeing the education of young people who are meant to become members of the ruling class must deal closely with the fact that education and training on the one hand and work on the other are linked, and hence must provide guidance, taking into account external demands and job placements for those who have completed their studies. Those who use the 'output' are for the most part companies and administrative authorities who require that their employees possess the skills that are required in their specific sector and their organization. Moreover, this output consists not only of the skills of men and women but often also of the knowledge that is produced by research conducted by university institutes and laboratories, which can be transferred and applied in the production of goods and services. Finally, the state, which is almost always the major funder of higher education systems, is obviously interested in the optimum use of the – usually increasing – resources that are made available, and hence in subjecting higher education institutions to periodic evaluations and systematic controls. In some countries of Southern Europe, including Italy, the considerable public budget crises have led to a steady cut in resources allocated to universities and to research in the first two decades of the 21st century. It is to be hoped that the tendency to increase resources will pick up again in these countries.

The presence of external actors who are interested in the efficiency of universities (from their point of view) certainly has consequences for how they are run – their governance. The power of the academic component has been somewhat reduced and the management/administrative component has increased almost everywhere, which has led to tensions and sometimes actual conflict. In some cases, external stakeholders have become involved in administrative bodies, introducing a managerial way of thinking that has triggered strong reactions on the part of the more traditionalist elements of the institutions. The degree to which higher learning institutions are connected to external interests becomes particularly significant in the case of the higher technical education that has developed in many countries, such as France, with the creation of University Institutes of Technology, and, especially, Germany with its Technische Hochschulen (polytechnic universities) and Technische Universitäten (universities of technology).

The amount of – invariably public – resources requested by systems of higher education and research in tandem with budgetary necessities have induced different countries to create institutions that must evaluate the quantity and quality of their 'product', so as to make sure that resources are spent within ethical guidelines that are based on the principle of accountability. The first pertinent experiences focus on the assessment of research. These were conducted in England with the so-called Research Assessment Exercise. Many countries have followed suit, often prompting contrasting reactions, especially on the part of those who are assessed. Assessment of the quality of teaching – apart from the objective difficulty of actually carrying this out – has also met with substantial resistance and has rarely been performed so far.

Finally, for a couple of decades, various agencies have been compared on a global scale, various institutions being evaluated on the basis of a number of criteria and the issuing of 'report cards' and rankings that generally draw much media attention. Although the criteria of these rankings are rather questionable and their application sometimes not free of obvious errors, they have the effect of generating a sense of competition among institutions. They consequently attempt to improve or maintain their own position in the ranking, with the effect that they tend to adapt their behaviour to the requirements that are established by the classification criteria. These ranking and evaluation systems inevitably generate competition, mainly on three fronts: first, access to national and international research resources; secondly, recruitment of teachers and research staff; and thirdly, recruitment of the most promising students. This last requires student services (residences, cafeterias, equipment, including sports facilities, etc.) that grant a sufficient degree of mobility and reduce the considerable cost advantages of choosing to live closer to one's family. In various countries, the increase in the student population has not gone hand in hand with a corresponding increase in, say, residential services. This has led to a decrease in territorial mobility, one of the original characteristics of the university since medieval times. Not all universities allow themselves to be measured on these fronts, and not all of those who do have the success they aim for, with the result that internal differences between various systems of higher education are tending to grow.

Despite the push toward convergence, systems of higher education in Europe still remain quite different from one another, and this is actually not a bad thing. Europe will, in fact, be able to achieve unity if it manages to maintain a high level of internal differentiation and heterogeneity without becoming fragmented. The need to create networks of collaboration among academic institutions does not mean that a tendency toward internal homogeneity among the various systems of higher education must prevail.

CHAPTER 6

The Cities

1   From the Ancient City to the Medieval City

"How is it possible to envision Europe without the cities?" wonder Bagnasco and Le Galès in their introduction to a book of studies of the contemporary European city (Bagnasco and Le Gales, 2001). In fact, it is impossible. There is no other place in the world where the urban phenomenon has such marked features as in Europe. Not that there are (or have been) no cities elsewhere; on the contrary, historically the first cities originated in the Middle East and not in Europe. And today, with the exceptions of London and Paris, the largest cities are outside Europe, and this will remain the case in the future.

What distinguishes European cities from those in other parts of the world? Compared with American cities, there is no doubt that almost all European cities can boast of having been at the same location for a much longer time, that they have a long history that is inscribed in the space they occupy, one that has left traces not only in the form of archaeological finds but also in artefacts that have changed their function and significance, living testimonies to the transformations they have undergone. The remains of the cities of the Incas and Mayas are evidence of a vanished culture. The societies that produced the Forum in Rome and the Acropolis in Athens also no longer exist, but other societies have lived around them for centuries, almost without any break in continuity – societies that have occupied the same space, inherited traits of the cultures that preceded them and which have been conserved and passed on through traditions. However, it is important to note that a large number of contemporary European cities are located on the sites of Roman forts, which in actual fact were cities that were built so the military and the administration connected to it could rule and ensure stability in a given territory, could wage war if necessary, or guarantee peace. Apart from the Italian peninsula, where there are numerous cities that date back to Roman times, we find examples in every province of the Empire: in Great Britain (London, York, Colchester), in Spain (Barcelona, Tarragona, and Cordoba), in France (Carcassonne, Narbonne, Paris), in Portugal (Évora, Braga), in Germany (Bonn, Cologne, Aachen, Trier, Regensburg, Mainz), in Austria (Vienna), in Pannonia, now Hungary (Sopron and Aquincum, today at the border of Budapest), not to mention areas outside Europe, in North Africa, the Middle East, and Anatolia.

As Max Weber (1999) tells us, ancient cities, and many others before and after, were largely cities "of consumers"; they needed a population in the countryside to produce things that would satisfy the needs of their inhabitants, whose productive activities were confined to the generation and satisfaction of consumption by the ruling classes. With the decline and fall of the Empire, the connective fabric of streets and aqueducts that ensured the movement of soldiers, foodstuffs, information, and water around cities also began to crumble. During the long centuries that followed this development, until the demise of the Empire, urban life certainly did not stop, but the weakening of networks doubtless set in motion a shrinking process and impoverishment. Cities decayed, roads became impassable for a good part of the year, and potentates locked themselves inside their castles, where it was easier for them to defend themselves. A stereotypical image of the Middle Ages is of a dark age, with people divided into small and more or less self-sufficient units, with local rulers fighting one another; a violent epoch where whatever little civility remained withdrew into abbeys and convents. More informed historiography has modified this stereotypical image more than a little, and has given us a different and more positive notion of the medieval period, one that no longer squeezes it between what no longer was (classical antiquity) and what was yet to come (the Renaissance). Different schools of historiographers differ in terms of the emphasis they put on the discontinuity of the age on the one hand and its continuity on the other. There can be no doubt, though, that several centuries had to pass before urban life could begin to flourish again and the city could reclaim its role as an engine of social change.

Even if we do not agree with the entire line of argument of those who see in the reawakening of the city from the year 1000 the beginning of a new age that for centuries brought great transformations and the development of capitalism, it is nonetheless certain that roughly from that point we can witness a new quest for the importance of cities. According to Henri Pirenne (2027), it was especially the new urban classes of merchants and artisans that gave new impulse to the economy. Cities are typically places that are populated with people who do not produce their own means of subsistence. The city always needs the country and the rural areas from which farmers arrive to sell their products every day, or at least every week. Normally, this type of local commerce requires no intermediaries: producers and consumers meet in person in the marketplace. There are, however, goods that are not produced locally and must be brought from far away, and that therefore require merchants who are able to assume the physical as well as economic risks of intermediaries. Salt and pepper, for example, important as food preservatives, were often not found within the limited areas of local merchants. With the increase in traffic, there began to develop a new form of territorial division of labour, where some cities specialized in certain products to satisfy the needs of consumers who were spread across ever wider territories. The number of artisans grew, which in turn led to an increase in merchants, and vice versa – and both classes organized in professional associations to regulate their internal relations, avoid competition, and contribute to the growth of the city.

To use a distinction proposed by Max Weber, while the ancient city was one of consumers, the medieval city was one of producers. Yet merchants and artisans were not the only city dwellers. Apart from those who worked in their workshops (workers, apprentices, clerks, etc.), there was almost always an aristocracy of landowners and proprietors of urban real estate, as well as owners of landed properties who, rather than living in their castles, preferred to live in the city, as well as an ever conspicuous number of representatives of the clergy who worked in Church administration. These classes did not necessarily have, perhaps almost never had, the same interests, and therefore they regularly clashed with one another in the government of the city, in which many different configurations were marked by alliances and compromises.

We can distinguish between two basic models. The first prevailed in Southern Europe, with the conspicuous presence of a land aristocracy during the growth of the city. The second prevailed in Northern Europe, where the merchant class was pre-eminent. The latter model especially is marked by a fundamental interest that united the urban classes: that of asserting, protecting, and defending the autonomy of the city against feudal power. This is the meaning of Max Weber's thesis, according to which the origin of the modern Western city contains an act of insubordination (a *coniuratio*, or conspiracy) on the part of the citizens, who armed themselves to gain their freedom from their territorial lords and/or the imperial power itself.

On what did this freedom rest? Above all, on self-government; in other words, in the freedom to choose one's own government, collect customs and fees on merchandise and the people who entered and left the city, impose taxes on the citizens, regulate economic activities, mobilize people in case of an attack, and sometimes even coin money or organize tribunals to resolve controversies. Those who wanted to escape serfdom had to try to flee to a city where, even though they had to submit to its rules, they would sooner or later be able to enjoy the privileges of its citizens. The motto *die Stadtluft macht frei* (city air makes you free) clearly expresses the contrast between the urban and feudal element during the period of the urban rebirth after the turn of the millennium. However variable and relative the concept of self-government was, it was the true distinctive characteristic of the medieval city in Europe in comparison with other continents. The Orient, India and China, also had cities, merchant classes, and associations, but there the city always remained an entity that was dominated by the central administration of the empire, which consequently left little room for self-government by the citizens.

There was also a striking difference between city and country in sheer physical terms, as the city was surrounded by a wall that delimited its territory, defended it when it was attacked, allowed it to control who entered and who left, who was obliged to pay a fee, and so on. The city gates were typically closed at night and reopened in the morning and were guarded by armed staff who were employed by the city. Eventually, wall and gates were to disappear in an age closer to ours, but this is an issue to which we will return.

In certain aspects, the medieval city has some similarities with the city-state of ancient Greece: relationships marked by conflict, competition (and sometimes alliance) with other cities, and the aversion to superior powers that threatened its autonomy. Yet while the aristocratic and military element dominated in the Greek city-state, the most important element of the medieval city was its economic dimension in terms of production and trade. Some cities specialized in port-related activities and long-distance trade (e.g. Genoa, Venice, Amsterdam, and Lübeck), others in the manufacture of certain products, and still others in the dissemination of knowledge as seats of universities (Bologna, Paris, Padua, Salamanca, Coimbra, Prague, and many others). Apart from sharing some features, their dissimilar backgrounds and internal structures ensured that there were marked differences between them in terms of time and space, and consequently we can say that each city has its own history. In Europe, particularism and localism are embedded in the past of the medieval cities. Until approximately the end of the 19th century, almost all European cities – excluding those that go back to Rome – have a history that dates back to the Middle Ages; there are only few with a history of under 500 years.

2   State and Industry during the Formation of the Modern City

The formation of modern territorial states marks the end of the Golden Age for medieval cities. This process did not happen simultaneously and at the same pace in all of Europe. In England, France, Spain, and Portugal in the west, in Sweden in the north, and in Russia in the east, the unification of large territories in a single kingdom and under the rule of a single dynasty took place in the 16th and 17th centuries. This did not happen in Europe's central area, which was occupied by Germanic and Italian populations, and where the fragmentation into small states lasted a long time and political unification, as we well know, did not happen until much later. The consolidation of central power through the expansion of the administrative apparatus and, above all, the build-up of military organization reduced the autonomy of the city considerably. The enormous military expenditure of the state imposed financial burdens on the cities that they were unable to effectively defy, despite their resistance. The monopoly of legitimate force held by the state, just like the monopoly of imposing taxes, rendered obsolete the towns' defences that the city walls provided. As a result, they were gradually torn down or no longer guarded. However, the cities that benefited from these transformations were those that became capitals, seats of courts and state bureaucracies. These capital cities were the first to experience major demographic growth in the course of a few decades, anticipating the explosion of urbanization that characterized European society from the second half of the 18th century onwards (Lenger, 2013).

In the mid-17th century, London had 350,000 inhabitants, one century later 700,000, two centuries later 2.3 million, and three centuries later – in 1950 – over 8.2 million. The population of Paris grew between the beginning of the 19th century and the First World War from 850,000 to 2 million, and during the same period, the population of Vienna nearly doubled. In the first decades of the 19th century, Berlin doubled its population (from 200,000 to 400,000), but from 1850 until 1913 it multiplied ten times. Madrid has seen its population grow 20 times between the mid-19th century and today, and Rome is at least ten times more populated today than when it was only the capital of the Papal States, in 1870.

If the development of state bureaucracy was the prime mover that made the capital city the element that put the urbanization process of the Modern Age in motion, the second was the Industrial Revolution. In Europe, industrialization almost always developed in an urban fabric that had already been woven during the preceding eras. Only a few cities were founded and grew solely because of industrial development. The list of European cities of a certain size that were founded after 1500 is tiny: Birmingham was not an important centre until the 18th century, and the same holds true for other British cities, such as Sheffield, Bradford, Wakefield, and Leicester; in Germany we find only Essen and Wuppertal, the sole urban centres that were almost completely insignificant prior to the Industrial Revolution; and no Italian, French, Spanish, or Portuguese city, or any city of a certain size in the East, with the exception of Katowice, was founded in the 19th century. Manchester, a symbol of the industrial city par excellence, was already an extremely important centre of textile production in the 14th century. Leeds was not much more than a village prior to 1400, but it expanded with the wool industry after the 18th century.

In England, the industrialization/urbanization process took place about half a century earlier than in the rest of Europe. Towards the mid-19th century, one in two English men and women lived in cities, while this was only true for one in four French or Germans. This process was fed by a strong influx of people migrating from the country to the city: rural areas, where agriculture was developing toward capitalism, drove out parts of the population who, attracted by the opportunities for making a living that industry offered, poured into the cities. Not far from the factories, overcrowded quarters for workers sprang up. Living conditions and hygiene were anything but ideal, with the result that there were frequent epidemics that claimed thousands of lives among the poorest part of the population. Commercial activities were concentrated in certain areas where the middle class lived as well, at least those who had chosen not to live in the suburbs that were surrounded by green fields, woods, and gardens. The city became ever more diverse – physically as well – with a greater or lesser degree of segregation between the different social classes. The city has always been a place where diverse social groups meet and often have different and sometimes antagonistic interests. The industrial city of the 19th century was where the 'social question' arose and the class struggle between the middle class and the industrial proletariat developed.

The speed with which urban development took place often caused a delay in the provision of and a shortage of essential services, such as water, the sewerage system, garbage disposal, healthcare, road conditions, the transportation system, and schools. This created the most acute problems for city governments, which had the difficult task of balancing public and private interests. There was hence a need to steer urban development on the basis of a plan for the spatial organization of different functions, with the demolition or regeneration of old neighbourhoods, new guidelines for expansion, and the provision of infrastructures and services. We are familiar with the plan that was carried out in Paris under Napoleon III by Baron Haussmann, who radically changed the shape of the city, which has remained nearly unaltered to this day, or the construction of the belt around Vienna, the *Ring*.

Industrial city and bureaucratic city models dominated the urban scene for about a century, in some countries earlier and in some later, after the consolidation of the nation state and the industrialization process had taken place. Obviously, not all cities followed these two models in their pure form; often they were mixed, with the industrial component more or less strong. Not all cities are like Wolfsburg in Germany or Turin in Italy, to name just two examples that are emblematic for the strong presence of the automotive industry. Anyway, in the second half of the 20th century, as the post-Ford era approached, the situation began to look different.

3 The Contemporary European City

3.1 *Specific Features of the European Model*

"The form of a city changes faster, alas, than the heart of a mortal". This quote by Charles Baudelaire, as recalled by Walter Benjamin, perfectly pinpoints the extraordinary dynamics of the urban reality ever since, barely more than a couple of centuries ago, history has been marked by formidable acceleration. While during the pre-modern era the context in which the life of every person developed changed imperceptibly between the moment he or she was born and his or her death, today – also because of the extension of the average lifespan – the memories of childhood of someone who has reached a mature age are of a world that has irretrievably disappeared. We have difficulty finding the houses, the gardens, the streets, and the squares in which we used to play as children. The shops, the theatres, the trams, the buses and bus stops are almost never where they used to be, quite apart from the fact that our way of looking at them has changed as well. If the average human life expectancy has increased, that of the buildings that populate the cityscape is considerably shorter. Urban renewal has almost become a duty, not only for the dynamics generated by real estate speculation, but also because a large percentage of people prefer living in a modern residential setting where they have the services and facilities available that used to be the exclusive prerogative of the upper classes.

In one way or another, these transformations have impacted all cities of a certain size in every part of the world, but they have by no means destroyed the specific character of European cities. First, despite the recurring processes of urban renewal, you will find reminders of past epochs in almost all European cities. These are not only archaeological finds primarily of museum value but objects with functions, even though these may have changed over time. As already noted, aside from the few industrial cities that only date back to the 19th century, almost all other European cities date back to the Middle Ages or the Renaissance. Secondly, the number of populated centres that have the features of a city is vast. In the European Union (EU), there are 3,500 urban centres with over 10,000 inhabitants (compared with only 1,000 in the United States), with centres of medium size being in the majority. Europe has about 40 cities with over 1 million inhabitants, and only five of them exceed the 2 million mark. In the list of the 20 demographically largest cities, Europe is only represented twice (with London and Moscow), or three if we want to include Istanbul. Thirdly, Europe has many 'regional capitals' with one centre, where the administrative and church buildings are concentrated (the city hall and the cathedral). Above all, in Germany and Italy, where national unification was delayed, many cities used to be state capitals, some of whose characteristics they still possess. A city without a true centre, such as Los Angeles for instance, would be inconceivable in Europe. Fourthly, the current spatial division in European cities is far less pronounced than, for example, in North American cities. With few exceptions, the upper social classes tend to prefer the city centres, where the value of apartments and rents are higher. The suburbs, where housing costs are lower, are inhabited by young couples. Workers' districts have been subjected to the erosion of the working class and are no longer distinct from middle-class districts. Immigrants have begun to occupy city areas in decline, at the city borders but sometimes also in the centres, which have been partly abandoned by the local population and where their arrival is speeding up a renewal process that has often already been under way for some time. We will shortly return to this aspect. And finally, fifthly, compared with North American society, European societies have considerably more welfare institutions, in particular when it comes to governing and aiding poor districts. Invariably, the primary institutions of welfare policies are primarily rooted in cities.

3.2 The City in the Post-industrial Age

From the last decades of the 20th century onwards – sooner in some countries and later in others – many large cities that had grown by riding on the wave of industrialization entered into a phase of decline, and others had to go in a different direction if they did not want to collapse but continue to grow. There are multiple causes for this phenomenon, but all have directly or indirectly to do with the transformations that took place on an international scale regarding the division of labour and, especially, the relocation of much industrial production to areas of the world that offered more favourable conditions for investments. In some countries industrial production declined drastically: in the past 25 years the contribution of industry to the gross domestic product (GDP) in the United Kingdom dropped from 37 per cent to 19.2 per cent, in France from 29 per cent to 19.4 per cent, in Italy from 33 per cent to 23.9 per cent, in Spain from 24 per cent to 22 per cent, and in Germany from 39 per cent to 30 per cent. The percentage of people in the agricultural sector has plummeted, and the percentage of those working in industry is decreasing considerably, whereas the service sector is growing, both for services supplied by the market and by public (government as well as local) authorities, to the benefit of citizens as well as businesses.

As a consequence, the social structure of every city is being transformed according to the kinds of changes that are taking place. In the manufacturing industry, many processes are becoming automated and performed by robots, which entails a drastic reduction in unqualified labour and an increase in the number of experts and technicians. The Fordian model has not disappeared entirely, but is tending to move to areas of the world where production costs, especially salaries, are lower. The price for this is therefore mainly paid by the traditional working class and, as a consequence, also the working-class neighbourhood, whose composition is changing. The service sector is dominated by the so-called middle class, which is strongly polarized between salaried, public, private, and self-employed work on the one hand and the large social discrepancy between, for example, a high-level employee in a multinational company, a middle school teacher, a saleswoman in a supermarket, an employee in a fast food outlet, or one in a cleaning business on the other. As we know, the social gap tends to turn into a spatial gap in an urban geography that is constantly changing (Magnier, 2005; Dematteis & Lanza, 2011).

These developments obviously also affect the ruling classes, which partly advance them and are partly subjected to them, in a constant regrouping process of those who are on the rise and those who are in decline. The deindustrialization and expansion processes in the tertiary sector reflect a general transformation of Western societies towards a capitalist economy that experiences unprecedented financial growth and a reduction in the manufacturing sector. The financial markets are eminently globalized, and within them a financial bourgeoisie is growing that is distinct from the industrial bourgeoisie and typically works from a transnational perspective. What impact are these globalization processes having on the structure of the city?

3.3 *The Response of Cities to the Challenges of Globalization*

Globalization processes are not a recent phenomenon. Immanuel Wallerstein (2013) speaks of 'world economies' having existed since the 15th century, and history has known alternating phases of expansion and contraction in the networks of relationships between the world's large geopolitical and geo-economic areas. Still, there is no doubt that these processes have considerably accelerated since the 1990s owing to the division of the world into two opposing blocks and the entrance onto the world stage of new economic and political powers, such as Brazil, Russia, India, China, and South Africa, to which we might now add Turkey.

Globalization is, above all, a question of markets. The market that is most globalized is certainly the financial market, where capital circulates in search of more or less speculative investment opportunities. It is followed by the commodities market and then the manufactured products and services markets. The market in which globalization has major difficulties in trying to establish itself is the labour market. Despite the increasing flow of temporary and permanent migration and the increase in geographic mobility, labour markets tend to be local because the majority of human beings exhibit a resistance to abandoning the place where they were born. Geographic mobility is concentrated at the two extremes of the social hierarchy: those who flee hunger and misery on the one hand and those who are members of the cosmopolitan elite of finance professionals, managers of multinational corporations, scientists, diplomats, functionaries of international organizations, and film and theatre stars on the other. It is this globalized bourgeoisie that makes its mark on what sociologist Saskia Sassen, in a splendid 1991 publication, has called the global city (Sassen, 1991).

Since Sassen's book was published, different attempts have been made to establish classifications of cities according to their degree of integration in the globalized economy and culture. The criteria on which these classifications are based vary, but they generally take indications of the following kind into account: the presence of a large range of international financial services (such as banks, insurance companies, internationally operating real estate agencies, consulting and marketing firms), seats of important multinational corporations, stock exchanges where these corporations are listed, production centres of goods for export markets, large infrastructure for the transportation of people and things (ports, international airports, etc.), centres for technological, economic, and financial development and innovation, centres of global information and communication networks, institutions of education and research that can attract students, teachers, and researchers from the rest of the world, and premium legal and health services.

One of the most best-known assessments (and most reliable, within the limits of this type of ranking) is the one that has been promoted, since 2008, by the periodical *Foreign Policy* in collaboration with a large consulting firm (Kearney Ltd) and the Council on Global Affairs in Chicago, with which Sassen collaborated. The Global Cities Index is based on a number of indicators that are grouped into five categories: economic activity, human assets, exchange of information, cultural events, and political influence. The index lists 84 cities and is updated every other year, therefore also assessing the dynamics of cities that are growing or shrinking in terms of globalization. The location as well as ranking of the major European cities, even within a very short time period, is interesting to note. Among the top ten in 2016 we find London in first and Paris in third place, with New York between them, having dropped one place since 2008, whereas London has moved from second to first place. Between places ten and twenty, we find Brussels, Madrid, Vienna, Moscow, and Berlin, together with the others shown in Table 6.1.

The criteria for making up this index are certainly debatable. However, if we balance our conclusion with some caution they allow us to make out a few relevant aspects. With a few exceptions, European cities have moved down several places on the list, and none of them appears in another index compiled by the same firm that classifies emerging cities, in other words, those that delivered a remarkable performance during the last few years and have a good chance of approaching the top rank of global cities in the near future. This does not mean that European cities are cut off the globalization

TABLE 6.1 European metropoles in Global Cities Index

Ranking	City	Country	Climb or drop between 2008 and 2019
1	London	UK	+1
3	Paris	France	=
12	Brussels	Belgium	+1
14	Berlin	Germany	=
15	Madrid	Spain	+1
18	Moscow	Russia	+1
19	Amsterdam	Holland	−2
23	Barcelona	Spain	+1
25	Vienna	Austria	+1
31	Zurich	Switzerland	−5
32	Stockholm	Sweden	−8
33	Munich	Germany	−2
35	Rome	Italy	−5
36	Geneva	Switzerland	−4
42	Copenhagen	Denmark	−6
45	Milan	Italy	−6
44	Prague	Czech Rep.	+4
44	Dublin	Ireland	−4
54	Budapest	Hungary	−3 (2014)
55	Warsaw	Poland	−2 (2014)
67	Düsseldorf	Germany	−1 (2015)
68	St. Petersburg	Russia	+2 (2015)

SOURCE: A.T. KEARNEY, GLOBAL CITIES, 2019 (https://www.kearney.com/global-cities/2019) https://www.kearney.com/global-cities/previous-indices

process, but that in this area the rest of the world is advancing with greater speed, also because the economic-financial crisis has hit harder and longer in the EU. In Europe, there are more than a few cities that are unable to keep up with the dynamics of globalization, while others endeavour to do so more or less successfully. There is a sort of ongoing competition and, as in every competition, there are winners and losers as well as some who decide not to compete at all.

3.4 The City, the Nation-State, and European Integration

The fact that cities, or at least some of them, can compete for the opportunities that globalization offers indicates that they can adopt strategies, coordinate the activities of different interest groups, and activate resources – in short, they can become collective actors that are able to move on a broad playing field often crossing national borders. We have seen that for cities, the formation of nation states has translated into a loss, or at least a lessening, of their autonomy. As Le Galès has written, with the consolidation of the nation-states, "the cities have become agencies of the state which are charged with putting national programs into action and legitimizing the control exercised by the state" (Le Galès, 2006: 67).

The phase of the relative decline of the nation states that commenced with the end of the Second World War reopened spaces of autonomy from which cities may or may not benefit. The nation state has seen its sovereignty curtailed legally and factually: it is not able to carry out a true foreign policy of its own in an age where there are great continental powers; it has armed forces whose capacity to intervene is reduced, to say the least; it has formally renounced its right to mint; it has subjected itself to severe budget constraints even though it has maintained its fiscal sovereignty; it acknowledges – within the limits of its own rules and regulations – directives that are issued on a supranational level; and its borders have become more permeable. The Schengen Agreement has greatly reduced the controls at internal border crossings even though, after a flood of asylum seekers, refugees, and migrants in 2015 and afterwards, some states have re-established barriers and controls. In any event, borders no longer constitute insurmountable obstacles that cannot be crossed by people and goods. Finally, states are no longer – if they ever were – integrated institutional machines where single devices function neatly, but rather a whole that consists of different agencies, all of which function independently, within certain limits, of the others.

The countries that are part of the EU and particularly those that belong to the so-called eurozone are in reality states of limited sovereignty. The gradual crumbling of the sovereignty of nation states runs in parallel to the creation and consolidation of European institutions. However, the integration process is anything but finished, nor can we exclude the possibility that it might be reversed, as Brexit has somewhat unexpectedly reminded us. Despite its limited sovereignty, the nation state maintains an institutional apparatus, has enormous fiscal resources at its command, and for the most part democratic political battles take place on the domestic front. The strengthening of the power of the European Parliament and its direct election has not created a true federal

European political power. Weakened but not vanished, the nation states have ceded their sovereignty both at a higher, supranational level and at a lower level, to subnational territorial authorities, which have seen their power increase somewhat everywhere. In different ways, shapes, and forms, their importance has grown in many countries, regions, and communities.

The cities have thus regained their role as protagonists. By definition, the city is, and always has been, a place of diversity and conflict, the latter between classes and among various groups and fractions of the ruling classes. However, these conflicts do not necessarily destroy social cohesion, even though they may do so. If they are under control and, above all, if there are agencies that are able to mediate, negotiate, foster, and guarantee compromise, conflicts can generate a positive dynamic and contribute to the development of the city. The concept of governance expresses the coordinating function well: it allows different actors to cooperate with a view of common objectives, even if they are not necessarily based on the same interests and values. There is discussion about if and to what degree we can think of the city as a collective actor with one united purpose. It is clear that conflicts are at the core of a city's social and political dynamics, but only when a consensus on implementation strategies is achieved – however fragile and temporary – can the city operate as a collective actor.

The mediating function not only exists horizontally, among the different interests within a city, but also vertically, in the relationship between the various levels of government, the region, the state, and the EU. Direct recognition (i.e. without mediation by the states) of cities as negotiating partners by the EU (e.g. concerning structural funds and regional policies) has certainly contributed to the legitimization of local bodies as autonomous actors (Grazi, 2006).

Obviously, these are eminently political functions that require constant negotiation on various levels, among different organizations and institutions, both public and private, each of which is a stakeholder with whom conciliation is not a given. Let us take, for example, the pressing and problematic issue of formulating land use plans. For centuries, ground rent has been one of the engines but also one of the major impact factors of urban development. The value of land and of what is built on it varies tremendously based on many criteria: proximity to/distance from transportation networks, the availability/lack of public services, such as water mains, drainage systems, garbage disposal, quality of the soil, air quality, accessibility of commercial networks, sociocultural characteristics of the population, and so on. These are criteria that are crucially impacted by urban planning decisions, which disadvantage certain interest groups and benefit others, not only from an economic point of view but also in terms of security, power, and prestige. Very often, moreover, it is the responsibility of city administrations to provide assistance to individuals or families who are permanently or temporarily indigent. In this case, too, the definition of the area – whether large or limited – in which welfare services are provided is an eminently political function.

The art of urban governance consists precisely of the political capacity to act while staying on course despite turbulence and gusts of wind blowing in all directions. One not insignificant sign of the new impact of city administration is that more than a few leaders with responsibility on a national level used to be mayors of important cities for whom local administration served as a springboard for a successful political career. Yet the reverse is true as well: lack of success and failure at a local level may seriously compromise promising political careers at higher levels. The quarrels that are normally fought at election time for the municipal government of, say, Rome, London, Paris, or Berlin are testimony to the central political role of the major cities.

3.5 *The Fiscal Crisis of the City*

One of the crucial issues in establishing relations between city government and other levels of government concerns the distribution of public funds among state, region, and municipalities, and the right of local authorities to impose taxes. We find practically all possible combinations of taxation systems and methods of public spending in different European countries. A first possible classification divides federal and unitary states. Among the former are Austria, Belgium, Spain, and Germany, and among the latter Finland, France, Greece, Italy, the Netherlands, and Portugal. These are countries that were part of a study by the National Association of Italian Communities. It comes as no surprise that the countries with a federal organization have a higher percentage of local public spending when this is compared with total spending. In Spain, for example, local spending amounts to 54.5 per cent of total spending, and in Germany it is 45.7 per cent. In the unitary states, the proportion depends on the degree of decentralization: in Italy local spending makes up approximately one-third (30.6 per cent) of total spending, in France only a little more than one-fifth, and in Greece slightly over one-twentieth.

The situation is also complicated with respect to revenues. A first factor concerns fiscal pressure, or the rate of GDP that is collected by the state (in all its forms), which varies greatly from country to country: it ranges from 56.3 per cent in Denmark to 36 per cent in Ireland. The authority of the municipalities to impose taxes is variable as well. Obviously, the greater the ability of communities, and hence cities, to defray their costs with taxes levied directly on the income of their inhabitants, the greater is their autonomy. Yet if they must depend on transfers by the state or other intermediate territorial bodies, their autonomy is smaller. For instance, nearly all countries have certain charges on property and real estate, and generally the municipalities where these properties are located are the ones that are benefiting from these revenues. Another relevant aspect is the possibility of local authorities, and especially municipalities, to be involved in assessing taxable earnings. Theoretically, municipalities should have more efficient tools available for combating tax evasion, especially if this happens on a small scale – in instances where it is more difficult to hide one's earnings behind some form of anonymity. Yet proximity to the inspection agency may also have the opposite effect.

Fiscal revenues, both those that derive from an autonomous authority to impose taxes and those that depend on transfers by the state, are all too often insufficient to cover a city's administrative expenses. Sooner or later, almost all cities must borrow money, incurring debts both to banks and by issuing actual credit instruments on the capital market. A city that is well governed and managed often takes recourse to loans in order to finance investment in important infrastructure that will promote the development of the city itself. The situation is more problematic for those cities that must resort to loans to pay for current expenditure.

Large cities, above all capitals, have often accumulated enormous debts. The most glaring example is perhaps Berlin, which has amassed a debt of over €60 billion, an amount that equals more than €20,000 for each of the city's 3.5 million inhabitants. Such an enormous debt has no doubt also been brought about by the particular history of this city, which was reborn after 1989. In Italy, the capital, Rome, is the city with the largest debt (it has been calculated that this amounts to over €12 billion), chiefly because of the mismanagement of about 40 public/private companies in which the municipality has a majority stake. The same is true for London, Madrid, and Paris, where the debt was incurred for financing large infrastructures that greatly improved the quality of the environment and, specifically, the transportation system.

Hence, debts are not necessarily a negative indicator about the way in which a city is being managed. There are many favourable instances where a dynamic administration has been able to make investments that could boost competitiveness and moreover attract new private investment without having to resort too much to taking out new loans. There are the examples of Barcelona and Valencia in Spain and Lyon in France. In Italy, aside from Rome, Milan, Turin, Naples, and Genoa are the cities with the greatest debts. They are certainly not at the level of Berlin, but still, every inhabitant of Turin and Milan carries a debt of over €3,000.

The financial problem is particularly evident in those cities that carry out functions for and are a centre of attraction for an area that extends far beyond its administrative boundaries. As Martinotti has clearly shown, the two populations of those who avail themselves of a city's services (the 'city users') and those who live there, elect the mayor, and pay the city's taxes (the citizens in a strict sense) are in fact not the same (Martinotti, 1993). Every day a heterogeneous population arrives in big cities consisting of commuters, as well as those who want to make purchases, go about their business, avail themselves of professional and healthcare services that are unavailable where they live, and go to the theatre or an exhibition, and in addition any tourists who are passing through. This latter population certainly contributes indirectly to the city's wealth and fortune, but it also uses public services (e.g. transportation, city cleaning), which it does not help to fund with the taxes it pays. This is an aspect of a phenomenon that has significant dimensions and provokes much interest, appearing in different forms on all continents, including Europe: the formation of metropolitan areas.

3.6 *Major Cities and Metropolitan Areas*

The urbanization process throughout the world and specifically in Europe has been steadily moving forward. By 2019 almost the entire population of the so-called First world lives in cities; yet it is in the areas of the so-called Third World that cities are growing at a more accelerated pace. However, if all (or almost all) of us live in cities, it certainly makes a great difference in which city we live. Specifically, there is a difference between living in a metropolis, a metropolitan area, or in a city that has difficulty in availing itself of the advantages of metropolitan life. No doubt, the transformation brought about by globalization that has already been mentioned first of all concerns the large cities, or rather the metropolitan areas. These, while often expanding even across national borders, enter into global economic competition, giving substance to the notion of 'glocalism', which blends aspects of globalism and localism.

We can define a metropolitan area as the territory that is connected to one or more central cities in a functionally interdependent way. This definition conjures up the image of a large urbanized area with a main centre and an extended area of minor centres that are connected via a transportation and communication network. It turns out that defining what a metropolitan area is, where it begins, and where it ends is not easy. There are numerous criteria that can be applied, and scholars, in particular urban geographers, are not in agreement on which criteria to consider over others.

In Europe, most metropolitan areas are around capital cities: Moscow is surrounded by an area with almost 15 million inhabitants (the population of the city of Moscow is 11.5 million). Greater London is in the same ballpark (14 million inhabitants, of whom 7.5 million are in central London). The Paris greater metropolitan area has 11.8 million inhabitants, but the city of Paris 'only' 2,275,000. The metropolitan area of Istanbul also exceeds 14 million inhabitants if we include the districts that many geographers consider to be part of Asia. There are also some areas with many centres among the most urbanized territories in the world, such as the one north of Cologne that has the centres of the Ruhr region (Cologne, Düsseldorf, Dortmund, Essen, Duisburg, Wuppertal, Bochum, and other, smaller cities, which are an average of 50–60 km apart) and which have almost 12 million inhabitants, or Randstad, the 'Ring City' in the Netherlands (which includes Amsterdam, Rotterdam, The Hague, Utrecht, Leiden, Haarlem, and Hilversum), with over 6.5 million inhabitants. Although Milan is not a capital city, a vast area gravitates towards it: this includes practically all of Lombardy, with over 8 million inhabitants, whereas the city itself has only 1.3 million people: a relatively small municipality at the centre of a large metropolitan area. By contrast, almost the opposite is true for Rome and Berlin, two capitals where the city itself makes up most of the metropolitan area: in Rome, the city has 2.8 million inhabitants and the metropolitan area 4.4 million; and in Berlin, 3.4 million people live in the city and 4 million in the metropolitan area. Then there are some large, combined metropolitan areas that cross national borders: Copenhagen and Malmö are separated by a small strait and linked by a bridge, and are at the centre of an area of 2.4 million inhabitants; the conurbation Aachen, Liège, and Maastricht connects three countries (Germany, Belgium, and the Netherlands) and has 2.2 million inhabitants.

As already mentioned, these indications and these large figures must be viewed cautiously, as the definition and calculation criteria for metropolitan areas are anything but homogeneous. Still, with this caveat firmly in mind, it is useful to see where the large European cities are ranked in the context of major global cities. Among the first ten, we find only Moscow (in tenth place), and among the first twenty, there are also London, Paris, and Istanbul; of the rest, ten are in Asia, three in North America, two in South America, and one in Africa. What are the conclusions we can draw from this ranking? It is clear that the expansion of metropolitan areas is a global rather than a European phenomenon, and that, overall, Europe is the most urbanized area in the world, yet – disregarding Africa for the time being – the one with the fewest metropolitan areas. Therefore, we can conclude that the city remains a distinct trait of European identity and is destined to remain so in the future, even though our cities continue to be protagonists of constant change, at least those that are not turning into museums. For a number of cities across the continent, this is not an entirely remote risk.

CHAPTER 7

Population and Family Structures

1 How Many Europeans Are There and How Many Will There Be?

In 2018, with 512,4 million inhabitants, the 28 countries of the European Union (EU) constituted the third largest political entity in the world, after China (1,398 million) and India (1,335 million), ahead of the United States (USA) (323 million), Indonesia (258 million), Brazil (205 million), Pakistan (184 million), Bangladesh (155 million), Nigeria (147 million), Russia (140 million), and Japan (127 million). The Union achieved this size after a long series of enlargements, which saw various countries join the original core of France, Germany, Italy, Belgium, the Netherlands, and Luxembourg. In 1973, it was joined by the United Kingdom (UK), Denmark, and Ireland; in 1981, Greece; in 1986, Spain and Portugal; with the reunification of Germany in 1990, the population of the former German Democratic Republic was added; in 1995, Austria, Sweden, and Finland joined; in 2004, no fewer than ten new members acceded: Cyprus, Malta, Hungary, Poland, Slovakia, Latvia, Estonia, Lithuania, the Czech Republic, and Slovenia; in 2007 Bulgaria and Romania joined; and finally, in 2013, Croatia became a member as well. Once the exit of the UK takes effect, following the June 2016 referendum, we will need to subtract 65 million British citizens.

If we also want to include the countries that have applied for EU membership (Turkey, Macedonia, Montenegro, Serbia, and Albania) and the countries that are part of the area defined as Europe (Russia west of the Urals, the European nations of the former Soviet Union that have not joined the EU: Ukraine, Belarus, Georgia), and the countries that are closely connected to the Union even though they are not members (such as Switzerland and Norway), we arrive at a figure of no fewer than 750 million inhabitants. Even so, unless there is an unlikely reversion of the current trend, the proportion of Europeans in the world population, which today is a little over 11 per cent, is bound to continue to shrink.

The demographic tendencies reveal important traits in these societies. In this chapter we will take a look at the dynamics of the European population that is part of the EU both before and after its major expansion at the beginning of the 21st century, with references to the neighbouring populations of

Russia, Turkey, and the southern shore of the Mediterranean, when appropriate, in order to better grasp the similarities and differences.[1]

When speaking of Europe, occasionally the expression 'Old World' or 'Old Continent' is used in order to distinguish it from the 'New World' of the Americas. Today, the expression 'old world' sometimes has a different meaning, namely that of a world inhabited by a very aged population. Yet the expression is ambiguous, as it suggests a rearguard world in contradistinction to other worlds that consist of young people who constitute the avant-garde. In a certain sense, the very opposite is true. European society is among the first in the history of the human species that has a population whose low birth rates go hand in hand with low mortality rates, and where, therefore, the percentage of the young population is tending to shrink while that of the elderly is steadily expanding. European society shares these characteristics with Japan and, to a lesser degree, with the USA, and increasingly so with China as well, these two countries, in this respect, also belonging to the 'old world'.

According to the theory of demographic transition, as they modernize human societies pass from phases of high birth and mortality rates to periods in which first the mortality rates and then the birth rates decline until both are finally balanced at a low level. This theory has been questioned, as it is not able to adequately account for the great variety of demographic dynamics that exist in today's world. Nonetheless, the theory is partly valid, and from this point of view, European society appears to be in the forefront, in the sense that it must confront unprecedented problems. These are connected to the fact that it has a huge proportion of elderly and a small proportion of young people. In fact, we are learning to live in a society with few children and many old people, whereas societies of the past and much of today's world are the diametric opposite: many children and young people, and relatively few old people. This development may be slowed down and corrected by specific public policies, and perhaps even temporarily reversed, but it is highly likely that it is bound to become the general direction, at least in the long run, in other societies that are currently passing through intermediate phases of the transition process (Golini, 2009).

Looking at the current situation, what are the foreseeable developments and potential consequences for social organization? To answer these questions we must examine population dynamics – on the one hand, the structures of household units and families, and on the other the quantitative and qualitative

---

1   Since the modalities of the exit of the United Kingdom are still under discussion, it does not seem to be appropriate to exclude its population in presenting the demographic situation in European society.

aspects, which crucially depend on three factors: birth rate, mortality rate, and migration movements.

2   Household Units and Family Structures

The figures in Table 7.1 indicate the mean size of what the French call *foyer* and the Italian *unità domestica*, what in English is simply called the *household*. This is an artificial variable whose profile is determined by a number of different factors (birth rate, existence of cohabitants, number of couples without children, number of singles), and yet it is highly significant in that it reveals a general tendency of shrinkage across Europe during the first 15 years of the 21st century. This is not the case in other countries, most notably North and Sub-Saharan Africa (Saraceno, 2012).

The artificial figures for median household size do not give us a full picture of various family structures in different countries and regions. Europe also appears highly diverse from this point of view. To begin with, let us take the figure for single households. This is a highly heterogeneous group, because it includes young people who no longer live with their family but have not set up house yet, widowers, divorced individuals and divorced people without children, and unmarried women and men who have decided, more or less voluntarily, to live by themselves. Today, one-third of Europeans live alone, but the figure ranges from the northern countries (Denmark, Sweden, Finland, and Germany), where their proportion exceeds 40 per cent of total households, to Ireland, Spain, and Portugal, where it is only 25 per cent. The fact that a considerable proportion of Europeans in all countries live by themselves cannot be ignored. This is a population with special needs concerning housing, food, communication, and relationships that social policies often do not take into account.

The number of households consisting of one person who lives with one or more minors, children or adolescents, is one measure for the instability of marriage, for instances where one partner in an unmarried couple has left, or for early widowhood. The figure for this category is moderate in Europe (4.5 per cent), but in some countries (e.g. Denmark) it exceeds 9 per cent.

The model that in some ways is considered 'normal', where a couple lives with their minor children or the children of one or other of the spouses, is in fact becoming more uncommon. In Europe, it represents about 20 per cent of all households, but the number is smaller in the Nordic countries, in Bulgaria, and in Germany, and only somewhat higher in Latin countries, where young people tend to live longer in their parents' home. The 'normal' families now also include households where a couple lives with children from other

TABLE 7.1   Mean household size in some countries

Country	2000	2015
Croatia	3.12	2.86
Slovakia	2.90	2.80
Poland	2.86	2.80
Ireland	2.97	2.73
Ukraine	2.79	2.68
Romania	2.90	2.70
Greece	2.70	2.60
Portugal	2.83	2.55
Spain	3.08	2.57
Russian Federation	2.75	2.57
Italy	2.63	2.44
Hungary	2.65	2.34
United Kingdom	2.41	2.35
Belgium	2.42	2.34
Czech Republic	2.66	2.40
Austria	2.47	2.23
Netherlands	2.34	2.23
Norway	2.29	2.22
France	2.30	2.20
Switzerland	2.24	2.18
Sweden	2.03	2.10
Germany	2.16	2.02
USA	2.69	2.63
Turkey	4.25	3.66
Egypt	5.19	4.36
Algeria	6.51	6.25
Morocco	6.40	6.58
Tunisia	5.48	5.51

SOURCE: EUROSTAT, (ONLINE DATA CODE: 'LFST_HHNHTYCH'), https://appsso.eurostat.ec.europa.eu/nui/show.do?dataset=lfst_hhnhtych&lang=en

marriages, a category that is growing owing to the instability of relationships between couples. The couples without children amount to about 25 per cent.

The other types of households – with or without children, shared living conditions (e.g. student housing, homes for the elderly), but also newly founded or

POPULATION AND FAMILY STRUCTURES 145

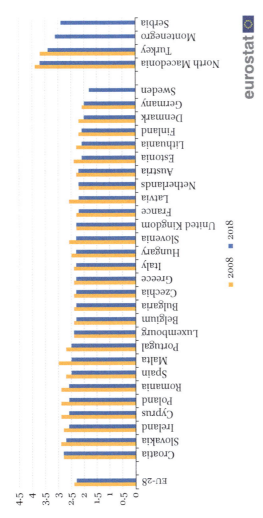

FIGURE 7.1   Average household size, 2008 and 2018 (average number of persons in private households)
Note: EU-28 2009 data instead of 2008.
https://appsso.eurostat.ec.europa.eu/nui/show.do?dataset=ilc_lvphon&lang=en

enlarged multi-family units – make up 17 per cent. Most individuals go through several of these forms of cohabitation, but it is still interesting to note how the type of household that is dedicated to the social reproduction of the population is only one of these forms, and not even the most frequent one, in Europe.

3   Declining Birth Rates

In France, birth rates (calculated on the basis of number of live births per 1,000 population) were already beginning to drop during the second half of the 18th century. In other countries of Northern Europe, the decline started in the second half of the 19th century. The trend has continued to this day and has spread at different rhythms and speeds in almost all other countries. If we take the example of France, we see that in about 1750, approximately 35 children were born per 1,000 population every year; a century later, the number declined to 20; and it reached its lowest point in history in 1994, with 12.7 births per 1,000. In the beginning, this development took place almost simultaneously with the industrialization process: in farming families, more children basically meant more hands to work the earth, and in working-class families, more children meant more mouths to feed. This explains, if only roughly, the driving force behind this process. The decline has continued until today, although it was suddenly interrupted by the wars that marked the history of the European continent in the 20th century. These saw men dying at the front and women taking their place in factories and offices – not very favourable conditions in which to bring children into the world. During each post-war period, however, the birth rate recovered almost everywhere, which at least in part made up for the lack of births during the armed conflict. These events characterized populations in practically all European countries, with the exception of those few who managed not to become involved in the hostilities.

Once these epochal convulsions were over, the long-term trend of declining birth rates resumed its course, albeit not linearly, under the impact of politico-cultural factors that differed from country to country. An indicator that is often used to illustrate the trend of shrinking birth rates is the fertility rate, which measures the average number of children per woman of childbearing age (between 15 and 49 years). A fertility rate under 2.1 signals demographic decline, as it means that a population cannot replace its own members and that sooner or later there will be a negative natural balance; that is, the number of newborns in a specific period does not offset the number of deaths. The populations in European countries have crossed the decisive threshold to fewer than two children per woman several times in history. The Nordic countries and France were first, and the Southern and East-Central European countries have followed over a number of decades. The latter quickly made up for the delay, drifting toward the all-time lowest birth and fertility rates in human societies.

At around the end of the second millennium, the fertility rate recovered again in the Scandinavian countries, Ireland, and France, and in some cases (e.g. in France) it almost reached equilibrium. In France, the birth rate climbed within a mere quarter of a century from 1.66 in 1993 to 2.03 in 2010, declining again thereafter to 1.90 in 2017. This recovery, which was also recorded in Northern European countries, is almost certainly because of the success of social policies that, as mentioned earlier, were geared toward the support of young couples and in this way generated favourable conditions or removed obstacles to procreation. In the countries that, like Italy, had seen a more drastic drop in the birth rate, there were also signs of a modest recovery (for the most part, however, owing to the greater fertility of the immigrant population), but the economic crisis brought a sudden halt to this: in 2013, 514,000 children were born in Italy and the fertility rate dropped to 1.39, and in 2015 there were 485,780 births and the fertility rate finally dropped to 1.32 in 2017.

Research that was conducted at the Organisation for Economic Co-operation and Development (OECD Family Database http://www.oecd.org/els/family/database.htm) clearly indicates a discrepancy between the number of wanted children (both male and female) and the number actually produced, and shows that this discrepancy is particularly pronounced in countries with a higher drop in the birth rate. Hence, we can predict that this discrepancy can be eliminated, or at least reduced, by pertinent social policies.

Currently (2017), the total fertility rate for the 28 countries of the EU is 1.59. It is interesting to note in Table 7.2. which countries are substantially above

TABLE 7.2 Fertility rates (2017)

Above the EU-28 average		Below the EU-28 average	
France	1.90	Spain	1.31
Sweden	1.78	Italy	1.32
Ireland	1.77	Greece	1.36
Denmark	1.75	Portugal	1.38
United Kingdom	1.74	Croatia	1.42
Belgium	1.65	Poland	1.48
Netherlands	1.62	Finland	1.49
Germany	1.57	Slovakia	1.52

SOURCE: EUROSTAT (ONLINE DATA CODE: 'DEMO_FRATE'), https://appsso.eurostat.ec.europa.eu/nui/show.do?dataset=lfst_hhnhtych&lang=en

(+10 per cent) or below the average (−10 per cent). The birth rate crisis is more pronounced in the Mediterranean countries, in some eastern and the German-speaking countries, whereas it is much less strong in the Nordic countries (except Finland), in the UK, and, above all, in France, the only European country that, as we have seen, currently has a fertility rate that almost (not quite) ensures an equilibrium between births and deaths.

4   Couples, Families, and Reproductive Decisions

The modifications of the index figures that show the transformations in the reproductive behaviour express, and are connected with, profound changes in social organization. In the first place, the female role in the family and in society has changed, and no longer revolves exclusively around reproduction and taking care of household and family. Rather, women often assume an active role in the productive and, more generally, the public sphere. These transformations are a consequence of and accompany women's growing access to education, which constituted the prime and powerful engine of this transformation. The decline in fertility rate and the increase in education levels among the female population are two phenomena that run parallel to one another, and even though there is no automatic cause and effect link between them, there is no doubt that the phenomena are directly connected. More education translates into more autonomy, more access to out-of-home labour, and hence – unless other factors intervene – greater difficulty in spending time on childcare.

When and how new family units have formed are also connected to reproductive behaviours and the decline or recovery of the birth rate in various ways. With different degrees of intensity, a crisis in the institution of marriage can be observed more or less everywhere in Europe. The proportion of single-person households is growing, and not only because one partner in the couple – almost always the woman – survives the other by several years; there are also many singles who are not old. As Table 7.3. shows, the marriage rate is declining, the number of couples living together is growing, and consequently the number of children born to unmarried couples is also increasing. This phenomenon cannot be sufficiently explained from a strictly utilitarian perspective: not getting married in fact entails both extra or fewer expenses and tax advantages or disadvantages that are not always easy to determine. That many young couples are abandoning the institution of marriage – at least in the current period – seems rather to reflect an individualistic concept of

TABLE 7.3 Marriage and divorce rates (per 1,000 population) in some countries of the EU

	Marriages			Divorces		
	1965	2000	2017	1965	2000	2017
EU-28	7.0	4.4	4.4	0.6	2.6	1.9
Bulgaria	8.0	4.3	4.0	1.1	1.3	1.5
Belgium	7.0	4.4	3.9	0.6	2.6	2.0
Czech Rep.	8.4	5.4	5.0	1.7	2.9	2.6
Denmark	8.8	7.2	5.5	1.4	2.7	2.6
Germany	8.3	5.1	4.9	1.0	2.4	1.9
Ireland	5.9	4.3	4.6	0.7	0.6	0.7
Greece	9.4	4.5	4.7	0.4	1.0	1.8
Spain	7.1	5.4	3.7		0.9	2.1
France	7.0	5.0	3.5	0.7	1.9	1.9
Italy	7.7	5.0	3.2		0.7	1.5
Hungary	8.8	4.7	5.2	2.0	2.3	1.9
Netherlands	8.8	5.5	3.8	0.5	2.2	1.9
Austria	7.7	4.9	5.1	1.2	2.4	1.8
Poland	6.4	5.5	5.1	0.7	1.1	1.7
Portugal	8.4	6.2	3.2	0.4	1.9	2.1
Romania	8.6	6.1	7.3	1.9	1.4	1.6
Slovenia	9.2	3.6	3.1	1.1	1.1	1.2
Slovakia	7.0	4.8	5.8	0.6	1.7	1.8
Finland	7.0	5.1	4.8	1.0	2.7	2.4
Sweden	7.8	4.5	5.2	1.2	2.4	2.4
UK	7.8	5.7	4.4	0.7	2.6	1.8

SOURCE: EUROSTAT https://ec.europa.eu/eurostat/statistics-explained/index.php?title=Marriage_and_divorce_statistics&oldid=438517

couple relationships that in a certain sense is removed from the sanction of and control by society and has been relegated to the private sphere. If we take the figures for the period 2000–14, we can make out fluctuating behaviour: the marriage rate experienced a sudden recovery of brief duration in Eastern and Northern European countries, whereas almost everywhere in the countries of Southern and Western Europe a constant drop was recorded. As the number of marriages declines, so does the number of divorces. In fact, divorce rates tend to be constant and sometimes even declining, contrary to the widespread perception of a growing trend for the dissolution of the bond of marriage.

Where the institution of marriage is still firmly established, it nonetheless often comes later in life. Currently women in Europe get married at an average age of about 30 years, and men two to three years later. Italy is a case in point. With the transition from agriculture to industry, people exhibited a trend toward getting married at a younger age. This development came to a halt toward the mid-1960s, from which point on people started getting married later and later in life (and in Italy this number is still large). Within an 11-year period (2004–15), the average age of people getting married for the first time went from a little under 29 years for women to 32 and from a little over 32 to almost 35 for men. In Europe, people get married the latest in the Nordic and Mediterranean countries. In Eastern Europe, people married younger before 1990 – women around the age of 22 (in Sweden, the marrying age was already 27 at that time), but in the last 25 years weddings have been taking place later in the east as well, and in a few years the gap will probably be closed.

Europeanization and globalization processes impact the marriage marketplace and hence the choice of spouse. The number of mixed marriages, where one of the spouses was born in a country other than the one in which the wedding is held, is growing over time, and so is the number of spouses who were born in different countries, which, however, are part of the EU. In other words, true European families are being formed into which bilingual and bicultural children are being born. Their number is small as yet, but in 2014 a total of 5.2 per cent of new births in an EU country were delivered by mothers who were born in another EU country. It comes as no surprise that the country with the greatest incidence of mixed marriages is Luxembourg (no less than 34 per cent), but in Holland one in 20 marriages is also mixed.

In any event, bringing children into this world has on the one hand become more and more an informed decision on the part of the couple (in terms of using birth control) and on the other is often being delayed until the situation has become more favourable. In Italy, for example, until a few decades ago, the first child was born an average of nine months after the wedding, which means that in some instances the wedding indicated a situation where the decision to get married had been forced by a pregnancy. Today, the first child is often born when the couple is older and has lived together for several years (married or not), which explains the increase in the number of only children. The large families that we saw so frequently in the rural regions of Southern Europe until a few decades ago are becoming a rarity, and tend to be concentrated in areas in which the tradition of the Catholic Church is more deeply rooted.

As for reproductive behaviour, we see various models in Europe that in geographical terms are distributed on a north–south and east–west axis. In the Northern European countries, more and more couple relationships are formed and children are born outside marriage. Consequently, this happens at a younger age than in southern countries. This development has led to a substantial recovery in the birth rate, as family support measures have been extended to common-law couples. These trends are also taking place in Southern Europe, but there they meet with greater cultural resistance, which explains why the decline in the birth rate is fairly consistent and the recovery is still quite moderate.

As Table 7.4 shows, there are some countries where more than half of all children are born to unmarried couples (Estonia, Slovenia, Bulgaria, Sweden). In most other countries their proportion is more than one-third (UK, Netherlands, Portugal, Latvia, Hungary, Czech Republic, Austria, Spain, Ireland, Germany), and in a few countries it is less than one-third, but increasing over time (Romania, Lithuania, Italy, Poland, Greece).

It is not surprising that with mass education, especially that of women, we notice almost everywhere a delayed onset of the adult phase in life, and this impacts the assumption of parental roles. Yet the effects vary a great deal from society to society; specifically, in the societies that border the northern shore of the Mediterranean (excluding France and including Portugal, which joins this group in this respect) we find that young people, especially males, stay longer in their parents' family (Table 7.5). This cohabitation of two generations of adults generally lasts as long as the younger party does not get married – a familial as well as cultural model that would be deemed unacceptable in Northern Europe by most parents and young adults alike. While in this part of Europe becoming independent of one's birth family is considered a positive value, a necessary important step on the way to adult life, in Southern Europe the condition of young adults is chiefly defined in terms of acquiring a sphere of autonomy not from but within the family. It is an autonomy that obviously exists only in part, as it does not include the assumption of responsibility for managing one's home life and the family budget.

The extended time that young people spend living with their original family could be shortened by educational policies aiming at linking education and work, and by active labour and housing policies that address the needs of young couples, all the way to, say, rent control measures.

Another issue that goes in the same direction deserves attention as well: the phenomenon of NEETs (those who are Not in Employment, Education and Training) appeared in all its dramatic force during the economic and financial crisis that erupted in 2008, which saw an increase not only in youth

TABLE 7.4 Percentage of live births outside marriage of total births

	1990	2012	2018
Estonia	27.2	58.4	54,1
Slovenia	24.5	58.0	57,7
Bulgaria	12.4	59.1	58,5
Norway	38.6	54.9	56,4
Sweden	47.0	54.4	54,5
Belgium	11.6	52.3	49,0 (2016)
United Kingdom	27.0	47.6	48,2 (2017)
Netherlands	11.4	47.4	51,9
Portugal	14.7	47.6	55,9
Latvia	15.9	45.0	39,5
Hungary	13.1	44.5	43,9
Czech Republic	8.6	43.2	48,5
Austria	23.5	41.5	41,3
Luxembourg	12.8	37.1	39,5
Spain	9.6	35.5	47,3
Ireland	14.6	35.1	37,9
Germany	15.3	34.5	33,9
Romania	–	31.0	30,9
Lithuania	7.0	28.8	26,4
Italy	8.5	26.9	34,0
Poland	6.2	23.4	26,4
Greece	2.2	7.0	11,1

SOURCE: EUROSTAT (ONLINE DATA CODE: 'DEMO_FIND'), https://appsso.eurostat.ec.europa.eu/nui/show.do?dataset=demo_find&lang=en

unemployment but also in the proportion of disillusioned young people who left school between the ages of 15 and 24. The number of young people who found themselves in this situation reached its highest level in the Mediterranean countries (approximately 20–25 per cent of young people aged between 20 and 24), in particular in Spain, Italy, and Greece, and it is much lower in almost all northern countries, particularly in the Netherlands, Sweden and Germany. With the crisis slowly returning, the phenomenon is diminished, but remains considerable, results in additional expenses for families, and is certainly not conducive to forming lasting couple relationships and bringing children into the world.

TABLE 7.5 Age at which young people leave their parents' home, start living with a partner, and become parents (2013)

Country	Leaving home		Living with a partner		Birth of first child	
	M	F	M	F	M	F
Austria	25.9	23.3	29.6	26.5	33.5	29.8
Belgium	24.6	23.2	28.1	25.6	34.2	29.4
Czech Rep	28.1	25.4	29.9	36.8	32.9	28.8
Greece	31.5	26.8	34.5	29.8	37.0	31.8
Spain	28.3	26.4	31.1	28.8	36.1	32.6
France	23.2	22.0	26.6	23.3	32.4	28.8
Italy	29.6	26.8	33.8	28.9	37.2	31.8
Netherlands	23.4	21.5	28.7	26.1	33.5	30.0
Poland	29.1	26.4	28.9	26.4	31.4	28.2
Sweden	20.8	19.9	28.5	25.7	31.8	28.8
United Kingdom	25.1	23.0	27.7	25.3	33.6	29.2
EU-27	26.3	23.8	29.4	26.4	34.3	30.1

SOURCE: EUROSTAT https://ec.europa.eu/eurostat/web/products-eurostat-news/-/EDN-20190514-1

The trend towards differences between East and West, however, has been profoundly influenced by historical events that have upset the political and economic systems of the eastern countries and symbolically culminated in the fall of the Berlin Wall (in 1989). In fact, while in the mid-1960s birth and fertility rates gradually declined in the West, the birth rate recovered in the eastern countries in the late 1960s, a trend that lasted, albeit with fluctuations, until the mid-1980s. Then it suddenly declined, reaching an absolute low at the end of the 1990s. This was followed by a slight recovery and great stability at very low levels. The phenomenon appeared even more pronounced in Russia, where within a span of a mere eight years, between 1988 and 1996, the overall fertility rate dropped from 2.13 to 1.28 children per woman, with a further decline in the following years until the turn of the millennium. This extremely pronounced drop can be explained by a convergence of different factors. First, the end of the near isolation in which the societies of Eastern Europe were kept may signify emulation of Western models of smaller family households within a more individualistic framework. Secondly, it may indicate a response to a situation of uncertainty created by the disappearance of a system of guarantees that

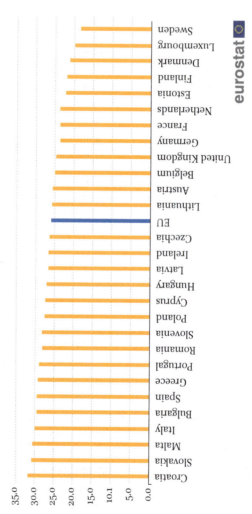

FIGURE 7.2 Estimated average age of young people leaving the parental household, 2018
SOURCE: EUROSTAT

the regimes were able to impose. Thirdly, the specific economic difficulties in many social areas during the transition period toward a capitalist economy may play a role. The costs ran up quickly, but the wait for benefits – if there were any – was long. Bringing children into the world under these conditions – always a show of confidence in the future – may have constituted too great a risk for many couples. Figure 7.3 illustrates very clearly how the expansion of the EU modified its demographic profile.

5 Fewer People Die and Live Longer

If the first component of the demographic dynamic is the birth rate, the second one is obviously the mortality rate. Taking a long-term historical view, the beginning of the decline of the death rate in Europe dates back to a remote period. In England and Wales, there were 30 deaths per 1,000 population annually in the mid-18th century. Two centuries later, that figure was 11. The other countries in Northern Europe followed the same trend. Yet in Italy too, and in the countries of Southern Europe, where that trend established itself with some delay, the mortality rates at the beginning of the 21st century were less than half of what they had been in 1950. To explain the stages of this process in more detail, it is helpful to take a look at the development of mortality rates for different age groups. Everywhere, the first figure to decline was infant mortality rate, as Table 7.6 shows. Initially, an elevated birth rate corresponded to an elevated morality rate in the first year or first years of life, which was primarily a consequence of the precarious hygienic conditions to which children were exposed in both urban and rural settings. Gradually, fewer children were born, but many more of them survived. The times and modes of the decline of the infant mortality rate varied according to social geography: the process was always led by the countries of Northern Europe, followed by those in Southern Europe. A reduction in infant mortality is moreover a clear indicator of the degree of modernization (UNICEF, 2014). The rate is dropping everywhere in Europe, including in Eastern European countries, which still had fairly elevated rates when they joined the EU (Table 7.7).

In a second phase, the mortality rates of people of a more advanced age began to decline as well. It was chiefly the drop in this age category that generated the ageing process in the population that now characterizes all European societies. However, if we look at the life expectancy at the time of birth during the past half-century (i.e. the average number of years that every new born

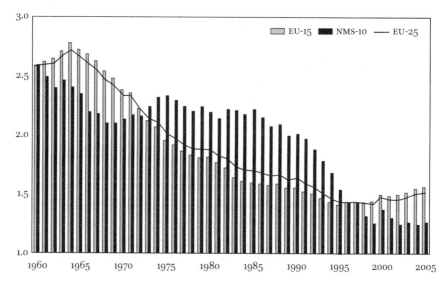

FIGURE 7.3 The demographic situation in the European Union (total period fertility rate)
SOURCE: https://www.cairn.info/revue-population-2004-2-page-361.htm#

could expect to live), we notice quite pronounced differences between the countries of the EU before and after its expansion in 2004. Among the members of the EU-15, the increase was linear throughout the period under consideration: life expectancy for both men and women grew by almost ten years. In the countries that joined more recently (almost all of them from Eastern Europe), the increase was not linear and even shows a sudden inversion of the trend, especially with respect to the male population, in the years of the Great Turnaround of 1989 caused by the crisis of the USSR. In any event, the discrepancy in life expectancy between the two groups of countries is remarkable: men in Western Europe have a life expectancy that is 6.5 years longer than that of citizens in the East (for women the discrepancy is smaller, at 4.0 years). If we then also consider the difference between the countries with the longest life expectancy (i.e. Sweden for men at 80.7 years and Spain for women at 85.5 years) and the countries with the shortest life expectancy (Lithuania for men at 68.1 years and Bulgaria for women at 78.0), we note a strong inequality between regions that in fact splits the population of the Union in two parts. A Swedish man lives an average of 12 years longer than a Lithuanian and a Spanish woman 7.5 years longer than one from Bulgaria.

The phenomenon can also be observed on a larger scale in the Russian Federation, where the median life expectancy for the male population dropped by 7.7 years between 1987 and 1994; for women the decline was more modest (4.0

TABLE 7.6 Infant mortality rate in Western Europe (deaths in the first year of life per 1,000 births)

Western Europe	1900	1950	Average 2005–10	Average 2011–15
Sweden	96	22	2.56	2.80
Netherlands	147	26	4.42	3.46
Norway	88	27	3.00	2.50
Denmark	126	32	4.04	3.47
Switzerland	139	32	3.75	3.68
United Kingdom	145	33	4.91	4.19
Finland	135	42	2.81	2.26
France	149	53	3.64	3.34
Belgium	153	53	3.81	3.33
Ireland	102	47	4.04	2.93
Germany	207	55	3.71	3.10
Austria	221	66	3.97	3.09
Italy	168	68	3.51	2.8
Spain	195	69	3.76	3.00
Greece	–	60	4.65	2.84
Portugal	–	93	4.45	3.29

SOURCE: UNITED NATIONS WORLD POPULATION PROSPECT (2015 REVISION), https://population.un.org/wpp/DataQuery/

years). This decrease appears to be attributable both to the rapid deterioration of the healthcare system after the sociopolitical crisis that took place towards the final days of the USSR and to increased alcohol consumption (with an associated climb in cardiovascular diseases) that mainly affected working-age males. These are signs of a dramatic social anomie.

Low fertility and increasing longevity are the signs of ageing that distinguish the European (and Japanese) populations from those in other parts of the world. From this point of view, Europe, as already mentioned, must now and in the immediate future confront the problems that the other parts of the world will face in the long run. The United Nations Statistics Division calculates the ageing index of the population as the number of people over 60 per 100 young people between 0 and 14 years of age. An index above 100 is interpreted as a sign of ageing, and the countries of the EU (which have a median index of 136), with the exception of Luxembourg, Cyprus, and Ireland, are all above this threshold, with the figure being way above this level in Italy (190) and Germany

TABLE 7.7 Infant mortality rate in Eastern Europe (deaths in the first year of life per 1,000 births)

Eastern Europe	1955	Average 2005–10	Average 2011–15
Romania	100	13.87	9.64
Bulgaria	91	10.21	9.02
Latvia	68	7.51	6.49
Slovakia	74	7.27	4.91
Hungary	72	7.44	4.62
Poland	95	7.21	4.58
Estonia	77	7.39	3.2
Lithuania	93	7.68	3.76

SOURCE: UNITED NATIONS WORLD POPULATION PROSPECT (2015 REVISION), https://population.un.org/wpp/DataQuery/

(182). The other countries whose situation approaches that of the EU are Japan (201), the Russian Federation (114), and Canada (110), whereas Australia (95) and the USA (84) are still below this threshold, if only slightly. China (55), Brazil (34), Turkey (29), Mexico (28), and India (26) are societies that are characterized by a huge young population vis-à-vis a still moderate number of elderly people (Kunisch et al., 2011). We arrive at the same conclusions when we look at the percentage of the population that is above a certain age. For example, in Italy and Germany more than one-fifth of the population is more than 65 years old, whereas in Ireland, Slovenia, and Cyprus this figure is barely 12 per cent.

Yet it is above all the future trend of the ageing process that is remarkable. Projections for 2050 (fairly realistic projections, too, as those over 65 years old have already been born) indicate that for many European countries, including Italy, there will be three times as many elderly than young people, unless a solid increase in births takes place, such as happened in France and the Scandinavian countries, where it was still not sufficient to turn the situation around.

The ageing of society is also directly reflected in the dependency ratios, which are calculated by comparing the number of people under 20 years old and 65 and older (i.e. people not yet and no longer able to generate wealth) and those in the middle age class between 20 and 65 years. Of the two figures in the numerator, one is diminishing (newborns, children, and adolescents) whereas the latter is growing more than the former is declining. The dependency rate therefore shows an upward trend, with obvious repercussions on pension schemes and on healthcare. Albeit with differences in time and intensity from country to country, the European population is tending to shrink and become older. There is, however, another phenomenon that will certainly alter the demographic situation on the European part of the Eurasian continent. It is of course that of migration, which is examined in Chapter 8.

6   Social Policies for the Family

The drop in the birth rate and the ageing of the population are issues that apply to all of Europe, but we cannot say if there is, or has been, a uniform response to the challenge this trend poses. The European Council has addressed the issues of a social European agenda on various occasions and has suggested targets that member countries should pursue. In fact, however, the mix of policies that individual countries have enacted and the objectives of these policies vary considerably owing to different priorities, and sometimes they are incompatible with one another. The objectives of stimulating a recovery of the birth rate, facilitating women's access to the labour market, and reducing the inequality of parenting and, more generally, running a household are rarely pursued without inconsistencies and ambivalence.

An examination of the policies in this area illuminates the considerable heterogeneity between countries. Let us start with one of the older measures, which was intended to prevent working women, after giving birth, from either handing their child to their original family (i.e. almost invariably their own mother) or to some charitable institution, or from leaving their job voluntarily or being let go by their employer. I am talking about maternity leave, a practice that was established for the first time in the 19th century and whose duration varies from country to country and in different historical periods. It guarantees that the mother not only receives compensation but also gets her job back after giving birth. In the EU, maternity leave lasts an average of 19 weeks; that is to say, roughly two months before and three months after giving birth. A directive of the European Council establishes the length of maternity leave as 14 weeks, but there are differences from country to country that depend on voluntary provisions for parental leave, which assure that the parent can hold on to his or her job for longer periods (up to two or three years), either without or with reduced pay. In general, long leave periods come with a suspension or reduction of wages, whereas reductions in pay are smaller for shorter leave periods.

Parental leave is a right to which only a mother is entitled, or the father, or both parents, which can be exercised flexibly according to their needs and priorities. In fact, however, it is a right that fathers exercise less frequently; only in the Nordic countries, in Austria, and in Slovenia is the proportion of fathers who take advantage of paternity leave more than 20 per cent of those who are entitled to it.

These measures may have a positive impact, at least in the medium to long term, on a different gender division of labour and different relationships between the genders. The model that assigns the task of earning the family's living to the husband/father, who works in the labour and job market, and the task of meeting the emotional needs of and raising offspring to the wife/mother is doubtless in decline throughout Europe, and has been ever since women gained access to mass education and the labour market. The intensity of these transformations and when they take place, however, are certainly not the same.

It is obvious that these measures, which are intended to help families and raise the birth rate, can on the one hand help prevent a more balanced distribution of caretaking responsibilities among the parents and on the other constitute a disincentive to employing women and an obstacle to women having a career. Cases in which employers hesitate to hire women of reproductive age so as to avoid the economic and organizational costs that their periods of absence because of maternity might entail are not rare.

In any event, maternity, paternity, and parental leave are not the only measures designed to boost the birth rate. In some countries, particularly in France, the welfare state becomes involved when a girl or boy is born, giving parents whose income is below a certain threshold a subsidy called *prime de naissance*, in 2019 amounting to €944, which is meant to cover the major expenses a newborn incurs. Single parents especially, almost always the mother, are also eligible to receive the subsidy. In France, moreover, the subsidy increases with every subsequent child in order to boost the number of families with more than two children and in this way balance out the deficit created by single-child families.

Financial support, however, particularly one-off support, does not appear to be a very effective means to induce a substantial number of couples to bring children into the world. Much more effective are those child services that allow parents, especially mothers, not to interrupt their work after they have given birth – that is to say, nursery schools for children up to the age of three and preschools for children between the ages of three and when they enter primary school. As for the former, only five EU countries (Denmark, the Netherlands, Sweden, Belgium, and Spain) are able to meet more than one-third of the childcare needs for newborns, while another five are close to this threshold (Portugal, UK, France, Luxembourg, Slovenia), and other countries (including

Italy and Germany) cover roughly 20 per cent of needs; still others (including the countries of Eastern Europe and Austria) barely meet 10 per cent of needs.

The situation looks much better with respect to preschools, however. Most European countries offer preschool educational services for about 95 per cent of four to six year olds. Below the 80 per cent threshold are only Greece, Croatia, Poland, Slovakia, and Finland, but it is likely that this gap will be filled within the next few years. In a country such as Turkey, for which joining the EU is a problematic issue, the figure is still below the 50 per cent mark.

Yet often these resources are paid for entirely or partly by the family and are only available for part of the time that is needed for childcare when both parents work. As a result, even some preschool-age children are only taken care of by the family, especially in some eastern countries, such as Bulgaria, Croatia, Poland, and Romania. Moreover, numerous studies emphasize that children who have attended a preschool educational institution for at least a year will perform better in school later on. The same is true for children whose fathers have taken paternity leave.

The burden of childcare, which slows down the career mostly of women, does not, however, only apply to infancy, but also to the unequal distribution of other family-related responsibilities, for instance caring for the elderly when their health robs them of some of their autonomy. The elderly – grandparents – are certainly an important resource for taking care of infants. In many countries, without grandparents many mothers would be unable to have a full-time, or even part-time, job away from home. However, there is a threshold beyond which this resource becomes a burden, when old people need constant care – a task that depends on the individual country and one's social condition. This concerns the general issue of old age to which we referred at the beginning of the chapter. One study has shown that the typical American lives an average of 18 miles from his or her parents. There are no comparable figures for Europe, but it is likely that the average distance is even smaller. We know that one of the reasons for choosing one's residence is proximity to the parental home. With the increase in geographic mobility, however, this distance has probably tended to become larger. In any event, the variables of presence/absence, vicinity/distance, health/sickness, and autonomy/dependency of elderly parents are factors that heavily influence family decisions.

When we try to draw conclusions from an examination of family policies in European countries, the following picture seems to emerge:
- the northern countries (Denmark, Finland, Iceland, Norway, and Sweden) provide broad support for parents even of very small children through a combination of parental leave after the birth of the child and care services

during infancy, so that both parents can hold on to their jobs without having to jeopardize them;
- the UK offers financial assistance to families with small children and a small range of public services as well as parental leave;
- Germany and the eastern countries combine economic support with a limited range of infant care services;
- the countries in Southern Europe rely primarily on family support, offering modest economic subsidies and limited care services;
- France represents a special case in the Continental European panorama, with public investments supporting of young couples with small children, the primary goal being to allow working mothers to combine their jobs away from home with taking care of their children.

In conclusion, Europe presents a highly varied picture when it comes to family policies.

CHAPTER 8

Internal and External Migrations

1 A Challenge (Also) to the Sense of Identity

From many points of view, the issue of migration is crucial for the very existence of a society and a European identity. Someone who lives in Provence and moves to Paris, a Bavarian who relocates to Hamburg, or a Piedmontese who decides to spend his or her old age in the Aeolian Islands are all migrants, but since their migration takes place within the borders of a national state, it is by definition considered an internal migration as it does not challenge the principle of nationality on which the inclusion/exclusion of citizenship is based. Internal migrations within nation states, between different regions or city and countryside, have profoundly shaped the social and cultural profile of our societies.

In Europe people have also started talking of internal migration to indicate relocations between different countries, for instance in the case of a Neapolitan who manages a pizzeria in Berlin, or a Croat fleeing the Balkan war to France in 1996. Yet things are not that simple. If the "Pizzeria Napoletana" opened after 1992, the year in which the Maastricht Treaty formally established European citizenship, the pizza chef can (more or less) relax, as some of his fundamental rights are recognized just as if he had stayed at home, even though his new fellow citizens will consider him a foreigner for a long time, and perhaps forever. The Croatian refugee, on the other hand, was treated like a foreign citizen until the day his country of origin officially joined the European Union, that is to say, until 2013. Since that moment he has no longer been an immigrant from outside the Union, at least legally speaking, but acquired European citizenship. His condition would not have changed greatly, but he is now more protected compared to a Syrian refugee and subjectively may feel less of a stranger in the society which has received him.

The Anatolian peasant who has gone to work at Volkswagen in Wolfsburg, or the White Russian lady who took care of our mother in the last years of her life, or the Nigerian girl who was forced to emigrate to prostitute herself in some European city, and many others are all migrants who find themselves in a more or less permanent situation as strangers. The rights they enjoy depend on the laws of the respective country and can be granted them or revoked according to contingencies and without their consent. These examples give us an idea of the complexity of the issue of migration and how it is intertwined with the problems of borders, of inclusion and exclusion processes, and hence of identity, of the distinction between "us" and "them".

2   The Europe as an Area of Emigration and of Immigration

The pre-history and history of Europe is studded with migration movements, some of them slow and gradual, and others more intensive and of major proportions. As for the most remote ages, we know that homo sapiens arrived in Europe from Africa about 45,000 years ago. In the historic ages, the Greek colonies in Italy and the Anatolian peninsula, the Roman settlements from the British Isles to Persia, the migrations of people extended to the borders of the Roman Empire (which Italian school history books of a few decades ago called "barbaric invasions") testify to the fact that, next to sedentary populations, there always existed groups of people who moved about. On nearly all continents history tells us of ancient conflicts among populations of nomadic shepherds who came in conflict with agricultural populations, but also of wars among the latter about the use and conquest of land.

In the centuries after the discovery of America, the colonial expansion of the European powers entailed particularly large migratory fluxes from Europe to the rest of the world, but also enormous forced relocations of populations, if we think of the slave trade from Africa to the American continent. From 1800 onward, up until the First World War, Europe contributed to stupendous demographic growth owing to the beginning industrialization and modernization processes. This generated massive relocations of population groups from the country to the cities and the emigration of millions of men and women, mostly to the New World, Africa, and Australia. In the 19th century, an estimated 55–60 million people left Europe (Oltmer, 2016, p. 11). The two world wars, which drastically reduced the populations, more restrictive policies introduced by immigration countries, and the need for a labor force stimulated by economic development processes reduced the flow of migrants from Europe across the ocean considerably until it almost came to a halt in the last decades of the 20th century.

For half a millennium Europe had been an area of emigration for practically the entire rest of the world, especially the Americas and the regions that were more directly involved in the colonial expansion of the European powers and the development of trade relations. It was toward the middle of the xxth century that the direction was reversed and Europe began to become the destination of flows of immigration. The time when this process took place varies considerably from country to country. France, which in those days had the lowest natality rates in Europe, had already begun to receive many immigrants from

Poland in the last decades of the 19th century and before World War I, during which it suddenly lost a vast part of its population. This created a dreadful demographic gap, especially among its male population. During the postwar period, immigration came mainly from Armenia (after the 1915 genocide), from Southern European (Spain, Italy, Portugal, and Greece) and Eastern European countries (Poland, Hungary, Czechoslovakia, Bulgaria, Romania, and Russia). The United States of America is considered a country of immigrants, but actually, if we look at all the countries in the EU together (including the UK) the absolute number of immigrants in Europe (c. 47 million) exceeds that of immigrants in the USA (43 million), even though this is partly due to the fact that we also count those about 15 million people who were born in a different country of the EU than the one in which they are residing as "born abroad", and hence as immigrants. In any event, it is likely that the discrepancy between the USA and the EU is going to increase if the border controls or even the construction of walls effectively close the entrance gates for new immigrants from Mexico or other Latin American countries.

During the post–World War II period, the first countries which began to transform from countries of emigration to countries of immigration were the former colonial powers. In the course of the decolonization process, many former colonies and functionaries of the colonial administrations returned to their countries of origin, but many native inhabitants of the old colonies decided to follow them as well. As a result, hundreds of thousands of new citizens arrived in the United Kingdom from the countries of the Commonwealth, mostly Pakistanis, Indians, people from Bangladesh, Jamaica, Kenya, Nigeria, South Africa, and Australia. The same phenomenon affected France (from Indochina, the Maghreb regions, after 1975 particularly from Algeria), Belgium (from Congo), Holland (from Surinam, Indonesia, and the Antilles), Portugal (in addition to Brazil also from Angola, the Cape Verde Islands, Guinea-Bissau, and Mozambique) (Livi-Bacci, 2010).

Apart from decolonization, what created a strong push for migration was the long period of economic growth in the three decades following the war. After it had absorbed a large part of the 12 million Germans who were expelled or forced to flee from Eastern European countries (Russia, Ukraine, Poland, Czechoslovakia), the Federal Republic of Germany in particular began to import a labor force from Southern Europe (Italy, Greece, Spain, and Portugal) in the 1960s and, later on, above all from Turkey. We shall see how those who entered the country as foreign workers (*gastarbeiter*) became an element without which German society can no longer do today.

In the final three decades of the 20th century, immigration was also directed toward the Southern European countries which had traditionally and for the longest time been countries of emigration. Italy, Spain, and Greece found themselves in a situation where they had to deal with a completely new experience in their history. The fact that they had been countries of emigration did not necessarily help them become countries to receive and subsequently integrate immigrants. Populations rarely have a historical memory, and in all instances the memory of the difficulties which their own migrants encountered in the countries which received them is no aid in overcoming the mistrust of those who want to enter their own country today.

3   Internal and External Migrations to the EU

The 1992 Maastricht Treaty, which established European citizenship, set forth the freedom of movement and the right of residence in the European Union, and the subsequent Schengen Agreement abolished border controls for people coming from a signatory country (the United Kingdom did not sign the Agreement, whereas Norway and Switzerland, which are not part of the EU, did). Here the distinction is made between "external" and "internal" immigrants. Based on the principle of freedom of movement of workers, every citizen of one of the EU member states may enjoy the same rights as the citizens of the country in which he or she wants to reside, whereas the same may not apply to people coming from a non-EU or, more precisely, "external" country.

In reality, the migration flows between EU countries, which once mostly went from south to north and east to west, have shrunk considerably over the past few years and today mostly take place among the upper middle class of economy, technology, and science professionals. This is partly due to the fact that at a medium to high level, internal migrants are in competition with migrants from outside the Union. Non-Union migrants are willing to accept living and working conditions to which the majority of EU citizens are no longer used. Moreover, the countries with particularly generous welfare benefits do what they can to avoid encouraging migration motivated by the differences in welfare. Many EU citizens would probably like to immigrate to a country where they would receive special treatment in a system that offers social security, healthcare and/or unemployment benefits. It is no coincidence that before deciding in a referendum in June 2016 to leave the EU, the United Kingdom had negotiated regulations meant to mitigate the impact of the freedom of movement on the incentive for young people from the continent to emigrate to the other side of the English Channel so as to enjoy welfare benefits that are more favorable than those in their country of origin.

It is therefore not surprising that only a small part of the recent migration flows has occurred inside the territory of the 28 European Union member

TABLE 8.1 People born abroad and percentage of the total population of some European countries as of 1/01/2018

Country	Total population (x 1,000)	People born abroad (x 1,000)	% of people born abroad of the total population	% of people born in another one of the 27 EU countries	% of people born in a non-EU country
Austria	8,608	1,385	15.7	7.9	7.8
Belgium	11,264	1,366	12.0	7.9	4.1
Czech Rep.	10,521	515	4.9	2.1	2.8
Denmark	5,673	506	8.8	3.7	5.1
France	64,337	4,687	7.0	2.3	4.7
Germany	81,173	9,679	11.7	5.1	6.6
Greece	10,769	816	7.6	2.0	5.6
Italy	61,009	5,144	8.5	2.6	5.9
Netherlands	16,933	991	5.8	3.1	2.7
Poland*	38,494	239	0.6	0.1	0.5
Portugal	10,311	422	1.1	1.4	2.8
United Kingdom	64,915	6,286	9.5	5.8	3.7
Spain	46,335	4,563	9.8	4.2	5.6
Sweden	9,795	886	8.8	3.2	5.6
Switzerland	7,701	2,124	25.0	16.5	8.5
Norway	4,799	568	10.7	6.7	4.0

* temporary estimate
SOURCE: EUROSTAT (CENSUS HUB HC28)

countries (see Table 8.1) and that eastern countries (Romania, Bulgaria, and Poland) have outnumbered the western countries, except for relocations among neighboring countries, such as between Sweden and Finland, Austria and Germany, France and Spain, or Great Britain and Ireland.

Aside from migrations from East European countries, which in any event tend to decrease over the years (the invasion of "Polish plumbers" which xenophobic movements had feared never happened and, if anything, tends to diminish), there are also temporary migrations of people living near borders, of managers of multinational corporations and international organizations, and of students. In any case, the internal European migrations in the decades between the 20th and 21st centuries were relatively modest compared to those within a more extended area (although we cannot exclude the possibility that the data submitted to the registration offices of the respective municipalities were false, since, thanks to the freedom of movement, many migrants – especially if they only stay temporarily – do not change their residence in their country of origin). In other words, compared to the internal migrations, the number of those from outside of the EU is much larger, and the groups involved vary greatly from country to country.

If we look at where the people who reside in a country came from even though they were born in a different country, we quickly see that the direction of the migration flows is influenced by many different factors: the history of relations between country of origin and country of destination, the times when the various relocations took place, the immigration and residence permit policies, the permeability of borders, the labor market conditions, access to communication lines, and others. Let us take the example of three countries – the United Kingdom, Italy, and Spain – and look at where the largest immigration flows came from (Koser, 2009).

In the United Kingdom, people from the former colonial empire have more recently been joined by a large number of "Continental Europeans" who were attracted by a dynamic labor market, the importance of the financial centers of the City of London, or Britain's superior educational institutions. The presence of a large immigrant population from other states of the Union in the United Kingdom posed one of the major problems following the June 2016 referendum on the Brexit. In Spain factors that play an important role are certainly the language, which encourages the influx from Latin American countries, and the geographic vicinity to Morocco, but also the climate that attracts a considerable number of elderly Brits and Germans. Like Spain, Italy is preferred by people from Romania (mostly men) because of its linguistic affinity. Mostly men arrive from Albania and Morocco also due to the country's geographic vicinity, while mainly women arrive from the Philippines, Ukraine, and Moldova to care of the elderly. The reported data only concern regular immigrants, but we may presume that the places of origin of more recent arrivals – frequently irregular, without residence permits, and often also without documents – are in part different from those of immigrants who preceded them. The migration routes in fact follow routes of established "chain migration", where people who immigrated some time ago facilitate the arrival and reception of the newly arrived, of parents or friends who often come from the same village, but sometimes also new groups show up for the first time after following various migration routes.

TABLE 8.2 Origin of the population born outside of the United Kingdom, Spain, and Italy

United Kingdom (2015)		Spain (2014)		Italy (2019)	
Country of origin	No. in '000	Country of origin	No. in '000	Country of origin	No. in '000
India	776	Romania	730	Romania	968
Poland	703	Morocco	714	Albania	483
Pakistan	540	UK	311	Morocco	452
Ireland	503	Ecuador	213	China	210
Germany	322	Italy	182	Ukraine	201
Bangladesh	230	Colombia	172	Philippines	134
South Africa	216	China	165	Moldova	131
Nigeria	216	Germany	150	India	121
USA	212	Bulgaria	140	Poland	109
China	182	Bolivia	126	Tunisia	106
Jamaica	172	Portugal	110	Peru	99
Italy	152	France	100	Ecuador	92
Kenya	151	Peru	84	Egypt	90
France	150	Ukraine	82	Macedonia	89
Philippines	140	Argentina	81	Bangladesh	82

SOURCE: EUROSTAT (CENSUS HUB HC28)

4 The Reasons and Causes of Migration

The migration processes are set in motion by a complex network of push factors in the societies which the migrants leave and pull factors in the societies in which they arrive. Only some of those who are exposed to these push and pull factors – whether individuals, families, or entire social groups – decide to emigrate. Furthermore, the degree of willingness to emigrate depends on the type of migration. In any event, migrations are always selective: those who leave are in some ways different from those who stay, they tend to be younger, stronger, and more inclined to take risks. In many cases economic reasons/motives prevail, in others non-economic, political, religious, or moral reasons, and in still others it is quite difficult to distinguish between the different motives. In the case of unaccompanied minors who emigrate it is nearly impossible to decide if the decision was voluntary or forced. Moreover, often those who leave do not have an exact idea of which country they will end up in, the circumstances of the journey can be adventurous, the obstacles that must be overcome unpredictable, and the destination depends on the policies of the countries they pass through, plus the organization of the traffickers in charge of the route.

Often, however, it is economic reasons that start migration movements. Those who emigrate flee misery and aspire to better living conditions. If they find work that permits them to earn more than they need to survive, they can save money in the hope of returning to their motherland or send their savings home, or they will try to have the rest of their family join them later on. In certain cases the sums which emigrants send home constitute a not inconsiderable part of a country's earnings. According to data from the World Bank, India, China, the Philippines, Mexico, Pakistan, and Nigeria top the list of countries to which the largest amount of money is sent. It is estimated that in India, for example, it adds up to 4% of the GDP.

Often migrations hide behind a temporary plan which eventually becomes permanent. As already indicated, in the 1960s Germany, for instance, asked for about 14 million *gastarbeiter* from Italy, Spain, Greece, the countries of the former Yugoslavia, and Turkey, with the intention of sending them back to where they came from once they were no longer needed. Many – about 11 million – did in fact return, but three million of them stayed, got married, and had children whom they sent to German schools and who gradually became integrated in the new society while still remaining connected to their country of origin. Contrary to the migrations of the 19th and first half of the 20th century, the lower transportation costs and surge in communication which digital technologies have made possible, current migrations no longer mean definitive breaks with people's native culture. As a result, some people belong to two cultures, the one from which they came and the one of the country in which they have found their new home. In this sense the migrants become agents of change in two directions. They bring not only economic resources to their society of origin but also knowledge and a new mentality and attitudes which change the local culture. As for those who carry the innovations into their society of origin, the emigrants can often encounter resistance and even fierce opposition on the part of the traditional local culture, which may make their return problematical. Yet the effects can also be observed in the societies which have received them; just think of the way in which the presence of immigrants has changed many dietary habits of the population of European cities (Sciortino, 2016; Münkler, 2017).

However, its is not only economic reasons that set off migration processes. Aside from family reunifications due to the fact that the first to leave are typically young men and sometimes young women, many migrants are refugees who flee or are expelled from their country of origin for ethnic, religious, or political reasons. During the past few years, many people have fled the former Yugoslavia (Bosnia, Kosovo, Macedonia), Iran, Iraq, Afghanistan and, more recently, Syria and Libya, some of whom sought asylum in the European countries that were willing to receive them. In the case of Syria, the majority of refugees stopped in the neighboring countries Jordan, Lebanon, and Turkey. A large part of African migrants do not leave the continent, only some knock on the entrance gates of Europe, so to speak.

5 The Migration Emergency of 2015 and Subsequent Years

In the summer and fall of 2015 Europe witnessed a veritable onslaught of asylum seekers. Even though an enormous flow of people was predictable and was, in fact, predicted, especially as a result of the war in Syria and the collapse of Libya, its extent took the affected countries by surprise. The number of arrivals in the years from 2013 to 2016 left no doubt that this was not an isolated phenomenon and that, even though it was to vary considerably over time, it was not bound to disappear. In the face of the emergency situation, the countries reacted according to their own immediate concerns. In fact, the rules which the EU imposed in the Schengen Agreement and the Dublin Regulation suddenly turned out to be inadequate.

Often political reasons combine with economical reasons, for example in the case of those who arrive in Europe after fleeing dramatic situations, countries on the southern shore of the Mediterranean, but also from sub-Saharan Africa. Tragedies of boats sunk in the Strait of Sicily in an attempt to reach the Italian coast have abounded in the first two decades of the 21st century. According to UNHCR (the Office of the United Nations High Commissioner for Refugees) about 30,000 migrants have died in the past 15 years in attempts to reach the European shore and more than 1000 in 2019.

Even though it is difficult, and often nearly impossible, to draw a line between economic and political migration, it is a relevant distinction, because it is the basis of immigration policies. Over the years, the majority of countries have in fact adhered to the Convention Relating to the Status of Refugees (often referred to as the "Geneva Convention"), which stipulates that any person with a well-founded fear of being persecuted for reasons of race, religion, nationality, membership of a particular social group or political opinion by the state of which he or she is a citizen may request being recognized as a refugee and therefore demand political asylum. Aside from the Geneva Convention,

TABLE 8.3 Annual percentage of asylum seekers in some European countries

	2003/2013	2013/2015
Austria	−22%	389%
Belgium	−26%	212%
Denmark	65%	175%
France	1%	17%
Germany	117%	303%
Greece	0%	38%
Italy	91%	224%
Netherlands	7%	199%
Spain	−24%	224%
Sweden	73%	188%

SOURCE: UNHCR https://www.unhcr.org/statistics/unhcrstats/5do8d7ee7/unhcr-global-trends-2018.html

there are also other standards, both national and international, which grant protection to citizens of certain countries whose citizens are not granted basic rights or for humanitarian reasons, because they are not guaranteed living conditions that assure human dignity.

For example, the Constitution of the Italian Republic (art. 10, sentence 3) states that:

> A foreigner who, in his home country, is denied the actual exercise of the democratic freedoms guaranteed by the Italian constitution shall be entitled to the right of asylum in the territory of the Republic.

The affirmation of these principles, especially when we take into account the time in which they were formulated (right after World War II) doubtless signaled an epochal turning point in the area of global ethics as well as international law. Yet as we can easily imagine, problems arose the moment they were applied. Recognition of a person's refugee status implies on the one hand the assessment of effective economic, legal, and political conditions in the refugee's country of origin and, on the other, the assessment of biographical events in the life of the person concerned that would actually put him or her at risk upon returning to his or her country of origin. Both assessments take time and, above all, require a bureaucracy with a staff that possesses the adequate professional – not only legal, but also political, social, and possibly also psychological – skills. It is anything but easy, for instance, to reconstruct a person's political, educational, and legal background prior to his or her arrival, to determine what he has studied and what skills he possesses when, as is often the case, he has no documents, does not supply his personal details, and does not wish to stay in the country in which he has arrived because his destination is Germany, Sweden, or another Northern European country, where he already has friends or relatives. This does not even include the communication problems when there is no lingua franca or no interpreters and intermediaries are available who can serve as go-betweens during sensitive phases upon the person's arrival.

We often hear complaints about the excessive length of time the admissions process of asylum seekers takes. The medium duration varies from country to country, but often it can last up to several years (in Italy it ranges from about 15 months to two years). As a result, during that time the asylum seekers live in a

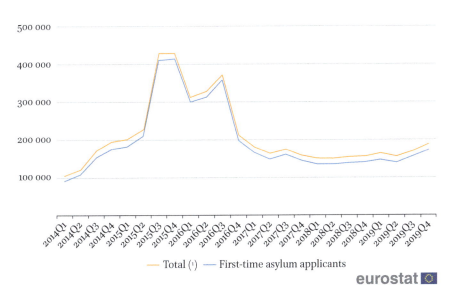

FIGURE 8.1 Asylum applications (non-EU) in the EU-27 Member States, 2008–2019
        [1] 2008–2014: Croatia not available.
        [2] 2008: Bulgaria, Greece, Spain, France, Croatia, Lithuania, Luxembourg, Hungary, Austria, Romania, Slovakia and Finland not available. 2009: Bulgaria, Greece, Spain, Croatia, Luxembourg, Hungary, Austria, Romania, Slovakia and Finland not available. 2010: Bulgaria, Greece, Croatia, Luxembourg, Hungary, Austria, Romania and Finland not available. 2011: Croatia, Hungary, Austria and Finland not available. 2012: Croatia, Hungary and Austria not available. 2013: Austria not available.
        SOURCE: EUROSTAT (ONLINE DATA CODE: 'MIGR_ASYAPPCTZA') https://ec.europa.eu/eurostat/statisticsexplained/index.php/Asylum_statistics

situation of great uncertainty about their own future, their dream behind the migration project is put on hold, they live in temporary quarters, rely on financial aid, or take on temporary part-time jobs, or beg for alms on the sidewalks. Or, in a worst-case scenario, they can turn to petty or major crime, pimping, and prostitution. In a best-case scenario, this time is used to learn the language of the receiving country to ascertain the educational level they have attained, and show and deepen their professional skills with a view toward future employment. Success or failure in the medium to long term of the integration processes in the host country largely depends on how the long months between the request for asylum and the decision of whether it is granted or denied are used. In Italy, for instance, there are currently discussions about the possibility to substantially reduce the processing time of asylum applications.

It is not surprising that the phases of the initial reception and subsequent integration differ greatly from country to country. The measures with which the EU has tried to confront the phenomenon in a generally homogenous and coordinated manner have turned out to have come too late and/or to be at least partially ineffective, with the upshot that the different countries have acted individually, looking after their own, short-term interests. This is illustrated by the so-called "Dublin Regulation" (repeatedly amended and supplemented until 2013) which establishes the criteria and mechanisms on whose basis the responsibility for examining applications for asylum lies with the member state in which the asylum seeker has first entered the EU, thus putting the main burden of the asylum procedures on the southern countries (Greece, Italy, and Spain). It is true that many immigrants arrive with temporary visas or residence permits (often as tourists) and once these expire automatically continue to stay illegally unless they submit an asylum request. Arrivals after 2014, however, for the most part came via the Balkan route (from Turkey to Greece) and the route across the Strait of Sicily.

The protection of the family unit and unaccompanied minors is the principal reason for exceptions to this rule. In practice, however, the responsibility for the vast majority of asylum requests falls on a limited number of member states, making this system untenable in the long run if the current migration trends continue, as is likely. Some of the arrivals elude – sometimes with the connivance of the authorities – the controls of the country which would have to process the registration, take the finger prints, provide the material necessities of life, lodging, and the preliminary examination of requests for asylum. It has happened that sooner or later they were detained and returned to the country where they had presumably disembarked.

Today about 5.2 million people have obtained a status as political refugees in one of the countries of the European Union, a number to which we must

TABLE 8.4 Countries of origin of asylum seekers in 2016

	Asylum seekers	Compared to 2015
Syria	339,265	−6%
Afghanistan	186,595	+7%
Iraq	130,015	+7%
Pakistan	49,840	+4%
Nigeria	47,710	+55%
Iran	41,340	+58%
Eritrea	34,480	+1%
Albania	32,335	−52%
Russia	27,605	+18%
Somalia	20,050	−1%

SOURCE: EUROSTAT (ONLINE DATA CODE: 'MIGR_ASYAPPCTZA'), https://appsso.eurostat.ec.europa.eu/nui/show.do?dataset=migr_asyappctza&lang=en

add those who have gone to Switzerland and Norway. At a global level, the High Commissioner of the United Nations for Refugees estimates the number of refugees for political reasons to be about 21.3 million.

In 2016 the EU member states received 1,249,955 asylum applications, a figure that far exceeds that for the years prior to 2015. Of those seeking temporary protection while waiting for an examination of their application in EU territory in 2016, more than one-quarter are of Syrian nationality. The second-most nationality among many refugees who have requested political asylum is that of Afghanistan: they were mainly received in Germany, Austria, Sweden, Italy, and Belgium. In 2016, 70% who applied for asylum in EU territory are concentrated in five of the 28 EU member states, most of them in Germany, Italy, France, Greece, and Austria. In proportion to the size of the population, Germany remains the country that received the largest number of applications, followed by Austria, Greece, Hungary, and Sweden (without considering Malta, Luxembourg, and Cyprus, whose populations are obviously smaller).

Despite the attempt to create as uniform examination procedures for asylum applications as possible, the acceptance rate varies considerably from country to country. The most recent data for 2017 indicate that Austria approved 55% of requests, almost the same the UK, Germany 40%, Italy and France less than 30%.

The policies adopted by the individual countries are not the only variable that influences the integration processes. Equally important are ways in which

TABLE 8.5 First time asylum applicants in EU countries 2016–2019

	2016	2017	2018	2019
EU	1.260.920	712.250	647.170	721.090
Belgium	18.280	18.340	22.530	27.460
Bulgaria	19.420	3.695	3.535	2.150
Czech Republic	1.475	1.145	1.690	1.915
Denmark	6.180	3.220	3.570	2.700
Germany	745.160	222.565	184.180	165.615
Ireland	2.245	2.930	3.670	4.780
Greece	51.110	58.650	66.965	77.275
Spain	15.755	36.610	54.050	117.800
France	84.270	99.330	120.425	128.950
Italy	122.960	128.850	59.950	43.770
Hungary	29.430	3.390	670	500
Netherlands	19.285	16.090	24.025	25.200
Malta	1.930	1.840	2.130	4.085
Austria	39.875	18.216	24.025	12.490
Poland	9.780	5.045	4.110	4.070
Sweden	22.330	26.330	21.560	26.255
UK	39.735	34.780	38.840	44.835

SOURCE: EUROSTAT, ASYLUM STATISTICS, 2020 https://ec.europa.eu/eurostat/statistics-explained/index.php/Asylum_statistics

the refugees decide to emigrate and start their journey as well as the particulars of the first phases of their incorporation in the country where they decide to stay. Crucial in this context are the migration chains of relatives and friends on the part of those who arrived first, are already settled, and who constitute a social network on which people can rely when dealing with the difficulties to be encountered in the initial phase of a process that is usually of an extended duration. The initial difficulties concern the chances of finding temporary accommodation, then a place to live and a job that provides enough to get by. Frequently, therefore, the migrants want to join family networks and/or people who are from the same village or region and who speak the same language. Very often, however, the events of the journey and the obstacles they have encountered in their passage through different countries keep them from reaching their goal and the migrants are unable to rely on financial community networks.

The actions of volunteer organizations and plain citizens of the host society are crucial and indispensible especially during the initial phases of a refugee's reception. They always, or very often, provide the most immediate necessities, such as food, lodging and clothing where the public organizations prove insufficient.

6   Models and Ways of Integration

Up until the 1990s, the influx of immigrants was for the most part looked at favorably by the advanced countries of Western Europe. The various states adopted different policies that tended to favor some form of integration. France aimed at assimilating the immigrants, i.e., at making them French citizens in all respects, expecting them to be proud of belonging to the French nation and wanting to make her national culture their own. Research conducted by Beauchemin, Hamel and Simon(2016), however, revealed that part of the North African immigrants, especially males, of the second generation (who were therefore born in France) had gone through painful schooling, suffered particularly long and frequent periods of unemployment, and felt like victims of forms of discrimination. This was the part of the population that fed the revolts in the Paris *banlieue* at the beginning of the new century and from which terrorist groups recruited some of their own followers.

In the United Kingdom, integration was seen as the formation of a collective multi-culture where every ethnic group may preserve its own original culture in addition to belonging to the collective of Her Majesty's subjects. The British model brings to mind the ethnic ghettos in the large American cities, but with one difference: in America the spatial segregation of the first generations of immigrants is usually a temporary aspect in a process of integration and sometimes social mobility, whereas in Greater London there is the danger that it may mean the relatively long-term social exclusion of entire ethnic groups, and it is no coincidence that in the case of Britain, too, the peripheries of cities have proven to be fertile ground for the recruitment of terrorist fringes.

In Belgium and Holland the situation is different for long-standing immigrants from the former colonial territories on the one hand and recent immigrants on the other. The multicultural model applies to the former, whereas the tendency for the new immigrants goes toward ways that speed up and mandate an at least partial assimilation to the native culture.

In Germany, on the other hand, integration was avoided in the initial phase as it was expected that immigration would be temporary, in continuous flows of people entering and exiting the country. Currently different forms of integration or semi-integration are being tried out in an attempt to avoid creating any forms of permanent spatial segregation. All three models – the British, French, and German alternative – and the Belgian and Dutch variants have at least partly failed to achieve their set goals. This is evidenced by the series of terrorist attacks (in Paris, London, Brussels, Berlin, and Nice) which often were carried out by second-generation immigrants who were born in the country in which they obviously did not succeed in becoming sufficiently integrated.

Italy and Spain have adopted emergency measures without developing medium- to long-term integration policies so far. Spain has practically blocked entry to its territory of people coming mainly from the outposts of Ceuta and Melilla on the African continent, in line with restrictive measures of the government of neighboring Morocco. Italy initially facilitated the transit its territory of those who disembarked on the Sicilian coast heading for Northern Europe. Gradually, after it had helped rescue tens of thousands of migrants at sea, it adopted a policy of distribution of arrivals waiting for a determination of their refugee status among small and large municipalities on its national territory. Many municipalities subscribed to a program which allowed the presence of two to three refugees per 1,000 inhabitants. The Italian government that took office after the elections in March 2018 and lasted until September 2019 adopted a very restrictive policy toward immigration, closing any landing opportunity even in cases of people rescued during the crossing of the see.

Establishing migration policies is a right which the different countries carefully protect. As we shall see shortly, forming a joint policy or at least coordinating the national policies meets with fierce resistance on the part of the governments (Basso & Perocco, 2000).

7 Stages and Obstacles in the Admissions/Integration Process

A basic prerequisite for initiating a process of integration in the host society is obviously a modicum of language skills. The success of the integration of Albanian and Tunisian immigrants in Italy is owed to a large extent to the fact that they had partly learned Italian through TV broadcasts which were available in their country prior to their departure. In Germany, learning German is considered likewise an obligation which the immigrants cannot avoid; language courses start a few days after arrival at the temporary lodgings that have been prepared for them.

The second prerequisite is the availability of lodgings. Recognizing the problems which segregated living of large groups of immigrants entails, the European countries currently tend to favor situations where the immigrants are more uniformly distributed across areas so they can on the one hand form a rapport with the local population and on the other maintain active networks of mutual support with relatives and friends, which are indispensable for mastering day-to-day life and for mental health.

The third prerequisite is obviously for the migrant to search for a job to earn a living for himself and any family members in his care that were often left behind in their country of origin. Obviously, the local labor market conditions on the one hand and the qualifications of the job seekers on the other are decisive variables. Countries such as Germany, with generally low unemployment rates, theoretically offer greater job opportunities than countries such as Greece, where there are few jobs even for the native population. It is well known, however, that the immigrant population is willing to perform kinds of work and at terms that are not really in competition with most available local job offers. This explains an apparently contradictory fact, which is that the employment rate is higher for non-EU immigrants in countries like Italy, Spain, and Greece but not in Germany, Austria, Belgium, or the United Kingdom. The existence of a large informal economic sector, of an agriculture that requires a workforce with few qualifications, and of small and tiny service businesses where little technology is involved, provides job opportunities that sometimes resemble slavery.

An extremely important channel for the assimilation/integration of the families of immigrants with school-age children is obviously the school. All countries have shown great disparity in education, both among different groups of immigrants and with respect to local students. The role of the school as a channel of integration cannot be denied, especially in early childhood, but it can also become a factor of exclusion and social discrimination. In some situations, for example, we can make out the tendency of native parents to keep their own daughters and sons away from schools with a growing proportion of children of immigrants.

Finally, a particularly pressing issue concerns the possibility or difficulty of obtaining citizenship rights on the part of the immigrants. The Maastricht Treaty recognizes European citizenship which grants some rights, but it is additional to and does not replace the citizenship of individual nations in the sense that it is automatically acquired but subordinate to the national citizenship. One cannot be a European citizen without also being a citizen of a member state of the European Union. The principles behind national legislation regarding citizenship are on the one hand *jus sanguinis*, which confers citizenship as a kind of hereditary right to the offspring of parents who already possess it, and on the other *jus soli* (or *jus loci*), which grants citizenship to those who are born in the country's territory. National legislations do in fact change the two principles in different degrees and ways which are sometimes closer to one and sometimes to the other. A typical application of the *jus soli* is the French law that recognizes the citizenship of all those who were born in the Republic (including its overseas territories), whereas Italian and German law (prior to 2000) are examples of the *jus sanguinis*. In Italy, people who were born there to parents of a different nationality may apply for citizenship if they have lived in the country for at least three years, whereas those who were born abroad must legally reside there for ten years before they can apply for citizenship. Yet citizenship is not granted automatically once these requirements are met and may be denied by the authorities. In Germany, the principle of *jus sanguinis* was recently curtailed, granting citizenship to those born in Germany to foreign parents who have resided in Germany for at least eight years. The admittance to the EU of the eastern countries that used to be part of the Soviet Bloc resulted in a partial and gradual expansion of the rights of European citizenship. Specifically, it was required that ten years must have passed to obtain the right to free movement.

We should also keep in mind the – often temporary – migration phenomena associated with diplomatic activities, international organizations, and multinational corporations. This concerns a cosmopolitan group of managers for whom geographic mobility comes with their job. We need not point out that the problems which this thin, albeit heterogeneous, class of people encounters when moving to a different location on earth have nothing to do with those of the migrants who flee hunger, war, or oppression. Nor do they have anything to do with the nomadic populations, such as the Roma and Sinti, whose migrations are clearly a different story altogether.

Of a basically temporary nature – although sometimes the cause of permanent relocation – are the migrations of students which are made possible by exchanges promoted by the European Union via its Erasmus program. Between its inception in 1987 and 2014, more than 3.5 million young Europeans benefited from this opportunity, and over 3,000 institutions of higher learning were involved (see also Chapter 6 on universities).

8   Xenophobic Movements and Welcoming Culture

Within the two decades between the 20th and 21st centuries, the slowdown of economic growth, the spread of collective fears and of hostile attitudes of native populations, the tensions generated by social movements rising from the heart of the groups of first- or second-generation immigrants have prompted the European governments to introduce restrictive measures in an attempt to reduce and select the immigration flows. In some strata of society the fear is spreading that the greater fertility rate of the immigrant groups will eventually lead to much faster demographic growth than among the native population, with the result that the national cultures are crushed. Even though these and other fears are often unfounded, as we know, for instance, that the natality rates among immigrants tend to adjust to the natality rates of the native populations within a few (two or three) generations, the emergence of xenophobic tendencies, especially during periods of economic and social crisis, can be observed in nearly all countries where the presence of immigrants reaches a certain level.

Opinion poll figures indicate that the influx of immigrants leads to considerable concerns in almost all EU states. Yet in the northern countries and in Germany, at least half of the population believes that they can enrich the respective society, while the majority of the Greeks, Eastern Europeans, and British believe the opposite. Terrorist acts and alarming news of the arrival of new waves of migrants have the effect of reinforcing the hostile attitude and conduct towards immigrants. It is interesting to note that the anti-immigrant attitudes are stronger in rural areas and in small towns, where the presence of immigrants is small, than in the large metropolitan centers, that is to say, they are more pronounced among the less educated and those who have few dealings in the international field. In any event, xenophobic sentiments are rather widespread and feed political movements which have taken up the battle against immigration as their cause and have chalked up significant successes in various national elections. These movements often cite religious motivations and frequently have anti-Islamic positions. That history offers not only examples of conflicts but also of populations with a Christian, Islamic, and Jewish tradition living together peacefully does not seem to mitigate the wave of anti-Islamic xenophobia which deeply pervades layers of public opinion in Europe and is closely linked to the growth of national-populist movements (see also the chapter on nationalism).

However, the picture we get from the xenophobic movements which oppose the acceptance of immigrants must not obscure the fact that their arrival has also given rise to a strong and widespread reaction of empathy and solidarity. In nearly all countries we have been able to witness a remarkable mobilization of volunteer organizations, but also of plain citizens organizing aid, arranging for lodgings, providing funds and goods to meet the primary and secondary needs of a population joined together in an unfamiliar place, deprived of resources and points of reference. Aside from a hostile Europe, there is also a sympathetic one (Ruemelin, 2017).

The immigrants are an indelible part of many European states. It is likely that the trend of the phenomena of desertification on the one hand and the economic cycles on the other will produce decelerating or accelerating phases of new arrivals, but it is highly unlikely that the flow is going to stop, at least as long as the great inequality in the distribution of wealth between rich and poor countries persists. Whether or not Europe wants to, it is going to be a multicultural, multi-religious, and multinational society. The European motto of "unity in diversity" would have to accompany as a matter of principle the formation of a society which recognizes and values the plurality of elements that belong to it. After all, just a few decades ago, in the last century, Europeans fought each other with unprecedented hatred and violence, but since 1945 they have shown that they can overcome the barriers which had been built in the course of the centuries. Why should they not be able to welcome in their midst and integrate new populations who bring new kinds of diversity? The new immigrants certainly fill the gap left by the decline of the European population and, in most cases, are willing to do the jobs the members of the native population no longer want to do. Nonetheless, it cannot be denied that the integration processes meet with strong resistance. Europe has no longer territories that can be colonized, the European continent is already densely populated and moreover recently underwent a long period of decelerated growth, if not in fact economic stagnation. Europe is faced with a dilemma: either to close itself off in a strong effort to defend its wealth and its own privileges or to open up toward that part of the world that also sees in Europe an opportunity of growth and emancipation.

9 Necessity of and Obstacles to a European Migration Policy

The protection of borders is doubtless one of the fundamental prerogatives of the Westphalian nation-state. With the Schengen Agreement (originally signed in 1985 by the Benelux countries, France and Germany, and in subsequent years extended to almost all countries of the European Union, with the exception of the United Kingdom and Ireland, plus – as already mentioned – Switzerland and Norway) the signatory states abolished national border checks of their citizens. Controls remain at the external borders, but after entering the Schengen area complete freedom of movement is in effect. The external borders continue to be controlled by the member states which have land borders with countries that are not part of the agreement as well as all countries with ports and airports that are open to international traffic. The agreement worked very well until the crisis caused by the migration emergency, which prompted a number of countries to suspend it for more extended or brief periods. The EU lacks the competence as well as technical, human, and economic resources to oversee its external borders and therefore cannot but leave this function to those member states that are the first to be confronted with the migration emergency. The only instrument the EU has been able to use is the Frontex agency, which can only provide technical assistance to the European countries suffering from the greatest migration pressure, such as sea rescue of boats in the Mediterranean. On the other hand the countries tend to pursue short-term national interests, especially in difficult situations, thus eroding the trust of their partners in a game in which ultimately there are only losers.

Confronted with the huge flood of refugees fleeing the war in Syria in the summer and fall of 2015, for instance, Germany declared that its own borders were open, without taking into consideration that in order to arrive in Germany, the refugees would have to pass through Greece, Macedonia, Serbia, Hungary, and Austria, countries which therefore would not only have to help with the transit but also receive those who might have wanted to stay in one of these countries. The inability and inefficiency of the EU concerning the political migrants was clearly revealed in the proposals to redistribute 120,000 refugees among the different member states according to their demographic weight and domestic income: not only were no more than a few thousand refugees relocated after several months, but a coalition of countries formed which refused to accept them, specifically the countries of the Visegrád Agreement, i.e., Poland, Hungary, the Czech Republic, and Slovakia. Even though the European Court of Justice condemned these countries, no effective means are available to force them to accept their due quota.

On the other hand, if the Union is unable to efficiently control its external borders, it is understandable if the individual member states try to control their own borders, even the ones with their neighboring partners. No country can allow people to live on its territory who have no legal residence permit, if only a temporary one. Illegal immigrants are incompatible with the idea of the state: either they become somehow legalized or they must be expelled. But who can do that if the Union is not yet a state and the states are no longer able to handle this phenomenon?

Let us postulate the hypothesis that, given the ageing of the population, the drop in the natality rate and the average living standard, the European Union, under a kind of development aid program, decides to accept one million refugees a year without too much resistance, or, alternatively, to give the amount of money it would cost to accept them to the countries from which the largest migration flows come, or to adopt some combination of the two strategies. The current institutional structure of the Union does not allow either of these two alternatives to be considered: the Commission might be able to propose this in a courageous step forward, but it is out of the question that a unanimous resolution could be achieved in the Council, and the European Parliament could at best make a recommendation.

If the members of the EU want to protect their power over the control of their borders and their immigrant acceptance policies (even if they ask for European aid when problems in dealing with the emergency occur), they are even more protective about the way they handle relations with third countries of origin or the transit of migration flows. The EU High Representative for Foreign Affairs and Security Policy is also the Vice-President of the Commission, but negotiations with Turkey, whose goal was to persuade it to keep the almost three million Syrian refugees staying on Turkish soil in 2015 and in this way to ease the pressure on the Balkan route, were conducted by the German Chancellor, and only later were the agreements ratified by Brussels. Regarding the countries of North Africa and especially Libya, too, from where the boats toward Lampedusa leave, the political initiative is not in the hands of the High Representative but rather those of the more influential national governments – almost invariably those of Germany and France, even though the Strait of Sicily is controlled by Italian ships.

The opinion that the migrations constitute a European issue – or rather, challenge – is widespread, but the EU has unfortunately played only a marginal role in dealing with this challenge as yet.

CHAPTER 9

The Dimensions of Inequality

1   Rich and Poor People in Rich and Poor Countries

When speaking about inequality, one immediately thinks of economic inequality. There is no doubt that the distribution of income and wealth is the primary source of inequality, and almost all other dimensions are connected with and partly dependent upon these economic inequalities. The common-sense notion of inequality refers to the simple fact that that there are wealthy and poor people, higher- and lower-paying jobs, and higher and lower consumption of goods and services. The experience of inequality in ubiquitous; perfect equality does not exist in human societies, as is blatantly obvious to anyone. We may wish to live in a world where inequalities are reduced or even absent, or alternatively we may not care about inequality, enjoying the benefits of being on the side of rich people.

In any case, if we want to live where inequalities are less pronounced there is no doubt that we should choose Europe. As Figure 9.1 shows, in Europe, the richest 10 per cent of the population receives 'only' 37 per cent of the gross domestic product (GDP), whereas in the United States (USA) and Canada the share of the top 10 per cent amounts to 47 per cent, in Brazil 55 per cent and in the Middle Eastern countries even 60 per cent.

Income inequality has increased all over the world in the last fifty years and the figures of the Oxfam Report (https://www.oxfam.org) for 2018 show that this trend is continuing. Europe is no exception, but the increase has been less dramatic than in other parts of the world, such as Russia, China, India, and also the USA. This outcome may reflect the different phases of economic growth that different countries have reached as well as the different economic and social policies that have been designed to protect the disadvantaged and fight against poverty. In the USA, the share of the national income of the top 1 per cent of the population rose from 10.5 per cent in 1980 to 21 per cent in 2015, and in Europe, it rose from 10 per cent to 12 per cent during the same period. The rise of inequality in China is astonishing, where the top 1 per cent of the population has profited most from development induced by the opening of the markets: its share in national income has doubled in 30 years, increasing from 6 per cent to 12 per cent.

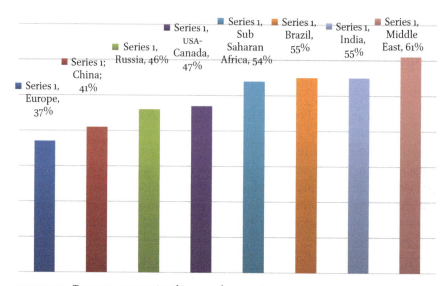

FIGURE 9.1   Top 10 per cent national income share, 2016
SOURCE: WORLD INEQUALITY REPORT, 2018

Comparing such vast territories hides the enormous differences within each of these areas. Even if Europe is only the rather small, western tip of the Eurasian continent, it is, as everybody knows, far from being economically homogeneous. In fact, there are very large differences both in income and in wealth among the European states, as Table 9.1 shows. As we shall see, Europe is divided across two main lines: a North–South and a West–East divide. Countries with a higher GDP per capita are almost all located in the north-western part; countries with lower income belong either to the South or to the East or to both at the same time. These cleavages are the product of centuries-old processes of economic development and of state policies intended to spur growth and/or reduce its social consequences.

The ranking does not change very much according to the income indicators used. However, if we want to tackle the economic inequality experienced by the people instead of looking at the per capita GNP, it is preferable to use the per capita household disposable income; that is, the money that people have to spend after taxes are paid and monetary benefits because of poverty or unemployment have been received. Whatever the measure of per capita income we use, it does not tell us how it is distributed. One crude but efficient measure of inequality is the Gini coefficient (Corrado Gini was an Italian statistician who first proposed its use). The Gini coefficient runs from 1 (total inequality when one single unit – person or family – receives the total amount of income or wealth and all others nothing) to 0 (complete equality, when everybody receives the same amount). Of course, there are no historical societies at either extreme

TABLE 9.1 European states by GDP (PPP) per capita

1.	Luxembourg	110,870
2.	Ireland	79,925
	Norway*	74,065
	Switzerland*	63,380
3.	Netherlands	56,435
4.	Sweden	53,77
5.	Germany	52,801
6.	Austria	51,936
7.	Denmark	51,643
8.	Belgium	48,258
9.	Finland	46,342
10.	UK	45,565
11.	France	45,473
12.	Malta	44,586
13	Spain	40,289
14.	Italy	39,499
15.	Cyprus	38,980
16.	Czech Republic	37,546
17.	Slovenia	36,566
18.	Slovakia	35,094
19.	Lithuania	34,596
20.	Estonia	33,842
21.	Portugal	31,964
22.	Poland	31,430
23.	Hungary	31,369
24.	Latvia	29,489
25.	Greece	29,057
	Russia*	28,957
26.	Croatia	26,215
27.	Romania	26,175
28.	Bulgaria	23,154

* Not EU countries
SOURCE: DATA IMF, OCTOBER 2018

of the continuum. There is, however, a sufficient range of variation to allow us to compare countries according to their degree of equality or inequality. Looking at the data in Table 9.2, one notes immediately that there is an almost negative relation between income and equality: with only a few exceptions, countries

TABLE 9.2   Gini coefficient of equivalized disposable income (2017) × 100

	Country	Value
	*Turkey**	42.8
1.	Bulgaria	40.2
2.	Lithuania	37.6
3.	Latvia	34.4
4.	Spain	34.1
5.	UK	33.9
6.	Portugal	33.5
7.	Greece	33.4
8.	Romania	33.1
9.	Italy	32.7
10.	Estonia	31.6
11.	Luxembourg	30.9
12.	Cyprus	30.8
13.	Ireland	30.6
	EU 28	**30.1**
14.	Croatia	29.9
	*Switzerland**	29.4
15.	France	29.3
16.	Poland	29.2
17.	Germany (1990)	29.1
18.	Malta	28.3
19.	Hungary	28.1
20.	Sweden	28.0
21.	Austria	27.9
22.	Netherland	27.1
23.	Denmark	27.6
24	Belgium	26.0
25.	Finland	25.3
26.	Czech Rep.	24.5
27.	Slovenia	23.7
28.	Slovakia	23.2
	*Norway**	22.5

*   Not EU countries
SOURCE: DATA IMF, OCTOBER 2018

with higher per capita income are more equal than countries with lower per capita income. The exceptions are on the one hand the United Kingdom (UK), with rather high inequality and high income, and on the other the Czech Republic, Slovenia, and Slovakia, with low income and low inequality. These exceptions can only be explained by referring to the specific historical circumstances that have characterized the policies of liberalization of the markets in these countries. It is remarkable how from the point of view of equality or inequality of income distribution a few Eastern European countries (Bulgaria, Lithuania, Latvia, and Romania) show a quite different pattern from the Czech Republic, Slovakia, and Slovenia, whereas Poland and Hungary are somewhere in between. The transition from a planned to a market economy apparently followed quite different paths.

We shall now look at the other dimension of economic inequality: wealth distribution. Income distribution and wealth distribution are not the same thing. Income is earned, whereas wealth is accumulated from one generation to the next. Wealth is the result of lifelong accumulation of earnings only in societies where the transmission of wealth from parents to sons and daughters and/or other relatives is impeded through high inheritance taxation. This is often no longer the case, since many countries in Europe as well as elsewhere in the world have reduced inheritance taxation in recent years.

Analysis of the distribution of wealth has some surprises in store: the ranking of wealth distribution is quite different from that of income distribution. To give just one example, as Table 9.3 shows, the per capita income of a German citizen is at present about 30 per cent higher than that of an Italian citizen, although Italians are slightly richer than Germans; the same holds true for Finland and Spain. We will see some of the causes of this discrepancy later on in the chapter. In general terms, Gini coefficients tell us that wealth is much more unequally distributed in societies than income.

There are some unexpected cases: wealth inequality is relatively high in Sweden and Denmark, countries that have the lowest income inequality ratings in Europe and, at the other end, Spain, which has lower wealth inequality than the average European countries. The top 1 per cent of rich Spaniards own 15 per cent of the country's wealth, but at the same time, the world's richest 1 per cent increased to 50.1 per cent its share of the globe's total wealth, according to Credit Suisse data.

2 Dualism and Territorial Inequalities

One should be aware, however, that what we are dealing with here is mostly inequalities between nation state members of the European Union (EU) and

TABLE 9.3   Wealth per capita and its distribution*

1.	Luxembourg	412,127	65.0
2.	Belgium	313,045	66.2
3.	Denmark	286,712	80.8
4.	France	280,580	73.0
5.	UK	279,048	69.7
6.	Netherlands	253,205	65.0
7.	Sweden	249,765	74.2
8.	Ireland	232,594	58.1
9.	Austria	231,368	64.6
10.	Italy	217,787	60.9
11.	Germany	214,893	66.7
12.	Spain	191,177	57.0
13.	Finland	161,062	61.5
	EU	**144,903**	-
14.	Malta	140,629	66.4
15.	Portugal	109,362	66.7
16.	Greece	108,127	65.4
17.	Cyprus	100,308	-
18.	Slovenia	79,097	62.9
19.	Czech Republic	61,489	62.6
20.	Estonia	57,806	67.5
21.	Hungary	37,594	65.1
22.	Croatia	35,951	65.4
23.	Latvia	33,958	67.0
24.	Slovakia	34,781	62.0
25.	Poland	31,794	65.7
26.	Lithuania	24,600	66.6
27.	Bulgaria	23,954	65.2
28.	Romania	20,321	65.1

* Wealth per capita (only adult Population) in US$ and Gini coefficient
SOURCE: CREDIT SUISSE, GLOBAL WEALTH REPORT, 2018

not inequalities within each of them. There are evidently large interdependencies between inequalities among and within societies. Comparing average figures for different countries, we obviously disregard by definition all regional and class inequalities within each country.

In order to develop a comparative analysis of the territorial imbalances in EU countries we can use a couple of indicators: the GDP per capita at equal purchasing power and the Human Development Index (HDI) at a regional level (for the construction of the HDI, see Hardeman & Dijkstra, 2014).

Taking the European average as a reference value equal to 100, we can calculate the width of the basic gap between the richest and the poorest region for each of the EU member states in order to identify the size of territorial imbalances.

The operation has a rather clear outcome: the countries with the greatest regional imbalances are the UK, Germany, Ireland, Italy, Spain, Portugal, and Poland. The UK appears in first place, but this is not because of the well-known separatist tendencies, especially of Scotland, but rather the large distance in terms of income between the most favoured and the least favoured region (even excluding London, the capital city, and its surrounding territory). Quest for greater autonomy is not based on economic claims. Scotland, after the London region and the south-east, is one of the richest areas of the UK. Separatism has distant historical roots that have little to do with economic imbalances. Economic factors should play a greater role in the case of Wales, which is in fact a relatively depressed area, but even there it is the historical/ethnic/cultural cleavage that is most determinant. The territorial imbalances in the UK are indeed quite marked, but the most depressed regions are not so geographically concentrated as to form a single contiguous territorial block.

The same can also be said of Portugal. In this case, the distance in terms of GDP per capita and HDI is very significant as well, but the economically backward areas lie partly in the north, partly in the central area and partly in the south, as opposed to the wealthier area that is around Lisbon. We cannot therefore speak of a territorial dualism, as there is no territorial contiguity among the backward areas. In Belgium, the gap between the Flemish and the Walloon regions is historically recent and rather contained, although quite clear. As is well known, this country presents a particular situation because its dualism is mainly due to linguistic, cultural, and religious differences. Among the other countries, true dualism only exists in Germany and Italy. Ireland is a small country of less than 5 million inhabitants that is split between a densely populated, richer, and more urbanized south-eastern region and a predominantly rural north-west. Even when it comes to Spain, we cannot speak of true dualism: there are at least two economically more backward regions, Andalusia and Estremadura, but separatist pressures come from the two richest regions, Catalonia in the south and the Basque country in the north. The reasons for the presence of centrifugal tendencies are embedded in the administrative political history of the Kingdom of Spain, which saw a strong centralization of the Castilian monarchy in Madrid. The economic reasons in both cases are secondary to the political and ethnic-linguistic reasons. Finally, the term 'dualism' does not apply to Poland, where the differences between rural and industrial districts do not produce a clear division of the country into homogeneous, territorially compact areas since the backward regions lie both east and west of the Mazoviewskie region of the capital, Warsaw. It is therefore on Germany and Italy that we must concentrate if we want to grasp the roots of territorial dualism.

In Italy in 2016, the disposable income per inhabitant, measured in nominal terms, was about €21,500 in the North-West, €21,000 in the North-East, €19,100 in the Centre, and €13,500 in the Mezzogiorno. The ranking of regions by income level available per capita in 2016 sees in first place the Autonomous Province of Bolzano-Bozen, with approximately €24,600, and in last place Calabria, with €12,400. Taking GDP (before taxation and welfare payments) instead of disposable income, the magnitude of the gap is even greater: in Lombardy, the GDP per capita amounts to €38,200, and in Calabria, it is less than half this at €17,100.

The gap between the richest region of the south (Bavaria) and the poorest region of the northeast (Mecklenburg–West Pomerania) in Germany is today in general less pronounced than between north and south in Italy, but it is still quite remarkable: the GDP per capita in Bavaria amounts to more than €45,000 a year, whereas Mecklenburg it hardly reaches €27,000.

3 Beyond Economic Inequalities in the EU

Economic inequalities have obvious consequences on multiple dimensions of life's conditions and, to a certain extent, these conditions have some impact on economic inequality; that is, on the ways economic goods are produced and distributed. The limits of a measure of equality/inequality based only on economic factors, such as income and wealth, have been recognized by several scholars as well as international institutions. To overcome these shortcomings, since 1990 the United Nations Development Program has published the HDI, which besides its economic dimensions also includes health conditions (calculated as life expectancy at birth) and education (in years of schooling of the adult population). The correlation between the ranking by income and by human development is no doubt fairly high, but there are a few interesting differences between the positions of countries on both rankings. Among non-EU countries, Norway and Switzerland keep their top position. Among EU countries, Luxembourg, which ranks first in income, drops to seventh position on the HDI (owing to the presence of a considerable number of immigrants with low education). Germany, by contrast, jumps from fifth to first position. Denmark, the UK, and France also improve their standing, whereas Austria loses a few positions. Slovenia and Greece far better placed on the HDI than in income terms, probably because of improved health conditions. The same does not apply to Slovakia, which loses a few positions, probably because of the negative impact of alcohol consumption on life expectancy. These considerations based on the HDI suggest that a closer look at the other dimensions of inequality should be taken. These are health, housing, education, and chances of social mobility.

3.1 *Health*

Compared with some other parts of the world, in terms of health conditions Europeans no doubt enjoy an enviable situation. One crude indicator uses World Bank data: while life expectancy at birth is about 72 years for the world population, Europeans of the EU live some eight and a half years longer, but the population of the USA only six and a half years longer. For Latin America and the Asian countries, the gap with the world average is only about two years, and the African countries are many years below the average. Yet life expectancy is not necessarily an accurate indicator of health. Therefore, in order to assess discrepancies among member states and suggest adequate policies, the EU produces a whole set of health indicators focusing on the quality of life spent in a healthy state. The EU average is 63.3 for females and 62.6 for men. Differences among countries are quite remarkable: a Swedish woman is expected to live in health more than ten years longer than a Slovak or a Portuguese woman, but even German women are not much better off. Life expectancy for women is 5.5 years longer than for men, but these additional years are not particularly healthy: the gender gap in terms of healthy life years is considerably smaller, just 0.4 years. In general, Eastern countries perform somewhat worse in terms of health conditions than Western countries, but there are some 'deviant' cases: Denmark, Finland, and the Netherlands do not follow the Swedish example (owing to different levels of alcohol consumption and smoking habits), and the Mediterranean countries (Spain, France, Italy, and Greece) show better health conditions than Austria or Germany, probably because of different dietary habits.

The state of the population's health is influenced by environmental, cultural, and socioeconomic factors, as well as the health care services available for disease prevention and treatment. healthcare systems are the products of long historical traditions connected with medical professions and the establishment and development of welfare institutions. A sign of the conspicuous differences among nation state systems is, to take just one indicator, the number of medical doctors per capita. In 2014, Greece, with 632 physicians per 100,000 inhabitants recorded the highest ratio among EU member states, followed by Austria with 505, Portugal with 443, Lithuania with 431, Sweden with 412, Germany with 411, Italy with 380, Spain with 375, and then all the others. Poland comes last, with only 231 physicians per 100,000 population. The health of a country clearly has no relationship to the number of medical doctors, so we should consider the number of physicians as only one of several factors pertaining to a country's overall health organization. A further factor is the way in which hospital care is organized.

Among EU member states, Germany recorded not only the highest absolute number of hospital beds (666,000) in 2015, but also the highest number relative to population size, with 813 hospital beds per 100,000 population. Austria and Lithuania recorded more than 700 hospital beds. The average for the EU-28 as a whole was 514 hospital beds (always per 100,000 inhabitants). Italy, Denmark, Ireland, Spain, Sweden, and the UK recorded the lowest number of hospital beds relative to population size, all under 300. (These figures should be taken with caution since the statistical counting procedures are not necessarily homogeneous.) This crude indicator too, like the previous one measuring the number of physicians, signals the structural differences of healthcare systems more than real inequalities in the way health is taken care of.

A more efficient indicator is probably health care expenditure per inhabitant and as a share of GDP. EU member states can be ranked in four categories:

1. top performers – countries spending more than €4,000 per inhabitant (Denmark, Ireland, Luxembourg, Netherlands, Sweden)
2. high performers – countries spending from €3,000 to €3,999 per inhabitant (Belgium, Germany, France, Austria, Finland, UK)
3. average performers – countries spending from €1,000 to €2,999 per inhabitant (Czech Republic, Greece, Spain, Italy, Portugal, Slovenia)
4. below-average performers – countries spending less than €1,000 per inhabitant (Bulgaria, Estonia, Croatia, Latvia, Hungary, Poland, Romania, Slovakia)

This ranking does not change substantially when we consider the share of healthcare expenditure of the GDP: ten countries spend more than 10 per cent of GDP on healthcare (Belgium, Denmark, Germany, France, Netherlands, Austria, Sweden), six countries spend more than 9.0 per cent (Ireland, Spain, Italy, Portugal, Finland, UK), and all other countries spend less than 8.9 per cent (Bulgaria, Czech Republic, Estonia, Greece, Croatia, Cyprus, Latvia, Lithuania, Luxembourg, Hungary, Poland, Portugal, Slovenia, Romania, Slovakia). Whichever indicator we use, the magnitude of the East–West and South–North divides in the EU is absolutely remarkable.

3.2 Housing

Food, clothing, and shelter are traditionally considered basic needs of the human species. The ways these needs are met vary considerably within each society according to lifestyles and economic conditions. Our concern, however, centres on some differences among countries. Among consumer goods, we shall focus on housing since it is specifically fit to highlight social inequalities. A significant variable is the tenure status of the inhabited space, which reflects housing policies, institutional and fiscal regulations, and the habits of the population. In the EU, the majority of the state populations (about 70 per cent) lives at present in ownership dwellings with or without mortgages and loans, and the minority are tenants (30 per cent, two-thirds of whom pay market prices and one-third reduced or zero prices). Housing property prevails largely in Eastern European countries (where public ownership was quite widespread during the communist past). Tenanted houses, by contrast, are more widespread in rich Western countries, where the market for rented dwellings is more dynamic: Germany has the largest share of tenant houses (close to 50 per cent), followed by Austria, Denmark, Netherlands, Sweden, UK, and France. In all other countries, approximately one house out of four is rented by its dwellers.

When looking at inequalities, a very eloquent indicator is the overcrowding rate, which is defined by the proportion of people living in the household and the number of rooms available. In 2014, close to 15 per cent of the EU population lived in overcrowded dwellings, but the differences among member states were conspicuous: high overcrowding rates (from 40 to 50 per cent) were recorded in Romania, Hungary, Poland, Bulgaria, Croatia, Latvia, Slovakia, and Lithuania; only two Western countries (Greece and Italy) show one out of four dwellings as overcrowded. Living in a house one owns does not mean living comfortably. In fact, the share of the population at risk of poverty living in overcrowded dwellings is very high, whatever the nature of the tenure arrangements.

3.3 Education

It goes without saying that when dealing with inequalities in education in particular, one should distinguish between inequalities within each country and inequalities between different countries.

Educational systems are very different among European countries. Some countries provide educational and care services for children aged 0–3 years, covering a more or less limited share of the population. In 2002, member states agreed in Barcelona to fix the target for 2010 at 33 per cent attendance among children under three (European Commission/EACEA/Eurydice/Eurostat, 2014). However, in 2011 only ten EU countries had reached the target. Denmark stands out with 74 per cent, whereas attendance was especially low (10 per cent or less) in the group of Eastern European countries. The situation is different for pre-primary education: 93 per cent of children attend school before starting primary education, but some countries still lag behind – participation rates were between 70 and 79 per cent in Greece, Croatia, Poland, Slovakia, and Finland. Data from the Program for International Student Assessment (PISA) and International association for the Evalutation of educational Achievement Progress in International Reading Literacy Study (IEA PIRLS) studies show clearly that attendance of pre-primary education and care institutions produces better performances in children's further educational career in both primary and secondary schools. We shall presently come back to the PISA data.

When comparing the performance of educational systems, one should be careful to choose the right indicators. It is, for example, misleading to look at the pupil–teacher ratio: in primary education: the UK and France show the highest number of children per teacher (about 20) and Greece, Hungary, and Poland the lowest (about 10). This indicator has little to do with the quality of teaching and depends primarily on organizational patterns and the labour market policy designed to help absorb teacher unemployment.

Another indicator of inequalities that is often used in education is the percentage of early school leavers: the quota of 18–24 year olds no longer engaged in education or training, who may face considerable difficulties entering the labour market. In 2016, the percentage for all 28 EU member states was 10.7. Most states ranked below average (Belgium, Czech Republic, Denmark, Ireland, Greece, France, Croatia, Cyprus, Lithuania, Luxembourg, Netherlands, Austria, Poland, Slovenia, Slovakia, Finland, Sweden), four were close to the average (Germany, Latvia, Estonia, UK), and the countries above average belong to Southern and South-Eastern Europe (Bulgaria, Spain, Italy, Hungary, Malta, Portugal, Romania). These countries present serious problems, with a not irrelevant share of young people entering adult life in a position of disadvantage.

Somehow connected with early school leavers is the so-called NEETs phenomenon (those who are Not in Employment, Education, or Training). This is the case for young people (more women than men) aged 20–34 who, having left school, are not only unemployed but also are not looking for a job. NEET rates depend on age and educational attainment. Within the EU, the phenomenon shows high degrees of variation: in some countries, its incidence is very limited (Denmark, Germany, Luxembourg, Netherlands, Austria, Sweden), in others, by contrast, it is very pronounced and is cause for serious concern (Bulgaria, Greece, Croatia, Italy, Romania). The EU-28 average amounts to 15.6 per cent; it is lowest in Sweden (7.2 per cent) and highest in Italy (26 per cent).

The picture does not change substantially when looking at life-long learning, the kind of educational activities designed for the population aged over 25 and below 65. The amount of the adult population engaged in such activities is in general quite remarkable, but the countries offering more opportunities in this field are not those where adult citizens would be in need of a rich educational supply, but those where the adult population has already reached a satisfactory educational level. Most Eastern countries (excluding Estonia and Slovenia) and most of the Mediterranean countries (excluding Portugal and also Spain) belong to the category where need is high but supply is limited.

The best way to assess inequalities between nation states in the realm of education is to look at the share of expenditures for education in the GDP or gross national income (GNI), which also includes income earned in the country by non-residents, and in public expenditure. The data in Table 9.4 is self-explanatory. There are few countries whose investment in education is significantly above the European average (Belgium, Denmark, Ireland, Cyprus, Malta, Sweden, Finland) and a rather large number where education does not seem to be a priority (Czech Republic, Spain, Croatia, Italy, Latvia, Hungary, Romania, Slovakia). All other countries keep close to the EU average. Again, there are evident causes of concern regarding education in most Southern and Eastern countries.

Taking the data of the well-known PISA study promoted by the Organisation for Economic Co-operation and Development, one can reach quite similar conclusions. PISA aims to measure competences in science, reading, and mathematics of 15-year-old boys and girls. The programme started in 2000 and is regularly repeated every three years. It is by far the most valuable endeavour ever undertaken to draw a comparative picture of educational performances on a worldwide scale. The latest published inquiry available was completed in 2015 in 72 participating countries, including all EU countries. The scientific educational community has lengthily discussed the methodology used, the choice of indicators, and the procedures of data processing. Notwithstanding the puzzlement of many commentators, PISA findings are widely used in orienting educational policies, and their reliability has been sufficiently tested. For each of the three skills assessed, an average score is calculated and countries are ranked according to the distance above or below this average. Each country is further ranked according to the proportion of top performer (in at least one of the skills considered), on the one hand and the proportion of low achievers on the other.

The following typology is highly significant regarding inequalities in education and gives some insights into the policy issues and targets in educational matters.

TABLE 9.4 Main indicators for public expenditure on education (excluding early-childhood educational development), 2012

	Expenditure as a share of GDP	Expenditure as a share of public expenditure	Expenditure as a share of GNI
EU-28	5.3	5.3	10.8
Belgium	6.6 +	6.6 +	12.0 +
Bulgaria	3.7	3.7	10.3
Czech Republic	4.3 −	4.7 −	9.7 −
Denmark[a]	8.8 +	8.5 +	15.2 +
Germany	4.8	4.7	10.8
Estonia[b]	4.8	5.1	12.3 +
Ireland	6.2	7.5 +	14.5 +
Greece	−	−	−
Spain	4.3 −	4.4 −	9.1 −
France	5.7	5.6	10.0
Croatia	4.2 −	4.3 −	8.7 −
Italy[c]	3.4 −	3.5 −	6.7 −
Cyprus	6.7 +	6.9 +	14.6 +
Latvia[d]	2.6 −	2.7 −	7.0 −
Lithuania[e]	4.8	5.0	13.4 +
Luxembourg	3.9 −	5.8	9.0 −
Hungary	4.1 −	4.3 −	8.3 −
Malta	6.8 +	7.2 +	15.7 +
Netherlands	5.9	5.8	11.7
Austria	5.6	5.6	10.8
Poland	4.9	5.1	11.6
Portugal	4.9	5.1	10.4
Romania	2.6 −	2.7 −	7.2 −
Slovenia	5.4	5.5	11.3
Slovakia	3.1 −	3.1 −	8.0 −
Finland[f]	7.1 +	7.1 +	12.6 +
Sweden	7.4 +	7.2 +	14.2 +
UK	6.1	6.0	12.7 +

+ above EU average
− below EU average

a Value also includes early childhood educational development; excludes upper secondary education. Expenditure as a share of GDP, GNI and as a share of public expenditure (2011);

excludes research and development expenditure; excludes independent private institutions.
b Expenditure as a share of GNI and as a share of public expenditure; includes early childhood educational development.
c Value: excluding short-cycle tertiary education. Expenditure as a share of GDP, GNI, and as a share of public expenditure; excludes tertiary education.
d Excludes tertiary education.
e Includes early childhood educational development.
f Includes expenditure by international organizations.
SOURCE: EUROSTAT HTTPS://EC.EUROPA.EU/EUROSTAT/STATISTICS-EXPLAINED/INDEX.PHP/GOVERNMENT_EXPENDITURE_ON_EDUCATION#EXPENDITURE_ON_.27EDUCATION.27

1. Countries ranking high in top performers and low in low achievers. These countries are successful in pursuing both excellence and equality (Estonia, Finland, Slovenia, UK, Germany, the Netherlands).
2. Countries high on top performers and ranking about average in the proportion of low achievers (Belgium)
3. Countries high on top performers, but with a high proportion of low achievers; the target of excellence is pursued at the expense of equality (France)
4. Countries close to the average on top performance, but trying to reduce the proportion of low achievers (Ireland, Denmark, Poland, Portugal)
5. Countries close to the average both in top performers and low achievers (Austria, Sweden, Czech Republic)
6. Countries ranking close to the average in top performers, but with a high proportion of low achievers (Malta)
7. Countries with a low proportion of top achievers, but successful in reducing the proportion of low achievers (Spain, Latvia)
8. Countries with a low proportion of top achievers and an average proportion of low achievers (Italy, Croatia)
9. Countries with very low levels for top achievers and high for low achievers (Luxembourg, Lithuania, Hungary, Slovakia, Greece)

3.4   *Social Mobility*

As we have seen so far, social inequalities in Europe, both between and within countries, are still quite remarkable. The same holds true if we look at inequalities in terms of social mobility. A widespread ideological belief in the tradition of Western societies supports the idea that social inequalities are acceptable to the extent that equal opportunities are assured by an adequate level of social mobility. In principle, all individuals should have the same opportunity to reach during their life regardless of their social position or that of the family in which they were born. Even if everybody knows that no historical society has ever realized perfect social mobility, meaning equal opportunities for all, this ideal still functions as a normative principle that social policies should aim to attain.

After the crisis at the end of the first decade of the 21st century, there is growing awareness among policymakers, scholars, and the public "that – for the first time in decades – younger generations of adults will have fewer opportunities for upward mobility than today's older generations enjoyed.... Young people find it increasingly hard to graduate from formal education without having accumulated debt, to find affordable housing and to get a job that will allow them a good standard of living" (Eurofound, 2017: 9) This awareness produces serious concern for the future of social cohesion, since it is questionable how our societies can hold together in the long run without the ideological underpinning of a belief in social mobility.

The traditional way to grasp the phenomena of social mobility distinguishes between inter-generational and infra-generational or career mobility. For our purpose, it is better to concentrate on the former in order to compare the occupation of one or both parents with the occupation reached by sons or daughters in a more or less stable stage in their careers, since occupation is thought to be the best indicator of social position and a reliable predictor of a variety of attitudes and behaviours. Sociological studies further distinguish between absolute and relative social mobility. Absolute mobility is produced by changes in the occupational and social structure over time. The decline in the rural population owing to industrialization, the rise of the service sector, as well as migration, are all instances of transformations that have an impact on the distribution of people in the social space and therefore on absolute mobility and the ability to change positions across generations. By contrast, relative mobility has to do with the probability that individuals will cross social borders and end up in a different position compared with their origins. In this case, one often speaks of social fluidity. Absolute and relative mobility are two analytical aspects of the same phenomenon that should be clearly distinguished from one another since they can vary independently: "In a society, it is possible for high levels of absolute mobility (large numbers moving up or down) to coexist with low levels of relative mobility (or social fluidity) and vice versa. The distance between occupational origin and destination is likely to be a combination of absolute and relative mobility" (Eurofound, 2017: 10). If society moves, if it is crossed by dynamic forces, individuals are pulled or pushed up (or down) by impersonal factors, operating in a certain way independently of individual will and action. By contrast, in a static society, one that does not change much over time between generations, individuals can move up and/or down the social fabric only if barriers between classes or strata are sufficiently fluid.

European societies show significant differences both in absolute and relative mobility, owing to different timing and shape of the social change they have undergone. Several researches on social mobility have been carried out in different countries, but there are only a few comparative endeavours (Golthorpe, 2016; Breen, 2004; Rose & Harrison, 2014). Fortunately, data from the European Social Survey (ESS, https://www.europeansocialsurvey.org) can be used to draw a tentative picture of the faces of social mobility in European society today.

Two dimensions should be singled out: gender and generation. The focus on gender is quite recent in research on social mobility, and it is not difficult to explain why: since the crucial variable in mobility studies is occupation, it is hard to assess mobility for the proportion of women not employed outside the domestic sphere. In this case, one way was to consider the occupational status of father and husband in the assumption that the path to mobility for women was primarily through marriage. This is clearly no longer the case in societies with a high proportion of employed women in both generations of mothers and daughters. Historical processes of social change have had a considerable impact on women's conditions in different European societies both in terms of timing and of pace, which explains why the patterns of social mobility for men and women can show significant differences.

The historical-generational dimension in mobility studies is of course relevant for both male and female populations. ESS data allow us to analyse three cohorts/clusters: 1. those born between 1927 and 1945 (this generation was called 'the silent generation' and comprised people born during the Great Depression and the pre–Second World War and immediate post-war period, who could pursue their careers amid the opportunities of the post-war expansion); 2. those born between 1946 and 1964 (called 'baby boomers', who grew up during reconstruction and the phase of rapid economic development, called 'les trente glorieuses' by Fourastié) (Fourastié, 1979); and 3. those born between 1965 and 1975 (called 'Generation X', the first to grow up without the expectation that they would improve upon the condition of their parents' generation).

An analysis of the data for 24 member countries (a few countries, among them Italy and Romania, were excluded from the sample owing to a lack of data) allows some interesting considerations on absolute social mobility in Europe over more than half a century. As Table 9.5 shows, the male population experienced a marked linear rise in downward mobility and a decline in upward mobility to the point that, in the case of the last generation considered,

TABLE 9.5 Absolute mobility statistics by cohort and sex (24 EU member states)

Men		N	A	B	C
Silent generation	1927–45	19,024	32.0	22.3	45.7
Baby boomers	1946–64	39,260	34.4	22.6	43.0
Generation X	1965–75	15,560	37.3	24.2	38.5
Women					
Silent generation	1927–45	19,079	37.9	21.5	40.5
Baby boomers	1946–64	42,938	35.8	19.2	45.0
Generation X	1965–75	17,771	37.3	20.5	42.3

N Absolute numbers
A Downwardly mobile (%)
B Immobile (%)
C Upwardly mobile (%)
SOURCE: EUROFOUND, 2017:22

the quota of downwardly mobile almost equals the quota of upwardly mobile people. The picture for women looks quite different: upward mobility prevails even if it shows a significant slowdown for Generation X. In fact, downward mobility increased for men in 18 out of 24 countries and only in six countries for women, whereas upward mobility increased in eight countries for women and in no country for men. Overall, women are experiencing successive mobility gains across cohorts in most countries, while men are more likely to experience downward mobility than previous generations.

If aspirations for social mobility are cement that holds society together and are instrumental in sustaining social cohesion, these data show that concern about the present phase of diminishing opportunities compared with previous generations is fully justified.

The picture, however, varies from country to country or, to be more precise, for different groups of countries. Absolute social mobility depends upon economic development and changes in the structure of social classes over the time period considered. There is a clear divide between 'firstcomer' and 'latecomer' countries as well as an East–West divide. Overall, Eastern and Southern countries show lower absolute (both upward and downward) mobility rates than Northern countries. The extent and the timing of modernization shape the ways of absolute social mobility, as pointed out in the conclusions of the Eurofound study:

> The more a society experienced shifts in its class structure between generations, the more upward mobility increased and prevailed over downward mobility. The more the class structure changed (or modernised due to the disappearance of low-skilled menial jobs and growth in service-class and highly qualified jobs), the more the extent of absolute social mobility among men and women became similar.
> Eurofound, 2017: 26

Looking at the issue in terms of equity and fairness, the relevant questions are related to relative social mobility (or social fluidity): does social origin become more or less important than education, personal achievements and career in reaching different positions in the social fabric? In other words, to what extent does social origin affect one's chances of being in a different occupational class than one's parents?

There are considerable differences between countries such as Sweden, where societal openness is very marked, and Italy, France, and Germany, where social fluidity rates are low. Similarly, there is a substantial difference between, for example, the Netherlands in the 1970s (which was quite a closed society) and in the 1990s, when it ranked among the most open (Breen, 2004). No doubt, equality of opportunities is unevenly differentiated among European societies.

Does fluidity increase or decrease over time? Further research taking cohort and gender as basic variables will help to answer this question.

3.5   *The Social Equality Index*

Starting in 2008, the Bertelsmann Foundation launched a programme to develop an index of social equality in EU countries; this is designed to monitor trends over time (Schraad-Tischler & Schiller, 2016). The index construction is quite complex and includes both quantitative and qualitative variables in six main sectors: poverty (population at risk of poverty and social exclusion, jobless households, percentage living in severe material deprivation), education (pre-primary education, early school leavers, less than upper secondary attainment), labour market (unemployment, long-term unemployment, youth unemployment, low-pay employment), social cohesion (Gini coefficient, gender equality, NEET), health (healthy life expectancy, access to healthcare systems) and intergenerational relations (greenhouse gas emissions, renewable energies, public debt, research and development expenditure, old age dependency). It is worth underlining the inclusion in the social equality index of indicators that show concern not only for present but also for future generations. From a long-term perspective, not only children's and youth's rights should be cared for, but also the rights of future citizens who have yet to be born.

As Table 9.6 shows and as could be expected, the first three countries with the highest scores of social equality belong to Scandinavia: Sweden, Finland, and Denmark (Norway, not being a member of the EU, was excluded). These countries were less severely hit by the crisis that started in 2008 and could keep, although with some restrictions, the provisions of a generous welfare state. In fourth place we find, somewhat surprisingly, the Czech Republic, which – unlike many other East European countries that used to be satellites of the Soviet Union – has high scores on successful antipoverty measures, on healthcare, and also a low rate of NEETS and early school leavers. Next we find, from 5 to 12, with the only exception being Slovenia, several Western European countries (Netherlands, Austria, Germany, Luxembourg, France, Belgium, and UK). Descending in the ranks follow a further number of East European countries (Estonia and Poland – just above the EU average – and Lithuania, Slovakia, Croatia, and Latvia – just below average) and three small West European countries (Malta, Ireland, and Cyprus). At the very bottom of this ranking are placed the so-called Mediterranean countries (Portugal, Spain, Italy, and Greece), together with the rest of the Eastern European countries (Hungary, Bulgaria, and Romania).

From 2008 (the year the ranking was first issued) to 2017 (the year of the last available issue), only a few countries improved their scores (Czech Republic, Germany, Luxembourg, UK, and Poland), while all others reduced their scores – (notably Ireland, Italy, Spain, and Greece). It goes without saying that countries that suffered the most during and after the economic and financial crisis were among the losers in terms of increasing inequalities. This confirms once again that the crisis had the effect of increasing inequality among EU societies.

4 Conclusion

There have been lively discussions during the last half-century about the existence of social classes in contemporary societies. Those who claim their persistency think that, despite changes in the transition from industrial to post-industrial society, social classes still exist. Others claim that in view of the

THE DIMENSIONS OF INEQUALITY

TABLE 9.6 EU Social Justice Index

	Country	Social Justice Index 2008	Social Justice Index 2016–17	Change 2008–17
1	Sweden	7.58	7.51	−0.07
2	Finland	7.22	7.17	−005
3	Denmark	7.35	7.16	−0.19
4	Czech Republic	6.74	6.85	+0.10
5	Netherlands	7.17	6.80	−0.37
6	Austria	6.88	6.67	−0. 21
7	Germany	6.23	6.66	+0.43
8	Luxembourg	6.41	6.57	+0.16
9	Slovenia		6.51	
10	France	6.27	6.27	
11	Belgium	6.19	6.18	−0.01
12	UK	6.02	6.16	+0.14
13	Estonia		6.15	
14	Poland	4.56	5.81	+1.25
	EU-average	6.06	5.75	−0.31
15	Lithuania		5.69	
16	Malta		5.57	
17	Slovakia	5.66	5.55	−0.11
18	Ireland	5.91	5.40	−0.51
19	Croatia		5.07	
20	Cyprus		5.04	
21	Latvia		5.04	
22	Portugal	4.97	4.97	
23	Hungary	5.08	4.96	−0.12
24	Italy	5.10	4.78	−0.32
25	Spain	5.45	4.76	−0.69
26	Bulgaria		4.03	
27	Romania		3.91	
28	Greece	4.44	3.66	−0.78

SOURCE: BERTELSMANN STIFTUNG, SOCIAL JUSTICE IN THE EU, INDEX REPORT 2019

major changes social structure has undergone, the concept of class has exhausted its utility. We can leave it to scholars to discuss the matter. However, everybody agrees that, whether or not in the form of social classes, inequality still exists. There is also consensus that nowadays inequality is rising, both within and between European societies.

However, the size and the shape of the inequality pyramid vary not only in space but also in time. Looking at the last two centuries, we can identify four phases. During the first, the process of industrialization was accompanied by an increase in inequality that was more gradual in countries where the process started earlier and sharper in 'latecomer' countries, such as Italy and Germany. This phase lasted approximately until the First World War. The second phase encompasses the period between the two world wars and was characterized by contrasting tendencies and differing outcomes in different countries: the economic crisis of the late 1920s led to sharp inequalities, plunging millions of people into extreme poverty. This was followed by the Second World War. Wars tend to destroy properties and can produce equalizing outcomes. Moreover, fiscal and social policies sometimes had the effect of reducing inequality during this phase. The third phase, between 1945 and 1975, was marked by both intensive economic growth and reduction in inequalities. For some analysts, the 30 years after the Second World War have been an unrepeatable exception in the history of capitalism. We will probably have to wait at least a century to test this hypothesis. Anyway, this period tells us that inequalities can be reduced when the cake to be distributed increases in size and when appropriate political fiscal and welfare measures are adopted. In fact, as we see in Chapter 11, in Europe, this was the period in which the welfare state model reached its peak. Since the end of the 1970s, the trajectory started to change and inequalities began to rise again. This is the fourth and last phase, continuing until the present time, which has seen a sharp acceleration of inequality following the financial crisis at the end of the first decade of the 21st century.

As discussed above, inequalities tend to increase not only within societies between the rich and the poor, the better and the less educated, the healthy and the sick, but also between states and regions within each state. The European integration process has no doubt contributed in general to the wellbeing of all Europeans, but not to diminishing the gaps that cut across Europe along the North–South and the West–East divides. The policy of the so-called 'structural funds' adopted by the EU was conceived to contribute to the development of backward regions and to increase social cohesion. They make up one of the largest items of the budget of the EU (about €350 billion in seven years). This is a considerable effort, but clearly insufficient to counterbalance the trend toward increased inequality within and between member states.

CHAPTER 10

The Political-Institutional Architecture of the European Union

The European Union (EU) has reached a crossroads. On the one hand, it can advance along the road of political union, complementing monetary union with a common fiscal policy and a common foreign and defence policy, and enhancing the European Parliament (EP) in EU decision-making, aware of the fact that deeper political integration is the best way to cope with the economic consequences of a long crisis, fragmented exit strategies, and their social implications in terms of inequality and unemployment. On the other hand, the EU can regress to a single free-exchange area, giving back to member states the portions of sovereignty that have been transferred at supranational level. But there is also a third alternative: the preservation of the status quo through a persistent decisional paralysis. This is the most risky since, according to a bicycle metaphor, if you stop pedalling you fall off.

In this chapter, we will outline the main interpretations of the nature of the EU political system, and the distinctive features of its basic institutions and decision-making processes. In Chapter 11, we will focus on European political parties and pressure groups; in the Conclusion, we will advance our proposals of institutional reform, to be achieved with or without the revision of treaties.

1 The EU as an Example of Bold Institutional Innovation

The EU is a complex, partially undefined, and constantly evolving political entity. It is one of the major institutional innovations in post-Second World War world politics. In order to understand its peculiar nature, we must look at the different views regarding its political institutions, governance structure, and multilevel and multi-agency decision-making. The EU is a political experiment that proceeds through accelerations and slowdowns, with continuous adjustments; it has been ironically defined as a UPO – an unidentified political object (by Jacques Delors) or a hornet that flies in spite of its structure. The EU is the outcome of almost 70 years of change, heated discussion, conflict, and compromise between competing visions concerning what it should be (single market/political union, confederation of sovereign states/federal union). Studies of the EU can only partially rely on models that analyse nation states, since there is no clear division of constitutional powers; the legislative function is actually performed jointly by the European Commission, the Council, and the Parliament, and, increasingly, by the European Court of Justice (ECJ) as well (through its power of judicial review), whereas the executive role is jointly performed by the European Council, which decides on strategic priorities, the Commission, and the regulating agencies that are engaged in policymaking.

In the vast multidisciplinary literature on the institutional structure of the EU, we find two main approaches:

a) the intergovernmental approach, which holds that the decision-making process is still predominantly based on agreements underwritten by sovereign states;

b) the approach that considers the EU to be a supranational community union;

The two main approaches largely reproduce the older controversy between neo-realists such as Waltz (1979) and neofunctionalists such as Haas (1958). Supporters of intergovernmentalism – among their number are most neorealist scholars of international relations – maintain that national governments continue to be the only relevant actors in the integration process, and sign treaties on the basis of national interests. According to them, the EU is an intergovernmental organization that does not strip member states of their sovereign power, but encourages them to use it in a different way (Millward, 2000). The EU works according to a logic of resource sharing rather than a logic of delegation of powers, with the consequence that policy areas in which the EU substitutes for the governmental action of member states are limited (Magnette, 2005). European decision-making is dominated by the national interests of the most powerful states, which have compensated in various ways the smaller ones and delegated very limited powers to community institutions, namely the Commission and the ECJ (Moravcsik, 1998). The liberal-democratic theories of preferences formation, rational choice, and intergovernmental bargaining combine in various ways in this approach, which finds empirical validation in the predominance of the intergovernmental method over the supranational 'communitarian' one and in the greater powers of the European Council – which represents member state governments – compared with those of the Parliament and the Commission.

In contrast, the neofunctionalist perspective and related approaches consider the EU to be a new, distinctive type of political system. The first and more prestigious proponent, Ernst Haas, sees European integration as the outcome of three main factors: actors with transnational goals and interests, supranational organizations endowed with the autonomous ability to produce norms and resolve controversies, and a normative structure that gives shape to the European polity. Integration develops insofar as economic interdependence and transnational transactions grow, thus revealing the potentiality of common benefits; political actors – governments, parties, business associations, trade unions – find in the integration a more effective way to pursue their own interests; and supranational governance bodies are granted the necessary powers to define the rules and procedures of integration and conflict resolution. A key element of this approach is the functional and political spillover; that is, the spontaneous, incremental feedback stemming from the inner logic of integration, which is both functional and political. The functional spillover derives from economic interdependence, since the decision to integrate given sectors in some member states implies the need to further integrate other sectors in more countries; political spillover is the outcome of the new political reality that derives from the transferring of a growing number of policy decisions from state level to European level, thus inducing powerful pressure groups to relocate their lobbying activities to the new supranational context and, in turn, for national governments to transfer further policies.

The empirical evidence backing this approach is abundant: the growing number of policies transferred at EU level, the deepening of integration from single market to monetary union, the enlargement (not without tensions) from the original six to 27 (after Brexit) countries. The vast ECJ jurisprudence, the extension of majority voting, the growing power of the EP, the creation of the euro and of the European Central Bank (ECB) are all instances of the fact that the EU is performing some of the functions that are typical of a national sovereign state. The EU is a constitutional system without a constitution in that it has its own judicial system, its own constitutional principles, and a normative body – the so-called *acquis communautaire* – made of the treaties signed by member states, the deliberations of community institutions, and the verdicts of the ECJ. As we will see, the ECJ in particular has played a fundamental role in legitimizing the supranational character of the EU through the constitutionalization of community law. All these facts have brought some to think that the EU can become an entirely autonomous political system (Wallace, 1983) with most of the features of a nation state (Gozi, 2001).

Both the neo-realist/intergovernmental and the neo-functionalist/supranational approach are, however, open to criticism, and do not provide a full picture of the actual functioning of the EU. The analysis of the complex interplay between the two models of governance they imply helps a lot, but is not enough. The former approach neglects the fact that the EU has a much more complex institutional structure than any other international organization (since it includes a directly elected parliament and a constitutional court) and is engaged in a much larger set of policies (Nugent, 1994). The latter approach neglects the fact that the EU differs from a full-fledged supranational union in some key aspects, such as the absence of a union president with executive powers and the requirement of unanimity voting on basic questions. The EU is not a mere intergovernmental organization with limited and strictly defined goals, unanimous approval of all decisions, and without autonomous institutions, but neither is it a federal union. In some respects the EU functions like a sovereign state endowed with the autonomous legitimate power that is necessary to impose its decisions on a given people and territory. Community laws are, in fact, legislative acts of general application, which must be incorporated into – and prevail over – member states' laws; the EU has responsibility in several matters that are typical of nation states, such as regulating market and currency, voting and managing budgets, implementing public policies, supplying public goods and services, holding elections, and participating as a single actor in international organizations. But, on the other hand, the EU still lacks some key attributes of the sovereign modern state as defined by Max Weber: the monopoly of legitimate violence, the power of taxation, effective institutions of law enforcement. Moreover, some critics argue that the EU has a deficit of democratic legitimacy and lacks several features of representative democracy, insofar as the European Council is not accountable to the EP for its decisions.

For these reasons, some scholars have suggested a third approach: the EU as a multilevel and multi-agency governance system with stratified levels of political authority. In reviewing the literature on the EU Pollack (2005) gives credit to the three types, affirming that some scholars consider the EU to be an international organization, others a political system, and still others a governance system. The last approach can effectively integrate the other two. But, rather than a third alternative it looks more a sub-type of the second (supranational union). Marks (1993), one of the main proponents of this approach, argues on the basis of his analysis of the planning and management of EU structural funds that the Single European Act introduced very relevant changes: national governments can no longer monopolize the representation of domestic interests and the choice of EU ends and means, European institutions have become largely independent in defining common preferences and strategies, decision-making power is diffuse through many public and private actors, and decision-making arenas are connected in networks that avoid control by national governments. The outcome is a model of multilevel and multi-stakeholder governance, in which nation states are no longer the exclusive link between domestic policies and intergovernmental negotiations, but interact at various levels with several other actors with overlapping competencies (regional and local governments, parties, unions, organized interest groups) in an integrated decision-making hierarchy. European policymaking is characterized by governance rather than government, regulation rather than rule, and by a proliferation of committees and workgroups formed by European and national officers together with experts and interest groups' representatives. Growing integration does not stem only and necessarily from intergovernmental bargaining; it can even take place without the conscious leadership of European institutions (Stone Sweet, Sandholtz, & Fligstein, 2001), thus explaining why integration – in terms of volume of cross-border exchanges and number of community laws – has continued to grow even in periods of 'Euro-sclerosis'. The non-governmental actors in transnational European society, who are engaged in community exchanges (trade and investment, social and political exchanges, cultural relations), directly or indirectly influence the integration process, since they generalize the demand for common rules and supranational policies. As a consequence, integration is not uniformly achieved in all sectors and across every policy area.

Majone (1996) goes further, arguing that the EU is not only a multilevel and multi-stakeholder system of governance, but also a regulatory state, different from both a supranational and intergovernmental political entity. A panoply of independent and quasi-independent regulatory agencies have developed, these aiming to correct market failures (such as monopolistic growth, environmental degradation, industrial crises) and to create a space open to normative innovation and to the harmonization of member states' laws and regulations. The main goal of the EU is the creation of a regulated single market on a continental scale. The common currency, social and environmental policies, budgetary regulation, and even the policies of the second and third pillars are to some extent related to the main goal. The EU has not replaced member states' governments, but has acquired unprecedented regulatory responsibilities. The decline of Keynesian economic policy has not only paved the way to some deregulation but has also fostered new regulatory activities. Majone's thesis that the EU does not rule but regulates is still valid, although it should be reformulated in light of the euro, the ECB, and the Stability Pact. In the new regulatory context, new forms of informal coordination have become essential for EU functioning, such as peer review, benchmarking, policy learning, and the open method of coordination.

Applying the perspective of multilevel, supranational governance helps us to analyse the EU political system by focusing on such aspects as interaction networks among a plurality of public and private actors, informal cooperation, and horizontal diffusion of power; but it is not without its critics either. First of all, it is argued that European governance has a democratic deficit, since decisions taken at supranational level cannot claim the same legitimacy as those taken at member state level, and are often the outcome of technocratic/elitist decision-making. The EU is, at best, a representative democracy of the second degree, since its most powerful body, the European Council, is composed of the heads and ministers of governments of the member states, and European Commission members are nominated by state and government heads and approved only afterwards by the EP. The answer given to this kind of criticism is that since the EU is not an input democracy but an output democracy, its legitimacy does not derive from the rules of democratic representation but from the results achieved, which are greater than those that could be achieved by the single member states in isolation. It is an argument that is only partially convincing since, first, the quality of a political system cannot be evaluated only in terms of its deliverables and, secondly, even if one accepts this evaluating approach, it is not easy to find objective measures to compare government achievements.

A second line of criticism concerns what is considered a point of strength of multilevel governance: the scope of consultation and participation of stakeholders, pressure groups, and lobbies at the various stages and levels of decision-making; it is argued that this practice risks fragmenting and stretching the whole process, and is likely to obscure the political responsibility of decision-makers. The most severe critics in this regard are Offe and Preuss (2006), who define governance in general as a style of government without a real opposition, an example of the depoliticization of contemporary democracies, a symptom of the absence of legitimate and effective power structures. According to them, so-called 'good governance' actually aims to create and maintain order in a highly interdependent world of blurred boundaries between public and private and national and supranational spheres, with many opportunities for veto playing and scarce resources of sovereign power. In the same manner, Crouch (2004) includes governance in his notion of 'post-democracy', arguing that it favours "the maximum level of minimal participation" and creates favourable conditions for the power of elites, which is not subject to democratic control, and for decision-making processes that are open to and permeable by organized lobbies.

For European citizens, it is hard to assign specific responsibilities to this or that level or institution of European governance, and they cannot reward or punish with their vote the parties that support a given EU government. As a consequence of this, a growing number of EU citizens show low levels of trust for European elites and institutions (Brussels Eurocrats, Frankfurt technocrats), and some even consider them easy scapegoats for their fears and frustrations.

The EU is increasingly considered responsible and continues to be inadequately accountable, thus fostering a legitimacy crisis (Hobolt & Tilley, 2014). The multilevel governance perspective helps us to give an account of a quite novel political system such as the EU, which is at the same time supranational and intergovernmental. Such a system should be reformed in order to increase both its legitimacy and its effectiveness.

2 The Main Phases of European Integration

The actual functioning of the EU provides some evidence for all the approaches we have discussed so far, and is characterized by the dialectical relation between supranational and intergovernmental models of governance. The predominance of one model or the other depends on the specific phase of the integration process and on the type of policies we consider. With regard to the various stages, initially, when the European Coal and Steel Community (ECSC), the European Economic Community (EEC), and the European Atomic Energy Community (Euratom) were formed, the communitarian supranational perspective was prevailing; later, at the time of De Gaulle's French 'empty chair' policy (i.e. systematically deserting EEC meetings), it was the intergovernmental one; then from the mid-1980s to the next decade, at the time of the Maastricht and Amsterdam Treaties it was again the supranational; then, in this century, with the failure of the Constitutional Treaty and exit strategies from the economic financial crisis, the intergovernmental perspective is leading once again.

With regard to the type of policy, we can adopt the language of the Maastricht Treaty and remark that the supranational perspective applies to the 'first pillar', the only one with legal personality, which regulates single market policies – consisting of the amended 1957 Treaty of Rome instituting the EEC (now the Treaty Establishing the European Community, TEC), the Euratom Treaty, and the 1951 ECSC Treaty (which expired in 2002), whereas intergovernmentalism applies to both the 'second pillar' on Common Foreign and Security Policy (CFSP), and the 'third pillar' on Police and Judicial Cooperation in Criminal Matters.

The transformation of the three communities into a single union took place through a series of agreements among member states. First, the Single European Act, signed in Luxembourg in 1986, celebrated the four freedoms of movement for goods, services, capital, and people that define the single market and introduced changes in governance. New powers were granted to the directly elected EP (as from 1979), such as the right to veto enlargements and international agreements and a required vote on legislation that related to the completion of the single market, on the basis of a legislative cooperation procedure between the EP and the Council. Decision-making rules within the Council were changed from unanimity to qualified majority voting; the cohesion policy aiming to reduce inequalities among member states was introduced; and the European Court of First Instance was added to the European judicial apparatus.

Strong acceleration took place in 1992 with the Maastricht Treaty, which marked a basic discontinuity in the institutional evolution of the EU. What made this possible were the momentous political changes of the time: the implosion of the Soviet Union, the end of the Cold War, and German reunification, which created the need to include a larger and more powerful Germany into a tighter institutional framework. Maastricht key innovations were the already mentioned three pillars structure, the co-decision legislative procedure in which the EP was recognized as representing the European people's branch of a bicameral legislative body, with the Council representing the member state branch, the further extension of qualified majority voting, the Committee of European regions, the Social Protocol (i.e. the legal mechanism adopted to resolve the impasse reached over the social provisions of the Maastricht Treaty), and the principles of subsidiarity and citizenship. In Maastricht, the Economic and Monetary Union (EMU) was also launched, a new sub-institutional system within the EU that defined aims, stages, and criteria for joining (the so-called Maastricht parameters). We will develop this aspect in Chapter 13 on the European economy, but here it is worth noting that a special regime was in fact decided for EMU, which combines the control of monetary policy by a supranational technocratic institution (the ECB) with the control of economic policies by an intergovernmental institution (the Council of Economic and Financial Ministers, Ecofin) operating under the supervision of the European Council.

The transformation of the three communities into a single union was a leap forward on the road to greater integration, that was made possible by a compromise between the supranational community method for the regulation of the single market and the intergovernmental method in the other policy areas. But this compromise, enshrined in the Maastricht Treaty, actually opened the way to the predominance of intergovernmentalism over communitarianism and of the European Council over the Commission and Parliament in EU governance. The policies of the second and third pillar (foreign and defense policy, internal affairs and justice), as well as monetary policy, are in fact key attributes of sovereignty and concern questions more directly relevant for the electoral fortunes of national governments, so that they prefer to keep decision-making on these matters within the European Council.

A third step in the process of European integration was the 1997 Amsterdam Treaty, which strengthened the legislative role of the EU through the extension of the co-decision procedure to new single market policies, introduced the flexibility of reinforced cooperation, extended the EP assent procedure for proposals submitted by the Council, and incorporated the Schengen Treaty on the free movement of people within the EU. The 2001 Nice Treaty recognized a Charter of Fundamental Rights (along the lines of the democratic constitutional charters of liberal democracies), and introduced institutional reforms in view of new enlargements. Finally, after the proposed Constitutional Treaty was not approved by French and Dutch referenda, in 2009 the Lisbon Treaty was finally approved, which includes the Treaty on the European Union (TEU) and the Treaty on the Functioning of the European Union (TFEU), reorganizes the whole matter of previous treaties, and introduces most of the new aspects that were already present in the aborted Constitutional Treaty. The Lisbon Treaty is now the institutional foundation of the EU.

Alongside the approaches and models of European integration developed by scholars, we must consider the views that are held by European citizens and their governments and reflect them more or less explicitly. The first view, which was upheld by the United Kingdom and is shared in varying degrees by other member states that do not belong to the eurozone, conceives of the EU only as an economic community, not as a political union however defined. They accept that preserving economic integration requires a supranational structure that can guarantee the respect of shared rules and the approval of common strategies concerning the single market, but they think that this structure was already put in place by the Maastricht Treaty and that the deepening of the integration process that has taken place afterwards is a threat to national sovereignty, which needs to be countered by pressing for further enlargement in order to increase the hybrid nature of the EU (Geddes, 2013).

The second view, shared by governments of the main eurozone states, acknowledges the need to put sovereignty in common, in other words to institutionalize member state cooperation, in order not only to preserve the single market but also to face global economic and political challenges. To this end, however, the intergovernmental method should be enhanced rather than community institutions.

The third view is held by those who consider themselves the heirs of Europe's founding fathers. They believe that the communitarian method should be enhanced, the role of the EU strengthened, sovereignty shared by national and supranational institutions, and that the process of integration must develop beyond nation states, although under their control.

The current Lisbon Treaty outlines an institutional architecture that aims to integrate and complement the intergovernmental and the community perspectives. The resistance to true supranational union by former EFTA states and new Eastern members has been and still is very strong, although it has not prevented the transfer of growing portions of sovereignty to Union level. The Maastricht Treaty tried to cope with the new challenges of the global market and post-Cold War politics by creating EMU and intensifying foreign policy cooperation. In 2008, the new critical juncture of the global financial crisis once again complicated the road towards closer integration (which had already received a blow from the failed EU constitutional treaty). As we argue in Chapter 14 on the EU exit strategy from the economic crisis, in order to counteract supporters of policy renationalization, pro-EU governments have chosen to reinforce the intergovernmental cooperation enshrined in the 2009 Lisbon Treaty and in other economic/financial treaties such as the European Stability Mechanism and the Fiscal Compact, on the assumption that the Europeanization of financial policies can be decided only by member state governments coordinated by the European Council and Ecofin. Ironically, the European integration that was intended to surpass the nation state is actually ensuring the latter's survival in a very complex world (Badie, 1995). The intergovernmental model is, however, exposed to both an efficiency and a legitimacy crisis: it is often not very effective since decisions come too slowly and solutions have undesirable consequences; and it suffers from a democratic deficit because of the excessive role played by technocratic and judicial bodies in ensuring compliance with intergovernmental agreements.

The intergovernmental model, functional incrementalism, and multilevel governance are key factors in explaining why and how European integration has moved on in spite of many obstacles, but cannot assure transition to a real political union. To achieve this goal, we need to develop a truly democratic polity, with political parties competing for EU government and active citizens in a pan-European public sphere, a process that in its turn requires the formation of a shared European identity alongside the various national and local identities.

3   The Basic Institutions of the European Union

The EU is a peculiar political entity, at the same time supranational and intergovernmental, a unique type of organized power; it shares some important features with sovereign nation states, but lacks others, and is constantly evolving towards an undetermined future. It is, however, less peculiar that most people think, since it can be considered an example of compound democracy, similar to the United States (USA) and Switzerland. Governance in a compound union is based on the principle of horizontal and vertical separation of powers, in order to accommodate cultural diversity and territorial and demographic asymmetries of member states. It is assured by separate institutions with distinct roles and different forms of legitimation, sharing power resources in a system of checks and balances in order to achieve common goals (Martinelli, 2007; Fabbrini, 2010). The similarity with the USA should not, however, be pushed too far, and it is very unlikely that the institutional architecture of the EU will evolve in an American direction, since the history of European states has been much longer and diverse, their claim of autonomy is much stronger, and the influence of path dependency in the integration process is greater. The EU will be able to become less exceptional in the future if it becomes a model of democratic global governance successfully adapting to the new global context to be initiated in other regions of the world (Martinelli, 2008). As Beck and Grande argue (2004), European integration stems from the desire of European nations to unite in order to be active participants in rather than passive subjects of global politics.

The legal foundation of the EU is the Lisbon Treaty, which was signed in 2007 and came into force on 1 December 2009. It consists of a series of amendments to the TEC (Rome, 1957), being renamed the Treaty on the Functioning of the European Union (TFEU), and to the TEU (Maastricht, 1992) and gives legal value to the Charter of Fundamental Rights (Nice, 2001). The Lisbon Treaty has reorganized the existing treaties, trying to put in order the institutional complexity acquired by the EU, includes most of the content of the abandoned Constitutional Treaty with the exception of such symbols as the flag, the anthem, and the preamble, and has given legal personality to the union when conducting international affairs.

However, the EU remains a very complex political entity because it is the outcome of compromises stratified in time, where the new is often added to the old rather than replacing it, and because, notwithstanding the formal suppression of the three pillar structure, the basic dualism between the intergovernmental and supranational models of decision-making is not bypassed but enhanced.

The Treaty establishes that integration proceeds through the law for most single market policies. EU legal activity consists of: (1) regulations, which are legal acts, binding, directly applicable, and immediately enforceable in all member states simultaneously; (2) directives, which set binding common goals and deadlines and may concern only a subgroup of member states, but leave to member states the choice of means and methods; they must be transposed into national law; (3) decisions, which are also binding, but refer to individual member states or economic subjects; (4) recommendations and opinions, which are not binding and provide guidelines for interpreting and implementing legislation.

There are five key governing institutions (the European Council, the Council, the Commission, the Parliament, and the ECJ), and one (the ECB) only for the eurozone states. There are a dual legislative (Council and Parliament), a dual executive (European Council and Commission), and a judiciary (ECJ).

3.1   *The European Council and the Council of Ministries*

The European Council, formed by the member countries' heads of government and heads of state who also play a government role (France, Finland, and Poland) and by the President of the Commission, "defines the general political directions and priorities of the Union" (TFEU, art. 15.1). More specifically, it outlines basic goals and strategies (even in areas not included in the existing treaties), contributes to set the agenda, takes all relevant decisions on the functioning of the union, international crises, objectives, procedures and outcomes of the open method of coordination, and can allow a simplified procedure for the revision of treaties. The Lisbon Treaty has given the European Council a permanent political head, a president elected by a qualified majority of its members for a term of two and a half years, renewable once (TFEU, art. 15.5), who should ensure the external representation of the Union on issues concerning its common foreign and security policy (TFEU, art. 15.6). The decision-making style of the European Council is consensual and based on unanimity, but qualified majority and simple majority voting are expected too. The European Council has played a crucial role in most controversial issues raised by the integration process since its informal institution in 1974. The Lisbon Treaty has enhanced its role as a kind of collective presidency of the Union and has formalized the distinction from the Council in its various formations (TFEU, art. 15.1 states that the European Council "shall not exercise legislative functions").

The Council (or Council of Ministries or Council of the Union) is made up of functional configurations (according to subject matter) of member state ministries together with the General Affairs Council that coordinates them, and exercises legislative functions. The Council and the European Council can no longer be considered as different expressions of the same institution, as they were in the past, since now the former is performing only legislative functions and the latter only executive functions (Kreppel, 2011). Although its members hold executive powers in their national governments, are not directly elected as in the American Senate and do not handle most issues relating to their states as the German Bundesrat does, the Council can be assimilated to an upper chamber that represents the governments of member states. Together with the EP, the Council forms a bicameral system that legitimates the lawmaking process through the representation of both voters and member states, as stated in TFEU, art. 289: "The ordinary legislative procedure shall consist in the joint adoption by the EP and the Council of a regulation, directive or decision on a proposal from the Commission". It should be remarked, however, that the Council is a particularly strong upper chamber, above a much weaker lower chamber; the EP may be formally "an institution of equal standing with the Council" (Fabbrini, 2010: 36), but it is not yet substantially so. The Council in its various configurations debates and approves laws, the community budget (together with the Parliament), deliberates on foreign and common security policy (on the basis of European Council resolutions), and coordinates judiciary and police cooperation, and international agreements. The Council meetings are closed and proceedings are secret, although the voting of member states is public. In relation to the importance of the issues being discussed, some functional configurations of the Council such as Ecofin have become more and more important, while others such as the Agriculture Council have kept their relevance, and still others, such as the Council of General Affairs and External Relations, have modified their role.

The activities of the Council are supported by the various Committees of Permanent Representatives of the member states (Coreper), which include both the permanent representatives of national embassies at the EU (in charge of preparing the work of the Council of General Affairs and External Relations) and lower level officers who prepare the works of the other councils. Coreper has a de facto decisional power, which stems from preparing in detail ministers' meetings, choosing procedures, making compromises on controversial issues, and confirming agreements reached in ad hoc working groups (Gozi, 2001). There are mixed feelings about the increasingly important role of Coreper; some perceive it as being a technocratic competitor for the Commission, others a defender of the Commission vis-à-vis national governments and their bureaucracies. The role of Coreper members is actually somehow ambivalent; they wear two hats, one intergovernmental when they defend national interests, the other communitarian when they prepare Council meetings (de Zwaan, 1995). But one has the impression that on the whole national interests outweigh those of the community. The tension between the intergovernmental and the communitarian perspective is also evident in the activities of the 'sherpas' – the officers of Brussels bureaucracy and member state ministries who do much of the work for the meetings of approximately 250 working groups, both permanent and ad hoc, more or less specialized, more or less influential, more or less open to pressure groups. The general coordination of this complex political/administrative machinery is assured by the secretary general, who organizes meetings, prepares minutes, and distributes approved documents; he is a kind of historical memory of the process of European integration.

3.2 *The Commission*

The Commission has the monopoly on legislative initiative, but its role is mainly executive, both in the narrow sense of acting as a kind of secretariat for the Council and in the large sense of acting as a federal government in embryo. It is in fact the principal executive body of the EU and holds important executive powers for policies such as competition and external trade. It is an institution that developed from the High Authority of the ECSC (instituted by the 1951 Treaty of Paris) and performs the tasks defined by the EEC: monitoring the implementation of EU law by member states, representing the EU in trade negotiations with other countries and in international organizations, and making new policy proposals. By virtue of these tasks, the Commission can be considered the engine of European integration. The Treaty of Lisbon has further specified the Commission role by designing a dual executive in which the European Council defines the general political directions and priorities of the Union, whereas the Commission monitors the implementation of Union law, under the control of the ECJ, and playing a coordination and management role. In some domains that have grown in time, such as the single market and the protection of competition, the Commission acts as a regulatory agency. In other policy areas, it chairs the committees responsible for the implementation of EU policy by member states. In still others, as those concerning the enlargement of the Union, it manages European Council decisions. But the Commission performs other important tasks: communication between EU institutions and European citizens, and mediation among different community institutions, being the only party present in all the phases of the legislative process and in the drawing up of the budget, which it proposes to the Council and Parliament. Moreover, the Commission has a role in managing EMU, since it submits to the Council recommendations for the draft guidelines for member states' economic policies, and warnings if those policies are likely to be incompatible with the guidelines; suggests measures to be taken if a non-eurozone member state is in difficulties as regards its balance of payments; recommends the exchange rate between the single currency and other currencies and provides general orientations for exchange-rate policy; assesses national policy plans and country-specific draft recommendations falling under the European Semester; and submits proposals to enable the Council to determine whether a member state has an excessive deficit.

The Commission is formed by a college of members with a President as primus inter pares and the assistance of an administrative body. The performance of the 12 presidents and their commissions since 1958 has been uneven; the success of Hallstein and Delors was the outcome not only of personal qualities but also, and even more importantly, of favourable economic and political conditions (sustained economic growth, political stability, and the will of member states – around the French–German axis – to uphold the integration process). The Treaty of Lisbon originally stipulated that the membership of the Commission, from 1 November 2014, was to be equivalent to two-thirds of the number of member states, but allowed the European Council to determine the number of commissioners; and, as expected, in 2009 the Council decided that the Commission would continue to consist of a number of members equal to the number of member states. The European Council, taking into account the results of the European elections, after appropriate consultations with political groups and acting by a qualified majority, proposes the candidate for President of the Commission to Parliament. The candidate is then elected by a majority of its component members; and the European Council, acting by a qualified majority and by common accord with the President-elect, adopts the list of the other persons whom it proposes for appointment as members of the Commission, on the basis of suggestions made by member states (which strongly influences the President's choice to distribute them in the various sectors of activity). Since the Treaty of Maastricht, a Commissioner's term of office has matched the EP's five-year term and is renewable.

The President and the other members of the Commission, including the High Representative of the Union for Foreign Affairs and Security Policy, are subject as a body to a vote of consent by the Parliament and are then appointed by the European Council, acting by a qualified majority. The role of Parliament has been growing in this respect, as shown by the resignation of Santer's Commission and the withdrawal of Buttiglione's candidacy by the Italian government because of the threat of a no-confidence vote by the Parliament (Buttiglione had been criticised by the Civil Liberties Committee of the EU for his views on homosexuality and the traditional role of women in the household which run contrary to those of the EU). The choice of Juncker was made on the basis of an agreement among the main European party federations to present their candidates and select the candidate of the party that received more votes in the elections. This procedure meant a further step toward the parliamentary legitimation of the Commission's President, although it seems premature to speak, as Gozi does (2001), of a fully fledged parliamentary system.

Members of the Commission form a collegium that is collectively accountable to Parliament and can decide by a simple majority vote, but actually has a consensus decision-making style and is at times characterized by a non-voting culture. Commissioners – and members of their cabinets – are required to be completely independent in the performance of their duties, in the general interest of the Union; in particular (besides being forbidden to engage in any other occupation, whether gainful or not), they may neither seek nor take instructions from any government or other external body. But this does not always happen, and national interests matter. This is the reason why Prodi's 1999–2004 Commission established the rule that cabinet chiefs and deputy chiefs had to be nationals of a country different from that of their commissioner and set limits to the number of cabinet members. But even these rules do not guarantee that the Union's interest always prevails.

The Commission's administrative apparatus consists of 33 departments (directorates-general, DGs) and 11 special departments (services), including the European Anti-Fraud Office, the Legal Service, Historical Archives, and the Publications Office. DGs and their general directors are not politically dependent on the commissioners of their sectors, although their task is managing the issues on an agenda that is defined by the commissioners themselves. Relations can often be tense, also depending on the type and degree of conflicting loyalty to the Union and the country of origin of the commissioners and of their cabinet members, and these can vary according to the nature of the policy and the political contingency.

The Commission's bureaucracy is too big and too small at the same time, too big with regard to Jean Monnet's original idea of a very agile coordinating body, and too small, since the average number of DG officers, between 400 and 900, must manage complex, time-consuming questions. Moreover, there are several instances of overlapping competences and conflicts among functional interest and decision-making styles, which the coordinating role played by the secretary general and the weekly meeting of DG general directors and deputy directors (inter-service consultation) often cannot solve.

3.3 The Parliament

The Treaty of Lisbon has sanctioned the increasingly important role of the EP. It is the institution that has evolved most in the 40 years of its life, and it now enjoys a status parallel to that of the Council in the European decision-making process. The main change introduced by the Maastricht and Amsterdam Treaties has been the procedure of co-decision that has granted the Parliament – already influential in agenda-setting – an absolute veto power in some policy areas.

In 1952, with the establishment of the ECSC, a common assembly was created, composed of 78 members nominated by the national parliaments of the six founding countries as a proportion of their population. Only in 1979 the first EP directly elected by citizens was formed, as required by the 1957 Treaty of Rome. Since 1979, there have been nine elections. Starting with the elections of May 2014, the EP consists of 751 members. The parliamentary seats are only partially apportioned according to the criterion of population of the member states, in the sense that the criterion applied is that of degressive proportionality. The seats distributed on the basis of 2019 EP election results were still 751, but after Brexit takes place, the already agreed redistribution of 705 will be: Germany 96, France 79 (+5), Italy 76 (+3), Spain 59 (+5), Poland 52 (+1), Romania 33 (+1), The Netherlands 29 (+3), Belgium, Czech Republic, Greece, Hungary, and Portugal 21, Sweden 21(+1), Austria 19 (+1), Bulgaria 17, Denmark and Finland 14 (+1), Ireland 13 (+1), Croatia 12 (+1), Lithuania 11, Latvia and Slovenia 8, Estonia 7 (+1), Cyprus, Luxembourg, and Malta 6.

EP prerogatives and responsibilities have been growing, from the first significant decision (the 1970 Budget Act) to the 1986 Single European Act, which gives the EP the power to directly amend legislation (although with the Commission's consent), to participate in the Conciliation Committee, and veto the access and association of new states. The Amsterdam Treaty consolidated the EP's equal status with the Council in the activity of conciliation and increased its role by establishing that the Commission's President nominated by the Council and all commissioners shall need approval of the EP as well. The Lisbon Treaty made co-decision the ordinary legislative procedure and extended it to new areas: according to TFEU, art. 289, "the ordinary legislation procedure shall consist in the joint adoption by the EP and the Council of a regulation, directive or decision on a proposal from the Commission". To conclude, the EP, although still enjoying less institutional power than national parliaments, is gradually transforming itself from a consulting body into a real legislative assembly, which actually approves about two-thirds of all laws concerning the lives of EU citizens. The EP and the Council in its dual form of state's and government's heads and ministries concur to the double legitimation of the European decision-making process by representing both EU citizens and member states.

3.4   The Court of Justice

The term Court of Justice of the European Union officially designates two courts and specialised tribunals. The Court of Justice of the European Communities – later the Court of Justice but commonly referred to as the ECJ – was born in 1952 in Luxembourg and officially instituted by the 1957 Treaty of Rome with the task of interpreting community norms and solving disputes among member states. It is composed of one judge for each member state, who stays for six months in the office, together with 11 advocates general. Since the number of cases the ECJ has to discuss has greatly increased over time – as well as the slowness of the trials – owing to the growth of community competences, a second court was created, the Court of First Instance, renamed the General Court by the Lisbon Treaty, which is formed by 47 judges, to be increased in 2019 to two judges for each member state. The Court of Justice deals with requests for preliminary rulings from national courts, certain actions for annulment, and appeals. The General Court rules on actions for annulment brought by individuals, companies, and, in some cases, EU governments. In practice, this means that this court deals mainly with competition law, state aid, trade, agriculture, and trademarks. The Nice Treaty established the institution of specialized tribunals, the first of which, the Civil Service Tribunal, from 2005, is concerned with disputes between EU institutions and their employees.

The ECJ is similar to a national constitutional court and has made a fundamental contribution to the constitutionalization of community law. In its first decades, the ECJ established with some famous verdicts the supremacy of community law over the law of member states and its direct applicability for individuals and corporations, arguing that "member states have limited, although in circumscribed domains, their sovereign rights and have therefore created a set of rights which is binding for their citizens and themselves" (van Gend & Loos vs. the Dutch government 1962 and Costa vs. Enel, Simmenthal vs. Commission 1964). Profiting from the institutional impasse between the Council and the Commission during the 'empty chair' conflict, the ECJ assumed an increasingly important role in adjudicating disputes between EU institutions and the member states. Union law supremacy allowed the Commission to deregulate national legal regimes, while defining a supranational regulatory structure. Later on, in the late 1970s, the ECJ contributed to the further constitutionalization of the common market by establishing the mutual recognition principle, which states that a product legally produced and commercialized in a given member state shall be accepted in any other member state (Cassis de Dijon, Commission vs. the German government, Francovich & Bonifaci vs. Italian government).

The ECJ provides the authentic interpretation of European treaties and legislation (preliminary rulings), determines whether a national law or practice is compatible with EU law, defines the powers of EU institutions and their mutual relations, enforces the law (infringement proceedings) whenever a national government fails to comply, annuls EU legal acts (actions for annulment) whenever an EU act is believed to violate EU treaties or fundamental rights, and ensures the EU takes action (actions for failure to act) when the Parliament, Council, and Commission must make certain decisions under certain circumstances. If they don't, EU governments, other EU institutions, or (under certain conditions) individuals or companies can complain to the Court and sanction EU institutions (actions for damages), since any person or company who has had their interests harmed as a result of the action or inaction of the EU or its staff can take action against them through the Court.

There are two ways in which a private individual or a company that has suffered damage as a result of action or inaction by an EU institution or its staff can take action against them. First, this can be directly before the General Court, if a decision by an EU institution has affected the plaintiff directly and individually (direct appeal). Secondly, it can be indirectly through national courts, which may decide to request a preliminary verdict by the ECJ on the interpretation of community law related to the case (reference for a preliminary ruling). In this way, EU law is made much more stable through its decentralized application, which is indirectly given to a great number of national judges, beyond their governments (Mancini, 2000). In spite of some disagreements with the ECJ, national judges have often seen in the Court an opportunity to strengthen their role vis-à-vis their national parliaments and governments.

The role of the judiciary is particularly important in the division of powers in the EU. The ECJ has the primary responsibility of verifying whether decisions taken by both EU institutions and member states comply with the basic principles of EU treaties. The Commission's treaty infringement procedures against a member state are the last step in the ECJ process of control. National sovereignty is no longer limitless, since member states must respect Union laws and implement their policies according to those laws if they want to avoid ECJ sanctions.

3.5 The Central Bank

The ECB is the central bank responsible for monetary policy of the nineteen EU member countries that have adopted the euro as their currency. The principal goal of the ECB is to maintain price stability in the euro area, thus helping to preserve the purchasing power of the euro. Its primary responsibility, linked to its main goal of price stability, is formulating monetary policy. This involves making decisions about monetary objectives, key interest rates, the supply of reserves in the euro system, and establishing guidelines for implementing those decisions. The ECB was established by the Maastricht Treaty, which affirmed its institutional, instrumental, personal, and financial independence after an explicit request by the German government (the German request for a politically independent central bank was matched by a French request to keep control of economic policies at national level, a compromise that has affected EU economic policy effectiveness and coherence). The ECB President and Executive Committee members are nominated by national governments with a non-renewable eight-year term and the ECB is committed to presenting a yearly report on its activity to the EP, the European Council, and Ecofin. In addition, the EU President and the Commission President participate in the meetings of the ECB's Executive Committee and the ECB President takes part in Ecofin meetings. The ECB – headquartered in Frankfurt am Main – has been responsible for monetary policy in the euro area since 1 January 1999, when the euro currency was first adopted by some EU members.

The ECB Governing Council is the body within the ECB that takes decisions on eurozone monetary policy. Monetary policy decision meetings are held every six weeks, and the ECB is transparent about the reasoning behind its decisions. It holds a press conference after each such meeting, and later publishes the minutes of the meeting. The Eurosystem comprises the ECB and the national member states' central banks. The Eurosystem is responsible for the practical implementation of ECB policy (such as implementing policy, holding and managing foreign reserves, operating in the foreign exchange market, and ensuring the payments system runs smoothly). The ECB is also the EU body responsible for banking supervision. In conjunction with national central bank supervisors, it operates the Single Supervisory Mechanism (SSM), which began in November 2014. The decisions involved in this function are mainly aimed at ensuring the safety and soundness of the European banking system. Part of the rationale for the SSM is to ensure consistent banking supervision practices across member country banking systems.

A delicate problem raised by the creation of the ECB has been the relations with EU member states that have not joined the common currency and are afraid of being excluded from vital decision-making. The solution to this problem has two elements. First, there has been the formation of the Euro Group, made up of the finance ministers of the eurozone member states, which meets before Ecofin meetings and postpones decisions to when all EU member state ministers are present (in reality, eurozone ministers' decisions are simply ratified by Ecofin). Secondly, an articulated structure has been set up, with three elements. The Executive Board consists of six members with permanent voting rights (President, Vice-President, and four members jointly nominated by governments), and is responsible for the implementation of monetary policy defined by the Governing Council and the day-to-day running of the bank. The Governing Council is formed by the Executive Board and the governors (or equivalent) of each member's national central bank, in this way regaining some of the power lost: as membership of the eurozone has expanded, so the governing council has increased, making necessary a system of rotating voting rights among the national bank governors (Executive Board members have permanent voting rights, as the Governing Council is now too large for all members to vote at each meeting). The General Council is a body dealing with transitional issues of the euro (such as fixing the exchange rates of currencies being replaced by the euro), which will continue to exist until all EU member states adopt the euro, at which point it will be dissolved. It is composed of the

President and the Vice-President together with the governors of all the EU's national central banks, including non eurozone member states.

ECB decisions are collectively taken, in spite of key strategic differences on monetary policy between supporters of fiscal austerity and supporters of economic and employment growth (both aims are legitimized by EEC, art. 105).

4 EU Decision-making

The EU decision-making process reflects the dualism between the supranational method and the intergovernmental method and is influenced by the complexity of multilevel governance, which implies a joint exercise of competences and responsibilities. In single market-related policies, the Treaty of Lisbon has codified a supranational institutional system of shared power between the Union and member states with a dual executive formed by the Commission and the Council of Ministers and a dual legislative body formed by the European Parliament and the European Council of heads of state and government. The division of labour in policymaking among EU institutions and member states is in these policy areas sufficiently clear: the Commission has the power of legislative initiative, the Council the power to discuss key questions and to approve the norms, the Parliament is involved in the process of co-decision with a possible veto power, and member states implement policies, both individually and collectively, in the Council of Ministers. On the other hand, in policy areas that are either fundamental in the exercise of sovereign power, such as foreign and security policy and fiscal policy, or electorally more delicate areas, such as labour and welfare policies, integration is pursued through the voluntary policy coordination by national governments. In this respect, the Lisbon Treaty has reproduced the Maastricht compromise. There is no standard decision-making process that applies to every policy and for all occasions, but a variety of decisional modes and paths that are influenced by the dialectic between the supranational and the intergovernmental regimes.

Various typologies of EU policymaking have been suggested. Wallace (1983) lists, alongside the communitarian and intergovernmental method (always adopted for constituent policies), the regulatory method (as in the policy of competition), the distributive method (as in agricultural policy), policy coordination (as in the EU employment strategy), and intensified transgovernmentalism (as in the Schengen Agreement and other instances of reinforced cooperation). Peterson and Bomberg (1999) distinguish between: 'historical' decisions – such as the signing of treaties or enlargement to include new member states – that are taken according to the intergovernmental method, and see the Council of heads of states and governments as primary actors; policy-setting decisions – such as the approval of a directive aimed at creating the single market in a given economic sector, where the intergovernmental method prevails again (with a key role being played by the Council of Ministers and Coreper), but acts together with the Parliament in the growing number of matters that are subject to co-decision; and routine decisions or decisions that have a more limited, technical nature – such as the adoption of a new manufacturing or marketing standard – where the communitarian method prevails with the active involvement of various Commission DGs, Parliament's permanent committees and Council's working groups. Nugent (1994) in his turn focuses on the principal factors impinging on the policy process: the procedures envisaged by the treaties – consultation, cooperation, co-decision and assent procedure, and reinforced cooperation (the important innovation introduced by the Amsterdam and Nice treaties); the areas to which the object of the decision refers, distinguishing between the supranational policies of the first pillar (exchange liberalization and single market) and the governmental policies of the second pillar (foreign and security policy) and third pillar (justice and internal affairs); the degree of generality/specificity of questions and the degree of political relevance (macro-, meso-, and micro-level policies); the preservation or change in the balance between different levels of governance; and, finally, the role played by exceptional political events, such as, for instance, the implosion of the Soviet Union, which opened opportunities for EU enlargement to the East, or the 2001 terrorist attacks, which prompted urgent resolutions concerning the second and third pillar.

But the most effective criterion for defining the type of decisional process remains the dichotomy between supranational communitarian method and intergovernmental method. The basic distinction is between policies: those related to the single market, which can be transferred to a higher level, and policies that cannot be delegated because they are considered (or at least have been until now) to be essential components of national sovereignty. The dichotomy is not absolute, however, since most policies are of a mixed nature and can be defined either quasi-intergovernmental or quasi-supranational.

It was the Maastricht Treaty that established different policies should be regulated by different institutional regimes. The supranational communitarian method is clearly predominant in the core areas of European integration, the policies of the so-called first pillar, single market and foreign trade, but also in regional and environmental policies. Here, legislation must be co-decided and pass through approval by the EP and the Council, while the Commission keeps the monopoly of policy initiative. On the other hand, the intergovernmental method is exclusive in the revision of treaties and in questions of enlargement, and is predominant in the policies of the second and third pillar; that is, foreign and security policy and judicial cooperation in criminal law (referred as justice and internal affairs policy before the Amsterdam Treaty), as well as in social policy (Chapter 12) and in several aspects of economic policy (Chapter 13 and Chapter 14).

As noted in TEU, art. 22, it is the European Council that defines the principles and general guidelines of foreign and security policy, decides common strategies, and determines ends and time frames, meaning that the Union and member states must commit and take common actions, thus assuring effectiveness and coherence. The coordinating role is performed by the High Representative for CFSP, who is also Vice-President of the European Commission; given the still considerable fragmentation in European foreign policy, however, the High Representative enjoys less power than the foreign ministers of the most important member states. Here the EP and the Commission are kept at the margins, although members of the EP (MEPs) claim their competence over crucial international issues such as human rights. In Maastricht, it was established, however, that the economic and monetary policy of the EU would be defined and regulated in a separate institutional regime that, although within the first pillar, was intergovernmental in nature.

The most important decision-making processes take place in the intergovernmental conferences that can amend treaties and thus modify the institutional structure of the EU. Here the approach is clearly intergovernmental; the constituent power rests in the member states, proving the non-federal character of the EU. Any reform of the treaties is the outcome of a negotiation among member states that have to approve unanimously and then ratify the approvals one by one according to their own procedure (parliamentary vote or popular referendum). These decisions are taken outside the ordinary institutional framework. Parliament and Commission have no power, although the latter can propose a constitutional revision by asking one or more member states to bring up the matter (the Council can decide by a majority vote whether to proceed). Moreover, the Commission informally participates in the negotiation, through research centres, experts, and ad hoc groups, with the aim of analysing key issues, suggesting possible agreements and compromises, involving European civil society, and with the constant attempt to expand EU competences to new areas and extend the field of application of qualified majority voting in the Council. Even the EP is not completely cut off; some member states, such as Italy, consider the approval of a new treaty by the EP a de facto ratification, although legally not binding. Since the 1980s, the rhythm of treaty revision has accelerated, with a continuous referral to intergovernmental conferences in order to solve problems where agreement has not been reached. The Single European Act referred the monetary question to a further conference, while the Maastricht Treaty referred to an intergovernmental conference that led to the Amsterdam Treaty, which in its turn set up a new conference, resulting in the Nice Treaty.

The community method is, on the other hand, clearly predominant in the EU legislative process, which is rather complex. The Lisbon Treaty foresees several decision-making procedures for the formation and adoption of EU laws, which involve European institutions in various ways and to varying degrees. The Commission has the monopoly on legislative initiative, and formulates an initial proposal to indicate the legal basis; that is, the treaty's article. In the course of time, the Commission has developed increasingly institutionalized consultation mechanisms with member states' governments and bureaucracies, and a variety of non-governmental stakeholders (organized interests, pressure groups, lobbies of various kinds), created policy networks, mobilized expert groups, drafted white and green papers, and developed multi-annual strategies such as Europe 2010 and Lisbon Strategy 2020. The Commission sends its proposal to the Council and the Parliament, which discuss it and can present amendments in the form of consultation, cooperation, assent procedure, and co-decision.

Consultation is the original form of procedure, and until 1987 the only one involving the EP, but today it is residual. Accordingly, the Commission should present a proposal to the Council, which makes a decision about it and can modify it only by an unanimous vote, after acquiring the opinion of the Economic and Social Committee and of the Committee of Regions and after consulting the EP – which can express only non-binding suggestions and amendments.

Cooperation, although not explicitly envisaged in the Treaty, is based on the previous procedure but with a greater role for the EP, and concerns only questions of EMU (TEU, art. 99.5 and 106.2). The Commission's proposal is sent first to the EP and then to the Council, which decides with a qualified majority vote and submits the proposal for a second reading to the EP; within three months the EP can either approve it or not express its opinion (in which case the Council approves), or reject the proposal (in which case the Council can bypass the rejection by a unanimous vote), or formulate amendments that are presented to the Commission; at this point, if the Commission endorses the amendments and the Council approves them by a qualified majority, the proposal is adopted; if the Commission rejects the amendments, but the Council approves them by a qualified majority, the decision is adopted; if the Council rejects the amendments a Committee of Conciliation is set up, where if an agreement is reached between the Council at qualified majority and the EP at absolute majority the decision is adopted; but if there is no agreement the Council confirms its rejection. As we can see, the EP plays a more relevant role than in the previous procedure of consultation, insofar as it can propose amendments, but the Council still has the last word.

The assent procedure is not employed for ordinary legislation (with the exception of cohesion policy), but extraordinary decisions such as the entrance of new member states, the signing of association and cooperation agreements with third countries, the imposition of sanctions on a member state for serious and continuing violations of fundamental rights, the approval of reinforced cooperation, specific tasks assigned to the ECB, statute modification of the system of central banks, and methods of election of EP members. The key actor is the Council here, since the Parliament can only accept or reject a proposal without amendments and the Commission can play a role only in cases in which the Council decides with a qualified majority, not a unanimous, vote.

The most important decision-making procedure is co-decision, in which legislative power is jointly exercised by the Parliament and the Council. The Commission presents a proposal to both bodies, and the Council can adopt it at first reading if it accepts EP amendments or the EP has not presented any amendment. In case there is no agreement, the Council adopts a 'common position' that it notifies to the EP, stating the reasons for it. At this point, it starts the second phase of the process: the EP can decide by absolute majority not to respond or to accept the Council's text, which is then adopted at second reading, or to reject it, with the consequence that it is not adopted, or to propose amendments, in which case the amended text goes back to the Council. Then, if, after hearing the Commission's opinion, the Council does not approve all amendments within three months, the third phase is opened, with the convening within six weeks of the Conciliation Committee. It is worth noting here the important role played by the Commission, since according to whether or not it approves or rejects the EP's amendments, the Council should decide by majority vote the amendments accepted by the Commission and by unanimous vote those rejected. The Conciliation Committee, consisting of one member for each member state and an equivalent number of MEPs, has the task of settling the controversial issues through a negotiation between the Parliament and the Council, with the Commission playing an unofficial mediating role. If the Committee finds agreement on a common text within six weeks, Parliament should approve it by absolute majority and the Council by qualified majority.

The co-decision procedure was introduced with the Maastricht Treaty and has increasingly widened its area of application in the Amsterdam and Nice treaties to the point of applying to most policies of the 'first pillar', with the relevant exceptions of agricultural policy, competition policy and fiscal policy (to which it applies the consultation procedure), cohesion policy (to which it applies the assent procedure), and EMU (to which it applies the reinforced co-operation procedure). Co-decision is in some respect similar to the legislative process in the USA, since in both cases the approval of a law requires a widespread and reiterated negotiation that aims at building the necessary consensus and involves a plurality of institutional actors in plenary sessions and subcommittee meetings, thus allowing an intense lobbying activity by interest groups. The key difference lies in the fact that in the USA neither the President nor the Congress enjoys a decision-making primacy, whereas in the EU there is an asymmetry of power between the Council in its double form, on the one hand, and the Parliament and Commission, on the other. In the EU, the centre is weak. As Giscard d'Estaing observed, in order to justify the compromise on the text of the Constitutional Treaty reached at the Convention, one has to acknowledge that nation states continue to exist, and in the end, the seat of decision is the Council where nation states are represented. Parliament legislates, the Commission identifies, suggests, and to some extent promotes the European common good, but decisions are in the final instance in the hands of the Council.

The EU is a complex political entity with a multilevel and multi-stakeholder governance, where national governments are key actors together with supranational institutions and the intergovernmental model of governance interacts with the communitarian one. It is a union in the making that goes on through a permanent institutional negotiation and a sequence of difficult compromises. It is today in a stalemate from which it should, and can, be released through a set of institutional reforms, such as those we suggest in the Conclusion of this volume.

CHAPTER 11

Parties, Elections, Pressure Groups

1 Transnational Party Federations and European Parliament Party Groups

There are two different and complementary types of European political parties: European level political parties – that are transnational party federations – and supranational party groups in the European Parliament (EP). To simplify, we will call the former 'europarties' and the latter 'EP party groups'. We will examine their interrelations as well their relations with the member states' national parties. Europarties are political alliances registered under EU law; they are officially recognized and codified political actors: Maastricht Treaty art. 138A – renumbered 191 in the Amsterdam Treaty – states: "political parties at the European level are an important factor of integration in the Union. They contribute to forming a European political awareness and to expressing the will of citizens of the Union". In 2001, on a proposal from the Commission, a second comma was added to art. 191, which states: "the Council, deliberating according to art. 251 procedure [co-decision with the EP], determines the statute of political parties at the European level and specifically the norms concerning their financing". Art. 191 has been implemented with the statute approved in November 2013 by the EP and Council and with the previously approved (December 2007) regulation, which together have established the public financing of European-level political parties as a specific item of the European Union budget (in order to distinguish them from EP groups); their absolute responsibility for campaign in EP elections; the prohibition on using the EU budget grants to finance national parties; and the creation of European political foundations. The Lisbon Treaty has transposed these norms in TEU art. 10, par. 4 (strangely enough, without the sentence: "important factor of integration in the Union") and in TFEU art. 224.

The formation process of europarties is, however, under way, since the Commission's proposal to modify their statute/regulation is still being discussed by the Council and the EP. In 2011, the Parliament adopted a resolution – known as the Giannakou Report – that suggests changes aimed at strengthening them. Parties and their related foundations are given a legal personality according to EU law; they are required to adopt rigorous rules of internal democracy and a common legal and fiscal status based on EU law; while less complex financing procedures and more effective sanctions for violations are established. In September 2012, the Commission resumed its discussion of EP proposals, and in March 2013 it enacted another communication that was aimed at affirming the key role of transnational federations "in making the citizens' voice heard and in bridging the gap between EU politics and the citizenship", and asking that citizens are informed of the relations between EP election candidates' affiliations to national parties and that europarties designate their candidates for the role of President of the Commission (a decision reiterated by the July 2013 EP resolution, which was met in 2014, but not in the 2019 elections).

On 27 February 2018, the Council and the Parliament reached an agreement on a targeted revision of the rules for European political parties, aimed at strengthening their European dimension, ensuring a fairer distribution of funds and modernizing EU electoral law. The new rules on elections to the EP received the consent of Parliament on 4 July 2018 and were adopted by the Council on 13 July. For them to enter into force, approval by all EU member states, in line with their respective constitutional requirements, is also required.

The amendments to the 1976 Electoral Act include new provisions on 'double voting', voting in third countries, different voting methods, and the visibility of European political parties in member states. An obligatory threshold of 2 per cent to 5 per cent is set for constituencies, including single-constituency member states, with more than 35 seats. Member states will have to comply with this obligation in time for the EP elections in 2024 at the latest.

Other changes concern conditions for registration of European political parties, the funding of parties and foundations, infringement sanctions, and transparency requirements. As far as registration is concerned, the Council and the EP have agreed that in future only parties – and no longer individuals – can sponsor the creation of European political parties. Sponsorship of several European parties is prohibited. This will put an end to multiparty memberships and the creation of pseudo-parties that are sponsored mainly by individual members. This is intended to make sure that European political parties have a genuine pan-European dimension.

The funding of European political parties will also become more proportional to their support at the European elections. The amount distributed in proportion to their share of members of the EP (MEPs) is increased from 85 per cent to 90 per cent. This will further discourage the creation of European political parties mainly for the purpose of receiving EU money, as the fixed amount is reduced from 15 per cent to 10 per cent.

The new rules will also make it easier for parties and foundations to access EU funds by lowering the cofinancing requirement. This will decrease from 15 per cent to 10 per cent for European political parties and to 5 per cent for European political foundations, enabling more public funding for their activities. This change recognizes the difficulties that parties and foundations have encountered in meeting the current threshold. It will mitigate the risk that they will use dubious financial practices to reach the required level for their own resources.

Other changes are aimed at better protecting the EU's financial interests in case of fraud. The EP has not been able to recover funds from some parties and foundations that have gone bankrupt. The new rules allow for recovery from natural persons in certain cases if they are responsible for the infringement. The European Public Prosecutor's office is called on to investigate alleged abuses in the future. The conditions for deregistering parties are also set out in more detail, which will simplify and speed up the process.

Finally, the new rules will increase transparency for citizens. Parties in EU member states will have to display on their websites the logo and the programme of the European political parties to which they are affiliated in order for the European parties to receive EU funding. The links between European political parties and their member parties have thus become more visible for the citizens ahead of the 2019 EP elections.

Once the amendments have entered into force, current European political parties will have two months to provide evidence that they continue to satisfy the conditions for registration. If they fail to do so, they and their affiliated foundations will be removed from the register. This will not affect funding for the budget year 2018, but in order to receive EU funds in 2019, parties and foundations will have to comply with the new rules.

In spite of these efforts to strengthen the role of European institutions, the context remains not very favourable for parties (Bartolini, 2012), and relations between europarties and EP groups are not yet completely clear.

Europarties and EP political groups are linked insofar as they are both expressions of Europe's various party families, but they are autonomous from each other and have different functions. Europarties can include parties of countries that are non-EU members, as in the case of the Ukrainian parties that joined the European People's Party (Timus & Lightfoot, 2014). Europarties are transnational party federations, whose members are national parties rather than individual citizens (but there are exceptions); their strength does not depend on the number but on the political and electoral power of their members and of their countries of reference; their main role is coordinating the political agendas of member parties, thus influencing EU strategic choices. They also tend to be elitist with a low participation rate (Van Hecke, 2010). EP groups are, on the other hand, groupings of EP-elected members: deeply engaged in parliamentary debates, they are the constituent units of a supranational party system (Hix, Noury, & Roland, 2007). Europarties work alongside the ideologically similar groups in the EP, but are distinct from them.

As of February 2020, there are ten registered Europarties, recognized and financed by the EU (Authority on European Political Parties and European Political Foundations, 2018), *which* differ in terms of their position in the right/left continuum, ideology, attitude toward European integration and number of MEPs and EU commissioners:

1) *The European People's Party (EPP)*, founded by primarily Christian democratic parties in 1976, has since broadened its membership to include liberal conservative parties and other parties with centre-right political perspectives. The EPP has been the largest party in the EP since 1999 and in the European Council since 2002, and it now includes 74 parties from 39 countries.

2) *The Party of European Socialist (PES)* from all EU member states plus Norway; other parties from non-EU European countries are admitted to the PES as associate or observer parties. It has been either the first or the second largest party in the EP. In 2019, EP PES is represented by the group Socialists and Democrats.

3) *The Alliance of Democrats and Liberals for Europe (ALDE)* was established as the first true transnational political party in 1993 and is now composed of 60 national-level liberal parties from across Europe, mainly active in the EU. In 2019, EP ALDE is represented by the group *Renew Europe* (we will use both names as it is done in the media).

4) *The European Green Party (EGP)* is a federation of pro-Europeanist political parties across Europe supporting green politics. The EGP cooperates with the European Free Alliance (EFA) to form the Greens/EFA group in the EP.

5) *The Alliance of Conservatives and Reformists in Europe (ACRE)*, which comprises 24 centre-right parties from EU and non-EU countries, is a conservative, centre-right to right-wing, soft to hard eurosceptic party, with a main focus on reforming the EU on the basis of anti-federalist, Eurorealism, as opposed to total rejection of the EU.

6) *The Identity and Democracy Party (ID)*, formerly known as the Movement for a Europe of Nations and Freedom (MENF), is an alliance of right-wing to far-right, national-populist, nativist, and hard eurosceptic parties founded in 2014. Its political group in the EP was Europe of Nations and Freedom, which was succeeded in 2019 by Identity and Democracy.

7) *The Party of the European Left (PEL)*, commonly abbreviated European Left, is an association of softly eurosceptic democratic-socialist and communist parties in the EU and other European countries. Elected MEPs from its member parties sit in the EP in the Left–Nordic Green Left (GUE/NGL) group.

8) *The European Free Alliance (EFA)*, pro-European, stands for "a Europe of Free Peoples based on the principle of subsidiarity", and brings together 40 progressive nationalist, regionalist, and autonomist parties from across the EU who represent stateless nations, regions, and traditional ethnic minorities.
9) *The European Democratic Party (EDP)* is a centrist, social-liberal, and federalist party that stands for a more democratic, integrated EU closer to its citizens. Between 2004 and now (end of 2019) the EDP has formed a joint European parliamentary group with ALDE.
10) *The European Christian Political Movement (ECPM)* is an association of national parties from across Europe that share traditional Christian politics; they are softly eurosceptic and generally more socially conservative than the EPP.

Moreover, there are four other parties, all hard eurosceptic, that are not recognized by the EU:

a) *The European Alliance for Freedom (EAF)*, a right-wing Eurosceptic political party, whose members are not national parties but individuals.
b) *The Europeans United for Democracy (EUD)*, a eurosceptic and self-described eurorealist alliance of parties and movements.
c) *The Alliance of European National Movements (AENM)*, a group formed in Budapest in October 2009 by a number of nationalist parties and national movements mostly from Eastern European countries, who conceive European integration as a confederation of sovereign nation states.
d) *The Alliance for Peace and Freedom (APF)*, a far-right party that works for the dissolution of the EU, which it considers as an obstacle to the Europe of nations, and for the permanence and safeguarding of 'ancestral' European traditions, such as the Christian heritage.

Two other parties were dissolved: the Alliance for Direct Democracy in Europe (ADDE), which was closed down in 2016 after an auditors' inquiry and legally dissolved on 24 May 2017; and the Movement for a Europe of Liberties and Democracy (MELD), which was opposed to further European integration, was dissolved in 2015 by the EP owing to misuse of EU funding.

These lists do not fully cover the diversified world of confederations, networks, and alliances organized at European supranational level; most of them are short lived, with very narrow support or becoming defunct after a very short period, such as Euronat, the Movement for European Reform, European Democratic Union, Platform for Transparency, and the European National Front. But others have better prospects, an example being the interesting case of Volt Europa, the first pan-European political party to run under the same name and on the same policy platform in local, national, and European elections.

2   National Parties, Europarties and EP Party Groups

Europarties (transnational federations) and EP groups (supranational parties) affect European politics less than the national parties of member states. With regard to the main criteria for assessing party relevance – such as influencing public choices, holding power positions, and gaining votes in elections – national parties are more relevant than europarties and EP groups. Europarties are not much involved in EP elections: they organize meetings, prepare ideological manifestos, and define priorities for EP groups' agendas, but they do not manage electoral campaigns nor select candidates – with the exception of those europarties that in 2014 chose their candidates for Commission President. All important EU governance roles – Commission President and Commissars, Council President, EP President, High Representative for foreign and security policy – are essentially decided by national parties. On the eve of Council's sessions, informal summits are held (on a regular basis for the three main federations of the People's Party, Socialists, and Liberal-Democrats) with the participation of national government heads, national parties' presidents, commissioners, and leaders of the transnational party federation and EP groups belonging to the same party family, with the aim of reaching an agreement on issues to be discussed and of coordinating the party's role in EU legislative and executive powers. These summits help connecting political leaders acting at the various levels of European governance (the more so with the growing importance of the co-decision procedure), but parties at the national level strongly influence europarties and government priorities of member states tend to prevail on the EU supranational agenda.

Transnational party federations and EP party groups suffer from the same crisis of representation as national parties do (ideological decline, organizational weakening, growing lack of confidence among citizens), but they are even weaker, more fragmented, and more poorly organized, owing to two main causes: the special nature of EU governance (outlined in Chapter 10) and the complexity of member states' party systems. The EU institutional framework does not favour europarties, especially insofar as the intergovernmental method prevails over the supranational one in policymaking, and the EP still plays an unaccomplished role. The political representation of EU citizens is ambivalent: on the one hand, it is directly rooted in the EP (TEU, art. 10, par. 2); on the other, it is mediated through national governments, which are member of the European Council and are accountable to their national parliaments and constituencies.

National parties, especially those of the most important member countries, have a great influence in European politics because they exert their power in the Council (in the dual capacity of state and government heads' council and ministers' council). On the other hand, transnational party federations are weak and heterogeneous aggregates of national parties, and do not control party groups in the EP. These latter are weak too, since the EP, although widening the scope of its powers, still lacks many key parliamentary powers, first of all the approval of the budget law, that has been the historical *raison d'être* of representative bodies, in accordance with the principle of no taxation without representation. The absence of common voting rules for electing MEPs also contributes to the explanation of why party groups, although more active than europarties, tend to be weak, heterogeneous, and hardly capable of developing a coherent pan-European strategy.

The weakness of europarties is secondly due to the quite different political histories, party systems and electoral methods of EU member states. Party systems have been structured in quite different ways depending on the timing and sequence of critical cleavages in nation-building and industrialization, on the Cold War division between Western and Eastern Europe and on the varying impact of the recent economic crisis.

The classic interpretation of European party formation is Rokkan and Lipset's theory of critical cleavages in the processes of nation-building and industrial revolution, which remained frozen for a long time after they had been formed (Lipset & Rokkan, 1967; Rokkan, 1970). The first two cleavages, linked to nation-building and the historical consequences of Protestant reform and the French Revolution, were the one between centre and periphery (i.e. the resistance by peripheral regions, linguistic, and cultural minorities to national elites and centre bureaucracies), and the one between church and state (i.e. the conflict between the sovereign state and churches' claims of autonomy, mostly in education). The new cleavages generated by the industrial revolution were then added to the old ones: the one between town and country and the one between the bourgeoisie and the working class. This situation was further complicated by ideological disputes between socialists and communists and between proletarian internationalism and 'socialism in one country'. From these five main cleavages stem the party families that for a long time – through various combinations – structured the party systems of European democracies: the family of liberal and radical parties and that of conservative parties (both secular and bourgeois), the family of socialist and social-democratic parties and that of communists (both originally being workers' parties), the family of Christian-Democratic parties (mostly Catholic, but also Protestant), the family of peasant parties, that of ethno-regionalist parties, and that of the radical right.

In the last decades of the 20th century, the party landscape changed again, as a result of two landmark events: one was inherently political, the collapse of the Soviet Union, and the other was primarily socioeconomic, the post-industrial revolution and contemporary globalization. The ideological appeal of traditional parties, first of all Christian and communist, which were related to the old cleavages, weakened, while, on the one hand, new political actors rooted in post-materialistic culture, emerged such as the Greens and feminist movements, and on the other hand, populist nationalism re-emerged, stressing national and subnational identities against economic and cultural globalization, such as Front National (FN), UKIP, Lega, Fidesz, PiS, and the Catalan parties.

If we apply the Rokkan/Lipset framework at EU level, we note that the cleavage between the centre and the periphery is by far the most important, much more relevant than the one between labour and capital. National interests and the related ideological justifications and policy priorities play a more relevant role than class interests and socioeconomic inequalities. The main cleavages in contemporary EU have been: (a) the cleavage between continental Europe and the UK (and between two varieties of capitalism) that has been ended by Brexit; (b) the cleavage between the 'Northern' member states, for which fiscal austerity and inflation control are policy priorities, and the 'Southern' member states, for which growth and jobs are policy priorities; (c) the cleavage between the older EU member states of Central and Western Europe, which support deeper political integration, and the most recent members of Eastern Europe, engaged in a complex transition to democracy and free market, which are eurosceptic.

Until recently, European elections have been considered less important than national ones. Europarties seldom offer voters clearly defined programmes and policy proposals on genuinely European issues. National parties mostly focus on domestic issues and voters' preferences are often based on domestic politics. As a consequence, adopting a supranational perspective in European policymaking is difficult for MEPs; this is also the case because their selection is seldom made taking into account their competence in European affairs. The link between voters' preferences and legislative production is weak, since competitors in the electoral arena are different from the actors in the legislative arena (Sozzi, 2013). This situation helps to explain the lower turnover in EP elections than in member states' national elections (about 20 points lower in 2014). Contrary to a fully fledged union such as the United States, where the elections for Congress are considered more important than those for state parliaments, the EP elections are often believed by political leaders, media, and the voters themselves as less relevant, and in essence second to national elections (Reif & Schmitt, 1980), being closer to an opinion poll that evaluates and sanctions national governments rather than an instrument through which a coherent majority in the EP is formed (Blondel, Sinnott, & Svenson, 1998). A vicious circle has taken shape: the limited role of the EP favours the continuing dominance by national parties, which do not intend to invest much in European politics; while weak transnational federations and EP party groups fail to form ideologically and programmatically coherent coalitions that are capable of developing an authentically supranational strategy. Their weakness fosters the EU democratic deficit, in the double sense that the EP does not control the European executive and europarties do not adequately represent citizens' will. Since parties at the European level are weak, interest groups are strong, actively lobbying at various points of entry in the decision-making process.

As we argue later, however, this situation is changing. The 2014 EP elections made a difference, since the aggressive campaign by europhobic parties forced all the others to focus on European issues. But a real change took place in the 2019 elections; after decades of steady decline, there was a high turnover increase, from 43 per cent in 2009 and 42.53 per cent in 2014 to 51 per cent in 2019, which can be explained by the fact that the core issue of the campaign was the future of the EU and the core cleavage was that between traditional pro-EU parties and national-populist ones.

However, europarties remain weak, also because of a limited financial and organizational autonomy. Until the approval of their statute in 2003, europarties were indirectly financed by EP groups. After this date, they have been directly supported by the EU budget with control by the Audit Court of legitimacy and regularity of income and expenditure on the basis of yearly reports drafted by an independent certifying authority: 10 per cent is distributed in equal shares among all beneficiary parties, while the other 90 per cent is distributed in proportion to their number of MEPs (with the provision that a member can only belong to one group). The costs that are regarded as eligible for financing must be directly linked to the goals of the party political programme (campaign costs, studies and research, administrative expenses, technical assistance, events, publications). Appropriations have more than doubled, but are still short of guaranteeing organizational autonomy from national parties (Schmitter, 2000), another reason for this being that national parties represent by far the most important among the additional financial sources. In conclusion, as stated by the 6 April 2011 EP resolution, parties at European level are umbrella organizations of national parties, not always homogeneous from a political and ideological point of view, not highly involved in EP election campaigns, and politically and economically dependent on national parties.

EP party groups are stronger than Europarties. They differ from each other in terms of size, resources, and relevance in European politics (only the largest have more than ten full-time employees, many fewer than organized interests groups at the European level and their corresponding parties at national level). National parties influence them less than they affect transnational party federations, being EP groups that are more remote and isolated from domestic pressures. Their degree of autonomy from national parties is directly related to the number of countries from which their members are taken: since a significant number of MEPs tend to depend on national parties of reference, the higher the number of countries the lower the dependence on one or other national party of reference; however, this runs the risk of greater fragmentation, thus making voting group cohesion more difficult.

The increasing power of the EP in the co-decision procedure has implied greater responsibilities for groups, whereas the power of individual MEPs has declined. The extension of majority voting in EP had the effect of strengthening the independence of groups – since it is no longer possible for a national party to block unwelcome decisions just through control of its country's MEPs – and of developing the groups' internal dynamics in search of agreements. Groups show the general tendency toward negotiation and compromise that characterizes European politics as a whole, and they tend to reject radical confrontation in favour of bipartisan and multipartisan cooperation. In the last legislatures, however, this tendency has come under growing stress.

The voting behaviour of MEPs has indicated considerable group cohesion (Raunio, 1996), greater than in the US Congress (Martinelli, 2007). In legislatures between 1989 and 1994, the three main EP parties showed a degree of cohesion in roll call vote that fluctuated between 0.90 and 0.91 for PES, 0.88 and 0.91 for EPP, and between 0.85 and 0.89 for ALDE (Hix, Noury, & Roland's agreement index, 2007).

Greater group cohesion fosters political moderation and intergroup cooperation, but this, however, should not be exaggerated. Hix and Lord argued in 1997 that in the EP there was no real government/opposition dialectic on key questions of European politics, but ten years later, Hix observed that the percentage of voting on the right/left axis was roughly equivalent to voting in the same way. In recent years, the conflict between traditional mainstream parties and national-populist parties has increased, but the former, especially EPP and S&D, have kept their attitude of cooperation and compromise, instead of allying themselves with radical forces on their right and left.

After the Single European Act, the strongest groups increased their power at the expense of other parties and non affiliated MEPs. New rules of strict numerical requirements have been approved, and weighted voting was introduced in the newly instituted presidents' conference. The new legislative procedure that requires an absolute majority of MEPs for passing proposals and amendments at different stages of the cooperation and co-decision process favoured until 2019 the two largest supranational groups, which could jointly guarantee their approval (the more so for resolutions that do not require a qualified majority). If Parliament wants to actively take part in EU lawmaking, it must rely on a 'grand coalition'. Until 2019, this was limited to EPP and S&D, but now has to be extended to Renew Europe and/or the Greens, since no single party has ever obtained an absolute majority. Radical left-wing or right-wing proposals would risk the marginalization of the Parliament, since they would likely be rejected by other European institutions, first of all the Council, where the balance of power between right and left always differs from the situation in the EP, owing to the different dates and shifting outcomes of member countries' elections. Given divergent national interests, EP groups are inclined to assume moderate political attitudes if they wish to exert some influence. This does not mean that traditional ideological left/right cleavages have no impact on EU decision-making, but that this impact is limited by the nature of EU governance and the role that national interests have in the Council.

The EP is evolving from a debating chamber into a real legislative body where power is concentrated in the hands of the most powerful parties. The future structuring of the European party system will continue to be based on the cooperation and de facto alliance between the largest parties. EPP and S&D, although facing a declining consensus, are still well established in several member states. But the outcome of the 2019 elections has brought to an end their self-sufficient duopoly of power and requires the enlargement of the majority to other pro-EU parties, Renew Europe and the Greens. An alternative model, based either on a centre-left or a centre-right coalition, seems rather unlikely, because of very different views on European integration. The radical alternative provided by right-wing national-populist parties, which challenge the dominant coalition with Eurosceptic and even Europhobic rhetoric, was put to a crucial test on the future of the EU in the 2019 elections, and failed.

3 The 2019 Elections of the European Parliament: Voter Turnout

Nine elections for the EP took place in the 40 years since the first 1979 election in nine member countries to the 2019 election in 28 member countries. The turnout declined from 62 per cent in 1979 to an all-time low of 43 per cent in 2014, but then increased eight percentage points in 2019. The nine member states that were already present in 1979 have constantly showed a higher turnout (a sign of greater involvement in the EU) than those that joined later. Compared with 2014, the 2019 turnout increased in 20 states, included all but one of the newcomers from Eastern Europe. In the largest EU countries, turnout increased 13 points in Germany, 8 points in France, and more than 20 in Spain and Poland, while it declined only in Italy (to 55 per cent, an all-time low since the 86 per cent in 1979, but still higher than the EU average). The turnout was lower in seven other states besides Italy: Belgium, Bulgaria, Greece, Ireland, Luxembourg, Malta, and Portugal. In the United Kingdom (UK), where turnout has always been low, it was 37 per cent, one point only higher that in 2014.

The much higher turnout in the 2019 elections can be traced to the greater importance given in the campaign to key European issues, thus changing the traditional opinion that for European voters EP elections are much less important than national ones, and that they consider the vote is only a way in which to express criticism for their country government without immediate consequences. The meaning of EP elections began to change in 2014; they were the occasion for national-populist parties, particularly strong in France and UK, to manifest their opposition both to their domestic governments – which were pro-EU – and to European integration. Among the largest EU countries, Italy was the exception, with the government party (Matteo Renzi's PD) obtaining 40 per cent of the vote on a pro-EU platform. In 2019, the trend was not in favour of government parties in Germany (with CDU and SPD gaining lower percentages of votes than in the last Bundestag elections), in the UK (where government parties suffered serious losses), and in France (where Macron came second behind Le Pen's FN, although for less than one percentage point). The almost generalized decline of government parties did not, however, only favour eurosceptic parties, but also pro-EU opposition parties such as the Greens. The main exceptions to the decline of government parties were again Italy (where Lega, the junior government coalition party, was the most voted with 34.5 per cent), Hungary and Poland, on the right, and Spain (where the pro-EU, Socialist leading government party was also successful), on the left.

Although the 2014 elections were the first to verify the political weight and influence of eurosceptic and europhobic parties, which had grown with the economic crisis and the immigrant question, it was only in 2019 that the future of the EU became the key issue in the campaign; the main cleavage was between supporters of deeper integration and supporters of restoring national sovereignty, with the effect of significantly increasing voter turnout after decades of declining participation. The national-populist upsurge brought pro-EU parties of member countries to pay more attention than in past electoral campaigns to pan-European issues (exit strategies from the crisis, the issue of refugees, the contradictions of the euro, policy renationalization, and declining participation).

The ninth direct elections to the EP were also the first after Brexit, but the clumsy management of Brexit by the UK government had the paradoxical effect of letting the radically anti-EU Brexit Party led by Nigel Farage to win 28 seats. At the end of 2019, the number of MEPs had not yet been reduced from 751 to 705, and the partial redistribution of UK seats among some member states that was decided by the EP and adopted in June 2018 by the European Council had not yet been implemented.

The 2019 elections were the second after the coming into force of TEU and TFEU Lisbon treaties, which attribute greater powers and prerogatives to the EP, although the Council still plays a greater role. They were also the second in which the main EU parties presented their candidates for President of the Commission on the premise that the candidate of the relative majority party would be designated for the job. But given the fact that PPE, although coming first, lost votes and seats, the European Council decided not to abide by this practice and proposed to the EP another candidate (instead of PPE president Manfred Weber), the former CDU Minister of Labour of the German government, Ursula von der Leyen. She was elected with 383 votes against 327, only nine more than the required majority (in 2014, Jean Claude Juncker was elected with 422 votes), since 75 members of the three coalition parties which agreed on her nomination (EPP, S&D, ALDE) did not support her, whereas MEPs of Italy's Five Stars Movement and Poland's PiS (both populist parties) voted in favour. However, the new College of Commissioners was approved with a much larger majority by the EP plenary of 27 November 2019, with 461 votes in favour, 157 against, and 89 abstentions.

4 The 2019 Elections of the European Parliament: Results and Recognized Party Groups

The best way to present the results of the ninth EP elections is the distribution of seats at the Constitutive session of the EP 2019–24 among seven recognized party groups and the relative percentages of votes (the number of seats based on the 2014 elections are in parentheses):

Seven political groups have been successfully formed, fewer than the 10 registered party federations, a small number given the great political and cultural diversity of European society (there are 380 possible translations from one

TABLE 11.1   Distribution of seats in the 2019–2024 European Parliament

EPP – European People's Party (Christian Democrats) 24.23% 182 (216)
S&D – Progressive Alliance of Socialists and Democrats 20.51% 153 (185)
  Renew Europe – Renew Europe group 14.38% 108 (69)
Greens/EFA – The Greens/European Free Alliance 9.85% 75 (52)
  ID – Identity and Democracy 9.72% 73 (42)
  ECR – European Conservatives and Reformist Group 8.26% 62 (77)
  GUE/NGL – European United Left – Nordic Green Left 5.46% 41 (51)
  NI-Non-attached Members 7.59% 56 * (21)

* In NI-Non-attached Members are 7 left-wing independent, 6 right-wing independent, 29 members of Nigel Farage's Brexit Party, and 14 members of Italy's Five Star movement. In 2014–19 Farage's Ukip and Five Star Movement formed the group Europe of Freedom and Direct Democracy (EFDD), which has not been reconstituted after the 2019 election.
SOURCE: NEWS EUROPEAN PARLIAMENT, 2019

recognized language to another!). As a consequence, transnational federations include parties with different political views on the EU, and voting discipline is not always guaranteed, a fact that makes even more necessary the formation of a stable coalition among major party federations (but two are no longer enough)

The already formed groups in the ninth EP are one less than the eight party groups of the eighth EP legislation (the one missing is EFDD). But the number of EP groups can increase if a sufficient number of non-affiliated members are able to form another group (according to Parliament's rules of procedure since 2009, a political group shall consist of at least 25 members elected in at least seven member states). The composition of EP groups can also change and will likely change, as in the past, since MEPs move from one group to another. If we calculate the gains and losses of various party groups by comparing the number of seats after the 2019 elections with the number at the end of the 2014–19 legislature, the decline of EPP and S&D looks greater (37 and 39 seats, respectively). The leaving of MEPs elected in the UK when Brexit is finalized will significantly impact on the composition of some of the political groups. The loss of 29 MEPs from the Brexit Party will make the reconstitution of the EFDD group impossible, in spite of one more MEP in Italy for the Five Star movement. In a similar vein, the Renew Europe (ALDE+) group will lose 16 UK members, but gain four thanks to new members being elected in France, Ireland, the Netherlands, and Spain. The Greens will lose 11 UK delegates, but gain five new MEPs from Austria, France, the Netherlands, Spain, and Sweden. The S&D will lose ten UK MEPs, but gain two new members elected in France and

Romania. The group of Conservatives, ECR, will lose four UK delegates, but gain one MEP from Croatia, whereas the left-wing GUE will lose one UK delegate, but gain two MEPs from Denmark and Ireland. Finally, EPP will lose none, being absent from the UK, but will gain five seats thanks to the election of new members in Finland, France, Italy, Poland, and Slovakia. On the whole, the eurosceptic component of the EP will be weakened, owing to the departure of Farage's party and the signs given by Italy's Five Star movement that it is changing its position on the EU through the vote for Von der Leyen's Commission.

The ninth EP 2019–24 is more fragmented than the previous ones, which have been characterized by the absolute majority coalition of the two largest parties, the PPE (centre right) and S&D (centre left). These two parties have together lost 76 seats (PPE changing from 216 to 182, S&D from 185 to 153), and are consequently 41 seats short from forming a majority by themselves.

The third major traditional European party, ALDE, renamed Renew Europe RE, obtained its best ever result with 108 seats (39 more than in 2014), thanks first of all to the 21 seats obtained by Emmanuel Macron's party En Marche in France (with 22,41 per cent of the vote), but also to positive results in several other member states. The Greens/EFA had a better result than expected, rising from 52 in 2014 to 75, thank to huge voting increases in France, Germany, Belgium, and Ireland (but not in Italy, where they did not take a single seat).

The necessity of relying on more than two parties to form a majority could open up a new, dynamic scenario, potentially more favourable to deeper integration, given the fact that within Renew Europe and the Greens–EFA groups there is a stronger pro-EU orientation than in EPP and in the S&D. On the other hand, it might be more difficult to form a cohesive majority, since a coalition of three or four partners increases the chances for disagreement on policy priorities and makes negotiations for key EU governance posts more complicated. Both the Liberals (who have already been party to EU governance, but not in an indispensable position) and the Greens will ask to focus on their policy priorities as a condition for their cooperation. An instance of this attitude was Renew Europe leader and confirmed Competition Commissioner Margrethe Vestager's first comment after the elections results: "I worked five years to break monopolies, that's exactly what happened to-night, monopoly is broken (i.e. the EPP-S&D monopoly). We can do things in a different way".

Just after the May 2019 elections, the leaders of the four pro-EU party groups – Manfred Weber (PPE), Udo Bullmann (S&D), Guy Verhofstadt (ALDE), Ska Keller and Philippe Lamberts (Greens/EFA co-presidents) – signed a document in which "they agreed to start a political process to define a common ambition for the next legislature and a basis for the future Parliament". We hope that "common ambition" is not a vague intention but a pledge to achieve concrete goals. We discuss these goals in the Conclusion, but can give some examples here. The first goal is increasing the EU budget, not through rising transfer payments from member states but through taxes going directly to the centre: a carbon tax on CO_2 emissions, a tax on financial transactions (as part of a larger policy aimed at completing the banking and capital markets union), and a web tax on the largest global software and web companies (Amazon – in first place with over $107 billion in sales and revenues of $70 billion in 2015-Microsoft, Google, Apple, Oracle, Facebook, WhatsApp, eBay, Priceline, Expedia, Netflix, Alibaba, Baidu, etc.). In the seven years of the long crisis, the 23 largest companies in this industry increased their output more than three times, but their labour force only 1.4 times, and had an average productivity 17 per cent higher than the average manufacturing firms' average, but paid taxes that were on average 23 per cent lower than the rest of the industrial sector. The second goal is a fiscal regulation that sets upper and lower limits to member states' corporate taxes in order to curb the interstate competition for attracting foreign direct investment. The third goal is a significant increase in EU investment in the green econoy and in material and social infrastructure (health, education, people, and housing). Finally, the fourth goal is the development of a common defence and security policy.

The point of departure of this ambitious programme is the legacy of the Juncker Commission, being based on the analyses and proposals of the White Book and Reflection papers written by the five high-level groups in 2017, which in their turn echoed the *Four Presidents Report* and the *Five Presidents Report* that between 2012 and 2015 made key proposals for the deepening of European integration. In her speech in the EP prior to the vote, Ursula von der Leyen has forcefully advanced some of these proposals, as we will see in due course.

The path of the potential new enlarged coalition will not be easy, as shown by the first test: the choice of the Commission's President. In the EP, the Greens hold a different position from the other three parties, voting against Ursula von der Leyen as a way to uphold the method of *SpitzenKandidat* (i.e. the European political party's lead candidate for the European Commission president). This disagreement, however, does not imply that they will not be part of the parliamentary majority – at least from time to time – in order to push their reformist agenda, which is the most advanced among pro-EU parties and focuses, above all, on climate change and sustainable development.

The selection of the top positions in EU institutions is the outcome of complex negotiations and compromises that reflect the relationships between member states in the Council and party groups in the EP. Those chosen for the new top jobs in the EU are the result of the alliance between the three traditional pro-European parties (PPE, S&D, Renew Europe) and the joint leadership of France's Emmanuel Macron and Germany's Angela Merkel, with the significant difference that, contrary to what often happened in the past, the roles are now reversed, with the French government pushing for acceleration in the reform of the EU and the German government asking for a more gradual approach. Holding a majority in the EP is not the only requirement when it comes to orienting EU decision-making; even more important are the relations among member states in the Council, given its prominent role in EU governance. Although in the new Council eurosceptic actors, marginalized in the EP, can make their voices heard, Macron's proposals for an ever greater union could rely on a majority of heads of government belonging to the same political groups that are dominant in the EP; a fact that makes even more relevant the formation of a stable three- or four-party EP coalition.

The five top positions in the new EU governance are the following:
- Ursula Von der Leyen (German, PPE, outgoing Defence Minister in Angela Merkel's government): Commission President
- Charles Michel (ALDE, outgoing Prime Minister of Belgium): Council President
- Josep Borrell (Spanish, S&D, outgoing Minister of Foreign Affairs in Pedro Sanchez' government): High Commissioner for Foreign and Security Policy
- Davide Sassoli (Italian, S&D): EP President
- Christine Lagarde (International Monetary Fund President, French): European Central Bank (ECB) President.

As we can see, no Green candidate holds a top position in EU governance, but, although the distribution of posts within the Commission is based more on national than party considerations, it is likely that some key DG directors will be Green. The new Commission took office on 1 December 2019 and reflects the fragmented and heterogeneous European political landscape (in spite of the new rules set by TFEU, there will be still 27 Commissioners, one for each of the 27 states).

The national-populist eurosceptic parties increased their votes and seats in the 2019 EP over 2014. They include the 73 seats of Identity and Democracy (mostly France's FN and Italy's Lega), which had a huge increase from the 42 seats won in 2014, the 62 seats of the European Conservatives (including the 26 seats of the Polish PiS), which declined from the 77 of 2014 (mostly owing to the very poor performance of UK Tories), and the 28 seats of Farage's Brexit Party (non-attached members), plus a few others. But given the fact that British MEPs will leave with Brexit, that the attitude toward the EU of Italy's Five Star movement is changing (as shown by the vote for von der Leyen), the truly eurosceptic parties will amount to less than 20 per cent of MEPs (even if we add eurosceptic MEPs in other EP groups like the European United

Left–Nordic Green Left, the percentage is slightly above 20 per cent). The decline of the more moderate ECR (owing to the weakening and future withdrawal of UK Tories) and the huge increase in the more radical component of ID, will make these party groups more strongly anti-EU, but with limited influence in Parliament. Even if they could overcome national interest-based conflicts (an international alliance of nationalist parties is an oxymoron), national populist parties cannot find allies in Parliament, the PPE having already excluded an alliance with them. These parties have more cards to play in the Council, where sovereignist governments of several member states are present (Austria, Bulgaria, Czech Republic, Hungary, Latvia, Poland, Slovakia) and can form a blocking minority on many policy issues, such as immigration. However, sovereignists do not necessarily oppose all reforms; for instance, it would be difficult for parties such as the French Front National, which often attack multinational corporations and international finance, to oppose decisions such as the introduction of a web tax or financial transactions' tax.

The rising tide of nationalist radical-right parties fed by anti-immigrant and populist sentiment was lower than forecasted on the increases of these parties in national elections (they won 16 per cent of the overall vote on average in the most recent parliamentary election in each member country, up from 11 per cent a decade earlier and 5 per cent in 1997). Although Eurosceptic parties were to some extent capable of defining the electoral agenda – with immigration and economic stagnation as key issues – the success of Renew Europe and the Greens more than compensated for the losses of EPP and S&D in the 2019 EP elections; and the attempt to weaken the traditional pro-EU stance of EPP and to shift the axis of the party to the right in the EPP did not succeed (Orban's Fidesz was suspended by EPP on 20 March 2019).

5   EP Elections Results in the Largest EU Member Countries

Since the confrontation between pro-EU and anti-EU parties takes place in the Council even more than in Parliament, it is necessary to include a brief overview of election results in the largest EU member countries in order to predict future political choices in the EU. These results are relevant insofar as they provide information about present and future government majorities in member states and their political attitudes within the Council.

Out of the 96 seats for Germany (the number will not change after Brexit), Angela Merkel's CDU came first and got 29 (six less than in 2014), with 28.9 per cent of the vote, and CSU got six (one more). The big winners were the Greens with 21 seats (ten more than in 2014) and 20 per cent of the vote (34 per cent among 18–24-year-old voters). The big loser was the SPD with 16 seats (11 less than in 2014) and 15.8 per cent of the vote (11 per cent less). The radical right party Alternative für Deutschland (AfD), increased from 7 to 11 seats with 11 per cent of the vote. The Liberal FDP increased its seats to 5 (2 more), while die Linke declined from 7 to 5, and the remaining 9 seats went to various smaller parties (5 of which have an environmental orientation).

In France, of the 74 seats (to become 79 after Brexit), Marine Le Pen's radical right Rassemblement National (RN), with 23.31 per cent of the vote, will get 22 (to become 23 after Brexit), the same number of seats as Emmanuel Macron's En Marche with 22.41 per cent of the vote will get 21 (to become 23 after Brexit). As in Germany, the big winners were the Greens (EELV) who doubled their seats compared to 2014, from 6 to 12 (13 after Brexit), with 13.47 per cent of the vote. Bad losers were the centre-right Les Républicains with 8.48 per cent, from 16 to 8 seats, and Le Partie Socialiste with 6.19 per cent, from 13 to 5 seats (6 after Brexit), while the radical left party La France Insoumise won 6 seats, with 6.31 per cent (much less than it had received in the last French presidential elections).

In Italy (73 seats, to become 76 after Brexit), it is worthwhile comparing the results not only with the 2014 EP elections but also with the March 2018 national elections, given the 'electoral revolution' that took place in Italian politics at that time. Matteo Salvini's Lega was by far the winner, with 28 seats and 34.49 per cent of the vote, a fourfold increase in comparison with 2014 (when he had only 6 seats) and doubling the vote of March 2018 (+15 per cent). The Five Stars Movement (5SM) with 14 seats and 16.84 per cent, did the opposite, halving the percentage of March 2018 (32.68 per cent), and declining 4 percentage points compared to 2014 EP election (mostly owing to a high abstention rate in the Mezzogiorno). Partito Democratico with 19 seats and 22.9 per cent lost 8 seats and 17 percentage points compared to 2014 (40.8 per cent), but regained some of the loss of March 2018 (18.7 per cent). Silvio Berlusconi's Forza Italia with 6 seats and 8.78 per cent lost 2 seats compared to 2014 (16.51 per cent), but declined from 14.1 per cent to 8.7 per cent compared to March 2018. The radical right party Fratelli d'Italia with 5 seats and 6.47 per cent grew significantly with regard both to 2014 (3 seats more) and March 2018 (4.35 per cent). The regional party Sudtiroler Volkspartei (SVP) won one seat. No other party got seats owing to the 4 per cent threshold of Italy's electoral law (the strongly pro-EU +Europa stopped at 3.09 per cent; the Greens, (Europa Verde), at 2.29 per cent; the radical left La Sinistra at 1.74 per cent, with a sharp decline compared to 2018 (3.4 per cent). The 3 extra seats after Brexit will be given one each to Lega, Forza Italia, and Fratelli d'Italia.

In Spain (54 seats, to become 59 after Brexit), PSOE, the Socialist party of the prime minister Pedro Sánchez, obtained 32.9 per cent of the votes and 20 seats (six more than in 2014). Second was the People Party PP, with 20.2 per cent and 12 seats (four fewer); third was Ciudadanos, the liberal centre-right party, with 12.2 per cent and 7 seats (one more); and fourth the leftist party Unidas Podemos, with 10.1 per cent and 6 seats (five fewer). Vox, the radical right party, got less than expected, with 6.2 per cent and 3 seats; while the alliance between the Greens and regional parties won 3 seats, with 5.6 per cent.

In Poland (51 seats, 52 after Brexit), the radical right government party PiS (Law and Justice) won 45.38 per cent of the vote and 26 seats (7 more than the radical right in 2014), and was 7 percentage points ahead of the European Coalition, the cartel of five pro-EU opposition parties, which obtained 38.47 and 22 seats (five fewer than 2014). The gap between right and left is actually smaller because KNP (Congress of the New Right), which won 4 seats in 2014, almost disappeared in 2019. The centre-left pro-EU party Spring, which decided to run alone, got 6.06 per cent and the remaining 3 seats.

In Romania (32 seats, 33 after Brexit) – where a huge increase in turnout from 34.6 to 49 per cent took place – the winner was the main opposition party (now in government), the moderately right-wing National Liberal party with 10 seats and 27 per cent(plus other 4 EPP seats form 2 minor formations) and its ally Coalition Alliance with 8 seats and 22.36, while the Social democratic party in government was second with 8 seats and 22.50 per cent, and ProRomania (Green Left) got 2 seatsand 6.4 per cent.

In the Netherlands (26 seats, 29 after Brexit) the Labour Party came first with 19 per cent (6 seats), prime minister Mark Rutte's centre party was second with 14.6 per cent (4 seats), Christian Democratic Appeal was third with 12.2 per cent (4 seats), while the eurosceptic Forum for Democracy obtained only 11 per cent (3 seats), contrary to the much more favourable forecast (the same of the Green Left 10.9 per cent, 3 seats).

In Belgium (21 seats, no change after Brexit), the vote was very fragmented between several Dutch- and French-speaking parties. The parties belonging to EPP group and ALDE groups won four seats each, parties belonging to S&D, Green-EFA, the two radical right eurosceptic groups, gained three seats each, and the radical left one. The Greens and Vlaams belang increased, while the Liberals declined.

In Portugal (21 seats, no change after Brexit), Prime Minister António Costa's Socialist Party gained 35.9 per cent (9 seats) and its main ally, the Left Bloc (BE), 10.6. per cent (2 seats), while the main opposition party right-wing PSD had the lowest result ever, with 23.6 per cent (6 seats) and Communist Party plus Greens got 7.4 per cent (2 seats).

In Greece (21 seats, no change after Brexit), the winner was the centre-right main opposition party Nea Dimokratia with 33 per cent and 8 seats (shortly afterwards it won the national elections). Prime Minister Alexis Tsipras' radical left party Syriza lost with 24 per cent(6 seats). KINAL (Movement for change) that was born from the ashes of the Socialist party PASOK, obtained 7.7 per cent (2 seats), the Communist Party 5.3 per cent (2 seats), and the neo-Nazi party Golden Dawn 4.9 per cent (2 seats).

In Hungary (21 seats, no change after Brexit), Victor Orban's radical right government party Fidesz won with the absolute majority (52 per cent) and 13 seats (one more than in 2014), to which should be added the seat won by the extreme right-wing Jobbik party(6.4 per cent), while 7 seats and 33 per cent went to three opposition parties.

In the Czech Republic (21 seats, no change after Brexit), 6 seats went to Renew Europe, 5 to the People's Party, 4 to European Conservatives, 3 to the Greens, 2 to 1 to Coommunists. The government ANO party lost half of its seats (from 4 in 2014 to two) to Voice, a liberal party that seceded from it.

In Sweden (20 seats, 21 after Brexit) Socialdemocrats was the first party with 23.6 per cent, ahead of the moderate centre-right party (16.8 per cent), while the radical right party Swedish Democrats, who in 2014 more than doubled their vote, further increased to 15.4 per cent.

In Austria (18 seats, 19 after Brexit), where there was the highest turnout (59 per cent) since 1996, Chancellor Sebastian Kurz' Österreichische Volkspartei (ÖVP) obtained 35 per cent (7 seats), while the Socialdemocrats, main opposition party, were second with 23.4 per cent (5 seats). The radical right party FPÖ lost 6 percentage points, from 23 per cent to 17.2 per cent (3 seats), owing to the scandal that engulfed the leader, concerning corruption and espionage connected with Russia. Finally, the Greens obtained 14.1 per cent (2 seats), and Neos (Alde) 8.1 per cent (1 seat).

For the sake of completion we report also the outcome of the UK: Nigel Farage's Brexit Party, founded only a few weeks before the elections, was the most voted-for party (30.5 per cent) and won 29 seats(out of 73). The Liberal Democrats, the historical third party in UK elections, which campaigned strongly against Brexit, came second with 20 per cent (the most voted-for party in London, ahead of Labour) and 16 seats (15 more than in 2014). Both the main traditional parties were big losers: Jeremy Corbyn's Labour was third with 13.6 per cent and 10 seats (ten fewer) and resigning prime minister Theresa May's Tories came in fifth place with 8,8 per cent and 4 seats (fifteen fewer). The Greens

TABLE 11.2 Number of MEPs for each member state by year of joining the EU, population in 2014 and 2019, and sequence of legislatures

Country	Year	Population 2014	Population 2019		
Germany	1951	82,428,000	82,521,653	18	36
France	1951	62,886,000	66,989,083	18	36
United Kingdom	1973	60,422,000	65,808,573		
Italy	1951	58,752,000	60,589,445	18	36
Spain	1986	43,758,000	46,528,024		
Poland	2004	38,157,000	37,972,964		
Romania	2007	21,610,000	19,644,350		
Netherlands	1951	16,334,000	17,081,507	10	14
Belgium	1951	10,511,000	11,351,727	10	14
Greece	1981	11,125,000	10,768,193		
Czech Republic	2004	10,251,000	10,578,820		
Portugal	1986	10,570,000	10,309,573		
Sweden	1995	9,048,000	9,995,153		
Hungary	2004	10,077,000	9,797,561		
Austria	1995	8,266,000	8,772,865		
Bulgaria	2007	7,719,000	7,101,859		
Denmark	1973	5,428,000	5,748,769		
Finland	1995	5,256,000	5,503,297		
Slovakia	2004	5,389,000	5,435,343		
Ireland	1973	4,209,000	4,784,383		
Croatia	2013	4,443,000	4,154,213		
Lithuania	2004	3,403,000	2,847,904		
Slovenia	2004	2,003,000	2,065,895		
Latvia	2004	2,295,000	1,950,116		
Estonia	2004	1,344,000	1,315,635		
Cyprus	2004	766,000	854,802		
Luxembourg	1951	460,000	590,667	4	6
Malta	2004	404,000	460,297		
Total		494,070,000	511,522,671	78	1

SOURCE: EP OPEN DATA PORTAL

TABLE 11.2 Number of MEPs for each member state by year of joining the EU, population in 2014 and 2019, and sequence of legislatures (*Cont.*)

36	81	81	81	99	99	99	99	99	99	99	99	96	96
36	81	81	81	87	87	87	78	78	72	74	74	74	79
36	81	81	81	87	87	87	78	78	72	73	73	73	N/A
36	81	81	81	87	87	87	78	78	72	73	73	73	76
			60	64	64	64	54	54	50	54	54	54	59
						54	54	54	50	51	51	51	52
								35	33	33	33	32	33
14	25	25	25	31	31	31	27	27	25	26	26	26	29
14	24	24	24	25	25	25	24	24	22	22	22	21	21
		24	24	25	25	25	24	24	22	22	22	21	21
						24	24	24	22	22	22	21	21
			24	25	25	25	24	24	22	22	22	21	21
					22	22	19	19	18	20	20	20	21
						24	24	24	22	22	22	21	21
					21	21	18	18	17	19	19	18	19
							18	17	18	18	17	17
10	16	16	16	16	16	16	14	14	13	13	13	13	14
					16	16	14	14	13	13	13	13	14
						14	14	14	13	13	13	13	14
10	15	15	15	15	15	15	13	13	12	12	12	11	13
										12	11	12
					13	13	13	12	12	12	11	11
					7	7	7	7	8	8	8	8
					9	9	9	8	9	9	8	8
					6	6	6	6	6	6	6	7
					6	6	6	6	6	6	6	6
6	6	6	6	6	6	6	6	6	6	6	6	6	6
					5	5	5	5	6	6	6	6

gained a significant fourth place with 11.8 per cent and 7 seats (plus four) and the pro-EU Scottish party SNP got 3.6 per cent and 3 seats (one more).

6 President Ursula von der Leyen's Programme Priorities and the Composition of the 2019–2024 Commission

In her pre-election speech (a 25-page document) in the EP on 23 July 2019, with the title *A More Ambitious Union. My Program for Europe*, Ursula von der Leyen presented a comprehensive five-year policy programme that tackled a wide range of economic, social, and environmental emergencies and reflected the priorities of Christian Democrats, Socialist, and Liberals, plus the Greens (as highlighted by the relevance given to environmental issues). She championed gender equality in her appeal to MEPs to back her as the first female president of the Commission, reminded them that exactly 40 years before, the first female president of the EP, Simone Veil, was elected, pledging to ensure gender equality among the 28 commissioners. She acknowledged a set of issues that have been on the agenda of European capitals and Brussels for years – such as common defence, fair taxation, education ("tripling the Erasmus+ budget"), the EU as the guardian of multilateralism in foreign policy, qualified majority voting, and Brexit (extending the withdrawal date to ensure a orderly exit from the EU), while putting less emphasis on other issues, such as the Common Agricultural Policy.

The most significant pledges of the speech were:

a) Climate change. "Our most pressing challenge is keeping our planet healthy. This is the greatest responsibility and opportunity of our times. I want a Europe *committed to sustainable policies* to become the first climate-neutral continent in the world by 2050". To this purpose, she announced a Green Deal for Europe in her first 100 days in office, then the first European Climate Law, a Sustainable Europe Investment Plan, the turning of parts of the European Investment Bank into a Climate Bank, and the introduction of a Carbon Border Tax to avoid carbon leakage.

b) Revitalization of the economy and digitalization. She pledged "to support our economies and our people in times of external shocks", to complete the capital markets union, to make use of all the flexibility allowed in the rules of the Stability and Growth Pact (SGP), to increase the funds for the Youth Guarantee and employment, to create a new European Unemployment Benefit Reinsurance Scheme (to bolster national insurance schemes for the unemployed), and to strengthen small and medium-sized enterprises ("backbone of our economies"). Digitalization was also a priority for von der Leyen, who stated that "We have to make our single market fit for the digital age, we need to make the most of artificial intelligence and big data, we have to improve on cybersecurity and we have to work hard for our technological sovereignty". She also pledged to adopt measures to support the single market, the energy market, and international trade.

c) Social issues. She committed herself to intensify the fight against poverty, with the proposal of a Child Guarantee ("to help ensure that every child in Europe at risk of poverty and social exclusion has access to the most basic of rights like healthcare and education"), to implement an action plan "to bring our Pillar of Social Rights to life", to achieve full gender equality (starting with the College of Commissioners), and to propose to add violence against women to the list of EU crimes defined in the treaty.

d) Immigration. Reminding MEPs that "in the last five years, more than 17,000 people have drowned in the Mediterranean, which has become one of the deadliest borders in the world" and that "at sea there is the duty to save lives and in our Treaties and conventions there is the legal and moral duty to respect the dignity of every human being", von der Leyen pledged to preserve the right to asylum and improve the situation of refugees (including via humanitarian corridors), to propose a New Pact on Migration and Asylum (including the relaunch of the Dublin reform), to reduce irregular migration, to fight smugglers and traffickers, and to boost the EU's border force Frontex to 10,000 staff by 2024.

e) Europe's values. She made a staunch defence of the Rule of Law (defining it as "our best tool to defend these freedoms and to protect the most vulnerable in our Union"), defining this as real democracy, an efficient public administration at the service of citizens, a judiciary independent of the executive, freedom of expression, freedom of the media, protection of minorities, and religious freedom. She also affirmed that no compromise can be made when it comes to infringement procedures such as those launched by the Juncker Commission (a warning to states such as Poland, Hungary, and Slovakia).

f) European democracy. She proposed that the EP is given "the right of initiative" (meaning the Commission would have to legislate on MEPs' resolutions, while currently only the Commission can draft laws), that the Commission and Parliament work together "to improve the *Spitzenkandidaten* system", and that a leading and active part of European citizens is restored in building the future of the Union (starting with the planned

Conference on the Future of Europe in 2020–22). Three 'technical' proposals were aimed at granting greater powers to Parliament and citizens vis-à-vis the governments of member countries.

Many of these commitments were reiterated by von der Leyen in her opening statement in the 27 November 2019 plenary of the EP, which, following the conclusion of the hearings process, approved the new College of Commissioners, with 461 votes in favour, 157 against, and 89 abstentions. Before the election at noon, political groups held brief meetings to decide on their voting intentions, which were followed by statements from their leaders in plenary. MEPs from EPP all voted in favour, together with almost all MEPs from S&D (only four abstained and one was against), and Renew Europe (only four abstained) also approved, the majority of MEPs form the Greens abstained (10 voted against and 5 in favour). The European Conservatives were very divided (30, mostly from Poland, voted yes, 17, mostly from Italy, voted against, and 14 abstained); all MEPs from the right-wing Identity and Democracy and almost all MEPs from the left-wing group GUE/NGL (only one abstained and one was in favour) voted against. Most (ten) MEPs from Italy's Five Star movement voted in favour, two against, and two abstained. We can argue that the more compact the vote is within an EP group, the more Union oriented is the political perspective of the parties forming that group, while the more divided the vote is, the more nationalistic is the political approach of the parties forming the group.

In her opening statement, von der Leyen pledged to put into place appropriate investment and regulatory frameworks for Europe to lead the way internationally on a range of critical issues: environmental protection and climate change, growth, inclusion, innovation, and digitalization, as well as the protection of democracy, European values, citizens' rights, and the rule of law. She stressed the fact that female representation in the Commission is the highest it has ever been: in addition to the President-elect, the current composition of the Commission comprises 11 female members and 15 male members. She confirmed one more portfolio change that Parliament had requested, adding Research.

Von der Leyen's Commission is thus in a continuous line with the legacy of the most relevant statements and reform documents produced in the 2014–19 legislature by the Commission, Parliament, and Council, as we argue in the Conclusion to this volume.

The composition of the new Commission (defined "*a balanced, agile and modern Commission,* tailored to what we want to achieve") reflects those priorities.

The criteria of equal representation for the 27 member countries (one commissioner each) and gender balance (11 women and 15 men) are met, as well as the marked predominance of pro-EU parties. The eurosceptic groups are present, with the commissioners designated by the Polish government party (ECR member), the Hungarian government party (suspended EPP member), by the Austrian, Bulgarian, and Latvian (belonging to the eurosceptic right wing of EPP), and by the Czech and Romanian government parties (belonging to the eurosceptic right wing of ALDE-Renew Europe). No commissioner comes from such parties as Italy's Lega and France's Rassemblement National, which belong to the most anti-EU group of ID.

The new Commission will have eight Vice-Presidents, with the three Executive Vice-Presidents each responsible for one of the three core topics from the President-elect's agenda. Frans Timmermans (Netherlands), S&D, will coordinate the work on the European Green Deal and be the Commissioner for climate action policy, supported by the Directorate-General for Climate Action;

Margrethe Vestager (Denmark), ALDE, will coordinate the agenda on creating a Europe fit for the digital age and will continue to be the Commissioner for Competition, supported by the Directorate-General for Competition;

Valdis Dombrovskis (Latvia), EPP, will coordinate the work on an Economy that Works for People and be the Commissioner for Financial Services, supported by the Directorate-General for Financial Stability, Financial Services and Capital Markets Union.

Josep Borrell (Spain), S&D, current Spanish Foreign Minister, is the High-Representative designate for Foreign Policy and Security Policy, A Stronger Europe in the World.

The four other Vice-Presidents, responsible for the other most important issues, are:

Maroš Šefčovič (Slovakia, S&D, who was Vice-President in the Juncker Commission): Inter-Institutional Relations and Foresight;

Věra Jourová (Czech Republic), ALDE, Commissioner in the Juncker Commission: Values and Transparency;

Dubravka Šuica (Croatia), EPP, Member of the EP: Democracy and Demography, and coordinator, from the Commission side, of the work on the Conference on the Future of Europe.

Margaritis Schinas (Greece), EPP, former Member of the EP, long-serving official of the European Commission: Protecting our European Way of Life;

The other Commissioners-designate are:

Johannes Hahn (Austria), EPP, a long-serving member of the Commission: in charge of Budget and Administration;

Phil Hogan (Ireland), EPP, current Commissioner for Agriculture: in charge of the Trade portfolio;

Mariya Gabriel (Bulgaria), EPP, current European Commissioner: in charge of the Innovation and Youth portfolio;

Nicolas Schmit (Luxembourg), S&D, national Minister for Employment and Labour: responsible for the Jobs portfolio;

Paolo Gentiloni (Italy), S&D, former Italian Prime Minister and Minister of Foreign Affairs: in charge of the Economy portfolio;

Janusz Wojciechowski (Poland), ECR, current member of the European Court of Auditors: in charge of the Agriculture portfolio;

Elisa Ferreira (Portugal), S&D, current Vice-Governor of Banco de Portugal and former national Minister for Planning and for Environment: in charge of the Cohesion and Reforms portfolio;

Stella Kyriakides (Cyprus), EPP, medical psychologist: in charge of the Health portfolio;

Didier Reynders (Belgium), ALDE, former national Finance Minister: responsible for Justice (including the topic of the rule of law, for which he has a joint responsibility with Věra Jourová);

Helena Dalli (Malta) S&D, former Minister for Social Dialogue, Consumer Affairs and Civil Liberties, and for European Affairs and Equality: in charge of the Equality portfolio;

Ylva Johanson (Sweden), S&D, former minister for Employment and Integration (2014–19): in charge of Home Affairs;

Janez Lenarcic (Slovenia), independent, Slovenia's former Permanent Representative to the EU: in charge of Crisis Management;

Jutta Urpilainen (Finland), S&D, former Finance Minister and a long-standing member of the Finnish Parliament's Foreign Affairs Committee: responsible for International Partnerships;

Kadri Simson (Estonia), ALDE: in charge of the Energy portfolio;

Virginijus Sinkevičius (Lithuania), Greens, national Minister for Economy and Innovation: responsible for Environment and Oceans.

In line with TEU Art. 17(7), before the European Council formally appoints the European Commission, the consent of EP to the entire College of Commissioners, including the High Representative of the Union for Foreign Affairs and Security Policy/Vice-President of the European Commission, is required. This is preceded by hearings of the commissioners-designate in the relevant parliamentary committees, in line with Parliament Rules of Procedure. Three designations were rejected by the EP for alleged conflicts of interest and had to be replaced: France's Thierry Breton, ALDE (former Finance Minister), was designated to the new Directorate-General for Defence Industry and Space, Industrial Policy and Digital Single Market, in place of Sylvie Goulard, ALDE (former national Minister of Defence); Hungary's Oliver Varhelyi, Fidesz, was designated Commissioner for Neighbourhood and Enlargement after an extended hearing to replace László Trócsány (former Minister of Justice in Orban's government, involved in the controversial reforms that were strongly criticized by the EU); Romania's Adina Valean, PPE, former MEP, was designated Commissioner for Transport and replaced Rovana Plumb. Finally, in spite of Brexit, the UK government should have nominated one commissioner as well, but Boris Johnson refused to do so before the UK's 12 December election. The EU decided not to wait, and the new Commission began work on 1 December 2019.

The first key issue addressed by the new Commission was the European Green Deal, which was presented at the 10 December plenary in Brussels. Von der Leyen affirmed that "our goal is to become the first climate-neutral continent by 2050, slowing down global heating and mitigating its effects. This is a task for our generation and the next, but change must begin right now and we know we can do it". It was argued that the European Green Deal is not only a response to the request for decisive climate action made by most European citizens and by the global environmental movement, but also by Europe's new growth strategy, that will cut emissions, boost the circular economy and preserve biodiversity while also creating jobs and improving the quality of life. It is the green thread that will run through all EU policies, from transport to taxation, food to farming, industry to infrastructure. It was further affirmed that the European Green Deal is not just a necessity, but it will also be a driver of new economic opportunities; many European firms are already going green, cutting their carbon footprint and discovering clean technologies. But what is needed is easy access to financing, and to this purpose the Commission will deliver a sustainable European investment plan, supporting €1 trillion of investment over the next decade. In March 2020, the first European climate law will be proposed, in order to define clear rules for investors and entrepreneurs so that they can plan their long-term investments. Moreover, since the transition to new ways of production and consumption implies human and economic costs for given social groups and territories, the Commission will propose the setting up of a just transition fund to mobilize, together with the leverage of the European Investment Bank and private money, €100 billion in investment over the next seven years.

The Green Deal is certainly a policy priority for the next five years, but consensus has not been reached. The EU's goal to become the first climate-neutral continent by 2050 is at the moment blocked by Poland, Hungary, the Czech

Republic, and Estonia. It will therefore be a key test for the willingness and capability of pro-EU parties and governments to achieve further supranational integration and a global role for the Union.

7 Interest Groups and Pressure Politics

The EU is a pluralist and competitive political system, open to a variety of pressure groups, more similar to the US system than to some European countries (Martinelli, 2007). The large number of lobbyists and the main points of entry into EU decision-making – which grow with the increased powers of EU governance – prevent the forming of monopoly positions. EU processes of governance in general, and specifically the Open Coordinating Method, envisage the required involvement of a variety of stakeholders through advisory committees, round tables, hearings, and public consultations, which are not systematically regulated except in the few cases in which the Commission must ratify the outcome of a negotiation (Pfeifer, 1995; Kholer-Koch, 2000). Not all scholars agree on the pluralist character of EU politics: some, such as Crouch (1999), have stressed the neo-corporatist influence of business interest associations and trade unions, while others, such as Georges (1996), note clear neo-corporatist aspects not at the macro-level, but at the meso-level of relations between pressure groups and government bodies. Still others, such as Michalowitz (2002), argue that neither pluralism nor neo-corporatism are actually compatible with EU governance, since both require the existence of a single reference point, the state; whereas at European level several governments have equal power and compete with a supranational 'umbrella' organization, and non-governmental actors are involved with diverse roles at different stages of decision-making. Parliament tends to be pluralist, the Commission leans towards neo-corporatism, while the Council is the least inclined to interact with pressure groups.

Unions and business interests associations, as the other major interest groups in the EU, are actually pluralist, that is, multiple, voluntary, competitive, and non-hierarchical. Any neo-corporatist attempt to attribute to EU institutions a ratifying role regarding their agreements would run into the opposition of national governments.

There is no agreement on the precise extent of the large and growing number of interest groups that are lobbying the Commission, Parliament, Court of Justice, and national governments (Broscheid & Cohen, 2006). It varies between about 3,000 groups and 1,000 employees, estimated by a Commission study in the early 1990s (Mazey & Richardson, 1993) and the 6,500 organizations that are listed in the 2014 Transparency Register. Numbers vary according to the definition that is used: should only economic and professional interest associations be included, or should non-governmental organizations, foundations, religious institutions, think tanks, and so on also be taken into account?

The most reliable numbers are the official data provided by the Transparency Register, which was created in June 2011 by the Commission and Parliament on the assumption that the activity of interest organizations, lobbies, and advocacy groups is legitimate and even necessary in democratic decision-making, provided these groups respect legal and ethical norms and are transparent and accountable to citizens. Registration is 'almost' compulsory in the sense that those who do not ask for it find it very difficult to access EU documents and activities. For this reason, the number of registered organizations has increased 60 per cent in three years, from 4,000 in 2012 to 6,500 in 2014. The Register is organized into six sections, the most crowded of which is the second, with 3,200 lobbyists and three-quarters of all commercial and professional associations of this type, and the third with 1,600 non-governmental organizations (NGOs), which amount to 60 per cent of all NGOs active in the EU (Greenwood & Dreger, 2013). As one can see, not all interest groups are represented in the same way: economic interest groups are more active and present, because firms move more freely in a supranational space, are endowed with greater human and financial resources, and are closer to the EU core, that is, market integration, which has been fostered by the alliance between political and economic elites.

European unions of business associations are more influential than other actors. In the early 1990s, industrial and commercial interest groups, either general, examples being the Union of Industrial and Employers Confederations of Europe (UNICE), the European Centre of Employers and Enterprises Providing Public Services, and Eurochambers, or sector specific, such as CEFIC in the chemical industry and ACEA in the automotive industry, or elitist, such as the European Round Table (which gathers together the biggest European firms), accounted together for 50 per cent of the total; agricultural and food interest groups for 25 per cent; groups in the service sector for 20 per cent; and labour unions, environmental, and consumer associations for the remaining 5 per cent (Mazey & Richardson, 1993). Public interest groups are weaker than private ones, but their influence has increased over time and their demands and opinions are more heard by the European Court of Justice, the EP, Commission, and Council (Majone, 1996). This picture has not substantially changed in the last 25 years.

Pressure politics in general – and the pressure of business interests in particular – is successful because decision-making is a long and cumbersome process in the EU, without a single locus of executive power, and is based on a broad consensus that requires the consultation of interest groups. The complexity of many issues requires a high level of specialized competence and technical know-how. The pro-business culture of several EU decision-makers and officers fosters the creation of policy communities where business representatives are regularly incorporated in decision-making. The European Single Act and the Maastricht Treaty widened the scope of EU intervention in policy areas such as environmental protection, scientific research, technological development, and social policies, giving rise to more than 300 harmonization procedures that require additional specialized knowledge and attract a growing number of new pressure groups. Moreover, criticism of the closed and non-transparent character of European policymaking has stimulated requests for extensive consultation, aimed at reducing the EU democratic deficit, further enhancing the role of interest groups.

Business interest organizations, both general and sectoral, can significantly influence European policymaking by virtue of their 'structural' power in the production process and of the availability of greater resources. Their influence is, however, limited by the conflicts of interest among member states that are often reflected in divergences between their entrepreneurial systems (which are quite different in terms of productivity and competitiveness, as we point out in Chapter 13 on the European economy), and by the fact that several big European firms prefer to deal directly and individually with EU institutions rather than acting collectively through their representative associations. Moreover, the influence of business interest organizations is counterbalanced by other pressure groups – initially labour unions, but also environmental, agricultural, and consumer groups – which we will now examine in more detail.

The European Trade Union Confederation (ETUC), born in 1973 in Brussels, has focused its action on the development of so-called 'social Europe' (see Chapter 12 on European welfare). ETUC has been able to overcome ideological divides and affiliate more and more unions (the French Confederation general du travail, CGT, joined as late as 1995). ETUC has acquired an increasingly communitarian – versus interstate – character, through the organization of the first 'European strikes' in the public services and transport sectors and the approval in the 1995 Brussels congress of a statutory amendment that introduced a required unanimous vote for agreements in the social dialogue with employers' associations; and it has become more authoritative not only for its business counterpart, but also for EU institutions. Relations with the Commission and the Council have become permanent in the framework of the 'macro-economic dialogue' that was introduced with the euro: twice a year, European social partners meet the Economic and Financial Affairs Council (Ecofin), the Labour Council, the Commission, and the ECB to discuss the effects of economic and monetary policy. Bourdieu's critique (2001) that the strategy of European trade unionism as engine of social Europe is still to be invented since it lacks the capacity to oppose UNICE's pressures and the related critique by CGT and Force Ouvrière that ETUC is not effective and autonomous in its relations with the EU are overstated. Unions' action in European policymaking has in fact not been without concrete results: there have been over 50 directives concerning the free circulation of workers, their health and safety in the workplace, gender parity, the fight against discrimination, the formation of European firm committees in multinational corporations, changes to the Services in the Internal Market Directive 2006/123/EC aiming at establishing a single market for services within the European Union (Bolkenstein Directive from the name of the former, i.e. the EU law), the measures of active labour market policy, and the modernization of social protection systems.

European trade unions and business associations were directly involved in the process for the creation of European Monetary Union and obtained that the governments of 11 member states out of the original 12 approved a Social Policy Protocol that was annexed to the Maastricht Treaty (the cleavage with the UK was bypassed by inserting the norms on social policies in the Amsterdam Treaty, art. 137–9). The Protocol, which reproduced the articles 12, 27 and 28 of communitarian Charter of Fundamental Rights that concern workers' rights, showed that European governments wanted to achieve economic and monetary union with the consent of workers, reaffirming the rights to free movement, fair remuneration, better working conditions, social protection, free association and collective bargaining, professional training, information, consultation and participation, work protection, and social security. All these rights and related goals were codified in the Amsterdam Treaty's Title XI (Chapter I on social provisions, Chapter II on the European social fund, and Chapter III on social policy, education, professional training, and youth), where social partners are empowered to implement, on entrustment of a member state or by their joint request, Council directives in the field of workers' social security and protection, employment conditions of third countries' legal migrant workers, as well as financial contributions aimed at promoting jobs and the collective interest representation of workers and employers (with the exception of wages, strikes, and lock-outs).

Labour unions are still more influential at national level than at European level, although their influence in the EU is growing at a time when unions' power in European countries is declining. Deindustrialization and the service economy developed later in European society than in America, but they occurred rapidly, and in some cases, as in Eastern European post-communist countries, very rapidly. These economic changes drastically reduced industrial jobs, exacerbated the dual labour market, and fostered working career shifts, which in their turn contributed to weaken the power of labour unions in different ways and degrees in various European countries (Visser, 2006). Northern countries and Belgium show high and rather stable rates of unionization (between 55 per cent and 78 per cent of the total labour force); in a second group of countries – UK, Italy, Ireland, and Austria – union members are still rather numerous (between 30 per cent and 35 per cent), but in constant decline and predominantly older workers and pensioners; a third group of countries – Germany, the Netherlands, Portugal, Greece – show declining numbers as well, but starting from lower membership thresholds (between 22 per cent and 25 per cent); finally, in countries such as France and Spain, unions recruit only small percentages of the active population (between 8 per cent and 15 per cent).

Trade unions should have a strong interest in pursuing a European strategy, given the transfer of decision-making to supranational level in a growing number of policy areas, and also in order to compensate for their declining power at national level. But this is taking place very slowly for the same reasons we observed for business organizations: because ETUC has limited control over the industrial relations strategies of national trade unions (as we can appreciate from the data of the European Industrial Report) and because national conflicts of interests make it difficult to agree on common European-level action.

CHAPTER 12

The European Welfare State

1 Welfare and the European Social Model

The European Union (EU), with less than 7 per cent of the world population and 22 per cent of world gross domestic product (GDP) (in US$, but only 17 per cent in purchasing power parity), has about 50 per cent of world welfare expenditure (2018 data). The welfare state, one of the most important institutional innovations of the 20th century, is a European innovation. Together with a market economy, it is a component part of the European social model, an original blending of capitalism and welfare. The concept is sometimes used to define both components, sometimes only one of the two, that is, the European variety of coordinated capitalism or social market economy (in contrast to the American variety of market-driven capitalism), or the welfare state, that is, the set of health, education, social security, public assistance services and benefits, labour market norms, and industrial relations practices. In this chapter, I will use the term mostly in the latter sense, with the further specification that 'European welfare state' can mean the national welfare regimes that EU member countries have in common; or the set of EU norms and policies that aim to coordinate, supersede, and integrate member countries' social policies (adding a new supranational layer to existing regimes); or a unified European welfare state with the same policies for all European citizens, which absorbs and integrates the various national welfare systems. I will refer to all three meanings, although the third reflects the current situation less than the other two.

The European Social Model is a distinctive aspect of European society in comparison with other major world societies, above all that of the United States (USA). The concept is omnipresent in EU documents, where is often used in a normative rather than a descriptive sense. It rejects the conception of the self-regulating market and aims to achieve economic competitiveness and social cohesion at the same time. It is an effective institutional device for remedying market failures and ensuring social protection, a major way of resolving conflict non- violently with the virtuous circle that connects social citizenship rights and representative democracy. The sharpening of competition in the global market and the rising costs of welfare threaten its survival, but the welfare state proves to be very resilient; and the belief that economic competitiveness and solidarity are complementary goals is still widely agreed upon by Europeans.

The European Social Model developed in different forms and along different paths in various EU member countries, but is based on a core of shared values that include representative democracy, individual rights, market competition, freedom of movement, collective bargaining, equal opportunities, social protection and solidarity. The model is based on the conviction that "economic progress and social progress are inseparable" (European Commission, 2014). Its main distinguishing characteristics are: a non-residual welfare system that is addressed not only to the poorest social groups and hence involves high social expenditure (between 20 per cent and 30 per cent of GDP); labour market 'flexicurity' aimed at ensuring both incoming and outgoing flexibility for firms and jobs, and wage security for workers; and institutionalized industrial relations, with inclusive representative organizations and collective bargaining for wages and working conditions. Other characteristics are present only in some countries, such as the involvement of trade unions and business interest associations in economic and social policymaking and workers' participation in corporate governance.

2   Welfare State Models

Speaking of a European social model does not imply that relevant diversity in member states' welfare systems will be neglected. As Figure 12.1 shows, there are still strong differences between member states in total government expenditure on social protection (Eurostat, 2018).

Well-known typologies of welfare ideal types can help us to appreciate this diversity, although a word of caution is in order: first, we should not neglect the discrepancy between ideal types and concrete arrangements when they combine in various ways; secondly, we should be aware of the inherently static character of ideal types and the false systemic coherence of their component parts: we should not consider one type to be the perfect model, evaluating all others in terms of their deviation from it. From the rich literature on comparative welfare systems (first of all, Esping-Andersen, 1990, 2002, but also, among others, Crouch, 1999; Pierson, 2001; Gallie & Paugam, 2002; Ferrera, 2005; Hemerijck, 2012), we can identify four main ideal types, which can be defined in terms of basic principles, institutional mechanisms, key actors, entitlements, and policy instruments. These are the liberal, market-oriented, Anglo-Saxon model; the Nordic, social democratic, full citizenship model; and the

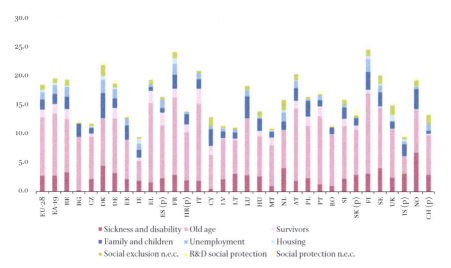

FIGURE 12.1 Total general government expenditure on social protection, 2017 (% of GDP)
SOURCE: EUROSTAT (ONLINE DATA CODE: 'GOV_10A_EXP')

communitarian, continental European model, which in its turn can be subdivided into Central European and Mediterranean.

In the liberal, Anglo-Saxon model, welfare benefits are granted in relation to basic needs, policies are targeted to well-defined social groups (the poor, the elderly), the labour market is largely unregulated, unemployment subsidies are modest and short term, the provision of health and social services is mostly private, and taxes are low. The ideological foundations are free enterprise and individual responsibility and the belief that the free market is the best source of welfare as state intervention threatens individual freedom (with the notable exceptions of government's key role in keeping law and order). The country welfare system coming closer to this first ideal type is in the world the USA and, in Europe, the United Kingdom (UK) since the Thatcher government, Ireland, and to some extent the Netherlands.

The second type, Nordic, social democratic, is a universalistic model of social citizenship with high standard government services provided to all, extended public employment, active labour policies, gender equality measures, unemployment benefits directly managed by trade unions, strong decommodification effects, and high taxes to finance all this. Its ideological assumptions are social democracy and Lutheranism with their principles of equality of opportunities and rewards, full employment, and the centrality of work as the core source of identity (Kautto et al., 2001). The Scandinavian countries are those that come closest to this second ideal type.

The third, the communitarian, continental European model (sometimes also defined corporatist or conservative) relies on employment-based, status-related, social insurance schemes. High employment levels are needed to subsidize services. It was first implemented in Germany at the end of the 19th century by Bismarck's reforms and concerned only male breadwinners, but was later gradually extended (keeping its professional base, instead of moving toward universal social security). Its ideological assumptions are rooted in Socialist trade unionism and Christian social thinking (communitarian in the Catholic variant, hybridized with some notion of individual responsibility in the Protestant variant), which support communitarian solidarity, autonomy from government of family, Church, and professional organizations, and subsidiarity. The welfare systems of Germany, Austria, France, the Netherlands, Belgium, Italy, and Spain show various elements of this ideal type, but their differences are so great that it is preferable to distinguish two variants or subtypes: Central European and Mediterranean.

The first variant, which includes Germany, Austria, France, and Benelux, is characterized by social security contributions as a non-wage component of labour cost, the participation of unions and employer associations in the management of pension schemes, rigorous norms on work safety, and sectoral industrial relations and bargaining. The second variant, which includes the Mediterranean countries and Portugal, is characterized by a strong dependence on social services provided by the family, which compensates for a scarcity of public services and implies a low participation of women in the labour market, a universal health system, and generous pension schemes, which foster intergenerational inequalities (Ferrera, 2005).

The relationship between social protection and competitiveness is different in the four models: the Anglo-Saxon model is marked by a trade-off between high competitiveness and low social protection; in the continental model, the reverse happens; in the Nordic model, levels of social protection and competitiveness are both high; and in the Mediterranean model, they are both low. When submitted to the check of national accounting, this typology is substantially confirmed (Martinelli, 2007). In the Anglo-Saxon model there are high levels of private spending for pension funds; in the Nordic high levels of social spending in general and for social services in particular; in the Continental spending for pensions is higher than that for social services; while the Mediterranean is characterized by high and essentially public spending for pensions compared with much lower spending for other social policies (to the point that, for instance, Italy's high-quality health system has been threatened in recent years by diminishing public investments).

After the implosion of the Soviet Union in 1991 and EU enlargement, with 11 new Eastern members (Czech Republic, Estonia, Hungary, Latvia, Lithuania, Poland, Slovakia, Slovenia in 2003, Bulgaria and Romania in 2007, Croatia in 2013), together with Cyprus and Malta, the question was asked whether a fifth welfare type should be added. Actually, in spite of their common historical experience of regime change from capitalism to real socialism and back, the welfare systems of these countries do not make up a fifth ideal type, but are the result of hybridizations between elements that belong to the other four. In more than four decades of communist rule, pensions, social assistance, full employment, health care, education, and family services were provided to all citizens, but in general involving low-quality services, low labour productivity, extended under-employment, and poor standards of living (Kornai, 1992). In the complex double transition from planned economy to market economy and from party state political regime to representative democracy, there has been a strong demand for better and more inclusive social policies, but the percentage of social spending on GDP has continued to be low (Inglot, 2008).

3 Challenges Confronting the European Welfare State

The welfare state typology outlined here has been updated and integrated against the dynamic background of globalization by transformative social policy reforms both before and after the global financial crisis, these reforms being based on a better understanding of the interaction between domains often treated separately in comparative welfare analysis (macroeconomic, fiscal, labour market policy and regulation, industrial relations, demographic shifts, changing family patterns, work–life balance policies). But the four ideal types still matter insofar as they help us to appreciate how national welfare regimes responded differently to the external and internal challenges of the last decades.

All EU countries had to confront the same challenges in a context of intensified European regional integration, but their policymakers made different, path-dependent attempts to redirect welfare efforts, redesign institutions, and elaborate on new principles of social justice. As far as external factors are concerned, international (global) competition challenges the redistributive scope and decommodifying power of national welfare states, and their capacity to shield people in need against the hard laws of the marketplace. Several scholars believe that the increase in cross-border competition in the markets for money, goods, and services has substantially reduced national welfare states' room for manoeuvre, and that tax competition between nation states in order to attract foreign investment results in an underprovision of public goods. Others credit to global competition the fact that decision-makers were led to adopt long-needed changes and innovations in welfare policies which were responsible of a rising public debt.

As far as internal factors are concerned, ageing populations (as a result of rising life expectancy and rapidly falling birth rates), changing family structures, the feminization of the labour market, changes in work organization, and skill-biased technological change are all processes that challenge the institutions of work and welfare inherited from the industrial age. Let us observe them in more detail. The reaching of retirement age by the post-Second World War generation of baby boomers has changed the ratio between the active and non-active population, greatly increased the number of pensioners, and exploded the cost of social security. The extension of average life expectancy thanks to medical progress and improved lifestyles impact on both health care and social security expenditure. This demographic cycle will last 30–40 years and have more or less severe consequences in different countries depending on birth rates (which are higher in countries such as France and lower in countries such as Italy and Spain).

Growing women's participation in the labour market is another cause of increasing social security and health care expenditure, since it transfers from families to state institutions the burden of caring for pre-school children and non-self-sufficient elderly. The transformation of family structures – in particular the growth of single-parent families that are more exposed to the risk of poverty and social marginalization – also contributes to increasing the costs of public assistance. Moreover, the prolonged economic crisis, closure of many factories, and job cuts all increase the costs of unemployment relief and vocational rehabilitation programmes.

On top of all these changes came the 2008 global financial crisis, the long economic recession, and the social and political aftershocks of these events. As we will see later, new and rising inequalities, youth unemployment, skill-biased patterns of social exclusion, and new sources of immigration and segregation, also taking place in the housing market in metropolitan areas, threaten social cohesion. Declining trust in representative democracy, rising populism, and neo-nationalism challenge the project of a closer political union (Martinelli, 2016). After a series of emergency bailout mechanisms and the monetary interventions of the European Central Bank (ECB) aimed at doing whatever it takes to defend the euro, a new imperative for the EU has been to mitigate the social and political repercussions of the long recession.

4 The European Social Model as Common Core of European Welfare Systems

European welfare is both diverse, because the national welfare systems correspond to the different ideal types already outlined, and unique, because a social pan-European dimension is always present in the treaties – member states therefore sharing a core of common characteristics as they face common challenges.

In the early decades of European integration, it was initially Germany that asked for and obtained agreement that in almost any area of social policy national governments could keep absolute discretion and sovereign power, even though greater social equality for European citizens was among the Community's goals. With the growth of the single market in the 1980s, worries of a downward alignment of social protection levels in the most advanced continental states were met with the principle of mutual recognition, which replaced the principle of rule harmonization. UK objections to the social chapter of the Maastricht Treaty were bypassed through the 'opt out clause', which allows a dissenting member state not to adhere to a specific policy while remaining a member of the Union. Only later, in the framework of the Lisbon strategy, were some competences and responsibilities concerning labour market and social security issues transferred to supranational institutions, which met them through open coordination among all interested partners.

The 'four freedoms' of the EU, which were at the core of the European Economic Community Treaty (underwritten in Rome in 1957 by the six original member states), are the free movement of goods, services, people and capital over borders. The convergence of social and labour laws and policies is a consequence, not a precondition, of the making of the European market. These norms and policies largely remain a matter for member states. But the notion of a social model was present from the start in order to meet the social costs of economic integration and was consolidated through the notion of social citizenship; that is, the right of all EU citizens to have equal opportunities in developing their skills and inclinations and equal access to services, resources, and job chances. The EEC Rome Treaty, the Charter of Fundamental Rights of the EU (approved at the Nice European Council in 2000), and European labour law have legitimized the social model. As early as the 1970s, several Community directives and European Court of Justice (ECJ) verdicts dealt with questions such as equal wages for women and men and employment protection. The European Single Act and the Maastricht and Amsterdam treaties introduced new opportunities for social policy standards harmonization. The creation of the single market, although giving priority to economic over social integration, was in fact accompanied by welfare norms and provisions at EU level and induced member countries to partially harmonize social and labour policies, social protection norms, and corporate governance practices, although national welfare policymaking remained predominant.

The Lisbon Treaty (TEU & TFEU) now in force emphasizes the social dimension of integration more than previous treaties. The main pillar of the European Social Model features the following in the current Treaty on the Functioning of the European Union (TFEU): "the Union, in all its activities, shall aim to eliminate inequalities, and to promote equality, between men and women" (art. 8); "the Union, in defining and implementing its policies and activities, shall take into account requirements linked to the promotion of a high level of employment, the guarantee of adequate social protection, the fight against social exclusion, and a high level of education, training and protection of human health" (art. 9); "the Union shall aim to combat discrimination based on sex, racial or ethnic origin, religion or belief, disability, age or sexual orientation"(art. 10); "the Union recognises and promotes the role of the social partners at its level, taking into account the diversity of national systems. It shall facilitate dialogue between the social partners, respecting their autonomy" (art. 152). TFEU also defines the legal framework for the European social dialogue (art. 154–5) and the European Employment Strategy with an open method of coordination (Employment title, art. 145–50).

European welfare systems, with relevant differences from country to country, have a common core of essential characteristics, the first of these being much higher levels of public spending, that separate them from all other countries in the world. While acknowledging national diversity in Europe, Hyman (2005) argues that the common features in continental Western Europe are strong enough to distinguish an a European model from the American model of largely deregulated labour markets and the Japanese model of management-dominated company employment relations. Europe is unique inasmuch as there are substantial limits to the ways in which labour (power) can be bought and sold. These limits constrain the autonomy of employers to "a degree unknown elsewhere in the world" and are primarily set through comprehensive employment protection legislation, as well as all-encompassing and centralized collective bargaining structures. The European Social Model is defined as a specific combination of comprehensive welfare systems and strongly institutionalized and politicized forms of industrial relations (Grahl & Teague, 1997).

In the same manner, Offe (2003) argues that in the European model of 'social' capitalism, economic transactions, including labour market exchanges, tend to be institutionally embedded and therefore more restricted than in other parts of the world. In addition, Schiek (2013) remarks that despite all the differences, European national social and economic models converge on a common core, above all on the idea of societal responsibility for individual well-being, with labour market corrections through legislation and collective bargaining, and transfer payments policy in periods of lost income.

The common features have been strengthened by the combined effect of the Europeanization of issues of work and welfare, which since the mid-1980s have become intertwined with the Single Market and the Economic and Monetary Union (EMU), and the attempts of policymakers to recast welfare policies as part of a successful transition toward 21st-century knowledge-based economy (the Lisbon strategy). These attempts have been caught between long-standing social policy commitments in the areas of unemployment and pensions, and the constraints of permanent austerity. We have entered an era of semi-sovereign welfare states in the EU. National welfare states can no longer behave as if they were autonomous and in full control. European economic integration has fundamentally recast the boundaries of national systems of social protection, constraining autonomy for domestic policy options, but also opening opportunities for EU-led multilevel policy coordination.

5   The Three Phases of European Welfare

If we look in more detail at the evolution of relationships between European integration and welfare, we can identify three main phases. In the first, from the 1957 Rome Treaty to the mid-1980s, high economic growth – favoured by trade liberalization in the common market – allowed welfare state expansion in member countries, embedded in the mixed 'administered' economy, according to the formula 'Keynes at home, Smith abroad'. The key aim of European social policy was to enhance the mobility of workers between the six (nine after 1973) member countries, by abolishing discrimination in working conditions and social security benefits based on nationality. But provisions were also made for workers' health and safety and equal employment opportunity, while issues of workers' participation and centralized collective bargaining between trade unions and employers' associations at the supranational level did not succeed.

Streeck (2017) identifies two stages in what we may see as a single phase: he distinguishes between a first stage, from the start to 1968 (in which social policy was embedded in supranational industrial policy in core sectors such as steel and coal mining of mostly national mixed economy), and a second stage, between 1968 and 1985 (characterized by labour-inclusive supranational welfare harmonization as a response to labour militancy of the late 1960s). I prefer to consider these three decades a single phase, since the attempt "to make the European community the right instrument for a supranational modernization of national social policy regimes", as Streeck puts it, did not travel too far (Streeck, 2017:8)

In the second phase, from the 1986 Single European Act, through the introduction of the euro in 1999, to the 2008 global financial crisis, accelerated economic and monetary integration, while increasing competition in the world market, constrained social policies and put them on the back burner. The construction of the EU has been a contradictory process from the start, since 'negative' integration, removing obstacles to the free circulation of capital, people, goods, and services in the single market, conflicts with 'positive' integration, which is achieved at the national level by fiscal policies, social security, public services, labour market regulation, and industrial relations (Scharpf, 2009). In this phase, the goal of completing the European internal market and the policies aimed at complying with the Maastricht parameters required to join EMU were given absolute priority over social policies. Moreover, instead of creating a common governance of EU money and economy, EMU chose to insert a kind of automatic pilot, based on pre-established rules and procedures and valid for all countries at all times, that severely limited member states' autonomy (T. Padoa Schioppa, 2001).

Welfare policies of EU member countries are subject to a twofold constraint: on the one hand, they are limited by the transfer of sovereignty to the supranational union, which implies constraints to their budget choices; on the other, these policies continue to be subject to the constraints of their welfare communities, which punish in elections any attempt to reform or downsize social programmes. Welfare is one area where the tension between supranational coordination and national specificities is most acute. Welfare policies are sensitive political issues, with implications that are directly felt in citizens' daily lives, where government parties risk more in terms of consensus. Moreover, the existence of different member states' welfare systems runs the risk of social dumping, which violates the rules of free competition in the single market, and the risk of welfare shopping, which stirs conflicts among the citizens of old and new member states and between natives and immigrants.

The Commission headed by Delors, although primarily focused on the completion of the single market, tried not to neglect the social dimension; to this purpose a Social Chapter was attached to the 1992 Maastricht Treaty, with a

Social Protocol that provides for a privileged role in social policy proposals for organized business and labour; but only a few directives were successful, among which were those on parental leave in 1995, part-time work in 1997, and fixed-time work in 1999, as well as the most important directive of this period: the one allowing member countries to make their labour regimes binding on all firms operating in their territory, including non-nationals, as a way to cope with increasing global competition. Issues of work and welfare became intertwined with the Single Market and the EMU instituted by the treaties of Maastricht and Amsterdam- a key step toward a closer union, better equipped to compete in a globalized world-, but a conscious effort to build a European Social Union alongside EMU was not made.

However, relevant welfare reform policies (active labour policy, flexicurity) were implemented at the member state level, with varying success, in different countries, within an EU framework of soft law, mutual learning, minimum standards, and an open method of coordination (OMC); in this way a new European space of social citizenship and solidarity has been gradually formed.

Implementing a common welfare system for EU states is not an easy task, but several steps in this direction have been taken, such as: the large number of ECJ verdicts and official documents from EU government institutions, initially with norms aimed at extending from one country to another the social rights of European citizens; the rich *acquis* in the area of labour, on the free circulation of workers, health and safety in the workplace, and gender equality; the European Social Fund (the oldest of European Structural and Investment Funds); the European Social Charter in the social chapter of the 1989 Amsterdam Treaty; the Treaty of Nice Charter of Fundamental Rights, the 2007 European Global Adjustment Fund; European legislation on non-discrimination, protection against dismissals, access to social transfers, and fiscal benefits for non-residents; the adoption of an open coordinating method in the field of employment, social inclusion, and the various attempts to coordinate health and pension policies in the 2000 Lisbon Strategy and 2010's 'Europe 2020'; and the long sequence of social agendas developed by the Director General Employment of the European Commission. Social policy measures have not only been a spillover effect of the single market, the completion of which has invaded the field of social policy (Leibfried, 2000); there have also been several instances of positive welfare integration, mostly in the direction of establishing uniform social standards at European level through Commission-initiated directives, developing a core of convergent measures of macro-social strategy, first of all for jobs, through social dialogue and the open coordinating method.

Streeck (2017) suggests that this phase should be divided into two stages by distinguishing between the years 1986–95 (which in his view were characterized by welfare subordination to the completion of the internal market) and 1996–2008 (when national governments were encouraged to reform their national welfare systems to adjust to global competition). I prefer to consider the period a single phase, because there is continuity in the EU strategy of single market completion and creation of EMU, as well as in welfare policy reform.

The third phase, marked by financial crisis, economic recession, and exit strategies from the crisis, is a contradictory one: on the one hand, social investments are considered an integral part of the Lisbon strategy (in the sense that in the knowledge economy they can foster competitiveness); on the other hand, social policies are seen as hardly compatible with fiscal austerity and public debt containment. Issues of work and welfare became more complex and controversial because of the global financial crisis and economic recession, as well as the social consequences of exit strategies. I will discuss this third, highly controversial, phase in more detail in Section 12.6, arguing that the key question is not whether to keep or dismantle the welfare state, but how to reform it in a viable, effective, sustainable way, passing from the passive defence of workplaces to active labour policies and flexicurity, and from distributive to retributive pension schemes.

6   The Effects of the Global Financial Crisis and the Reaction of European Welfare Regimes

The global financial crisis, which exploded in 2008, had relevant effects on the two main models of contemporary capitalism: while it downsized the alleged superiority of the Anglo-Saxon, market-driven, variety, it also put strong pressure on the European, coordinated market, variety, and on the welfare state as its key component. The thesis that identifies in the growth of the welfare state one of the main causes of the financial crisis does not persuade. Rather than the increase in welfare expenditures were management inefficiency, patronage politics, and corruption that aggravated the fiscal crisis of the state in the countries that were most struck by the crisis; but it was also the other way around: it was the financial crisis that badly worsened public finances and reduced resources for social policies. Low, and even negative, growth rates worsened the deficit/GDP ratio and increased the sovereign debt; deindustrialization and jobs losses reduced the tax base; and fiscal austerity policies cut welfare expenditure.

The global crisis has actually been a sequence of related crises, which did not affect with the same intensity and over the same length of time individual developed countries and emerging economies. The global financial crisis, triggered by the subprime crisis in the USA, caused a sharp decline in production in 2009 and provoked in the following years a series of negative effects, both social (rising unemployment, decline of disposable income, growing inequalities, and social malaise) and political (citizens' declining trust in policymakers, government crises, and neo-populist upsurges). The crisis hit the EU economy harder than other world regions. The recession lasted 15 months, with a −5.40 per cent record low in the first quarter of 2009; in that year there were 23 million unemployed, equal to 10 per cent of the active population. Still in 2012, GDP declined both in the EU (−0.4 per cent) and the eurozone (−0.91 per cent), in 2013, it declined by 0.26 per cent for the Eurozone and increased by only 0.3 per cent in the EU. The crisis has compounded serious difficulties for public finances in many EU countries and a sequence of sovereign debt crises (Greek Irish, Portuguese, Spanish, Italian) that have put the euro under heavy stress. Since 2008, there have been different phases in the management of the crisis: the early years were characterized by measures aimed at recapitalizing banks that were in trouble (amounting to 20–30 per cent of GDP in the UK, Belgium, and the Netherlands, and up to 100 per cent in Ireland; the EEU helped this process by th ECB supply of money at close to zero interest rates), and by relaxing the rules of the European Stability and Growth Pact, and favouring public investments and fiscal stimulus for jobs and growth (an example being the Brown government's £3 billion 'budget for growth' in the UK).

EU exit strategies from the crisis (fiscal consolidation, price stability, cost reduction, and efficiency increasing policies) have been successful. The European economy as a whole has overcome the crisis; in August 2018, Greece was the last EU country to end emergency measures. But social costs (for employment and welfare have been very high: youth unemployment and underemployment, increasing inequalities, growing disparities in growth rates and employment levels between member states, severe cuts in social spending for health, education, and public housing. Especially in those countries that received support from the European Stability Mechanism or from the International Monetary Fund (IMF) as stand-alone grants, austerity measures were coupled with far-reaching institutional reforms underwritten in Memoranda of Understanding by the receiving governments (Scharpf, 2011). The number of voices demanding structural changes has increased considerably during the crisis, as several commentators have identified the lack of structural reforms as a major cause of the crisis and as barriers to renewed growth in the crisis countries. But contrary opinions have also voiced, denouncing cuts in social benefits and pensions, the promotion of atypical employment and the erosion of employment protection, the decentralization of collective bargaining, and the weakening of workers' interest representation. It is open to question how different government coalitions influenced exit strategies and welfare cuts. Some researchers (Becker and Jager, 2012; Hermann, 2014) point out that reforms were similar, despite the fact that both the causes of the crisis (real estate bubbles, public debt, private debt, etc.) and the type of welfare systems differed from one country to another. But, although it is true that social policy was everywhere subordinated to fiscal stabilization policy, they actually overstate the similarities and understate the legacy of different welfare systems.

European welfare regimes reacted to the financial crisis and economic recession by enhancing different mixes of reforms that were already in place in the previous decades as a response to increasing global competition. Adopting Hemerijck's detailed analysis (2012), one can identify nine areas of policy changes and innovations:

1. More rigorous fiscal and monetary policies aimed at macro-economic stability, low inflation, and public debt reduction (such as the Maastricht parameters for joining the EMU).
2. Collective bargaining aimed at moderating the demands for wage increases, often achieved in tripartite negotiations between unions, employers associations, and governments.
3. Active labour market policies based on the principle of employment priority.
4. Flexicurity mechanisms in regulating the labour market, aiming at reconciling the flexibility required by employers with active support for temporarily unemployed workers to re-enter the labour market.
5. Tendency to consolidate unemployment relief with social assistance and to grant less generous unemployment benefits with the condition of attending courses of professional retraining and counselling (as in the French minimal wage reintegration system).
6. Reforms of social security, shifting to pay as you go pension schemes and rising the pension age, together with integration of the three pillars of social security (state, firm, and individual).
7. Upgrading social services for families and facilitating women's work, shifting from 'passive' monetary incentives to 'active' labour policies (preschool child-care, parental leave).
8/9. Related changes in the ways to finance and manage social policies (as in the new public management approach), which imply a redefinition of the relations between state, market, and civil society.

Various combinations of these policy changes were reinforced and hardened after the 2008 crisis, stirring widespread worries about the survival of the welfare state. To mention just one, Guy Ryder, Director General of the International

Labour Office, in introducing the volume *The European Social Model in Crisis. Is Europe Losing its Soul?* (Vaughan-Whitehead, 2017), argues that many elements of the European Social Model have changed dramatically over the last few years, especially in those countries facing fiscal consolidation, and, although he admits that pressure from demographic changes and long-term sustainability issues, as well as structural unemployment, may mean that reforms are required to ensure the sustainability of Europe's economic and social systems, he points out that many reforms in Europe have been implemented abruptly and in some cases arbitrarily, with important social costs. However, scholars and commentators of European politics differ on their evaluation of the performance of EU welfare during the crisis and, more significantly, on the best strategies to be adopted.

Space and time matter in evaluating the effectiveness of European welfare during the crisis; some countries, at least in the early stages of the financial crisis, weathered the storm better than others. Through the use of strong social dialogue and automatic stabilizers, many jobs were saved and household income protected. Social protection mechanisms acted as automatic stabilizers and greatly contributed to minimizing the social costs of the crisis. Unemployment benefits and relief measures helped to cushion the social shocks of massive job losses and increased poverty, and contributed to limit the economic impact of the crisis by avoiding a collapse in consumption. The fact that real public social expenditure, which was relatively stable in 2006–8, started to increase dramatically in 2009 shows that these mechanisms acted as automatic stabilizers, thus limiting the decline in citizens' purchasing power and global domestic demand. In 2009, social protection expenditure increased by around 6 per cent in the EU-27, an acceleration driven mainly by increases in unemployment expenditure, but also in health, disability, old age, and survivors' pensions.

The increase in unemployment expenditure mainly reflected increases in the number of unemployed. Significant differences exist between countries in their mitigation of the employment shock of the crisis. The 'employment miracle' in Germany – with not much employment reduction despite output contraction – was due in particular to the implementation of work-sharing schemes that could be negotiated through social dialogue at enterprise level and represented a credible alternative to layoffs. In France, partial unemployment schemes, with the state funding a shorter working week, also allowed some alternatives to unemployment. Other elements of the model such as the *Cassa Integrazione Guadagni* in Italy, helped to mitigate adverse effects on unemployment. The training system in Sweden together with its flexicurity system helped the country to avoid major unemployment effects. The external flexibility system combined with training mechanisms developed in Scandinavian countries contrasted with the type of external flexibility based on a high share of temporary workers in Spain, who not only lost their jobs in the crisis but also had difficulties finding another job, with a very high rate of long-term unemployment. In all countries where there was a tradition of social dialogue at enterprise level, layoffs were often avoided through the negotiation of agreements between management and unions on shorter working hours, as in Austria, and/or lower wages, as in France. By contrast, in those EU countries where social dialogue institutions were less developed, the crisis led to immediate and massive layoffs, as in Estonia, Latvia, and Lithuania.

The initial 'neo-Keynesian' response to the downturn, i.e. deficit spending in order to make up for the lack of private demand, did not last long, because it implied increasing budget deficits, which triggered sovereign debt crises in the most vulnerable EU economies, threatening the future of the monetary union itself. And the strategy of fiscal austerity and public debt containment became dominant; from 2009 onwards, the EU shifted from economic stimulation to financial consolidation (Bieling, 2012; European Commission, 2012; Theodoropoulou & Watt, 2011). One country after another adopted austerity packages, some of them several packages in a row. Greece and Ireland presented the most ambitious plans, cutting public spending by 18 per cent of GDP, while Portugal was aiming for 12 per cent (OECD, 2014). Social protection expenditure in the EU-27 increased by around 7 per cent in 2009, levelled out in 2010, started to decline in 2011, and continued to fall in 2012. The decline affected most member states but was particularly significant in Greece, Latvia, Lithuania, Hungary, Portugal, and Romania. Since 2011, the worsening of the sovereign debt crisis in countries such as Greece and Spain, after Ireland and Portugal, and the risk of further extension to other vulnerable economies, such as Italy, has made fiscal consolidation an absolute priority for the EU. The sovereign debt crises forced countries at risk to ask for rescue measures from supranational institutions (EU, ECB, IMF). These came in the form of conditional aid (fiscal austerity and public expenditure containment), which in turn implied severe cuts in welfare programmes, depressed investments, and reduced jobs at the very time they were needed more than ever.

The negative effects on welfare included: wage cuts (although Germany's decision to introduce a statutory minimum wage in 2015 went in the opposite direction), greater freedom for employers to unilaterally change working hours (as in Spain or Romania), restrictions on the right to strike (as in Hungary and Greece), cuts in firms' occupational safety and health budgets (as in Portugal and Croatia), the simplification of procedures for individual dismissals (as in Greece, Italy, Estonia, Portugal, and Slovenia) and cuts in both unemployment and social benefits, with stricter eligibility conditions and reduced duration (Vaughan-Whitehead, 2015). Hermann's study (2014) on reforms in social protection, pensions, labour markets, and collective bargaining in eleven EU countries severely affected by the crisis between 2008 and 2012 reported pension freezes in seven of them, while four actually cut pension benefits, a general fall in social expenditure, a decline both in in-kind and cash benefits in 2010–12 in most member states (particularly significant, around 5 per cent or more, in Greece, Latvia, Portugal, Romania, and, to a lesser extent, Spain). Employment security was reduced in the public sector, with adverse effects on women and the reconciliation of work and family. The UK applied unprecedented employment cuts, as well as a pay freeze across all areas of the public sector for 2011–13, followed by a 1 per cent cap on pay rises after 2013. At the other extreme, Nordic countries did not experience any employment or wage cuts in the crisis, although the share of employment in the public sector fell in the 1990s and 2000s in Sweden. Job cuts during the crisis were limited in the Netherlands, Croatia, and Germany.

Moreover, relevant structural reforms, including changes in welfare policies, have been implemented in several EU countries. Some had limited scope in countries where income taxes and non-wage labour costs were already high and could not be increased further in the highly competitive context of the global market. But other reforms were more far-reaching, such as the prolongation of working life (as the Monti government did in Italy in 2012), measures for streamlining health care, and pension and assistance expenditures.

Differences in the various types of European welfare states have influenced capacity to cope with the crisis, but common elements have been strengthened by the combined effect of the Europeanization of issues of work and welfare, which have since the mid-1980s become intertwined with the Single Market and EMU, and the exit strategies from the global financial crisis and economic recession.

7 The Critics from Opposite Sides

The reforms implemented (or suggested) before and during the crisis have stirred a lively debate about the need, feasibility, and type of welfare changes and the prospects of the European Social Model. At one end of the continuum are the neoliberal theorists who think that competitive growth is hardly compatible with existing social protection and that welfare needs drastic downsizing; at the other end, are the traditional Left's defenders of the pre-crisis European welfare state. Neoliberal theorists believe in the ability of markets to determine optimal levels of wages and employment, and argue that labour regulations, when they induce labour market rigidities, also accentuate the negative impact of crises on unemployment. Social measures to protect individuals from the consequences of imperfections of market forces are considered as having the direct effect of increasing the cost of labour and undermining economic and labour market performance. It therefore becomes impossible for employers to lower wages to a level at which excess labour supply would be restored to its 'natural' level. Moreover, public social transfers, such as unemployment benefits, would have the effect of disincentivizing work and encouraging voluntary unemployment. Comparing GDP growth rates and unemployment levels in Anglo-Saxon countries and in continental Europe, they trace the lower growth of the latter to the many interferences by the state and the higher unemployment levels to a poorly flexible, dual labour market, where unionized workers are opposed to all those who do not have the same guarantees, such as many youngsters, women, immigrants, and other 'weak' groups.

This critique has some truth, but largely underestimates, or even utterly ignores, policy innovations such as flexicurity, active labour policies, and new forms of social protection, which can be beneficial not only for workers but for enterprises and society as a whole. In spite of this underestimation and in spite of official EU documents (such as those of the Lisbon Strategy) that declare social progress is a 'productive factor', the neoliberal paradigm was hegemonic (although often formulated in less extreme forms). At first, it mostly targeted the largest EU economy, Germany, and mistook contingent difficulties linked to German reunification for alleged structural weaknesses of the social market economy model. Later on, after the 2008 crisis, it increasingly focused on the weakest EU member states' economies and their huge sovereign debts.

At the other end of the continuum, radical Left intellectuals stated that the key qualifying elements of the model had been sacrificed to neoliberal ideology (Gallino, 2013) to the point that the 'social model' had become a simple cover up of subjugation to economic neoliberalism (Scharpf, 2011). Structural reforms were severely criticized. Cuts in social benefits and pension payments, the promotion of atypical employment and the erosion of employment protection, the decentralization of collective bargaining, and the weakening of bargaining structures and interest representation reverse the decommodifying effect built into the model and fuel poverty and inequality. And the critique extends to the Open Method of Coordination, because through mutual learning and peer review structural reforms can spread to further countries (Hermann, 2014).

This view also has some truth, but it neglects the effectiveness of welfare policy innovations in various EU member states and the resilience of key aspects of the European Social Model even in the neoliberal climate, such as better industrial relations, more effective policies for human resources development, more balanced relations between the real economy and financial economy, and more careful regulation of financial activities by central banks.

8   The Reformers: The Social Investment Approach

The critical approach at one end of the continuum demands the drastic downsizing, or even dismantling, of the traditional welfare state, the approach at the other end staunchly defends the pre-crisis welfare state and wants to restore it. A third, in the middle, the social investment approach, focuses on the key question of welfare state reform, both persistence and change (Hemerijck, 2012). This approach was developed before the global crisis to account for the policy changes introduced in response to global competition, but was further refined during the global crisis. It argues that the welfare state has actually been undergoing deep institutional changes, trying to cope with new macro-economic and macro-political requirements, but keeping its basic goal of social protection.

The social investment approach marked a transition from the classical post-Second World War welfare state view to one more in line with contemporary globalization. Well before the 2008 crisis, the three pillars on which rested the 'Keynesian compromise' had been severely weakened, these being stable employment of all adult males in fast growing economies with a Fordist work organization; a stable family, based on gendered division of labour and intergenerational solidarity; and autonomous economic and social policymaking by sovereign states. These pillars were undermined by a combination of processes: firms' delocalization, flexibilization of labour, the transformation of women's role in the family and in the workplace, constraints of global competition on government decision-making. At the same time, new social risks had to be met by new welfare policies – such as health care for a fast-growing elderly population, assistance for severe disabilities, benefits for structural unemployment, day nurseries for working mothers – that conflicted with the traditional ones of social security, temporary unemployment, and anti-poverty. The need to cope with the new risks without neglecting traditional ones has been a key drive in developing the new perspective, where welfare is seen as a social investment rather than a social expenditure.

The study commissioned by the Belgian presidency of the EU in 2001, *Why we Need a New Welfare State* (Esping Andersen et al., 2002), affirms that new risks – stemming from social segmentation, erosion of professional skills, and structural poverty – make traditional passive social policies (such as unemployment benefits) inadequate and too costly, and suggests that individuals, families, and society should be prepared to adapt to the ongoing transformation (changes in career patterns and working conditions, aging population, and new social and environmental risks) through innovative policies aimed at long-term development of human capital: training, flexicurity, active employment policies, social services for the family, and rising retirement age. This proposal is very similar to the one outlined by Anthony Giddens as a qualifying aspect of Tony Blair's Third Way Labour government programme, with a significant difference: whereas for the Third Way ideologists the new social investment approach should replace the traditional social protection model, for Esping Andersen and his colleagues the new policy should work alongside the old one (and it is actually in line with the Nordic welfare model).

The need of reforming welfare systems has increased with the crisis. Institutional and policy innovations have been numerous and relevant, but unevenly distributed in states with different welfare systems. The social investments perspective can be more easily applied to the Nordic welfare model countries, which have healthier public finances. The governments of Denmark, Finland, and Sweden have implemented fiscal stimuli, active employment policies, initially for the young, new public and semi-public job opportunities, and infrastructural investments. Let us take as an example the Swedish attempt to fight unemployment in general and youth unemployment in particular. Between 2008 and 2009, unemployment rose from 19 per cent to almost 25 per cent. The government responded with a great expansion of active employment policies, the creation of new jobs in the public and private/public sectors, an increase in vocational college enrolments, the development of counselling for activating human resources, and the doubling of incentives for employers hiring new, mostly unemployed, workers.

Preventive policies aimed at keeping jobs and investing in human capital have also been developed in continental welfare model countries, such as Germany, France, Belgium, and Austria, with various measures aimed at supporting employment through the transfer of social contributions from industry to state, trade union agreements of wage freezes in exchange for no layoffs, and an increase in funds for professional training. In Germany, the Angela Merkel centre-right coalition government invested €12 billion in education, research, and development, together with a saving plan of €80 billion in the three-year period 2012–14 in order to assure a balanced public budget in 2016 (this included, among other measures, cutting 10,000 public jobs and reducing tax benefits for housing).

The social investments approach runs into greater difficulty in the other two European welfare models. In the UK, an Anglo-Saxon welfare model country, after the Labour party government headed by Gordon Brown had to implement a massive rescue operation for the banks, David Cameron's Conservative/Liberal coalition government adopted a neoliberal plan of public expenditure cuts of €20 billion in five years (13 of which of welfare cuts, including education, social protection, and fiscal incentives for families). In the Mediterranean welfare model countries hit by, or risking, a sovereign debt crisis, such as Greece, Portugal, Spain, and Italy, drastic fiscal austerity measures had to be implemented, such as raising the retirement age, cutting public employment, freezing wages and pensions in the public sector, increasing VAT, and liberalizing the labour market.

Although several European strategies embody elements of a social investment strategy (Kvist, 2013), the crisis will be felt in years to come with reduced life income for younger cohorts, lower fertility laying the ground for intergenerational conflicts, and the migration of skilled youth (implying that returns in social investments made in southern parts of Europe will benefit northern parts).

Overall, evidence points at the European social investment model taking a larger role in Europe after the crisis, but this is unlikely to become a generalized feature, since the countries most in need of social investments are also the countries least likely to develop high-quality social investment.

9 The Open Method of Coordination

Given that EU member states are unevenly suited to the adoption of a social investments approach in the recalibration of welfare, an essential requirement for its success would be a strategy coordinated across the EU. National governments are in fact squeezed between the so-called troika (EU, ECB, IMF) demand to reduce their public debts through fiscal austerity and pressure from their electorates, who are reluctant to accept new sacrifices. This situation fosters the rise of populist anti-EU parties that urge for nationalist closures (Martinelli, 2018). The answer to national populism can only be what constitutes the leitmotiv of this book: relaunching the European project and moving fast on the path of closer and deeper integration, starting with coordinated fiscal policy and investments in growth and jobs. What is needed is a daring political response to what has been a serious economic crisis and is still a serious social crisis. Welfare policies can be implemented at national level, by adopting a common strategy and a shared method. The open Method of Coordination

(OMC) appears to be the best and more viable in a field such as welfare, where member states intend to keep sovereignty but at the same time homogeneous choices at European level are required. We will examine this method with regard to a very important policy, that of employment.

The origin of the OMC goes back to the Delors Commission's White Paper on Growth, Competitiveness and Jobs at a time when, as we have already noted, intensifying competition on the global market induced an acceleration of economic and monetary integration with the risk of leaving social policies behind. The White Paper was focused on the link between economic policies and social solidarity, and proposed an investment of ECU 600 billion, with the aim of creating 15 million new jobs in five years, but member states considered it too costly and refused. The goals set in the following year (December 1984) in Essen by the European Council (improvement of employment opportunities, reduction of unskilled labour, active employment policies aimed at fighting unemployment, and measures for social groups risking inactivity) were not achieved. It was only with the 1997 Amsterdam Treaty (Title VII) that a European employment strategy was outlined, according to which the Commission proposes policy guidelines, the Council adopts them, national governments implement them, the Council evaluates their effectiveness, and suggests forms of cooperation and gives incentives to member states willing to cooperate. Title VII had the merit of institutionalizing a mutual learning process of best practices, adopting a middle-range perspective, and introducing the comparative evaluation of results achieved by member states; but it can be criticized for lacking rigorous measures and effective sanctions for defaulting states and for subordinating labour policies to macro-economic policies.

Drawing on the experience of coordinated employment policies over the preceding decade, OMC has been broadly applied to a great range of policy fields as part of the 2000 Lisbon European Council strategy (aimed at turning the EU by 2010 into the most competitive and dynamic knowledge-based economy in the world, with sustainable economic growth, more and better jobs, and social cohesion), and of the subsequent strategy known as 'Europe 2020'. OMC can be generally defined as a process based on the principles of participation, accountability and transparency, guidelines and timetables, indicators and benchmarking, regional and national targets and measures, periodic monitoring and evaluation by independent committees, automatic correctives, peer review and feedback, and mutual learning of best practices as key steps (Zeitlin & Pochet, 2005). In what is defined a deliberative poliarchy, EU institutions and member states jointly define the main goals and at the same time agree on procedures and indicators for the empirical evaluation of goals attainment. Several public and private actors can contribute to attaining agreed goals at different levels of authority and involvement. Each participant enjoys a high degree of autonomy in the choice of strategies and means, but has the obligation to report periodically and systematically according to the commonly agreed procedures and indicators, and to participate in peer reviews. Objectives, procedures, and measurement criteria can be periodically reviewed too, mostly due to the entrance of new actors who are considered necessary to achieve the agreed goals. Actors do not comply because of the threat of sanctions by a hierarchical authority, but because they feel obliged to give account and justify their own autonomous choices in front of their peers in terms of efficiency, effectiveness, and equity. This in its turn requires appropriate indicators.

On the one hand, OMC has been praised as a 'third way' for EU social policy between regulatory competition and harmonization, an alternative to both intergovernmentalism and supranationalism, an instance of public rule-making, a new way for enhancing democratic participation and accountability within the EU by opening up the policymaking process to inputs from nongovernmental organizations, social partners, and local/regional actors (Rodrigues, 2002). On the other hand, it has been criticized as an unnecessary 'soft law' option even in domains where the EU already possesses legislative powers, and as an exercise in symbolic politics where national governments repackage existing policies to demonstrate their apparent compliance with EU objectives (Radaelli, 2003). Although this kind of criticism has some grounds, OMC can be considered a valuable approach to coordinate at European level public policies that play a strategic role in enhancing EU competitiveness (research and innovation, infrastructures, digital economy) without downsizing welfare policies (social security, employment, social inclusion) at the national level. However, OMC has been applied only on a limited scale owing to the difficulty of adopting measures of positive integration, which require coordination between national and subnational governments and cooperation with key actors of civil society, and then run the risk of raising the opposition of neo-nationalist parties and governments.

The Lisbon Strategy, revised in 2005 on the basis of the Kok Report (2004), was consistent with the European Social Model but the outcome was unsatisfactory, owing to manifestation of the global crisis. A new strategy, 'Europe 2020', was then adopted in 2010, the EU reiterating its commitment to implement the model as part of the strategy to boost growth and employment (more and better jobs throughout the EU). The headline targets to be met by 2020 were: to raise the employment rate of the population aged 20–64 from the current 69 per cent to at least 75 per cent; to reduce school drop-out rates to 10 per cent from the current 15 per cent and increase the share of the population aged 30–34 completing third level education from 31 per cent to at least 40 per cent; to invest 3 per cent of GDP in R&D in particular by improving the conditions for R&D investment by the private sector, and develop a new indicator to track innovation; to reduce the number of Europeans living below national poverty lines by 25 per cent, lifting 20 million people out of poverty (or the risk of poverty and social exclusion). The actions outlined in the flagship initiative An Agenda for New Skills and Jobs are essential to meet these targets.

We are convinced that European Social Model can and should remain a key distinctive feature of the EU, provided that it reforms itself through the coordination of member states' policies of labour, pensions, health, education, in a way that can combine competitive growth and the protection of social rights. A necessary requisite for implementing these coordinated reforms is economic recovery, because stagnation has increased disparities in competitiveness among member states and aggravated social inequalities owing to welfare cuts in the economically weaker countries; but growth is a necessary, not a sufficient, condition to avoid a disconnection between 'economic' Europe and 'social' Europe, mitigate the conflicts between northern and southern states, and prevent 'welfare shopping' and the levelling down of social protection.

To counter these trends, it is necessary to outline a macro-social strategy for the eurozone, to complement its macro-economic strategy, also through the creation of a European Institute of Social Protection, as proposed by the European Socialists and Democrats (S&D). This macro-social strategy should include the setting of social minimum standards for national policies in the fields of unemployment, workers' reintegration and retraining, minimum wage, strengthened monitoring of social disequilibria between member states with accurate indicators, country-specific recommendations and infraction sanctions in all cases in which critical thresholds are bypassed (analogous to those inflicted in case of macro-economic imbalances), and the use of EMU fiscal resources for facing social crises that threaten eurozone growth and stability; making the Employment, Social Policy, Health and Consumer Affairs Council as institutionally relevant as the Economic and Financial Council (Ecofin).

10   Conclusion

EU welfare is both diverse and unique. Besides the common principles, goals, and norms written in the treaties (the current Lisbon Treaty emphasizes the social dimension more than previous ones), which outline the general framework, there are two main policy areas and some other social spaces. First, there is the complex of member countries' social protection systems that, although different, share a common core and should keep their path-dependent specificities, but at the same time strive to coordinate and adapt to each other on the basis of common goals and standards, and accept the sharing of some risks. Secondly, there is the EU's social policy, or the set of regulative, distributive, and redistributive policies, financed by the EU budget and based on EU law, that are addressed to all EU citizens. Thirdly, in the middle, there are: the intra-European mobility space, based on the principle of non-discrimination (upheld by several ECJ verdicts), within which all EU citizens are entitled, qua citizens, to social services and benefits in the place where they choose to live, work, and retire (the free circulation of workers is a key principle in the treaties, norms for the coordination of member states' social security systems go back to the 1960s, a 2011 directive regulates the trans-border mobility of medical patients); and subnational and trans-border social spaces resulting from EU regional cooperation policy (since Delors there has been a tendency to strengthen the third level of government and foster region-building in areas such as labour, health, and inclusion policies, because at the regional level there are relevant economic and demographic differences and it is easier to experiment with policy innovations such as the public/private mix), as well as from cooperation between professional organizations in health and social security (2004 directive). It is necessary to integrate and reconcile all these social spaces into a coherent whole. And it is necessary to further develop the European social union (ESU) to complement EMU.

European leaders such as the Belgian Frank Vandenbroucke suggest reconciling the pan-European and national levels through the open method of coordination; the EU should support and orient national welfare policies on the basis of agreed goals and standards, but leave them largely autonomous to define specific policy measures and organizational models. This can be done in many ways, but first of all through the recommendations of the European Semester and with a smart use of flexibility clauses in monitoring state budgets (in order to persuade leaders to decide social investments with long-term benefits and short-term costs, which they are not too willing to make owing to continuous electoral campaigns and anti-EU populist propaganda on social media).

The Rome Declaration, adopted by EU leaders on 25 March 2017 confirmed that delivering a more social and fair Europe is a key priority for the Union and outlined the importance of looking towards a strong social Europe, based on sustainable growth, which promotes economic and social progress as well as cohesion and convergence, upholding the integrity of the internal market and taking into account the diversity of national systems and the key role of social partners for the EU-27.

A step forward in this direction has been the European pillar of social rights, presented by the European Commission in April 2017 and proclaimed by EU leaders at the Gothenburg Social Summit in November 2017. The Pillar (primarily conceived for the euro area but applicable to all EU member states wishing to be part of it) was prepared in consultations with social partners and sets out 20 key principles and rights to support fair and well-functioning labour markets and welfare systems. It provides a framework for the upward convergence of national welfare systems and the modernization of the existing EU legal framework. The 20 principles are grouped in three sectors: work–life balance (with legal norms being parental leave and flexible working arrangements for providing personal care, and policy measures against discrimination and dismissal of parents); access to social protection for people in non-standard forms of employment and self-employment who, owing to their employment status, are not sufficiently covered by social security schemes and are thus exposed to higher economic uncertainty; transparent and predictable working conditions aiming at setting new rights for all workers, particularly addressing insufficient protection for workers in more precarious jobs, while limiting burdens on employers and maintaining labour market adaptability (such as a worker's right to more complete information on the essential aspects of the work and a limit to the length of probationary periods). The 2019–2024 Commission President Ursula von der Leyen pledged to implement an action plan "to bring our Pillar of Social Rights to life".

Specific directives can be approved or rewritten on this basis (such as the one in the making by the new Commission on reconciling family life and working life), as well as making recommendations and non-binding communications (soft law). National welfare policies can be evaluated in terms of their coherence with the 20 stated principles; programmes of social infrastructures can be financed using EU structural funds and schemes of cofinancing in the critical areas of education, health, and housing in order to make social rights really applicable to all (after the 2019 EP election, an interesting investment plan of social infrastructures has been proposed by two former Commission presidents, Prodi and Santer). A successful instance of EU-wide social program is the European Youth Guarantee, so that young people can benefit from decent wages and high-quality internships: since its start in 2014, more than 3.5 million youngsters each year have successfully participated.

The social investment paradigm and related policies (social dialogue, open methods of coordination) have produced relevant results, but have been less effective during the 2008 global crisis and its aftermath because the constraints on fiscal consolidation and public spending cuts have narrowed the space for innovative welfare reforms. It is now urgent to pursue the strategic goals of sustainable growth, jobs enhancement, and quality welfare (without abandoing fiscal consolidation), in order to avoid the vicious circle of cuts in public investments leading to low growth leading to increasing public debt leading to enhanced fiscal austerity; but, with some exceptions, this is not yet happening. In order to break the vicious circle, a paradigm shift in welfare policy is needed.

The EU is confronting a basic choice: either continue to sacrifice social policy to fiscal and monetary stability, running the risk of fostering national/populist protest parties and movements that want to renationalize policymaking and reduce the EU to a free exchange area; or significantly investing in the social dimension of European integration, coupling the existing EMU with an ESU, in other words gradually moving in the direction of a single federal welfare state – while helping at the same time the selective modernization of national welfare systems in a sustainable way, compatible with the requisites of global competition. This is not an easy task, but is far more desirable than the fragmentation of the EU into weak, conflicting sovereign states with obsolete and inadequate national welfare systems.

CHAPTER 13

The European Economy

1   Unity and Diversity of the European Economy

In the concluding chapter of *The European Economy since 1945*, written at the dawn of the global crisis, Barry Eichengreen (2007) compares the future of the European model with the American. He remarks that in the last decade gross domestic product (GDP) and productivity grew less in the European Union (EU) than in the United States (USA); and predicts that, if radical technological changes (in informatics, biotechnology, nanotechnology) continue with the same pace and scope of previous decades, the European economy – whose culture is more inclined to incremental rather than radical innovation – will continue to grow more slowly; but he adds that in the medium and long term there is no reason to expect a serious competitive crisis, because the fundamentals will still be there, such as a numerous, well-educated, and well-trained labour force, an effective enforcement of contracts and competition rules, good corporate governance, efficient and careful supervision and regulation, and, last but not least, stable macroeconomic policies.

Twelve years after Eichengreen's book was published, we can remark that these fundamentals of the European economy are still in place and the EU economy has recovered from the global crisis. With an estimated US$18.8 trillion GDP in 2018, the economy of the EU amounts to 22 per cent of global economy (but only 17 per cent in purchasing power parity). As Figure 13.1 shows, compared with the other major world economies, its performance in the ten years since 2007 (the last year before the global crisis) is similar to that of the USA, higher than Japan, and lower than China and emerging economies (IMF, *World Economic Outlook*, October 2017).

The EU GDP is higher than in the pre-crisis years; its rate of growth was 2.6 per cent in 2017 (2.5 per cent in the eurozone), the highest since 2007, and 2.1 per cent in 2018 (1.9 per cent in the eurozone). But, as Figure 13.2 shows, the recovery took an uneven path, marked by ups and downs, with years of anaemic growth caused by a series of debt crises and years of robust expansion, helped by very accommodative monetary policy, mildly expansionary fiscal policy, and a recovering global economy (World Bank, *Tradingeconomics*, 2019). In 2019, a new slowdown has taken place: forecasted growth is 1.4 per cent in 2019 and 1.6 per cent in 2020 (1.2 per cent and 1.4 per cent in the eurozone). Forecasted inflation rates are getting more distant from the desired 2 per cent

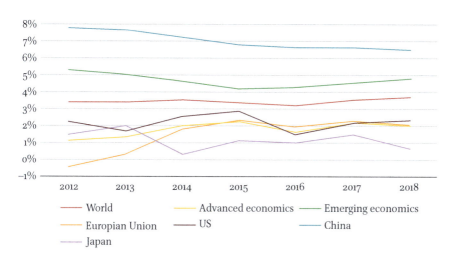

FIGURE 13.1 Growth rate of the world economy, 2012–2018
SOURCE: INTERNATIONAL MONETARY FUND, *WORLD ECONOMIC OUTLOOK*, OCTOBER 2017

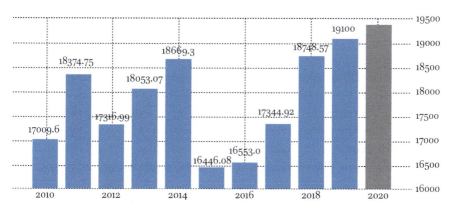

FIGURE 13.2 EU GDP in billion US dollars at current prices
SOURCE: TRADINGECONOMICS.COM / WORLD BANK

a year (1 per cent for the EU and 1.3 per cent for the eurozone in 2019 and 2020). As stated by the European Commission's Summer 2019 *Economic Forecast*, growth is clouded by external factors (the negative impact of protectionism and the ensuing uncertainty in trade tensions and investment, the consequences of Brexit, the more so for 'no deal' Brexit). In the near future, economic activity in the EU-27 and in the eurozone will show lights and shadows: the resilience of domestic demand, the services sector, and the labour market in the face of export-oriented activity and manufacturing weakness, and robust growth in Central and Eastern Europe in contrast with the slowdown in Germany and Italy.

The European economy has recovered from the long crisis, but economic and social consequences of the crisis are still being felt, in terms of growing divergence between the various EU national and regional economic reality and increasing cleavages in the economic policies of EU member states. Differences among member states and regions within them have existed from the start of the integration process, in terms of GDP, balance of payments, foreign investment, sovereign debt, primary budget deficit/surplus, structural unemployment, labour market participation, labour cost, labour productivity, import/export, investments in research and development (R&D), human capital, and so on (OECD, *Economic Outlook*, various years). Just to give an example, in the five years after the global crisis began, GDP grew mostly in Poland (+18 per cent), Slovakia (+10 per cent), and Germany, whereas it declined mostly in Greece (–20 per cent), Latvia (–13 per cent), Croatia (–8 per cent), Italy (–7 per cent) and Ireland (–7 per cent).

Even more significant are the differences in per capita income between regions (in terms of standardized purchasing power), from the highest (Inner London region 328 per cent more than the EU average, Luxembourg +266 per cent, Brussels region +203 per cent, Hamburg city state +203 per cent) to the lowest (the north-eastern region of Romania –30 per cent), Bulgaria's Severen Tsentralen –29 per cent, Severozapaden (–26 per cent). The same differences apply when we compare families' net purchasing power (which takes into account free welfare services and monetary transfers). As Figure 13.3 shows, in the ten years 2004–14, the total area of regions with less than the average individual purchasing power standard increased from 38 per cent to 45 per cent (Eurostat, 2004, 2014).

In 2018 economic differences among Eu member states remain large. GDP per capita (PPS) variates from 261% in Luxemburg to 51% in Bulgaria, The ranking of largest EU states GDP per capita is: Ireland (138, but this high value is partly misleading, due to the fact that the country's large share of crossborder workers in total employment, while contributing to GDP, are not taken into consideration as part of the resident population which is used to calculate GDP per capita), the Netherlands (129), Denmark (128), Austria (127), Germany (122), Sweden (120), Belgium (117), Finland(111) and France (105), all above average, whereas Italy (96), Spain and Czechia (91), Portugal (77), Hungary (71), Poland (70), Greece (68) and Romania (65) are below. Similar differences appear in actual individual consumption (AIC), that is a more significant indicator of households' material welfare. Nine Member States recorded AIC per capita above the EU average in 2018, the highest level being that of Luxembourg (34% above the EU average), ahead of Germany (20), Austria (117), Denmark (114), Belgium and the Netherlands (113), Finland (112), Sweden (108), France (107). Fourteen Member States recorded AIC per capita below the EU average: just below is Italy (98%), followed by Ireland (95), Cyprus (94), Spain (90), Lithuania (89), Portugal (83), Czechia (82), Malta (80), Slovenia (79), Greece (77), Poland (76), Estonia (74), Slovakia (73), Romania (71), Latvia (69); two countries, Croatia and Hungary, are 36% below average, and Bulgaria is at the bottom, 44% below average (Eurosytat Statistics, 2019).

Great disparities also occur in unemployment rates, which have further deepened during the crisis. In the crisi years, etween 2008 and 2012, it was Spain that showed the greatest increase (4 million, of which half a million were young unemployed), followed by Greece, Italy, the United Kingdom, and France, whereas in Germany there was the countertrend of 1,285,00 fewer unemployed (of which 216,000 were youngsters).

The long crisis has partially reversed the basic tendency toward greater homogeneity within the EU. Since the start of the European Economic Community, the economies of member states have grown more similar in terms of growth rates, GDP, per capita income, social protection, consumption patterns, and styles of life to the point that economic integration has appeared easier than political integration and as a major route to attaining the latter. The reduction of disparities between member countries has been a basic goal and a specific policy of the EU; the social cohesion policy has been implemented with the aim of attaining this, with the premise being that a society is more cohesive when inequalities are controlled and do not go above a certain level. The trend towards greater similarity has been interrupted – and even reversed in some aspects – as a consequence of the global crisis, which has deepened the cleavages between northern and southern countries and also within countries. The trend has continued with regard to the new EU members from Eastern and Central Europe.

At the roots of the increasing disparities and inequalities lies not only the global economic/financial crisis, which has affected in different ways and to different degrees the various member countries, but also the lack of a united and coordinated EU exit strategy. As we argue in Chapter 14, a single monetary policy coupled with 19 different macroeconomic policies does not allow an effective exit strategy from the crisis; a single currency shared by economies with different rates of productivity opens the way to financial speculation; a single monetary policy coupled with 19 different fiscal policies and corporate law systems pushes eurozone states to fiercely compete for attracting foreign investment. The creation of the euro was not wrong, since

298　　　　　　　　　　　　　　　　　　　　　　　　　　　　　　　　　　　　CHAPTER 13

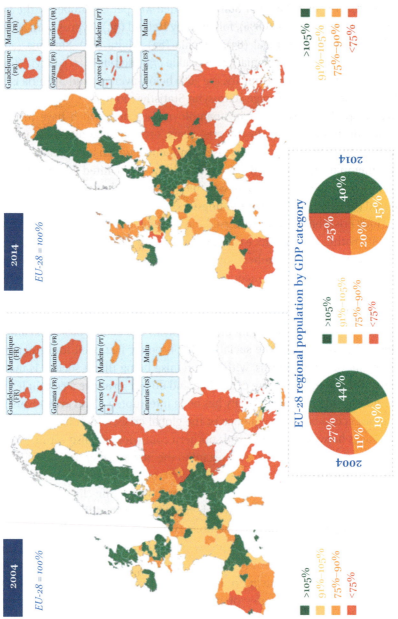

FIGURE 13.3 GDP in Purchasing Power Standard (PPS) per inhabitant by NUTS 2 region (% of the EU-28 average, 2004 and 2014)
SOURCE: EUROSTAT STATISTICS, 2014

benefits outweigh the costs, but it was a mistake not to complement it with a set of coordinated fiscal and macroeconomic policies, and with greater political integration.

2   European Economic Development since the Start of the Integration Process

The present state of the EU economy must be placed in the long-term perspective of Europe's economic integration, from the birth of the EEC to the present. Post-Second World War economic development is generally divided into two periods, separated by mid-1970s stagflation: the so-called *Les trente Glorieuses* (Fourastié, 1979), or the period between the end of the war and the first oil shock in 1973, and the other 30 years of contemporary globalization, from the late 1970s to the 2008 financial crisis. In the first period, the EU economy performed much better than the American economy, while in the second it lost ground with regard both to the USA and to the new emerging economies of China, India, and Brazil. The EU economy's pace slowed down especially in the so-called 'difficult' ten years between 1995 and 2005, then experienced a short recovery that was ended and reversed by the global crisis. The long stagnation is over, but the new phase of growth is precarious and unevenly affecting EU member countries.

The key elements of the first 'glorious' period have been the historical compromise between capital and labour and the complementary roles of market and state. On the one hand, trade unions and employers associations, strengthened by the Fordist model of production, engaged in collective bargaining and 'exchanged' wage moderation (at a time of significant productivity increases) for social security and employment growth. On the other, the Bretton Woods system favoured the opening of markets and free trade among nation states, but they remained fully sovereign in policymaking, implementing anti-cyclical deficit spending, full employment and welfare policies, and encouraging collective bargaining. This mix of national sovereignty and international liberalism is captured by the formula "Keynes at home, Smith abroad".

The 1957 Rome Treaty, which gave birth to the European Economic Energy Community (EEC) and European Atomic Energy Community (Euratom), as the previous 1951 Paris European Coal and Steel Community Treaty, were congruent with the new international economic order. In fact, the EEC was based on the customs union that resulted from removing domestic tariffs and quotas and adopting common external trade policies. In July 1968, after a series of gradual reductions, internal tariffs were completely abolished, 18 months ahead of the Treaty deadline. The economies of the six founding countries – Belgium, France, Germany, Italy, Luxembourg, and the Netherlands – gained considerable benefits in terms of high, rapid growth, low unemployment, and reduced inflation; Italy's GDP at constant prices grew 5.6 per cent a year on average between 1960 and 1967 and 4.9 per cent in the following six years. The equivalent data for Germany were 3.8 per cent and 5 per cent, and were similar for France (except in 1968). The German average unemployment rate was only 0.8 per cent in both periods, the French rate was 1.5 per cent in the first seven year period, and 2.8 per cent in the second six year period, whereas in Italy unemployment was higher (4.9 per cent and 5.7 per cent in the two periods, but lowest when taking a long-term perspective). Inflation was under control: the gross consumer price index increased on average between 1960 and 1967 by 2.5 per cent in Germany, 3.5 per cent in France, and 4.1 per cent in Italy; and increased somewhat more between 1967 and the 1973 oil shock, by 4.3 per cent in Germany, 5.8 per cent in France, and 5.1 per cent in Italy. In these years, the six EEC countries recovered half of their income gap with the economy of the hegemonic country, the USA: EEC per capita income, which was 40 per cent of the American figure in 1950, increased to 70 per cent.

In the early 1970s, at the end of *Les trente glorieuses,* the success of the European common market was evident. Trade among member countries had greatly increased; the opening of domestic markets forced the French and Italian industry and agriculture to restructure and rationalize in order to become more efficient and competitive; and the macroeconomic policies of the six member states were increasingly coordinated through the creation of the central banks' governors' committee and regular intergovernmental consultations. Indirect evidence of this success was the failure of the European Free Trade Association (EFTA) to become a real alternative to the EEC and the consequent request of the UK and other EFTA countries to join, as well as the negative reaction of French businessmen and farmers to De Gaulle's 'empty chair' policy.

Would Germany's, France's, and Italy's post-war reconstruction and economic growth taken place even without the European common market? Probably yes, owing to the combined effect of Bretton Woods monetary stabilization and trade liberalization, Marshall Plan aid, the growth in investments, and the diffusion of American technological innovation; but progress would not have happened on such a scale in the absence of the virtuous circle triggered by trade growth and integration among EEC member states, ensuring enhanced productivity and more efficient resource allocation. At the end of the first period, in the early 1970s, the degree of openness of EEC economies, measured in terms of the percentage value of exports on total production value, was up to 23.8 per cent (about half of which was due to infra-communitarian trade), much higher than the USA's 5.8 per cent and Japan's 10 per cent; and the EEC percentage of world trade was close to 30 per cent, the highest in the world. EEC countries enjoyed a *de facto* monopoly power in their internal market and a relative advantage in third countries' markets for a significant number of investment and durable consumer goods (Guerrieri & Padoan, 2009).

The varieties of capitalism theory that developed in these years compare the continental European coordinated market economy model (CME) or *Rheinische Kapitalismus* with the Anglo-Saxon 'market-driven' or liberal market economy model (LME). In the latter, the economy tends to be more competitive and dynamic, but provides fewer opportunities for employment stability and workers' union representation (while other firm's stakeholders, such as consumers and investors, are better protected by specific norms such as antitrust laws). The former is characterized by efforts to combine economic growth and social cohesion through the welfare state (a system of public services and monetary transfers for health care, social security, education, unemployment, minimal wage; see Chapter 11) or, in other words, the goal of developing a 'social citizenship' alongside a legal and political citizenship (T.H. Marshall, 1950). Workers are in this way integrated into the political system of representative democracy through an exchange of loyalty to democratic institutions with full citizenship rights and welfare policies.

The USA, but also the UK and other developed English-speaking economies such as Canada and Australia, are seen as examples of liberal market economies, in which firms organize their activities in competitive markets by top management authority, while the EEC countries, other continental European countries such as those in Scandinavia, Austria, Switzerland, and Japan are seen as examples of coordinated market economies, where business activities are based on a system of strategic institutionalized interactions among firms, unions, banks, and government agencies (Hall and Soskice, 2001). The competitive strength of an LME is based on sectors involving radical innovation, while that of a CME is based on sectors involving incremental innovation (engineering). As far as financial systems are concerned, LMEs are characterized by equity-based large stock markets, where it is easy for investors to switch assets, with consequent strong pressures for short-term profits, whereas CMEs are credit-based, providing an important role for banks, which often take a direct role in corporate decision-making-through their representatives in corporate boards – and take a long-term view of corporate success.

The role of the state in an LME is to ensure 'free and fair' markets, but otherwise intervene as little as possible, whereas in CME the state aims at establishing a framework by which authority can be delegated to corporate actors such as employers' organizations and trade unions. Unions are primarily occupational in LME and primarily sectoral in a CME (but not in Japan). Accordingly, wage bargaining is decentralized, at workplace or firm level, in the former and centralized, at sectoral or national level, in the latter. Relationships between employers and employees tend to be low trust owing to the 'hire and fire' principle and rely on numerical flexibility in LME, while they tend to be more high trust between co-workers and rely on functional flexibility in CME. Human relations in LME are characterized by individualized pay and career development, low level employment security, and declining trade union power, while in CME they are more collectively oriented, with higher levels of collective employee involvement, greater prevalence of autonomous teams, and less individualized pay.

Finally, relationships between firms are competitive and contract based in LME, with sub-contracting tending to be based on price competition and being relatively low trust, for example; whereas in CME they are collaborative, both in terms of building an institutional infrastructure (wage determination, bargaining, training, etc.) and developing long-term, high-trust relations across the supply chains of large firms. As for vocational training and education, in LME general education is provided by the state, while in vocational training large firms prefer to develop their own systems rather than contribute to sectoral/occupational systems; while in CME (but not in Japan) firms pool resources into highly developed vocational training systems, usually at sectoral level.

The two ideal types of LME and CME capitalism do not catch other significant differences between the EU and the American (US) and UK economy, such as, these two: first, the USA developed a large tertiary sector earlier than continental Europe and a great number of giant corporations, owing to the more active role played by financial markets in favouring corporate mergers and takeovers. Second, US firms are characterized by greater structural changes and organizational flexibility, while in Europe firms favour more long-term institutional stability, and growth through acquisitions is made more difficult by EU anti-trust legislation (Martinelli, 2007)..

More recently, a partial convergence has taken place between the US economy and the continental European as a consequence of globalization through such changes as a decline in the relative importance of the manufacturing sector, a growth of financial investments in the unregulated global market, a wave of mergers and acquisitions prompted by the need to develop bigger organizations, and more aggressive strategies in global competition (Crouch and Streeck, 1997).

3   The 1970s Regime Change in the World Economy

The golden age of post-war capitalism ended in the early 1970s owing to a few interconnected causal factors. On the one hand there was the growing deficit of the US trade balance (starting in 1971, with the first deficit since the beginning of the 20th century) and the inflationary push of the Vietnam war, which provoked a drastic change in American economic policy (the end of the convertibility of the dollar to gold and the start of floating exchange rates, and the implementation of monetary policy aimed at financing a growing public debt). On the other hand, there were rising wages, a fourfold increase in oil prices and related raw materials increases causing rising inflation, and declining productivity and balance of payments deficits in EEC countries. The outcome was stagflation, a dangerous combination of economic stagnation and monetary inflation. This critical juncture in the 1970s encouraged the regime change from the post-Second World War settlement between capital and labour to the neoliberal financial capital model.

The history of the paradigmatic change to hegemonic financial capital in the global economy and to the empowerment of central banks and international economic organizations has been widely described and need not be repeated here. Let us just point out that it implied both a policy change and a theoretical shift. Stagflation changed the primary focus of concern for government leaders and their scientific advisors from problems of aggregate demand and employment to problems with production's supply and cost. This policy shift went together with the intellectual shift from Keynesian economic theory to the Chicago School of supply-side economics.

In the following three decades, capitalism has changed, not in the sense of modifying its basic features (the key roles of market and entrepreneurship, the driving force of technological innovation, creative destruction, and periodic endogenous crises), but in the sense of being increasingly globalized because of the digital revolution in information and communication technology (ICT), the widespread adoption of neoliberal economic policies, and the failure of planned economies (with the collapse of the Soviet Union and the opening of the Chinese economy to the world market). Among the varieties of capitalism, the Anglo-Saxon market-driven neoliberal model seemed more fit for the new global context (sometimes even in the most radical form of 'market fundamentalism') and the other main models (*Rheinische Kapitalismus*, the Japanese model, the Nordic and the so-called Chinese 'market socialist economy') reduced their differences with respect to it and between themselves. However, in the 2008 global crisis, these other varieties of capitalism have reaffirmed their specific traits, such as a better balance between manufacturing and service, real economy and finance, and more effective government policies aimed at sustainable development and at reducing inequalities (although these goals have been unevenly pursued with ambivalent outcomes).

The 1970s regime change to the neoliberal model has been interpreted by some scholars as a strategic attempt by capitalists to buy time: "inflation, admitted to enable strong unions and weak employers to agree increases in nominal wages, ultimately resulted in stagnation as it distorted relative prices and undermined the confidence of owners of monetary assets" (Streeck, 2013: 48). Others see it as the result of governments' failure to reduce public spending and accept cutbacks in the budget-due to the electoral constraints of their welfare communities- which caused a neo-liberal anti-state reaction. Actually, as we remarked earlier, the 1970s stagflation can also be traced to other causes, alongside increasing wage demands and welfare expenditures: first of all, the very high increases in oil and raw material prices, and in the cost of money, these in their turn prompting supply-side economic policies.

In conclusion, the change that took place after this critical juncture can be explained in terms of structural economic variables (technological innovation, changes in relative competitiveness and world trade shares, expansionist monetary policy, and a huge increase in the volume of money looking for profitable investment) and key political transformations (China's shift to market socialism). All these factors contributed to corroding the oligopolistic assets of the previous phase. The push from below, made by the aggressive 'animal spirits' of new entrepreneurs, would not have been so successful without a dramatic change from above in the cultural climate and the government economic policies of developed countries. Keynesian theory seemed less fit to cope with 1970s stagflation and rising public debts. The Reagan administration in the USA and the Thatcher government in the UK – followed by the governments of several other developed and developing countries – adopted supply-side economic policies of extensive deregulation, privatization, tax cuts, and expansive monetary policy. A new policy regime, and within it a new growth model, prevailed (Magara, 2014).

The ICT revolution and global interdependence fostered a staggering growth in GDP and improved living conditions in emerging economies (especially China, India, and Brazil) as well as a more limited growth in developed countries; but, on the other hand, caused a growing asymmetry of power between capital and labour (through off-shoring and international supply chains) and between global market actors and national governments (which consciously reduced their regulatory powers or were unable to implement them). The increasing decision-making power of technocrats at the head of international organizations such as the International Monetary Fund (IMF), the General Agreement on Tariffs and Trade/World Trade Organization(WTO), the Organisation for Economic Co-operation and Development(OECD), and largely independent central banks significantly increased and coalesced in the so-called 'Washington consensus', whereas democratic controls were strongly reduced. Other consequences included the overexpansion of finance vis-à-vis the real economy (with an excess of wealth looking for increasingly higher financial returns), the predominance of financial control and short-termism in the conduct of the corporation, growing inequalities among and within national societies, and serious environmental threats.

The core of the cognitive framework that legitimized the new policy regime was the mainstream neoliberal economic theory of the self-regulating market, according to which markets are always capable of restoring their equilibrium whenever either rigorously exogenous factors or statistically unlikely events create imbalances. In a class analysis perspective, a shift took place from the Fordist compromise between managers and wage earners to an alliance between top managers and financiers (Boyer, 2012). With the opening of the world economy, foreign competition disciplined labour. The majority of wage earners were expelled from the dominant political bloc and reintroduced only as consumers. With long-term wage stagnation, living standards could only be sustained by working more hours and relying more on credit. Conversely, as regulations were removed, the financial system became dominant, imposing its logic on labour, the welfare state, and government policies, since it enjoyed an unchallenged mobility. The prosperity of the last decade of the 20th century was due to the growth of private and public finance, sustained by deregulation policies and legitimized by monetarist theory. The 1970s stagflation was interpreted as a state failure and fostered a neoliberal reaction, which changed the balance between market and state. Neoliberalism became the dominant ideology; Keynes was replaced by Hayek, Friedman, and the Chicago monetarist school. Deregulation, privatization, and liberalization policies were widely implemented with the aim of restoring market self-regulation.

The global economy grew owing to the increasing involvement of large 'emerging economies' (China, India, Brazil) and with the injection of large quantities of money into the advanced economies (quantitative easing). In these latter countries, social expenditure kept growing to compensate for the harsh effects of market discipline, resulting in ever increasing public debts; states became more dependent on the confidence of those market actors who bought their bonds and thus indirectly could dictate national economic policies. A parallel expansion of private debt took place – a "privatised

Keynesianism" (Crouch, 2004) – which was justified with the need to sustain consumption. These factors were at the root of the 2008 global financial crisis, which provoked the failures and bailouts of big American investment banks and spread to world finance. National governments had to pour a large amount of money into failing banks, thus increasing their debt (for some EU countries this meant moving from financial crisis to sovereign debt crisis). Huge state intervention clearly contradicted the orthodoxy of market self-regulation, but it was justified on the grounds of the exceptional character of the situation (the 'black swan' metaphor). The supporters of neoliberalism in central banks (Federal Reserve, Bank of England, European Central Bank, Bank of China, Bank of Japan), international economic organizations (IMF, World Bank) and national governments continued to argue that more liberalization and financial austerity (cuts in public expenditures) were necessary to avoid stagnation.

The resilience of the neoliberal policy regime, in spite of the global crisis, and contrary to Stiglitz's prediction that the failure of Lehman Brothers in 2008 would play a role equivalent to the fall of the Berlin Wall, is explained by the belief that capital, in particular financial capital, is the key driver of prosperity in the global economy. As Offe and Wiesenthal argue (1980), the influence of capital in the politics and policymaking in capitalist economies is inherently greater than that of labour, in whatever form it is exercised, in the market or in the political arena, by individual or collective actors (the latter being usually a second best choice, Martinelli, 2001). In an increasingly globalized economy, this asymmetry of power increases because entrepreneurs can not only threaten to start a 'capital strike', but also threaten to delocalize their activities (offshoring); in so doing they can play one state against another, one tax policy against another, in order to attract investments, and thus curtail the counter-power of unions and severely limit the regulatory power of governments. Since growing economic interdependence goes together with continuing political fragmentation, the democratic process of consensus formation that could limit the structural power of business is also limited. The international business class, and global finance within it, does not need to accept – or has less need to accept – a class compromise, since it is highly mobile and acts at a higher, global, level than political parties and voters who are still acting at national level. Business and financial elites are key components of the dominant social coalition in several countries, above all in the USA; but even governments, which have a political base that does not explicitly include these actors, cannot neglect them. The range of policy options for national governments, central banks, and international organizations are constrained by the interests of this dominant coalition, and neoliberal policies are often dominant.

The case of the EU in the global market is particularly interesting: we will try to assess how globalization implied opportunities and risks for the EU, whether it accelerated or slowed down the integration process, fostered greater unity or deeper cleavages; and we will review the responses of European institutions to global challenges and the strategic steps toward more integration – the completion of the single market and creation of the EU.

4 The EU in the Global Market

Contemporary globalization, from the late 1970s to the end of the long financial crisis, created significant opportunities for the EU economy, but also serious difficulties, greater than in the USA. European economic culture is less inclined to the radical technological and organizational innovation required by the digital revolution and more inclined to incremental changes that imply lower growth rates (Eichengreen, 2007). Investments in human capital and R&D are lower in the EU, as is the ability to attract investments, because of greater market rigidities and the stronger negative impact of financial austerity policies (Valli, 2002). The different performance of the EU and the US economy in this period is highlighted by the fact that gaps in per capita income and employment rate stopped diminishing.

The performance of the EU economy was much less sparkling than that of huge emerging economies, which were more and more open to the world market and characterized by large financial resources, lower labour costs, and fast scientific upgrading and technological learning (China after the Deng Xiaoping revolution, India after the shift from state planning to market, Brazil after the return to democracy and the neoliberal course of Henrique Cardoso's presidency). In an increasingly competitive scenario, European economies have been caught in between the more flexible and dynamic market-driven US economy and the aggressively competitive emerging economies. The response of EU institutions and member states governments has been only partially effective, sometimes inadequate, and often too fragmented.

We can distinguish three subperiods in contemporary globalization and in EU response: in the first, between the 1970s stagflation and the mid-1990s, EU countries effectively reacted to the challenges of the global market, as shown by significant GDP growth rates, and also because the potentialities of the newcomers in the world economy had not yet fully come to fruition. In the second subperiod, the so-called 'lost decade'– between the mid-1990s and the warning signs of the global financial crisis – the outcome was disappointing. In the third subperiod, that of the 2008 global crisis, the situation worsened. We will discuss the two first subperiods in this chapter and the global crisis in the next.

In the first subperiod, the economies of the EEC (which had been enlarged to UK, Ireland, Denmark, Greece, Spain, and Portugal) reacted to stagflation with diverse and disconnected policies, growth slowed down, inflation and unemployment rates were much higher than in previous years (although with significant differences between Germany and France and Italy). The process of convergence of productive systems was diminishing and even reversed its course in the following years; a sombre picture and a climate of pessimism were gaining ground, described by neologisms such as 'eurosclerosis' and 'eurodecline'.

However, EEC institutions were capable of reacting. First, the Group for Recovery of the European Economy (consisting of the chairmen of the six parliamentary committees on economic matters), led by Michel Albert and James Ball, was formed in the European Parliament with the aim of addressing the problem of "non Europe on the verge of non growth". The Group's final report *Towards European Economic Recovery in the 1980s* denounced the fragmentation of markets and the impotence of states, and suggested a community effectiveness multiplier, with supply-side strategies of negative integration and demand-side active policies of research, energy, and regional development.

Then, in June 1985, the Commission, chaired by the newly elected president Jacques Delors, published the *White Paper on the Completion of the Internal Market* with the proposal of abolishing by 1992 all obstacles to the free movement of goods, services, people, and capital: physical obstacles, such as administrative formalities and custom controls; fiscal obstacles, such as the huge disparities in member states' indirect taxation; and technical obstacles, such as different norms and standards implemented by member governments. Three hundred provisions for the creation of the European single market were implemented in the period following, the most important of which were the abolition and simplification of border formalities, the harmonization of technical standards of production and marketing, the liberalization of public procurement, the removal of all controls on capital movements, and the integration of capital markets. Although not all productive sectors were liberalized (most services sectors are still only partially so), the step forward was significant.

On 1 July 1987, the Single European Act (SEA) came into force (this had been approved on 28 February 1986). SEA substantially modified the Treaty of Rome, making a paradigmatic shift from common market to single market and introducing new institutional provisions. Decision-making rules within the Council were changed from unanimity to qualified majority in key matters concerning the completion of the single market, thus departing from the gentlemen's agreement that in the past had helped to bypass France's 'empty chair' strategy (the so-called 'Luxembourg compromise', which allowed a member state to continue negotiating an issue of national interest until unanimity could be reached). New powers were granted to the directly elected (since 1979) European Parliament, such as the right to veto enlargements and international agreements, and the required consent in the new cooperation procedure for passing legislation concerning the single market. The European Fund for Regional Development was created, and environmental and research policies were strengthened.

In June 1989, the chiefs of state and governments of EU member states received the Delors Report that envisaged the creation of the Economic and Monetary Union (EMU), later included in the February 1992 Maastricht Treaty, which would lead to the introduction of the euro in 1999. The year after Maastricht, a new Delors Commission white paper was published. This outlined several key aspects, still topical and urgent: the simplification of legal and fiscal frameworks; the implementation of more substantial trans-European information, energy and transport networks, to be financed through union bonds; the integrated development of small and middle-size firms; the creation of new workplaces; and the overcoming of the sub-optimal enhancement of EU human and natural resources.

The rapid acceleration and completion of the single market was aimed at fostering the productive growth of the EU economy, through increased competition, economies of scale, and the supply of a greater variety of products. Although there is no direct correlation between the completion of the single market and the growth of the EU economy (which had already recovered from the second oil shock in 1981/82 and started to grow again from the mid-1980s), it is undeniable that this decision contributed much to growth by fostering optimistic expectations for the success of European integration; these expectations fostered in their turn numerous mergers and acquisitions, and significantly increased direct investments aimed at achieving the minimum required size for EU firms successfully competing in a larger market (Guerrieri & Padoan, 1999). An indirect test of single market success was the decision taken by the remaining EFTA countries (Austria, Finland, and Sweden) to sign the agreement for the creation of the European Economic Area in 1992, and to join the EU three years later.

The end of the Cold War and the implosion of the USSR – which redesigned the new post-bipolar Europe – gave a further stimulus to the process of European integration. But it is worth emphasizing how EU institutions were capable of anticipating major political changes. The key Maastricht intergovernmental conference took place in 1991, its outcome would have been partially

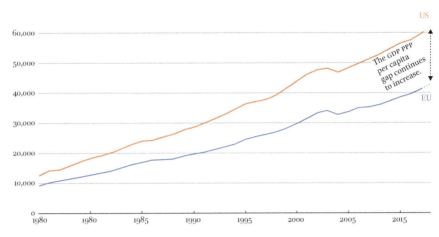

FIGURE 13.4 US vs. EU: GDP PPP per capita comparison 1980–2018
SOURCE: IMF WORLD ECONOMIC OUTLOOK, OCTOBER 2018. DATA ANALYSIS BY: MGM RESEARCH

different without this critical juncture of history; but the path toward Maastricht had already been traced.

And yet EU far-sightedness and confidence about its future were not confirmed in the 'difficult' ten years or 'lost decade' (1995–2005) following the completion of the single market. As Figure 13.4 shows, it is at that time that the gap between EU and US per capita GDP starts to grow (IMF World Economic Outlook, October 2018). This happened mainly for two reasons: first, the world market was becoming more and more competitive, as a result of the combined effect of the aggressive behaviour of great emerging economies and the skilful exploitation of the digital revolution and global finance by the US economy; and secondly, the building of the political union alongside the single market was largely incomplete and had negative implications, such as a single currency coexisting with many different national economic policies and member states keeping veto powers in strategic areas of EU decision-making. Without neglecting the first reason, we will turn our attention to the introduction of the euro and the incomplete process of integration.

5 The Choice of the Euro

The explanation given by the Delors Commission for introducing the euro is neo-functionalist, and reminds us of the spillover effect of communitarian policies: the creation of a common currency is functionally linked to the single market (instituted with the SEA) and is necessary to its success, since the pooling of member states' monetary policies into a monetary union is the only way to guarantee a stable exchange rate – and the consequent greater efficiency and lower transaction costs – that are required for the smooth functioning of the single market (according to the Mundell-Fleming macro-economic model). It was believed that it would be possible to solve in this way what Tommaso Padoa Schioppa called 'the incoherent quartet' formed by free trade, capital mobility, fixed exchange rates, and autonomous economic policies of individual states (1994).

The most persuasive interpretation of the successful negotiations for the Maastricht Treaty is, however, not economic but political: the decisive factor was the convergence between the French and German governments on a modified perception of their national interests in the face of extraordinary geopolitical changes. On the one hand, Germany wanted to obtain European consent for German reunification; on the other, France wished to guarantee European anchorage for a reunified Germany and recuperate a certain degree of control and decision-making discretion in monetary policy, which had been hegemonized by Germany (Andrews, 1993). Less convincing is Moravcsik's thesis (1998) that sees Kohl's decision on the euro as the outcome of domestic policy, more specifically as the result of a compromise between the German business community interested in having a weaker and more competitive currency and German public opinion predominantly favouring a strict anti-inflationary policy. The convergence between German and French interests was the key factor, but other factors played a role too, such as the pressure politics of large firms and banks active in the world market – although firms more oriented to the domestic market were indifferent or even hostile (Frieden and Jones, 1998), and the fact that other members states' governments wanted anti-inflationary policy to be imposed by an external authority in order to overcome domestic political opposition (Talani, 2016).

Whatever the reasons for and against the euro, the perception that benefits would outrun the costs was at the time largely predominant, to the point that, in order to meet the requirements for entry, in countries such as Italy a specific tax was accepted without much citizen protest, and in countries such as Greece were even manipulated official statistics. Later on, several early supporters changed their minds, but the original perception that benefts outrun costs has been weakened, not disproved by events (Dyson, 2012). Strong currency countries could get relevant competitive advantages, whereas weak currency countries could avoid an inflation/devaluation spiral caused by the global financial crisis. The abolition of currency exchange risks and reduced transaction costs had a positive impact on trade. Positive effects have been however unevenly distributed in the eurozone countries. The most relevant ones were concentrated in the former Deutschmark area, where both the intra-industrial trade and the synchronization of the economic cycle were strengthened, But outside this area the impact was uneven, and the single currency generated no generalized growth acceleration, or unemployment decline. What is worse, this lack of results stirred harsh conflicts between eurozone states, the northern countries blaming the southern ones, because either they do not want or cannot implement needed structural reforms, and the latter blaming the former because they impose excessive fiscal austerity.

What actually happened is that government and business in the various eurozone countries behaved quite differently, widening the productivity gap between countries such as Germany that, through a painful process of restructuring considerably increased growth and export rates, and countries such as Italy, where firms' productivity stagnated and governments did not take the opportunity provided by monetary stabilization to implement structural reforms and reduce the public debt.

Then, with the explosion of the global financial crisis in 2008 and the ensuing economic stagnation, belonging to the eurozone could no longer protect high public debt states from international financial speculation; capital funds, and other forms of portfolio investment put pressures on sovereign bonds of the most fragile states, even those in the eurozone, because the ECB had more limited powers than other central banks and could not act as a lender of last resort; as a consequence the spread between German sovereign bonds and those of the most indebted and fragile states significantly increased. The EU had to make costly bailouts (alongside those made by the IMF) of countries risking default, on condition that their governments implemented strict financial austerity policies, such as wage and pension cuts, the laying off of public employees, and reductions in welfare expenditure; policies of this kind, on the one hand avoided bankruptcy, but on the other, depressed economic growth and employment.

This is why the single currency continues to foster opposing points of view. Supporters of the euro consider it a decisive step towards a deeper economic and political integration. Although recognizing that the global crisis has made things more difficult, they continue to think that the decision to create EMU was correct, since a single currency and central bank provide a safety net for the weakest and more indebted member states and a strong stimulus for them to implement the needed structural reforms of pensions, labour market, public administration, and the judiciary system. The defenders of EMU are, however, divided over the question of priorities: the view that considers the policies of financial and fiscal austerity are more important is opposed to the view that argues that austerity should not take place at the expense of economic recovery and unemployment reduction.

Opponents of the euro think the single currency severely limits national sovereignty. But even most of those who consider the euro a mistake are persuaded that dismantling it now would imply very serious risks for the European economy in general and highly indebted eurozone countries in particular, that would suffer a strong devaluation of the national currency, high inflation, further increase in the public debt, and massive capital flight. It is estimated that the exit of one highly indebted eurozone country would not only cause immediate devaluation of between 30 per cent and 40 per cent averagefor the national currency and a high rise of debt interest rates, but also serious consequences for the countries whose banks hold sovereign bonds from the indebted country and for their exporting economies (Biasco, 2015). In the years of the long global crisis, however, critical voices became louder, maintaining that the eurozone is not an optimum currency area and is therefore not sustainable for the less competitive economies within it, as they can no longer use periodical devaluations in order to readdress trade balance deficits and have no other choice than resorting to public spending, wage cuts, and privatizations.

The sovereign debt crisis reinvigorated those advocating the renationalization of economic policies and fostered the growth of national/populist parties and movements, who oppose European political integration and blame the euro as well as Brussels and Frankfurt technocracies for economic stagnation and high unemployment. One has to distinguish, however, between parties such as Front National in France and Lega in Italy that want to get rid of the euro and parties such as Syriza in Greece and Podemos in Spain that want to change the eurozone's monetary policy but keep the euro.

The arguments of those who claim the benefits of the single currency and those who blame the costs both contain some truth. The decision to create EMU represented a necessary, although not a sufficient, step towards political union, but it was a mistake not to complement it with a banking union and common fiscal, budgetary, and financial markets regulation policies at the supranational level, sustained by effective sanctions for infringements of agreements. The reason why this coupling did not happen is easy to understand: it is difficult to convince citizens and governments of member states to accept further transfers of sovereignty without enhancing at the same time the institutions of supranational democracy, above all the European Parliament. This enhancement is necessary in spite of the strong opposition of sovereign parties and movements. In fact, without the deepening of representative democracy in a true political union, the risk exists of strengthening both the power of national/popular europhobic parties at national level and the power of non-elected technocratic elites at supranational level. But abandoning the euro would create much greater problems than keeping it.

In order to mitigate the global financial crisis – and the specific European variant of the sovereign debt crisis – EU governments have decided to strengthen intergovernmental cooperation among all member states and specifically among those belonging to the eurozone with devices such as the European Stability Mechanism, Fiscal Compact, and the Single Resolution Fund. The community model of governance has been increasingly subordinated to an intergovernmental decision-making regime. The latter relies on the assumption that integration should proceed through consensual policy coordination between member state governments within the European Council. Supranational institutions such as the Commission and the Court of Justice are still important, but they play a technical, not a decision-making, role (such as monitoring the economic performance of member states, controlling their compliance with intergovernmental decisions, implementing those decisions together with national bureaucracies, and settling disputes). To give an example, the Commission can recommend initiating a procedure against a member state running an excessive budget deficit, but only member states' finance ministers sitting in Ecofin can decide the appropriate measures, which may range from requests of information to sanctions (which are in any case subject to the will of Ecofin). Parliament has a secondary role in economic and financial matters, because national governments' heads and finance ministers have stronger legitimation than members of the European Parliament do; and this is all the more true for EMU matters, since a Parliament representing the citizens of all member states cannot decide on matters that concern only some of them.

The eurozone was born from the convergence of German and French interests, and is a compromise between a centralized monetary policy at supranational level and economic and budget policies at national level. Mostly at the initiative of Germany, the contradiction between a single currency and many national economic policies has been managed by introducing a set of rules and *ex-ante* and *ex-post* controls, in order to guarantee the coordination of formerly autonomous policies. The more difficult aspect is coordination – owing to the growing asymmetry between the 19 economies of the eurozone. The stricter the rules and controls become, the worse the negative implications are for employment and growth in the countries more severely hit by the crisis. The conflicts of interest and the lack of trust between member states with stronger economies and those with weaker ones would require a truly supranational governance, democratically accountable to the citizens of Europe, in order to facilitate necessary deals and compromises. In the absence of this, it is the German government that exercises reluctant leadership (conscious of the hostility that it implies), but the German government represents first of all German citizens, not the citizens of the whole EU, and behaves consequently.

To conclude, EMU requires that decisions are not left to technocratic elites and ministers of the most powerful member states. The problems raised by the global crisis, above all the growing productivity gap between member countries, will be solved neither by dismantling the EMU nor by relying exclusively on ECB monetary policy, but by developing common economic and fiscal policies and enhancing the institutions of EU democracy, as a counterbalance to the technocratic power of Brussels and Frankfurt. We discuss the latter question in Chapter 10, on the European political system and the former question in Chapter 14, on the management of the crisis, while in the Conclusion, we outline our proposals for reforming the EU.

CHAPTER 14

The Global Financial Crisis

1   An Interpretation of the Global Financial Crisis

There are several exhaustive accounts of the 2008 global financial crisis and the related economic stagnation. Although agreeing on the sequence of triggering events – from the real estate bubble to the Lehman Brothers default, to the generalized crisis in confidence of banks, firms, and families – the main interpretations of the crisis differ on such questions as its structural or conjunctural nature, the role of endogenous versus exogenous factors, the responsibility of various actors, and the type of domestic and international political strategies that should be implemented in order to manage the crisis and restart growth. Let us just mention the comprehensive *Final Report on the Financial Crisis* written by the National Investigation Commission of the US Congress (2011) that was established by the Fraud Enforcement and Recovery Act signed by President Obama in May 2009. The Report concludes that the crisis could have been avoided and lists a series of key causal factors: the excess of liquidity favoured by monetary authorities, the shortcomings of regulation and supervision of financial activities by government institutions, the lack of corporate governance, transparency and proper risk management in financial operations, the practice of easy credit and risky investments through such new financial products as derivative securities, the obstruction by rating agencies, and the general lowering of ethical standards. My interpretation of the crisis (in Magara, 2014) is similar to that of the Report. I will not reproduce it here, but instead will point out a few basic features.

Unlike the Asian, Mexican, and Russian crises in the 1990s, this was the first major crisis of contemporary globalization: it had structural roots; it exploded at the core of global capitalism and propagated very fast throughout the world. The interpretation of the crisis must be framed in a broader context and in a longer time perspective than is usually done, since it highlights key aspects of a 30-year phase of world capitalism (structural interdependence, unregulated growth of financial markets, inequalities and disequilibria at world level). The immediate cause was the real estate/sub-prime bubble in the United States (USA), which provoked a chain reaction affecting the widely extended and highly complex system of related financial products (mortgage back securities, collateralized debt obligations, credit default swaps, and other types of hedge fund). But the crisis developed in a context of great expansion of wealth and liquidity, and a growing financial interdependence at world level that had more distant causes: the new economic policies of privatization and deregulation starting in the early 1980s in the USA and United Kingdom and then propagating to other developed economies; the expansive monetary policy of the Federal Reserve and other central banks; excessive financial expansion (the leverage buy-out boom and the explosion in hedge funds mostly active in the derivatives sector).

The continuous expansion of credit, the unchallenged rise of shadow finance, the less and less cautious attitude of investors towards risk, the retreat of regulatory agencies, the maximization of share prices, and the windfall gains of chief executives and financial speculators were all phenomena contributing to a series of financial crises that monetary authorities seemed at first able to manage. But the 2008 crisis could not be managed – as the previous 'new economy bubble' was – through traditional monetary policy measures, and required massive injections of public money to save large financial firms from default, both in the USA and in Europe.

The crisis was the traumatic expression of the key contradiction of globalization, between increasing economic, financial, and technological interdependence, on the one hand, and continuing political fragmentation, on the other, with the consequent lack of effective global governance (Martinelli, 2005). In this sense, we can define this crisis as systemic, specifying that this term does not imply the collapse of global capitalism, since systemic crises are actually the way in which capitalism continuously transforms itself. The classics of social sciences, from Adam Smith (1776) to Karl Marx (1867), from Max Weber (1922) to John Maynard Keynes (1936), from Joseph Schumpeter (1942) to to Karl Polanyi (1944), have all argued, although in different ways, that capitalism is inherently contradictory and transforms itself periodically through processes of 'creative destruction'. Contrary to both the theorists of the market as a spontaneous order, on one side, and the theorists of the inevitable collapse of capitalism, on the other, crises are endemic in capitalist development, but do not destroy it. The crisis has not meant the end of globalized capitalism, but marked the advent of a new phase, after the previous two 30-year phases (first, *'les trente glorieuses'* from the Second World War to the early 1970s, then global capitalism from the late 1970s to 2008). The crisis does not imply a negative evaluation of the whole process of globalization either. Globalization per se can have both positive and negative consequences, in a varying mix for different countries and different social groups; but, what is needed in order to increase benefits and reduce costs for a large part of the world population is a better coordination of states' economic and social policies and regulation at global level.

The crisis was the expression of the gap between the unprecedented rate of growth of unregulated global finance and the erosion of national sovereignty that made governments' controls ineffective (with no new system of international regulation and global governance superseding them). Major disequilibria have arisen between creditor countries with fast-growing, export-led economies, high rates of savings, huge balances of trade surpluses, and reserves in dollars, such as China, as opposed to debtor countries with finance-dominated, mass consumption economies, high levels of public and private indebtedness, and a huge balance of trade deficit, such as the USA. The growth of global wealth dramatically reduced poverty in large countries such as China and India, but fostered new economic and social inequalities within national societies, both developed and developing, between privileged or protected social groups and marginalized social groups. Moreover, other tensions constantly arise from high fluctuations in energy and raw materials prices, which are stirred by the growth of demand in fast developing economies. The monetary crisis has developed in such a context.

In fact, the crisis was actually a sequence of interrelated crises (similar to the trans-species jumps of a Sars virus) that did not affect the various developed and emerging economies with the same intensity or for the same length of time. The 2008 global financial crisis provoked a strong decline in gross domestic product (GDP) in the following year, aggravating the difficulties of public finances in developed economies of the USA, the European Union, and Japan; then, starting in 2010, a series of sovereign debt crises exploded in Ireland, Portugal, Spain, Italy, and Greece, which put strong pressure on the euro; and finally, in the following years, there were negative implications for sustainable development and democracy, both social (growth of unemployment and underemployment, decline of disposable income, social uneasiness) and political (government instability, erosion of citizens' confidence in the political class and government effectiveness, growth of national/populist movements).

2 The Financial-Economic Crisis in the EU and the Predominance of the Intergovernmental Regime of Decision-making

The financial-economic crisis has been longer and harder in the EU, the more so in Southern European countries, as Figure 14.1 shows (Eurostat, 2019). Southern EU economies have not yet regained their pre-crisis real GDP level. Their difficulties are responsible for the lower GDP growth rates of the eurozone with respect to the EU as a whole: 1.9 per cent versus 2.36 per cent in 2015, 1.73 per cent versus 1.95 per cent in 2016, 2.5 per cent versus 2.6 per cent in 2017, 1.9 per cent versus 2.1 per cent in 2018, as well as for eurozone inflation rates that are at some remove from the desired 2 per cent for the EU.

The main causes of the euro crisis were not only the huge sovereign debt of countries such as Portugal and Greece, but also the current account and capital flows imbalances within the eurozone, largely due to higher competitiveness in labour cost productivity of the German economy in comparison with other member countries, and to the negative implications of the private banking sector's disequilibria (Viesti, 2015).

The financial/economic crisis, as any crisis, presented risks and opportunities: it risked the breaking up of the monetary union, and even the whole EU, but it also prompted many EU citizens and leaders to attempt to move forward with the process of political integration. These attempts – based on the argument that crisis governance would be easier in a more integrated union, where fiscal and macro-economic policies complemented the monetary union – have run into serious obstacles. On the whole, the implementation of exit strategies has been less effective and timely than it could have been, because of the EU's slow and complex intergovernmental negotiations and decision-making. But the worst has been avoided through a sequence of measures for both managing and preventing the crisis, based on the current Stability and Growth Pact and European Central Bank monetary policy.

Fiscal austerity was at the core of EU economic governance during the crisis, and still is in 2019, even at the cost of obstructing growth, reducing employment, and making the reduction of the public debt/GDP ratio more difficult (by depressing the denominator) for the most indebted member states. But awareness of these risks is growing, as well as support for a more flexible enforcement (and even a possible revision) of EU financial rules being favoured, resulting from a compromise between member states such as France and Italy that demand more effective employment and growth policies and member states such as Germany and the Netherlands that uphold a rigorous interpretation of fiscal austerity.

A clear consequence of the crisis and exit strategies has been a consolidation of the predominance of the intergovernmental method, which started with the Maastricht Treaty. The current Lisbon Treaty confirms the combination of the supranational and intergovernmental decision-making regimes decided in Maastricht. With the extension of the integration process to policies of the so-called second and third pillar – foreign and security policy, domestic affairs and justice – that are key aspects of sovereignty and that member states are very reluctant to transfer to the supranational level (as well as other sensitive economic and monetary, welfare and employment policies), the Maastricht Treaty intended to integrate the supranational method adopted for the single

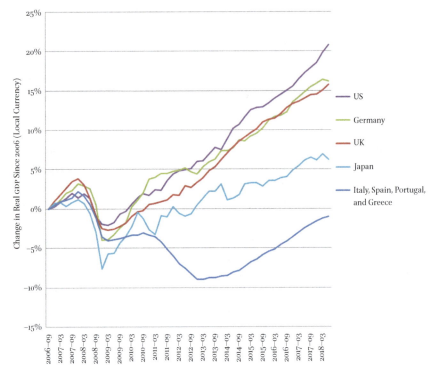

FIGURE 14.1 Real economic growth since Q3 2006
SOURCE: EUROSTAT, 2019

market with the intergovernmental method, based on the assumption that integration should proceed through voluntary and consensual coordination among the governments of member states; but actually laid the ground for the predominance of the latter. The sequence of measures aiming at managing the crisis, which we discuss below, implied a reduction in national sovereignty in financial and fiscal policy to the advantage not of community institutions such as the European Parliament (EP) and the Commission, but of intergovernmental institutions such as the Council and Ecofin.

A widely shared opinion is that the predominance of the intergovernmental method is the only possible way to take decisions in common in a union that is marked by strongly different views of integration, cleavages between old and new member states, conflicts between supporters of the single market versus supporters of a social Europe, and sovereignists versus federalists, which have become more acute during the crisis. Others scholars (Fabbrini, 2015) argue that this predominance is the outcome of a compromise between the two main member states, with France accepting the German economic paradigm of fiscal austerity (inscribed in the Fiscal Compact and related measures) and Germany accepting the French political paradigm (that favours the placing of most EU decisional power in the Council and Ecofin Fabbrini, 2015). Actually, the key reason was the shift from the European Economic Community to the European Union; somewhat paradoxically, advocates of a greater union such as Jacques Delors could achieve this goal only by granting more power to nation states in the Council.

In Maastricht, a compromise was reached that allowed the creation of the Economic and Monetary Union (EMU) through the euro and ECB, guaranteeing opting out for those member states who did not agree, a structure of variable geometry, in which supranational institutions formed by representatives of all EU member states cannot play a relevant role in decisions affecting only the eurozone. The Maastricht Treaty combined the centralization of monetary policy (which was to be exclusively controlled by the ECB) with the decentralization of economic, fiscal, and budgetary policies (which remained under the control of each national government). However, this combination had to take place within legally predefined parameters (the Protocol of the excessive deficit procedure), controlled by intergovernmental institutions (European Council and Council of Ministers), whereas the role of the Commission, the Parliament, and the European Court of Justice was downplayed. The coordination and control of domestic budgets was later institutionalized by the Stability and Growth Pact, which entered into force between July 1998 and January 1999 and was reformed in 2005. SGP rules were finalized by the Lisbon Treaty: the Treaty on the Functioning of the European Union (TFEU), art. 126.1 and 2, protocol 12, establishes that member states "shall avoid excessive government deficits and sets out the excessive deficit procedure to that effect", abiding by the Maastricht parameters, which are a yearly budget deficit not higher than 3 per cent of GDP ratio and a debt–GDP ratio not higher than 60 per cent; TFEU, art. 119 states that their economic policies should be strictly coordinated within the Union; and TFEU, art. 126 states that Ecofin approves (unanimously or with a qualified majority according to the nature of the issue) and adopts the appropriate measures to implement the agreed economic guidelines, after consulting the EP and the ECB. Actually Parliament is marginalized, and the Commission plays only a technical role, monitoring and controlling activity, as even more so are the eurozone member countries, whose finance ministers informally meet with a president elect who holds a two and half year term by a majority vote, with the participation of the ECB, but without the Parliament.

The intergovernmental method prevails also because the most important steps toward a deeper integration, such as the empowerment of the ECB, the establishment of the European Stability Mechanism (ESM), the creation of the Banking Union, have been made by eurozone states, which cannot do without it. But, as we have already remarked, heads of state and government and national ministers in the Council are more inclined to act in terms of the national interest than are Members of the EP or EU Commissioners. The democratic deficit of the European Council does not mean that its members do not have the mandate of their voters, but that the Council's legitimacy relies on a sum of mandates by separated constituencies. As a consequence, Council decisions are often felt in countries with weaker economies as imposed by the leaders of the stronger ones, in countries with stronger economies as unreasonable concessions, and in both types of countries sometimes even as decisions taken by a foreign government and implemented by technocrats who are not subject to democratic controls and are not motivated to listen to voters' demands. Hence, there is a need to rebalance the relationships between the intergovernmental and community method of decision-making and between the powers of the Council and those of the Parliament and Commission in order to increase the legitimacy of EU governance. But this rebalancing is difficult since it should be accomplished within the Council, being the very institution that would lose power in the change, whose members are heads of government afraid of sovereignist reactions in their own countries.

3   The Stages of the EU Exit Strategy

From 2010, the global financial crisis manifested itself in the EU mostly in the form of a sovereign debt crisis for the weakest EU member states, first of all Greece. It cannot be denied that the EU took many measures both to to prevent and manage the sovereign debt crisis, with a long and dense sequence of meetings and many decisions being taken since that year by the European Council and Ecofin. These measures were effective, but often too slow, costly, and with unintended negative consequences.

We can identify two stages of anti-crisis deliberations. The first, from 2010 to mid-2012, was characterized by new mechanisms of crisis management (the ESM) and increasingly stringent budgetary rules (the Fiscal Compact Treaty); the second, from the second half of 2012 to 2014, was marked by increasing disagreement among member states over growth versus fiscal austerity (with proposals to solve the contrast including the Four Presidents Report) and a focus on reforming the Stability and Growth Pact and creating the Banking

Union. The requests made by various member states, first of all Italy, to use the flexibility clauses of the SGP for exceptional reasons favoured a more pragmatic and softer interpretation of the Maastricht parameters and practical neglect of some of the constraints of the Fiscal Compact.

As far as goals are concerned, we can distinguish between measures, such as the ESM, aimed at crisis management, and measures, such as the European Semester, aimed at crisis prevention. As far as the governance method is concerned, we can observe that few decisions- the European Semester and Six Pack and Two Pack- were taken according to the community method, with the majority being taken according to the intergovernmental method.

Let us go briefly through the complex sequence of decisions. The first stage of anti-crisis deliberations took place between 2010 and mid-2012. At the Ecofin Council of 9–10 May 2010, it was decided to create the European Financial Stability Mechanism (EFSM) as a new EU legislative act. Then the 17 euro member countries of the Council 'switched hats', transforming themselves into representatives of their states in an intergovernmental conference. In this capacity, they decided to establish the European Financial Stability Facility (EFSF) outside the EU legal framework. The EFSF was not a new formal treaty, but an executive agreement that established a private company under Luxembourg law, authorized to negotiate with its 17 shareholders about how the crisis in countries at risk could be managed. The market welcomed the bonds issued by EFSF: in two years, bonds for about €200 million were issued for 25 years at moderate rates; 50 per cent of them were subscribed by the eurozone and 25 per cent by Asian countries, most by central banks and sovereign funds. On 16 December 2010, the European Council voted an amendment to TFEU, art. 136 that states "the Member States whose currency is the euro may establish a stability mechanism to be activated if indispensable to safeguard the stability of the euro area as a whole". As a result of this amendment, on 25 March 2011, the ESM was established by a European Council decision as a new treaty among the eurozone member states, endowed with its own institutions. The ESM was signed by all 27 EU member states on 2 March 2012, but had to wait for the positive decision of the German Constitutional Court and complex negotiations about its legal nature before it came into force on 12 September 2012. The ESM is a public law international organization, located in Luxembourg, which provides financial assistance to member states of the eurozone with a maximum lending capacity of €5 billion. It replaces the two previous temporary funding programmes, the EFSM and the EFSF (which continued to be concerned only with the previously approved bailout loans to Ireland, Portugal, and Greece).

In the Ecofin Council of 7 September 2010, an important crisis preventative instrument was approved: the European Semester had the aim of ex-ante coordination of the economic and budgetary policies of EU member states, in line with both the SGP and the Europe 2010 strategy. Between the two European Councils of 24–25 March 2011 and 23–24 June 2011, several other deliberations were taken. The most important of these was the Six Pack, consisting of a package of measures, adopted through the ordinary legislative procedure, that were aimed at further tightening the policy coordination required by both the European Semester and the SGP. The underwriting states committed themselves to a set of domestic reforms intended to improve their fiscal strength and competitiveness. Stronger economic policy coordination was pursued at the time with non-eurozone member states (Bulgaria, Denmark, Latvia, Lithuania, Poland, and Romania) through the Euro Plus Pact.

At the European Council of 8–9 December 2011, the increasingly worrying economic crisis prompted German Chancellor Angela Merkel and French President Nicolas Sarkozy to propose to amend the Lisbon Treaty in order to integrate member states' fiscal policies and impose automatic sanctions on member states that did not respect stringent budgetary criteria. Although it would have been possible to use the procedure of enhanced cooperation (according to TFEU, art. 32, a group of member states are allowed to advance toward deeper integration in policy areas that are not in the exclusive competence of the Union or do not concern the common foreign and security policy), it was preferred once again to adopt the form of a new intergovernmental treaty (owing to UK opposition and in order to avoid the active involvement of the Commission and Parliament that enhanced cooperation would require).

The new intergovernmental treaty, the Fiscal Compact, endowed with its own governance structure, had the aim of making the SGP parameters more rigid; it was signed by the 17 eurozone member states and all others (except the UK and the Czech Republic). The Fiscal Compact requires that all undersigning states, under strict Commission supervision and the jurisdiction of the ECJ, commit themselves to keep a balanced budget (i.e. a yearly budget deficit not higher than 3 per cent of GDP, a yearly structural deficit not higher than 0.5–1 per cent of GDP, the percentage varying in reaction to the entity of the debt, and a debt–GDP ratio not higher than 60 per cent, with the obligation to reduce one-twentieth of the excess stock every year); establishes fines up to 1 per cent of the GDP for states not complying with the rules; and requires that each member state introduces the constitutional rule of a mandatory balanced budget. The ESM and the Fiscal Compact were new intergovernmental treaties established outside the legal framework of the Lisbon Treaty. They significantly reoriented the politics of the EU. Although involving the Commission and the European Court of Justice the Fiscal Compact symbolized the predominance of the intergovernmental method and formalized the equally important – or even the more important – role of informal Euro Summits in the EU governance system. Just to give one example, to enter into force the Fiscal Compact required the approval only of a majority of 12 out of the at that time 17 eurozone states, fewer than half of the 25 EU member states at the time.

A second stage in intergovernmental cooperation aimed at coping with the economic crisis, still in the double register of deliberations of both the European Council and the Euro Group, developed in the second half of 2012, when it became clear that fiscal consolidation was not a sufficient exit strategy and that had to be integrated by effective growth measures in the whole EU in general – and specifically in a reformed EMU.

The 28–29 June 2012 European Council invited its president "to develop in close collaboration with the President of the Commission, the President of the Euro Group and the President of the ECB, a specific and time-bound road map for achieving a genuine Economic Monetary Union". A Report was presented at the 13–14 December Council (together with a more detailed *Blueprint for a Deep and Genuine Economic and Monetary Union*, 2012, prepared by the Commission on the basis of the document of the four presidents). The Report (and the Blueprint) draw the guidelines for setting an integrated financial framework (a banking union), an integrated budgetary framework (a budgetary union), an integrated economic policy framework (economic union), and, last but not least, a system of democratic legitimacy and accountability (a political union). The 'Four Presidents' Report has been defined 'the most comprehensive and strategic attempt by the European Council to identify the contours of a *de facto* euro-political union based on intergovernmental logic' (Fabbrini, 2015: 57). This is only partially true, since the Report also states that "one of the guiding principles is that democratic control and accountability should occur at the level at which decisions are taken", which "implies the involvement of the European Parliament as regards accountability taken at the European level, while maintaining the pivotal role of national parliaments, as appropriate". Fabbrini concludes that "intergovernmentalism requires interparliamentarism as its main check". Actually, there are two checks, since the role of the EP cannot be neglected, and seems even more important than that of national parliaments as the key actor in a supranational democratic accountability. The intergovernmental logic prevails, but it is once again inextricably connected with the supranational logic, and one can even perceive in the Report a timid step toward a supranational democracy.

In 2013 and 2014, the first proposal of the Report, the Banking Union, started to take shape, in order to prevent a connection between national banks and sovereign debt that threatens monetary stability (Barucci, Bassanini, & Messori, 2014). Three mechanisms were created: a Single Supervisory Mechanism

(SSM), a Single Resolution Mechanism (SRM), and a Deposit Guarantee Mechanism. Owing to the opposition of the German government, it was decided that the SSM, which entered into force in November 2013, under ECB monitoring, should concern only the main systemic banks and not the whole of the EU banking system (although it is authorized to intervene in other banks should national supervisory authorities prove unable to exercise their control). Eurozone states participate automatically, while other EU member states can request to participate as well.

It is worthwhile looking in some detail at the creation of the second mechanism, the SRM, since it highlights the conflict between the Council and Parliament over the predominance of either community method or the intergovernmental method of governance. The SRM was enacted in the double form of a regulation and an intergovernmental agreement, on the basis of a Bank Recovery and Resolution Directive approved in April 2014, after an understanding reached between the European Parliament and the Council in December 2013. On the one hand, the regulation – which was approved by the European Parliament in April 2014 and by the European Council in July 2014 – establishes uniform rules and procedures for injecting liquidity and recapitalizing credit institutions and certain types of investment funds under strict Council supervision and sets up a single resolution board, consisting of an executive director, four full-time appointed members, and the representatives of national resolution authorities, with broad powers in cases of banking disputes. On the other hand, the intergovernmental agreement instituted a Single Resolution Fund (SRF), situated outside the EU legal order, as a new intergovernmental treaty.

This decision was strongly criticized by the EP, which argued that member states do not need intergovernmental treaties to transfer funds to the EU budget, since they normally do so through the procedure of the Multinational Financial Framework. In a letter sent in February 2014 to Commission President Manuel Barroso, EP President Martin Schulz wrote: "The Commission should make use of all available means to defend the treaties and to stop the Council from setting a disastrous precedent through the adoption of an intergovernmental agreement to regulate matters that are part of a Commission proposal and on which the European Parliament has voted as co-legislator in committees and plenary"(European Parliament Documents, 2014). But the letter had no effect, and at the end of 2014, 26 member states (without the UK and Sweden) signed it. The SRF establishes the transfer and mutualization of funds from national authorities to a distinct organization with its own governing body, the Single Resolution Board, which can decide to borrow in financial markets, with the purpose of making available medium-term funding to banks. In this way, the European banking sector is subject to a dual system of governance: a system of financial supervision that applies to the EU as a whole and a banking union that applies only to eurozone member states (and all those willing to be part of it).

The concern with financial stability and member states' budgetary compliance with EU norms continued to be strong. In May 2013, two new regulations were approved (Two Pack) through the co-decision procedure, aimed at strengthening crisis prevention and crisis management with measures applicable to eurozone member states only (on the basis of TFEU, art. 136). On the basis of the Two Pack, eurozone member states are subject to a reinforced European Semester, an extended to ten-month cycle: by October, eurozone member states must publish their draft budgetary plans for the following year, by the end of November, the Commission has to make its remarks about rule complying, and by the end of the year, member states must finally adopt their budgets.

After 2014, the first signs of economic recovery in the EU together with the deepening of internal cleavages among member states fostered a discussion over the reform of the SGP and the interpretation of the Fiscal Compact, with requests by governments of the countries most affected by the crisis, such as Italy, to use the flexibility clauses of the SGP for exceptional reasons. This resulted in a more pragmatic and softer interpretation of the Maastricht parameters, a practical neglect of some of the constraints of the Fiscal Compact, and a more active role of the ECB, through the policy of quantitative easing (QE), but proposals such as the November 2015 legislative proposal by the Commission aimed at establishing a common deposits guarantee system had no result.

4 The Crucial Role of the European Central Bank

The ECB has been a crucial actor in the management of the crisis. Although lacking some of the powers of other central banks, the ECB has successfully defended the euro and protected eurozone member states, which are more exposed to the sovereign debt risk from financial speculation. Its effective measures included loans to banks at subsidized rates, a programme of unlimited buying of government bonds on the secondary market, the strategy of QE. At the Global Investment Conference in London, 26 July 2012, Mario Draghi officially declared: "Within our mandate, the ECB is ready to do whatever it takes to preserve the euro. And believe me, it will be enough". On 22 January 2015, the ECB joined other central banks in implementing QE through an asset purchase programme (APP) as part of its non-standard monetary policy measures, with the aim of supporting economic growth across the euro area and helping it to return to inflation levels below, but close to, 2 per cent. The APP – which is part of a package of measures that also includes targeted longer-term refinancing operations – expanded the ECB's existing programmes of private sector assets purchases (the asset-backed securities purchase programme and the third covered bond purchase programme) to include purchases of sovereign bonds (through the public sector purchase programme). The net purchases of public and private sector securities have put €2.28 trillion into the eurozone economy by the end of 2017, at an average rate of €60 billion a month over an initial period of 18 months. At that date, continuing economic growth in the eurozone and inflation comfortably above 1 per cent prompted some ECB policymakers to suggest winding down the programme and shifting from asset purchases to the use of interest rates to regulate the economy. But the ECB declared its intention to continue the QE programme until inflation rates were close to 2 per cent, and extended QE until the end of September 2018 at a new monthly level of €30 billion a month (starting in January 2018) and to December 2018 with bond buys at €15 billion. Then, at the end of 2018, the €2.6 trillion bond-buying programme drew to a close (although the ECB decided to reinvest funds from maturing bonds accumulated under QE in the debt market for an extended period of time).

Owing to the slowdown in the eurozone economy, the Governing Council of the ECB decided, at its monetary policy meeting held on 12 September 2109, to restart net purchases under its APP at a monthly rate of €20 billion as from 1 November 2019, expecting them to run for as long as necessary to reinforce the accommodative impact of the policy rates, and to end shortly before key ECB interest rates were raised again. The ECB also decided to continue reinvesting, in full, the principal payments from maturing securities purchased under the APP for an extended period of time past the date when key ECB interest rates started to be raised again, and in any case for as long as necessary to maintain favourable liquidity conditions and an ample degree of monetary accommodation. Moreover, the ECB decided to lower the interest rate on the deposit facility by 10 basis points to −0.50 per cent, and to leave unchanged both the interest rate on the main refinancing operations and the rate on the marginal lending facility at their current levels of 0.00 per cent and 0.25 per cent respectively (expecting these rates to remain at their present or lower levels until the inflation outlook converged on a level sufficiently close to 2 per cent), as well as taking other measures aimed at preserving favourable bank lending conditions, ensuring the smooth transmission of monetary policy and further supporting the accommodative stance of monetary policy.

ECB President Mario Draghi explained that these decisions were taken in response to the more protracted weakness of the euro area manufacturing sector, the continued shortfall of inflation, and the persistence of prominent downside risks and muted inflationary pressures. In his view, the euro area continues to be a resilient economy, but prospects for growth risks remain on the downside, owing to the prolonged uncertainties related to geopolitical factors, such as the rising threat of protectionism and vulnerabilities in emerging markets. He also affirmed that both economic and monetary analysis confirmed that an ample degree of monetary accommodation is still necessary, and that the comprehensive package of monetary policy decisions taken by the ECB aims to provide substantial monetary stimulus to ensure that financial conditions remain very favourable and support eurozone expansion, the ongoing build-up of domestic price pressures, and, therefore, the sustained convergence of inflation on the 2 per cent medium-term target. But Draghi also warned that benefits from monetary policy measures are not enough, and must be complemented by other structural policy decisions aimed at raising long-term productivity and growth potential, supporting aggregate demand, reducing structural unemployment vulnerabilities, and increasing resilience.

5 Fiscal Stringency and a Difficult Return to Economic Growth

EU regulations, the fiscal compact, and the strategy of the ECB have avoided the failure of the euro and have helped the EU economy to enter a new phase of growth, but at the cost of increasing social inequalities and disparities between member states. Monetary policy has been the only available instrument so far to guarantee liquidity to market. ECB Qunatitative Easing has had a dual positive effect: first, the reduction of the euro/dollar ratio that favoured EU exporting firms in the US market and other dollar area countries; and secondly, the contrast of deflationary trends and their depressive impact on consumption and investment.

Monetary policy alone is, however, not enough to achieve sustained economic growth. It is necessary to complement it with a policy of private and public demand, aimed at expanding consumption, first of all in trade surplus countries such as Germany – in order to rebalance macroeconomic disequilibria in the eurozone – and with an investment policy aimed at completing the internal market with infrastructure connecting the transport, energy, and telecommunication sectors and other strategic services (Micossi, 2015). On the contrary, as a consequence of fiscal austerity, public investments in the EU as a whole decreased by 17 per cent, in Italy by 33 per cent, and in other Southern

European countries by 50 per cent between 2009 and 2013. Policies that could foster economic recovery such as education research, health, environment, and public housing suffered most from the crisis. Investments reached an historical low, below 20 per cent of EU GDP. Private investments and credit declined as well, resulting in deindustrialization.

Industrial employment also declined, by 10 per cent in the EU and much more significantly in the Mediterranean countries. There are growing cleavages within the EU: unemployment and underemployment (mostly of young people and women) and risks of poverty and social exclusion are on the rise in the weakest economies, and the human development index has worsened. The policy of fiscal austerity creates a deflation risk that further reduces internal demand, and when internal demand declines even increasing export rates – fostered by low oil prices and declining euro/dollar ratios – are not enough to guarantee a stable recovery. It is true that in 2019 this situation has to some extent reversed, in the sense that domestic demand looks more resilient than export-oriented activities, which are weakened by the negative impact of protectionism and trade tensions. But the outcome is still anaemic growth; therefore, more public and private investments, first of all in the green economy, continue to be needed, mostly in surplus budget countries such as Germany.

The EU has tried to cope with the social consequences of the long crisis, including growing disparities among member states, through ambitious investments plans such as the 2000 Lisbon Strategy (that had the declared aim of transforming the EU economy into the most competitive and dynamic knowledge-based economy in the world within ten years), Europe 2020, a ten-year strategy for growth and employment, Horizon 2020, an investment programme in research and infrastructural networks, the Transeuropean network, the Connecting Europe Facility, the 2015–17 European Commission Investment Plan for Europe (or the 'Juncker Plan'). All well intended programmes that however achieved less than expected. Let us discuss in some detail Europe 2020 and the Juncker Plan.

Europe 2020 was agreed upon in 2010, acknowledging the shortcomings of the Lisbon Strategy and with the aims of finally getting out of the crisis, overcoming the weaknesses of the present growth model, and achieving clever, sustainable, and inclusive growth. The five primary goals – employment, research and development, climate and energy, education, social inclusion and poverty reduction – had to be achieved in ten years through exemplary initiatives to be taken jointly by the EU and member countries' governments in the areas of innovation, digital economy, job creation, programmes for youth, industrial policies, poverty eradication, and efficient use of resources. As usual, goals were better specified than the means to achieve them; references were made to the single market, the EU budget (which was, on the contrary, reduced for the years 2014–20 to €960 billion in financial commitments and €908.4 billion in payments, although allowing greater flexibility), the monitoring of member states' economic and public financial policies, and EU political relations with third states. In March 2014, the Commission presented its evaluation of the programme to the Council (European Commission, 2014), observing that goals had been almost achieved for education, climate, and energy, but not for employment (in spite of the funds allocated by the EU budget and the European Investment Bank for youth employment and small and medium-sized firms), research and development, and poverty reduction. The Commission's provision of an average 1.3 per cent EU growth rate in the 2010–20 GDP is well below the average 2.3 per cent rate of the pre-crisis 2001–07 period, which means that the crisis destroyed part of Europe's productive potential and that huge investments are needed in order to rebuild it.

The Juncker Plan, approved by the Council in December 2014, aimed to deal with the investment gap left as a result of the financial and economic crisis (European Commission, 2014). The Commission's agreement with the European Investment Bank (EIB), which received a guarantee of €16 billion from the EU, gave birth to a European Fund for Strategic Investments (EFSI), which was projected to mobilize around €315 billion in investments and involve 700,000 small and medium-sized companies that were set to benefit from improved access to finance. In spite of limited resources, EFSI was successful: between 2015 and 2018, 898 operations were approved, being expected to trigger €335 billion in investment across the 28 EU member states, more than the original goal of €315 billion. The European Council and the European Parliament decided to extend its duration and capacity to €500 billion by the end of 2020. The Plan also had the merit of making clear the Commission's belief that a fiscal shock was necessary to help the ECB support structural investments and enhance competition in the single market. Recalling the 'golden rule' of the June 2012 Compact for growth and jobs, it was decided that public deficits resulting from financing the Plan would be exempted from the constraints of the SGP (or at least accounted for differently from those financing consumption). A new type of regulated flexibility was thus introduced, making possible growth policies compatible with budgetary discipline. The Plan should be appreciated also for avoiding geographical earmarking; for not requiring that a member state's contribution to EFSI is necessarily matched by the Fund's investments of equal amounts in that country; and for encouraging public/private cooperation by establishing that the Plan focuses on investments of community public interest in the private sector (especially in favour of small and middle-size firms), and also able to be financed by private capital (Bruni, 2015).

The Plan is, on the other hand, open to criticism, for two primary reasons. First, it did not envisage additional resources: the €16 billion guaranteed by the EU was obtained through a reduction in other appropriations of the EU budget, including those for research. This was because of the chronic lack of resources for the EU budget, which will be solved only when the EU has the autonomous power to raise taxes and creates a European Treasury that issues eurobonds. Secondly, given the political rather than technical nature of questions such as whether to invest and how to distribute investments, the management of the Plan, instead of being given to the EIB (through a fiduciary fund), should have involved high-ranking representatives of member states' treasuries, in a kind of extended directorate or European fiscal institute – as a step toward the creation of a single EU Treasury (on the model of the European monetary institute that led to the creation of the ECB), which at first could concern only the countries of the eurozone (Maiocchi, 2015).

The negative implications of fiscal austerity are only partially neutralized by the monetary policy of QE and by investments programmes such as the ones we have discussed. Therefore, it is urgent to ensure that budgetary rules are more flexible for those low growth member states that intend to implement difficult and costly structural reforms. It is also time to acknowledge that the criteria so far adopted to assess member states' compliance with the SGP (the debt/GDP ratio and the deficit/GDP ratio) are inadequate and should be integrated with other significant criteria, such as structural surplus or deficit, private indebtedness, and export growth rates. Adding these other criteria could assure a more accurate measure of the macro-economic fundamentals of various countries, changing the evaluation of the performance of economies like Italy's and thus making possible a greater flexibility in governments' fiscal policies and public investments for growth and jobs. Finally, a better coordination of member states' industrial policies is required, which could further stimulate economic interdependence and the creation of value chains in the European industry, as argued by business interest associations in the eurozone countries.

These proposals and recommendations have been met with scepticism by all those who think they cannot be implemented until the key contradiction that is entrapping the EU is solved. Claus Offe, for instance, affirms that the road towards deeper integration is blocked by the fact that "what should be urgently done is mostly unpopular and practically impossible in a democratic context" (Offe, 2014: 20). What should be done is debt mutualization and productivity increase. But, on the one hand, a large scale and long-term mutualization of the debt, which would have strong redistributive effects between member states and among social classes, is rejected by most citizens of core

Northern European countries who have been less affected by the economic and social crisis; whereas, on the other hand, peripheral Southern European countries should pursue policies aiming at enhancing productivity and achieving compatible unit labour costs in order to make their economies more competitive and put less pressure on their public accounts, but their electorates are hostile to such policies. There is a divorce between politics and policy in the sense that policies necessary to achieve sustainable growth are neither supported by most voters of member states, nor put at the centre of EU strategy.

National/populist parties and movements in Northern EU countries – and pro-EU government parties that fear their competition in the polls – refuse to guarantee the debt of indebted countries with the money of their taxpayers. Their national/populist counterparts in the South oppose fiscal austerity and financial stability policies when they are in opposition and implement them inadequately when are in government, while pro-EU government parties are torn between compliance with EU rules and the risk of losing votes. In this situation, representative democracy is under severe stress: as we argue in Chapter 2, populist politics provides a simplified, distorted portrayal of the crisis and identifies easy scapegoats in the EU and the euro; while crucial decisions of monetary and fiscal policies are taken by supranational technical bodies (the Commission, the ECB), without adequate control and supervision by the EP, thus fuelling further the national populist protest.

The whole process of European integration is at risk. The integration crisis is the last stage in a sequence that began with the real estate subprime crisis and big US investment banks and quickly contaminated the global economy. The crisis of European integration consists of a renationalization of the culture of solidarity of the strongest EU states that impose fiscal austerity on the weakest ones in order to regain the trust of international finance; but the austerity cure risks to kill the patient, since it hinders domestic demand, restricts the tax basis, and makes the debt situation worse, thus forcing the indebted countries to depend even more on their creditors (the EU, ECB, and IMF troika). The rest of Europe cannot succeed in restoring growth without Germany, and Germany remains wedded to the austerity cure. Pro-European parties, still a robust majority in the new Parliament elected in May 2019, should therefore take a new course: an effective strategy for stimulating growth and jobs that could compensate for the negative effects of fiscal austerity (however important that might be) and a democratization of decision-making processes in EU governance.

The president of the 2019–24 Commission Ursula von der Leyen announced in her first speeches in the European Parliament a programme of policy measures aimed at revitalizing the European economy, speeding up digitalization, implementing a green deal for Europe, bringing to life the Pillar of Social Rights to life, and providing common solutions for immigration. She also pledged to strengthen European democracy by granting greater powers to Parliament and citizens vis-à-vis the governments of member countries. As we argue in more details in Chapter 11, it is an ambitious programme that can rely on the support of a three/four-party coalition (EPP, S&D, renew Europe, Greens), but that, given the strong intergovernmental character of EU governance, needs to be effective to be pursued by the European Council as well. In the Council an effective strategy to relaunch the European project will find the support of leaders such as Emmanuel Macron and most member states (first of all the largest ones, France, Italy, and Spain), but also the resistance of eurosceptic governments and the cautiousness of the German government, although the recent stagnation of the German economy fosters a changing attitude towards its huge public budget surplus (as with the already announced €60 billion plan to fight climate change). However, for the moment, the main policy decisions to help growth and employment remain those of the ECB (such as the restarting of the QE programme, announced by Draghi in September 2019 and likely to be continued by new president Christine Lagarde). But monetary policy is a necessary, not a sufficient, condition for revitalizing the European economy. The cleavage between financial austerity-minded governments and public investment-minded governments is here to stay, but a new compromise is possible based on huge public and private investments in the green economy, physical and social infrastructures, digitalization, science and technology, and on a trade-off between the flexible application of fiscal rules and the implementation of structural reforms.

Conclusion

1 External Constraints, Internal Cleavages, and Reform of the European Union

The economic and political geography of the European Union (EU) is constantly changing. In the past, many of these changes concerned the accession of new member states in a series of successive enlargement processes. At the time of writing (2019), there are five formal candidate countries: three with whom accession negotiations have begun (Serbia, Montenegro, and Turkey) and two (North Macedonia and Albania) that are still on the waiting list. Bosnia-Herzegovina and Kosovo are only potential candidates. It is highly unlikely that further enlargement is going to take place within the next few years, especially after the authoritarian turn the Turkish government has taken. Rather, after so many enlargements, the exit of the United Kingdom (UK), will represent the first, and hopefully last, 'shrinkage' of the Union.

The geopolitical order is not going to change as a consequence of the enlargement but because of internal and external dynamics. Among the external dynamics the most important new fact is certainly Trump's turnaround in American politics toward European unification: after always being in favour of a solid alliance with a strong and united Europe, under the Trump administration the United States (USA) has become an obstacle, focusing on bilateral agreements with individual countries, especially in trade matters, and trying to create division and conflicts of interests within the Union. The open support offered to the proponents of Brexit is a signal that could not be any clearer.

On the opposite front, and for different reasons, Putin's Russia does not look favourably upon the creation of an EU that is able to effectively oppose the ancient hegemonic, imperial aspirations that had begun to decline with the end of the USSR. For now, the new global powers that emerged when the bipolar order crumbled (in particular India and China), and that must now manage a multipolar order, do not yet really know whether they have to deal with a united Europe or a band of large–medium–small nations that are incapable of speaking with one voice and hence have basically no impact.

Beside the external factors, there are also internal factors at play within the Union that tend to increase rather than reduce its heterogeneity. The figures concerning public finances are perfectly clear: in 2018, the countries with the highest national debt in relation to the gross domestic product (GDP) are, in the following order: Greece, Italy, Portugal, Cyprus, Belgium, France, and Spain.

With the exception of Belgium, they are all Mediterranean countries. All other indicators, from per capita income trends to productivity, reveal a clear division between North and South that shows no sign of diminishing (despite the intervention of the Structural Funds) but rather tends to be deepening.

The Union as a whole and the subset of the 19 countries in the eurozone have survived the economic and financial crises of the past decade, but they have emerged from them with major or minor difficulties. To prevent possible future crises from undermining the foundation of the single currency, the European Stability Mechanism was established to help member states that are in serious financial difficulty. Yet the banking union could not be completed by authorizing the Central European Bank to supervise all banking systems of the individual countries, especially because of the reservation shown by Germany and Finland (which are part of the eurozone) as well as Denmark and Bulgaria (which are not).

We cannot know whether the measures taken will be able to master possible serious future financial crises that befall one or several member states of the eurozone. The risk that, when confronting upheavals brought on by new crises, short-term strategies based on the 'my country first' principle will win out is, unfortunately, realistic in a union where divergence often outdoes convergence. The short-term concerns of different countries do not tend to converge spontaneously to form a shared harmony, and in difficult situations short-term interests usually outweigh long-term concerns. Moreover, in an emergency such as the 2015 migrant crisis, when thousands of refugees, asylum seekers, or plain fortune seekers pressed against the borders, each country acted on its own, putting up barriers, barbed wire or walls, and suspended – at least partially and temporarily – free movement within the Schengen Area. Sweden and Denmark, which adopted different political migration policies, even had to reinstate border controls on the bridge that connects the two sea arms separating them.

The issue of whether or not to take in migrants has glaringly brought to the surface another deep fault line that divides the part of Europe that, for 40 years since the end of the Second World War, had remained within the orbit of the Soviet Union and the part of Europe in which the process of integration had begun. The political and cultural differences between East and West remain substantial, and it is only in the field of economy where we can discern signs of convergence. However, efforts to stop the flow of migrants, whether they come from the turbulence of the Middle East or from the African continent, do not characterize the Eastern countries alone. In the UK, the issue of migration has played a decisive role in strengthening the proponents of Brexit, and in Italy, it was a crucial factor in the formation of a government where, until the crisis of

September 2019, populist forces united with nationalist forces. In all other countries, the groups that demand a return to national sovereignty have been remarkably successful, even though they are still rather effectively kept in check, at least for the time being. In France, Emanuel Macron's victory against Marine Le Pen in the 2017 presidential election revealed that the populist wave can be stopped by offering a clear-cut European alternative. In Germany, despite the considerable approval the neo-nationalist *Alternative für Deutschland* has received, especially in the eastern part of the country, and even though it has won a large number of parliamentary seats, it does not look as if it is able to move the country in a direction away from Europe.

At this historical stage, it is difficult to make out which countries may become the 'engine' that can restart the unification process. Macron's France alone – apart from internal problems that beset him periodically – lacks the strength to pursue its vision alone (or even leading an alliance of Mediterranean countries). France seeks a dialogue with Germany, which is however more reluctant than in the past to assume the responsibility its position, size, and economy accord it almost naturally, and often prefers to side with Northern countries' financial rigour hardliners. Italy, which historically had an important role in counter-balancing the weight of the Paris–Berlin (and earlier Paris–Bonn) *entente*, has a limited room for manoeuvre, being constrained by its huge public debt and attempts to delay the task of balancing its budget.

We are doubtful about the future of the EU and its ability to reform itself. Yet the need that we take a few steps forward in order to avoid having to take even more steps back seems so obvious to us that we cannot shrink from the task of concluding our work by proposing a few lines of reform concerning both the institutions and the economic and financial policies of the EU.

Before presenting our proposals, we need to state four points:

1. The May 2019 elections to the European Parliament (EP) and the beginning of the 2019–24 European legislature bear the risk of a stalemate or of regression, but even more the opportunity for the European project to evolve further. The elections have brought more clearly to the fore the contrast between pro-European and sovereign governments that can paralyse decision-making within the EU. But the sovereign and eurosceptic parties received only slightly more than one fifth of the votes, and there continues to be a solid majority of pro-European parties, although the self-sufficient majority of popular and social democratic parties has melted away, which forces them to broaden the front that favours an ever deeper union.
2. The EU has overcome the global financial crisis and the long stagnation, although at obvious social cost; yet in the face of new crises, any response

by a single nation state would be inadequate or downright dangerous. The market power of transnational corporations and global finance, and the great political power of countries including the USA and China require the formation of a real supranational union as a counterweight, not the renationalization of political choices, because no European country, however strong, can ensure its own sovereignty all by itself.

3. We must realistically note the current state of European governance and propose a path that uses the intergovernmental method, despite the risk it contains, in order to rebalance it with an appreciation of supranational institutions. We must accept a union of two speeds (Scenario 3 in Juncker's White Paper: "Those who want more do more"), because enhanced cooperation among the countries in the eurozone allows for the implementation of necessary and urgent reforms, pending a systematic revision of the treaties, which will take more time and require more complex negotiations.

4. Our reform proposals are not meant to to outline a detailed and thorough blueprint for chenge,this will require the work of a large group of experts aimed at putting the particulars of the political will into specific action toward the completion of the Union. But we do not either limit ourselves to formulating general aspirations that do not reflect the complexities and critical issues we will encounter in the course of our argument.

2 Amending the Treaties

Some of the reforms we propose do not require a revision of the treaties that are in force and can be implemented on the basis of the provisions regarding the euro (Treaty on the Functioning of the European Union, TFEU, art. 352) and 'enhanced cooperation' as long as a significant number of member states possess the political will to implement them relatively quickly. Others, however, need the modification of existing treaties pursuant to the procedure outlined in art. 48, Treaty on the European Union (TEU), or one or more new treaties only for some countries, as was the case with the treaties that established the Economic and Monetary Union and the European Stability Mechanism. Art. 48, in fact, provides that the draft amendment be submitted by the European Parliament, the Commission, or a national government; that the European Council shall decide by majority if it is in favour of examining the proposed amendments, and if yes, that it convene a convention to prepare the draft by consensus; that it convene an Intergovernmental Conference (IGC) to approve, amend, or reject the draft unanimously; and that, finally, if it approves the draft, it also be approved by all member states according to their own legal requirements (with the safeguard clause that in the event of approval by at least four-fifths of the member states – currently 22 out of 27 – the draft be returned to the Council). The last two paragraphs, unanimity within the IGC and veto power even of a single member state, make any revision of treaties quite difficult (even though Brexit overrides what would have been a highly likely British veto)

This difficulty may be overcome in three ways: (a) guaranteeing that when the amended treaty is adopted, it contains an opt-out clause for dissenters; (b) passing a treaty within the existing treaty (based on the international Vienna Convention on the Law of Treaties); (c) agreeing on a new treaty that replaces the existing ones and provides for the withdrawal of countries that approve and those that reject the amendment, while resolving the problem of preserving the unified market for the time being. It is obvious that all these options require decidedly more time and more complex negotiations than the reforms that can be implemented under existing treaties.

Despite the difficulty and slow speed of the treaty amendment process, let us outline the key features of desirable amendments, starting with the Fundamental Law of the EU as drafted by the group of experts coordinated by Andrew Duff (2011) and approved by the Spinelli Group of the EP, whose two most important proposals we endorse: applying the procedure of co-decision by the Council and the Parliament to all legislative activities of the EU, and at the same time abolishing the veto power of the Council of Ministers. This suggested new legislative procedure (called a special procedure to distinguish it from the ordinary one) stipulates that a super-majority is needed in matters of major importance, both in the European Council and the EP. These are substantial modifications that try to rebalance the relationship between the intergovernmental method and the Community method (not the replacement of the former by the latter, which is now unrealistic) by overcoming the veto power in the Council and involving the Parliament. It would be a great step forward regarding the Union's decision-making capacity as well as its democratic legitimacy.

More specifically, the systematic proposal to amend the treaties in order to establish a new Fundamental Law for Europe should redefine the power of the institutions in the EU as follows. The current EP should become a genuine chamber of representatives who are elected according to criteria of proportionality by all European citizens on the basis of a uniform election law and unified candidacies; a pan-European electoral method would encourage the formation of genuinely European parties (which is true if the EP should give the Commission a vote of confidence, and even more so in the not very likely event that the law should provide for the direct election of the president of the

Union). The EP should be given the power of co-decision regarding all activities of the EU, including proposals to amend treaties; it should exercise democratic control over the governance of the EU; and it should be vested with powers that are typical of other democratic parliaments that it currently does not possess, always in co-decision with the Council – to wit, the power of taxation and the power to determine the amount and allocation of resources in the European budget; the power to determine its own borrowing capacity, within the limits set by the treaties, so it can make investments of European interest for which a supranational level is most adequate (the subsidiarity principle); the power to approve foreign and security policy lines in cases where the Commission does not accept the invitation to draft a specific law; the same power as the Council to appoint the president of the Commission (which it does not have today), passing a vote of confidence in the entire Commission. The EP should moreover approve with a qualified majority its own guidelines for establishing parliamentary and operating procedures. Our proposal for a fundamental reform concerning the EP is clearly eyeing a generalization of the principle of co-decision, to put it on an equal footing with the European Council.

The current European Council should preserve its character as a 'collegial presidency' of the Union and the chief political driving force, and it should continue to exercise a central governing role in such key areas as foreign and security policy, in collaboration with the Commission. The fundamental reform concerns the introduction of the principle of majority vote (both of the population and the number of member states) – either a simple, qualified, or a super-qualified majority, depending on the relevance of the issue at hand, without the unanimity requirement. Furthermore, it should become possible (as already provided in the TEU) for the European Council to nominate by qualified majority the president of the Commission as its own president. This would give the European leadership greater strength and unity (even without electing the president of the Union by direct popular vote, a very difficult option because it contradicts the character of the Council's 'collegial presidency').

The Council of Ministers should be transformed into a Senate of the Union and include members of national governments on the basis of weighted proportionality, with representatives of the respective parliaments being chosen based on their experience in the various parliamentary committees (hence constituting a highly competent second chamber). The Senate president should also be vice-president of the Union. The minutes of the meetings of the Council of Ministers should be made public within a specified time frame to ensure democratic transparency, yet without curbing the freedom of discussion in the Council's work.

The Commission should consolidate its role as government of the Union, but in collaboration with the 'collegial presidency' of the European Council, a collaboration that is facilitated and enhanced if – as we propose – the president of the Commission, who should be elected on the basis of the number of votes for his or her party in the elections for the EP (as happened for the first and only time in 2014), is also the designated president of the European Council. The president should be the head of the European government, present a legislative programme to be approved by the EP, choose his or her ministers, including the minister of foreign affairs and the minister of the treasury, and report to the two chambers of the EP.

The European Court of Justice, which currently consists of two courts, should, in its function as a constitutional court, have the power to repeal national laws that contradict the Treaties of the Union.

The participation of a democratically informed and active European citizenship should be boosted by holding referendums on the most important issues on the political agenda and the reform of electoral processes.

3   Reform Proposals under Existing Treaties

The modification of European institutions outlined above require the amendment of the treaties, and not only cannot be quickly implemented, but also, above all, must undergo a difficult approval process on the part of all member states. The most realistic option in order to strengthen the supranational union is therefore to proceed from the existing treaties (Treaty of Lisbon): first, the competencies in the chief policy areas can be expanded at the supranational level by realizing the evolutionary potential of existing treaties, first of all through the EP's full exercise of its powers (passing a budget, appointing the president and members of the Commission), with the aim of promoting sectoral authorities for common policies in the fields of energy, environment, immigration, technological development, common security, and foreign policy.

Second, the method of enhanced cooperation should be pursued by groups of member states who decide to advance in the road of supranational integration. The group of countries that is most able, as well as likely, to advance on the road toward integration is the one that consists of the 19 member states of the eurozone (and their representatives in the EP). These countries must act in concert since they are living the contradiction between a single currency, 19 sovereign debts (on which the financial markets speculate freely), and 19 fiscal and public spending systems, often in fierce competition with one another.

They must agree to complete the Economic and Monetary Union and the authority of the European Central Bank (ECB), and to step up the joint regulations where necessary (for instance in the fight against tax havens both outside and inside the EU and the eurozone), and to reduce them where not. But other members states' groups can enhance cooperation in other policy sectors, such as the institution of a single European army (which will replace the armies of the different countries, transferring to it a major part of the budgetary resources currently allocated to national defence, and will lead to more efficient European defence and reduced spending for the member states).

However, the method of enhanced cooperation must not put the single market at risk, nor bring advantages only for the citizens of the relevant countries, nor limiting citizens' democratic control. It is a pragmatic choice owing to the difficulty of achieving unanimous consensus in the struggle to achieve political union; it must anticipate choices (such as the one already made – that of establishing the ECB, and the ones yet to make – such as strengthening the autonomous budget of the Union with its own resources, which will replace some of the tax revenues of the member states rather than be added to them). We hope that these choices will gradually spread from those vanguard countries that cooperate more closely with one another to all member states.

The need to reform the Union has been reaffirmed by the President of the new Commission, Ursula von der Leyen in her first speeches to the EP, where she defined priority goals: Green Deal for Europe, digital economy, Pillar of Social Rights, defence of European core values, development of European democracy (upholding rule of law, enhancing the role of Parliament, developing citizens' participation), and highlighted the appropriate investment and regulatory frameworks to achieve them so that Europe can lead the way internationally on a range of critical issues.

Von der Leyen's Commission appears to be in a continuous line with the legacy of the most relevant statements and reform documents produced in the 2014–19 legislature by the Commission, Parliament, and Council, such as the 2015 Five Presidents Report; the Rome Declaration of EU Heads of State and Government on 25 March 2017; the Juncker Commission 2017 White Paper on the Future of Europe and the Way Forward (with its five scenarios and the proposals made in reflection papers by the five High Level Groups).

The 2015 Five Presidents Report, based on a previous analytical note prepared by the 2012 Four Presidents Report, set out a series of policies to be undertaken between 2015 and 2025, arranged under four main headings: Economic Union; Financial Union; Fiscal Union; and Democratic Accountability, Legitimacy and Institutional Strengthening. In particular, the Report puts forward actionable ideas on how to strengthen the euro and make the Economic and Monetary Union more resilient to future asymmetric shocks.

The 27 heads of state and government of the Union who reconvened in Rome on 25 March 2017, the 60th anniversary of the Treaty of Rome (EU 2017), stated that they were in fact taking "pride in the achievements of the European Union", "a unique Union with common institutions and strong values ... [that] started as the dream of a few [and] became the hope of the many", one that is the fruit of "a bold, far-sighted endeavor". Aware of the unprecedented challenges the Union must face ("regional conflicts, terrorism, growing migratory pressures, protectionism and social and economic inequalities"), they promised to make the EU "stronger and more resilient, through even greater unity and solidarity amongst us and the respect of common rules".

Unity, they declared, is "a necessity" (because it is "our best chance to influence [global dynamics] and to defend our common interests and values"), and to "act together, at different paces and intensity where necessary, while moving in the same direction, as we have done in the past, in line with the Treaties and keeping the door open to those who want to join later". They pledged to work toward (a) "a safe and secure Europe" that is determined to fight terrorism and organized crime, one in which all its citizens feel safe and can move freely, and whose "external borders are secured, with an efficient, responsible and sustainable migration policy"; (b) "a prosperous and sustainable Europe: a Union which creates growth and jobs", with a single market and currency, investments in innovations, "structural reforms and working towards completing the Economic and Monetary Union"; (c) "a social Europe: a Union ... based on sustainable growth" that "promotes economic and social progress as well as cohesion and convergence, while upholding the integrity of the internal market; a Union taking into account the diversity of national systems and the key role of social partners; a Union which promotes equality between women and men as well as rights and equal opportunities for all; a Union which fights unemployment, discrimination, social exclusion and poverty", one that offers the best education and training and that "preserves our cultural heritage and promotes cultural diversity"; (d) "a stronger Europe on the global scene" that develops existing and new partnerships, promotes stability and prosperity in other regions of the world, takes more responsibility for safety and common defence (including a defence industry) in cooperation with NATO, defends rule-based multilateralism, and promotes free and fair trade and a global climate policy. Finally, they said, "We want the Union to be big on big issues and small on small ones. We will promote a democratic, effective and transparent decision-making process and better delivery".

These are good intentions and objectives one can surely endorse, but they fail to indicate a clear and common political strategy for achieving them and risk to remain solemn words that are not translated into coherent policy choices, The Commission's White Paper and the reflection papers written by five High Level Groups, however, do offer pertinent suggestions (in particular on EU finance and social policy).

The White Paper first identifies the critical policy areas of the EU (single market and trade, economic and monetary union, migration, security and Schengen Agreement, foreign and defence policy, EU budget, plus the effective realization of the Union itself in general). During 2017, five so-called reflection papers were produced under the direction of one or two presidents, together with the pertinent commissioners, which formulated specific proposals for the relaunch of the Union for each of these critical areas: the social dimension of Europe with the proposal of a European Pillar of Social Rights, which was discussed in November at a conference in Gothenburg; the methods, rules, and tools for controlling and enhancing globalization, with respect to the Italian-led G7 summit at the end of May 2017 and the German-led G20 summit the following July; the strengthening of the eurozone in light of the Five Presidents' Report; European defence, in preparation for the conference in Prague on that controversial issue; and the budget of the Union. The results of the five working groups were summarized in the September 2017 speech by Juncker on the State of the Union.

The White Paper goes on to delineate five scenarios or courses of action, their respective impact on the above critical areas and their ability to achieve results, as well as their respective roadmap for the future. The first scenario ("Carrying on"), which foresees the continuation of 'small steps', day by day, with the consent of all, is clearly inadequate to manage crises and the post-Brexit negotiations with the UK effectively, because all decisions are in danger of being paralysed by differences among member states or of being slowed down greatly by difficult downward compromises. The second scenario ("Nothing but the single market"), which predicts the deepening of the liberalization of the market and the renationalization of some policies, amounts in fact to a return to the European Community before Maastricht, including the end of the euro, the ECB, and of the common defence and security policy, and is, realistically speaking, not acceptable to the countries of the eurozone. The third scenario ("Those who want more do more") is of a multi-speed Europe or one with a variable structure, constituting a possible compromise between the countries that want greater political integration and those who only want a single market (such as the UK prior to Brexit and the countries of Eastern Europe). The fourth scenario ("Doing less more efficiently") has a suggestive title but is rather vague in content; it probably means that the integration process should focus on a few strong objectives (trade, currency, defence) and relinquish those that are pursued with weaker forms of integration (such as the open form of coordination), which generally pertain to social policies. The fifth ("Doing much more together"), which hints at the integration of all areas and therefore constitutes a complete federal union, is the preferred option of the federalists, but today does not look very likely as it would require all member states to want it very strongly.

Since the first scenario signifies the mere continuation of the status quo and cannot properly deal with the current crises, number two and four risk the deepening of inequality and rifts between the member states and the fifth scenario will be very difficult to put into action, the preferred scenario is the third one, "Those who want more do more", that of building a multispeed Union by way of enhanced cooperation. It is the one that can bring about reform most realistically, might offer the chance to get out of the current stalemate and manage ongoing crises without exacerbating the existing differences among the member states, acknowledge existing differences, and head in a direction of federal union (without calling it that), with a hard core of member states within a wider, larger economic community. We wish to point out, however, that this is only the second best, after the fifth scenario, and indicates a route that all member states should take together. This preference seems to be shared by the leaders of the four largest countries in the EU and is reiterated – although with great caution – in the Rome document signed by all 27 member states.

The definition of the proposed working groups seems to clearly identify the policy areas in which integration is to be deepened. The relaunch will succeed if a group of countries (all or most of those in the eurozone) decide to share in a supranational union not only the regulatory policies of the single market (shared by all 27 member states) and not only the central currency and central bank (shared by the eurozone countries), but also other fundamental policy areas.

First, the recommendations regarding fiscal and budget policy on own resources made by the High Level Group, which was chaired by Mario Monti ("The future financing of the European Union", 2016): after affirming the need to undertake the budgetary reform and that of expenditures jointly in response to new priorities of contemporary Europe, the guiding principles of the reform are defined (European added value, subsidiarity, the unchanged overall fiscal burden on the EU taxpayer, synergies between national and the European budgets in achieving the EU's objectives, transparency, and readability). Specifically, the report proposes the introduction of new own resources (a financial transaction tax, a reformed value added tax, a CO_2 levy). In this way, it is possible to overcome the current system of national contributions, which intensifies tensions among the member states that are net contributors and those who receive more than they pay. Even though the report does not mention federalism, it notes that fiscal autonomy of the Union is a crucial prerequisite for ensuring its autonomy from the member states.

Second, common macroeconomic and social policies, whose implementation would be possible with the resources given directly to the federal government and finance counter-cyclical measures, strategic investments in infrastructure, research and innovation, as well as health, education, social housing policies, and other social policies such as European unemployment insurance, measures for the social integration of immigrants, and environmental and energy saving policies. The EU government should also establish a European Treasury that can issue its own bonds to finance the most important activities and allow for a partial mutualization of member states' debt.

The third group of policies to be implemented at a supranational level is that of foreign and security policy (border control, common European army, integrated intelligence system, global network of diplomatic representations).

We thus have a trove of analyses and proposals, documents and declarations that can guide the reform plans of the new Commission and the pro-Europe majority in the Council (which, however, is divided between those who, such as Emmanuel Macron's France, want to refound the European project and those who, such as Angela Merkel's Germany, prefer a gradual continuity). Yet, as we argued in Chapter 11, what elements of these proposals that are realistically feasible, given the two alternatives for the entire EU and the eurozone, depends not only on new balances that emerge from the European governance institutions following the May 2019 EP elections, but also on many other factors at European, national, global, and local level, which may mitigate or deepen the rifts and conflicts within the EU.

4 Key Decisions for Moving Forward a Greater Union

In consideration of all this, we identify the most important decisions and their order of priority, specifying whether they be carried out by all member states or only by some of them through enhanced cooperation.

The first decision of high symbolic significance is to increase the EU's tax revenues (leaving unchanged the overall fiscal burden on the EU taxpayer), which can take various forms: from new ones as a common CO_2 levy and web tax (which would be difficult to vote against even for sovereign governments) to reformed ones as a reformed value added tax and financial transaction tax

(FTT). Let's consider the last one in some detail: eleven countries of the eurozone have already decided on enhanced cooperation (even though agreement on whether the taxation of derivatives should be based on country of issue or place of residence has yet to be reached). Even if the tax rate is set at a very low level so as not to slow down the development of the European financial market, the tax revenues would suffice to ensure the issuing of Eurobonds at an adequate price to collect at least €100 to 150 billion a year; however, since the FTT is designed as a national tax, a political decision is required to allocate part of the revenues to the European budget.

But the eurozone countries should go further, implementing a partially common fiscal policy, in the sense that they must establish a strictly regulated, common corporate income tax of 10 per cent-which can contribute to independent tax revenues for the eurozone so that programmes can be enacted that stimulate growth and employment; and that the part of the corporate income tax that remains available to national governments must be uniform (another 10 per cent to be added to the percentage that goes to central government) to avoid financial competition between countries.

With independent tax revenues partly replacing those of member states (without adding to them) and the issue of Eurobonds by a European Treasury, the countries of the eurozone could establish an autonomous budget, creating a Development and Employment Fund to be managed by the Commission and controlled by the Parliament of the eurozone. It would be able to make appropriate investments in the completion of infrastructure networks and the creation of public goods (health, higher education, research and development, vocational training and instruction, green economy) in order to promote structural change within Europe's economy, build the competitive capacity of companies, and improve citizens' quality of life.

Agreement must be reached on a common macro-economic policy, first of all by eurozone countries, whereas those economic, fiscal, and budgetary policies that remain within the competence of individual countries should be co-ordinated at a supranational level based on integrated guidelines in order to prevent decisions by one member state from having a negative impact on another one.

The macro-economic strategy must be complemented by a macro-social strategy that defines the common rules and minimum standards for social policies in the areas of health, education, care, unemployment, reintegration and retraining, and minimum wages, which will continue to be the responsibility of member states.

This fiscal and spending policy must be decided and controlled by a democratically collected body, that is to say, for some policies by the existing EP and for others by a parliament of representatives of the eurozone countries (both endowed with genuine fiscal power based on the principle of no taxation without representation and vice versa). The eurozone countries' representatives could meet as a subset of the existing EP, in which decisions on these and other matters specifically concerning them are made by double majority vote (by the citizens and member states following the Swiss model). To make sure this process is coordinated with the current EP, the members of parliament elected in the other EU countries could attend meetings, but without having the right to vote. This solution is preferable to the proposal by former German Foreign Minister Joschka Fischer, among others, of forming another chamber that is made up of parliamentarians appointed by the national parliaments of the eurozone countries, a solution which would further complicate the institutional architecture of the EU.

The ECB is to be vested with the full powers granted to other central banks, including that of being the lender of last resort, which is essential to ensure fiscal stability, in the context of the democratic control exercised by the House of Representatives of the eurozone. In addition, the European Banking Union is to be fully realized. The share of the debts of the member states exceeding 60 per cent of GDP, furthermore, is to be pooled. This has already been initiated with such tools as the ECB's Outright Monetary Transactions programme, the European Stability Mechanism, and the European Debt Redemption Fund (proposed at the end of 2011 but not implemented). If the countries with the lowest debt cannot be persuaded to accept part of the debt of the countries with the highest debt, at least a single interest rate on the sovereign debt government bonds of all eurozone countries should be agreed upon.

If the EU as a whole does not proceed, or proceeds too slowly, common policies at a supranational level must be advanced using the method of enhanced cooperation in the fields of foreign policy (starting with the formation of a European army that is less expensive and more efficient than the 27 existing national armies), common security, energy, environment, immigration, and technological development (instituting authorities for the different sectors so they can be coordinated).

There is also the major issue of migration. The inability to take this on is the chief cause of the spread of the populist sovereign parties that threaten the robustness of the democratic governments in many EU countries. It is very likely that the issue will come up again as a consequence of war or climate emergencies that are going to happen in the regions beyond the south-eastern and southern borders of the EU. Who will guard the external borders, and who, how, and on the basis of what criteria will have the power to decide who can legitimately enter, stay, and settle in the territory of the Union? The solutions that were adopted with the Treaty of Dublin and with the establishment of Frontex have turned out to be completely inadequate. It was a mistake to abolish internal borders among the member states (Schengen) without making provisions for guarding the external borders together. Greece, Italy, Malta and Spain cannot take on the task of border police for the Union. On the other hand, the current Union lacks both the competencies and the resources to face a challenge that has all the signs of becoming permanent.

The issue is one of foreign policy toward the countries of origin as well as one of domestic policy that determines the right of citizenship. Currently, European citizenship is acquired by way of citizenship of a member state. It is not inconceivable that the Union can manage external border controls, organize its own camps for first asylum, manage the application of asylum standards concerning the right of asylum and refugee and asylum seeker status, establish quotas based on place of origin and characteristics of the people who want to enter, and, ultimately, decide to whom to grant citizenship even beyond national laws.

A broad consensus can be achieved concerning these proposals – and similar ones, such as those made by Notre Europe (the think tank founded by Jacques Delors in 1996), the Spinelli Group in the European Parliament (since 2010), the Glienicker Group of von Bogdandy, Calless, and von Weizsacker (2013), the New Pact for Europe Project (2013,2014), the Piketty–Rosanvallon Group (2014), the Enderlein–Pisani–Ferry Report (2014), the "Empower Citizens for the Future of Europe" Group (2019), as well as those of other groups and individual scholars with similar objectives and proposals. Clear, viable proposals must be formulated that are discussed with Europe's citizens at public events and at meetings with the political representatives in the EP and the national parliaments. The recent elections to the EP have documented the victory of the supporters of the European project over the national-populist eurosceptics and therefore constitute the precondition for a refoundation of the EU. However, consensus among public opinion groups and think tanks is not enough. What is really relevant is the attitude of the European people at large and the decisions taken by the institutions of EU governance.

As we argue in Chapter 11, the key issue of the 2019 EP elections was for the first time the future of the Union, that is, the choice of whether to build an ever closer union or return to a mere free-trade economic area. Pro-EU parties and Eurosceptics confronted each other on this issue. In the end, the former were victorious, although the decline of both the European People's Party group and the Group of Socialists and Democrats now requires an enlarged majority coalition in the EP. The upsurge of the sovereign national-populist parties did not happen, despite their success in the Visegrád Group countries and in Italy, the rise of Marine Le Pen's Front National in France, and the Alternative für Deutschland in Germany.

As usual, France and Germany are key players concerning the future of the EU, but they have switched roles, with Emmanuel Macron pressing for an EU overhaul (see the Sorbonne speech of September 2017) and Angela Merkel pursuing a more cautious strategy of change. Macron can play a key role both in the EP through France's leading position in the Renew Europe (former Alde) Group, the third party required for a majority, and in the Council owing to the country's political and military power as a permanent member of the UN Security Council and its role as a nuclear power, which traditionally counterbalances the greater economic power of Germany. But the role of Germany is also crucial.

Yet the impact on the relaunch of the EU by political events in the member states, especially the largest ones, is not limited to France and Germany. The sovereign front of Eurosceptics has not won, and it has become weaker on account of Lega's departure from the Italian government, but the governments of the Visegrád Group countries as well as a few others are against any increase in the decision-making power of the EU. On the other hand, the Northern European countries (the Scandinavian countries and Holland have produced a document in response to Macron) oppose any revision of the Stability Pact that attempts to weaken the budgetary discipline for the sake of facilitating the economic recovery, as France, Italy and Spain request. Since some countries are experiencing high political instability, the relationship between pro-EU and eurosceptic countries may change frequently, which will make internal relations in the Council – the body with the greatest power in the European government – even more complicated.

In conclusion, we must acknowledge that Europe is an ever more diversified union of countries that have different concepts of the European project owing to their own history and the strategy of their ruling classes, and that the mix of economic crisis and migration pressure deepens the rifts. Even though the outcome of the EP elections has been favourable to the pro-European forces, and even though the 27 member states are able to demonstrate unity – for example, in the difficult negotiations with the UK concerning Brexit – the refoundation that we hope for will be a process fraught with difficulties. The prospect of a multispeed Europe, which was already realized with the creation of the Monetary Union, appears to be the most feasible way to proceed. But the refoundation must involve all member states and all EU citizens. The only effective response to the ongoing crises is an authentic political union that develops democratic representative institutions along with policies that are already held in common (such as those concerning competition and the common currency) and others that are necessary, such as policies concerning taxes, migration, welfare, green economy, security, and defence, and which can effectively guard the borders of the Union. The building of this greater EU is the historical responsibility of European leaders, but requires the active involvement of all citizens in the European democracy, the development of their loyalty, and their dedication to the implementation of the joint project, which remains the greatest political ideal of Europeans of the 21st century.

Afterword

Just after editing the final version of this book, the crisis of Covid19, unexpected and unprecedented, exploded. The deep changes in European society caused by Coronavirus do not make our book already obsolete. The thorough appraisal of long term trends (identity and nationalism, universities and cities) and current developments (demography, migrations, inequalities, economic imbalances) describe the context in which the Covid19 challenges are developing. The detailed analysis of key institutional, economic and welfare reforms throw light on the constraints and opportunities of a joint response to the pandemic, and on the main political cleavages, conflicts of interests and visions among member states; particularly relevant in this respect is the critical assessment of the EU management of the previous euro crisis (in Chapter 14), together with the proposals to reform the Union under existing treaties in the Conclusion.

It is hard to predict what will the near future of the European project look like. EU member states can either try to recapture portions of their lost national sovereignty even in front of an epidemic which knows no borders, or they can decide to face the challenge pushing the integration a step forward. There are signs in both directions, but the latter attitude prevails.

As it is often the case, the crisis opens up disastrous outcomes and unexpected opportunities. What we write in the Introduction, that the EU is facing risks that threaten its very existence and that its future depends on the decisions that political leaders are able to take under the pressure of this emergency and on the support of all European citizens is even more true after Covid19 outbreak. What we write in Chapter 2 that the transfer of growing portions of national sovereignty from state level to supranational level requires a parallel transfer of commitment and loyalty from member states' citizens to the evolving supranational community and European institutions is even more true now. Covid19 is a dramatic test bench for the European project. The pandemic threatens not only the euro, but the whole Union, and at the same time opens the way toward a fullfledged political union. Let's briefly consider both threats and opportunities in the light of our book.

During the pandemic and for long time after (nobody knows how long) a serious financial, economic and social crisis is going to hit almost every country, albeit with different timing, sequence, speed and intensity. Facing very serious health emergency and very severe recession and unemployment, all governments almost at the same time are asked to act quickly, mobilizing resources to provide health systems (hospitals, doctors, health personnel and services) with the necessary facilities and to help people meeting basic needs and companies to avoid bankruptcy. Where are they going to find the money? If member states (and first of all the largest ones) do not agree to develop a large emergency financial plan to support a common effort, each member state will be forced to act alone with poor results and the risk of breaking the union. Should the crisis get out of control, should the interests rates on public debt of some countries diverge too much, should some governments be unable to keep the number of unemployed within reasonable limits, the public opinion could be strongly pushed toward anti-European and nationalistic solutions.

However some positive signs can already be observed: first of all a widespread attitude to take common action through the key institutional mechanisms and policy choices adopted to manage the financial crisis (that we discuss in Chapter 13 and 14). They are once again debated to-day, showing once again the cleavages among Northern and Mediterranean countries, with some significant continuities, but also remarkable changes. Some decisions were agreed upon by all: in a line of continuity was ECB' decision to buy further 750 billion bonds to finance member states' extraordinary expenditures for health and economic recession (ECB will buy this year a total 1,110 billion bonds beyond maturing debt refinancing), thus assuring liquidity to the market and preventing the spread between bonds to rise. A remarkable change was the Commission's decision to suspend the Stability and Growth Pact i.e. to grant member states greater freedom to stimulate their economies, also by relaxing state aid rules if the aid is intended to compensate citizens or companies affected by Coronavirus. It shows that the epidemic emergency has prompted some changes of view (even of the German dogma of zero budget deficit).

However, forgoing enforcement of our common fiscal and state aid rules is not a coordinated action at the EU level. It is just letting member states act as they see fit. It is not enough. What is necessary is to pool member states resources together for a joint response. But at this point, old cleavages and conflicts came to the fore. In fact, the other two main measures to manage the crisis, besides ECB QE and relaxing SGP rules, the large use of the European Stability Mechanism (ESM) and the issuing of "Eurobonds" have stirred heated conflict among member states. Northern countries (the Netherlands, Sweden, Denmark, Austria and, until recently, Germany) strongly oppose any financialization of the debt and are reluctant to renounce to conditional requirements of stringent budgetary rules for ESM lending. In the opposite camp, the government heads of nine Southern eurozone countries (Belgium, France, Greece, Ireland, Italy, Luxemburg, Portugal, Slovenia and Spain) signed a joint letter to Charles Michel, President of the European Council, calling for the creation of 'Coronabonds' to face the economic crisis caused by the pandemic and requesting that ESM financing is subject only to the condition that they are invested to help coping with Covid19. At the European Council meeting of 23rd April 2020, an important agreement was reached by the 27 EU heads of state and government: first, the decisions taken a few days earlier by Ecofin were confirmed: a 540 billion rescue package to start on June 1st 2020, that includes ESM 240 billion financing with the only condition that is aimed at funding healthcare systems; the Commission's 100 billion Sure program to finance national plans aimed at helping firms and workers on the model of Italy's redundancy fund; the European Investment Bank's (EIB) 200 billion loan guarantees for small and medium-sized enterprises. Second, and more important, the decision was taken to create a common EU Recovery Fund for relaunching the European economies struck by the virus, charging the Commission to work out a detailed proposal about the amount (it is estimated that about 1 trillion will be necessary), timing and targets (investments in health, research&education, the Green Deal for Europe). The key questions to be solved are how much of the funding will take the form of grants and how much the form of loans, On May 27th the Commission proposed a €750 billion recovery plan, called Next Generation EU, that would provide €500 billion in grants to countries hit hardest by the pandemic, and make another €250 billion available as loans.The rescue and recovery plan is bolted onto a revised seven-year budget proposal — the EU's Multiannual Financial Framework (MFF) — totaling €1.1 trillion for the years 2021 to 2027 and would use an unprecedented scale of joint debt incurred by the EU 27 member countries. The grants portion largely reflects the proposal put forward a week earlier by German Chancellor Angela Merkel and French President Emmanuel Macron and would allow the Commission to borrow on the financial markets, using national commitments to the EU budget as a guarantee.

The Commission also argues that new own resources -such as a digital tax, a carbon border tax or a tax on operations of large enterprises- could cover the repayment and interest costs of the entire amount of money borrowed for the recovery plan.

Although the Recovery Plan will be subject to fierce negotiation among EU heads of state and government, between the 'Southern' group of countries (first of all France, Italy, Spain) and the 'Northern' group (Austria, Denmark, the Netherlands, Sweden), the decisive step taken by Angela Merkel to come closer to the position of the first group makes likely the approval of the plan by summer (in spite of the fact that it requires unanimous approval).

As we forcibly argue in this book (and in previous writings), issuing eurobonds and linking this operation to a long-term EU budget, revamped with new own fiscal resources are two key decisions that would usher in a new, long-overdue era of greater fiscal solidarity and cooperation within a greater union.

EU countries have been caught unprepared by the dramatic crisis of Covid19, their responses have been until now less effective than needed, not because their sovereignty is limited by the Union, but, on the contrary, because the Union is still unaccomplished and not enough policy decisions are taken at the supranational level (just to make one example, the lack of a European industrial policy- that could foster European supply chains- has severely limited the availability of key drugs, health equipment and devices). There are however clear indications of a renewed spirit of European cooperation.

The challenge is very serious, prospects uncertain, the best hope to cope with the devastating consequences of Covid19 is greater integration, cooperation and solidarity among the governments and citizens of the European Union.

Bibliography

Albertini, M., 1981, *Lo stato nazionale*, Napoli, Guida.

Aldridge, A., 2000, *Religion in Contemporary World*, Cambridge, Polity Press.

Anderson, B., 1991, *Imagined Communities: Reflections on the Origins and Spread of Nationalism*, London, Verso, 2nd edition.

Andrews, D.M., 1993, "The global origins of the Maastricht Treaty on EMU: closing the window of opportunity" in A. Cafruny, G.G. Rosenthal, *The State of the European Community: the Maastricht Debate and Beyond*, Boulder, Lynne Rienner Publishers.

Armstrong, J.A., 1082, Nations before Nationalism, Chapel Hill, University of North Carolina Press.

Assman, J., 2008, *Of God and Gods: Egypt, Israel, and the Rise of Monotheism*, Madison, The University of Wisconsin Press.

Assmann, J., 1998, *Moses the Egyptian: The Memory of Egypt in Western Monotheism*, Cambridge, Mass. Harvard University Press.

Atkinson, A., 2015, *Inequality, What can be done*, Cambridge Mass. Harvard University Press.

Authority on *European* Political Parties and *European* Political Foundations, 2018, "*List of registered European Political Parties*", appf. Europa. eu *Retrieved 1 January 2018*.

Badie, B., 1995, *La fin des territoires : essai sur le désordre international et sur l'utilité sociale du respect*, Paris, Fayard.

Bagnasco, A., Le Galès, P., eds., 1997, *Villes en Europe*, Paris. La Dècouverte.

Ballas, D.D. Dorling e Hennig B., 2014, *The Social Atlas of Europe*, London, Polity Press.

Banfi, E., Grandi, N., 2003, *Lingue d'Europa. Elementi di storia e di tipologia linguistica*, Roma Carocci.

Bartolini, S., 2012, "The strange case of europarties" in E. Kulahci ed. *The Domestic Party Politics of Europeanisatiom: Actors, Patterns and Systems*, Colchester, ECPR Press.

Barucci, E., Bassanini F., Messori M., eds. 2014, *Achievements and Open Problems of the Banking Union*, Roma, Astrid.

Basso, P., Perocco, F., 2000, eds., *Immigrazione e trasformazione della società*, Milan F. Angeli.

Bauer, O., 1907, *Die Nationalitatenfrage und die Sozialdemokratie*, Wien, Verlag der Wiener Volksbuchhandlung.

Beauchemin, C., Hamel, Ch., Simon, P., eds 2016 *Trajectoires et origines: Enquête sur la diversité des populations en France*, Paris: INED.

Beck, U., e Grande E., 2006, *Cosmopolitan Europe*, Cambridge, Polity Press.

Beck, U., 2008, *Der eigene Gott. Von der Friedensfähigkeit und dem Gewaltspotential der Religionen* (English translation, 2010, *A God of One's Own: Religion's Capacity for Peace and Potential for Violence*, Cambridge, Polity Press).

Becker, J., & Jäger J., 2012, "Integration in crisis: A regulationist perspective on the interaction of European varieties of capitalism", Competition and change 16(3): 169–187.

Benjamin, W., 1997, *Charles Baudelaire. A Lyric Poet in the Era of High Capitalism*, Verso, London (German edition, 1974, *Charles Baudelaire. Ein Lyriker im Zeitalter des Hochkapitalismus*, Frankfurt/M, Suhrkamp.

Berger, P., Davie, G., Fokas, E., 2008, *Religious America. Secular Europe?*, Ashagate, Aldershot.

Bertelsmann Stiftung, 2017, *Social Justice in EU*, Berlin.

Biasco, S., 2014, "Abbiamo l'opzione di uscire dall'euro?", Il Mulino, genn. 2014.

Bieling, H.J., 2012, "EU facing the crisis: Social and employment policies in times of tight budgets", *Transfer* 18(3): 255–271.

Blondel, J., Sinnott R., Svensson P., 1998, *People and Parliament in the European Union*, Oxford, Clarendon Press.

Bourdieu, P., Passeron, J.C., 1964, *Les Héritiers. Les étudiants et la culture*, Paris Editions de Minuit, (new enlarged edition, 1985). English translation, 1979, *The Inheritors: French Students and Their Relations to Culture*, Chicago, The University of Chicago Press.

Boyer, R., 2012, The present crisis. A trump for a renewed political economy, Paris, Institut des Ameriques.

Brass, P.R., 1991, Ethnicity and Nationalism: Theory and Comparison, New Dehli, Sage.

Breen, R., ed. 2004, Social Mobility in Europe, Oxford, Oxford University Press.

Breuilly, J., 1982 (2nd edition 1993), *Nationalism and the State*, Manchester, Manchester University Press, tr.it. *Il nazionalismo e lo stato*, Bologna, Il Mulino, 1993.

Breuilly, J., 1996, "Approaches to Nationalism" in G. Balakrishnan ed. *Mapping the Nation*, London, Verso.

Broscheid, A., e D., Coen. 2006, *Lobbying Systems in the European Union: a Quantitative Study*, MPIfG Working Paper 06/3.

Bruni, F., 2015, Tra austerità, solidarietà e crescita: compromesso (im)possibile?, Ispi Commentary, 12 January 2015.

Bukodi, E., & J.K., Goldthorpe, 2018, Social Mobility and Education in Britain, Cambridge, Cambridge University Press.

Calhoun, C., 2007, Nations Matter Culture, History, and the Cosmopolitan Dream, London, Routledge.

Carr, E.H., 1945, Nationalism and After, London, Macmillan.

Cavalli, A., 2005, "Social science and European society on the making", in European Review, XIII, 3: 327–335.

Cavalli, A., & A., Martinelli, 2015 *La società europea*, Bologna, Il Mulino.

Cavalli-Sforza, L.L., 2001, *Genes, peoples and languages*, Berkeley, University of California Press.

Cerulo, K.A., 2001, "Nationalism and Expressive Forms", International Encyclopedia of the Social and Behavioral Sciences, Amsterdam, Elsevier.

Cerutti, F., E., Rudolph eds. 2001, *A Soul for Europe. On the Political and Cultural Identity of Europe*, Leuven, Peeters.

Chattergie, P., 1993, The Nations and its Fragments: Colonial and Postcolonial Histories, Princeton, Princeton University Press.

Churchill, W., 1946, Speech delivered at the University of Zurich, 19 September 1946, https://rm.coe.int/16806981f3.

Chiesi, A., 2007, "The economy" in A. Martinelli, Transatlantic Divide, Oxford, Oxford Universty Press.

Clark, B., 1983, *The Higher Education System. Academic Organization in Cross-National Perspective*, Berkeley University of California Press.

Cohn-Bendit, D., e G., Verhofstadt. 2012, *For Europe!: Manifesto for a Postnational Revolution in Europe*, CreateSpace.

Crouch, C., 1999, *Social Change in Western Europe*, Oxford, Oxford University Press.

Crouch, C., 2004, *Post-Democracy*, Cambridge, Polity Press.

Crouch. e W., Streeck eds. 1997, *Political Economy of Modern Capitalism*, Londra, Sage.

Cvajner, M., Echeverria, G., Sciortino, G., 2018, "What Do We Talk when We Talk about Migration Regimes? The Diverse Theoretical Roots of an Increasingly Popular Concept", in Pott, A., Rass, C., Wolff, F., eds., *Was ist ein Migrationsregime? What Is a Migration Regime?*, Baden VS Verlag für Sozialwissenschaften.

D'Andrea, D., 2001, "Europe and the West. The identity beyond the origin" in Cerutti, F., E. Rudolph eds. *A Soul for Europe, An Essay Collection*, Leuven, Peeters.

Delanty, G. & K. Kumar eds. 2006, The Sage Handbook of Nations and Nationalism, London,Sage.

De Mauro, T., 2014, *In Europa son già 103. Troppe lingue per una democrazia?*, Bari, Laterza.

De Swaan, A., 2001, *Words of the World. The Global Language System*, Cambridge UK, Polity Press.

Delanty, G., and K. Kumar eds. 2006, *The Sage Handbook of Nations and Nationalism*, London, Sage.

Draghi, M., 2012, Speech at the Global Investment Conference in London, 26 July 2012.

Duff, A., 2011, *Post-National democracy and the Reform of the European Parliament/La démocratie postnationale et le reforme du Parlement Européen*, Paris, Notre Europe, Policy Paper 42.

Dyson, K., 2012, "Economic and Monetary Union" in Jones E.A. Menon & S. Weatherhill eds. The Oxford Handbook of the European Union, Oxford, Oxford University Press.

Eco, U., 1993, *La ricerca della lingua perfetta nella cultura europea*, Bari Laterza. English translation, 1995, *The Search for the Perfect Language (The Making of Europe)*, Hoboken, Wiley.

Eichengreen, B., 2007, *The European Economy since 1945*, Princeton, Princeton University Press.

Eisenstadt, S.N., 1987, *European Civilization in Comparative Perspective*, Oslo, Norwegian University Press.

Eisenstadt, S.N., 2001, "The civilizational dimension of modernity. Modernity as a distinct civilization", *International Sociology*, vol. 16 No 3, Sept. 2001, pp. 320–340.

Eliot, T.S., 1948, Notes Toward the Definition of Culture, London, Faber & Faber.

Enderlein H., e J., Pisani-Ferry J., 2014, *Reforms, Investment and Growth: An Agenda for France, Germany and Europe, Report to Sigmar Gabriel (Federal Minister for Economic Affairs and Energy) and Emmanuel Macron (Minister for the Economy, Industry and Digital Affairs)*, 27 November.

Esping-Andersen, G., 1990, *The Three Worlds of Welfare Capitalism*. Princeton, NJ, Princeton University Press.

Esping-Andersen G., D., Gallie, A., Hemerijck, J., Miles, 2002, Why we need a new welfare state, Oxford, Oxford University Press.

Eurofound, 2017, *Social Mobility in the EU*, Publications Office of the European Union, Luxembourg. Report written by Ludwinek A., Anderson R., Ahrendt D., J-M. Jungblut, Leoncikas T. European Commission, 1985, *White Paper on the Completion of the Internal Market*.

European Commission, 2004, Facing the Challenge, The Lisbon Strategy for Growth and Employment (the Kok Report).

European Commission, 2012, *A blueprint for a deep and genuine economic and monetary union. Launching a european debate*, Bruxelles, 28 novembre, 2012.

European Commission, 2014, *Taking stock of the Europe 2020 Strategy*, Bruxelles.

European Commission, 2014, Investment Plan for Europe ("Juncker Plan").

European Commission, 2015, The Five Presidents Report.

European Commission, 2016, "The future financing of the European Union" (High Level Group Report).

European Commission, 2017, White Paper on the Future of Europe and the Way Forward.

European Commission, 2018, Government Expenditure in the EU, Classification of the Functions of Government (COFOG).

European Commission's Summer 2019 Economic Forecast.

European Council, 2012, *Toward a Genuine Economic and Monetary Union*, 5 dicembre 2012.

European Council, 2012, *Blueprint for a Deep and Genuine Economic and Monetary Union*.

European Council, 2017, The Rome Declaration of 25 March 2017, issued by the Heads of State or Government of the EU-27 on the occasion of the 60th anniversary of the Treaties of Rome.

Eurostat, 2019, *Real Economic Growth since Q3 2006*.

Fabbrini, F., 2010, *Compound Democracy. Why the United Statdes and Europe are becoming similar*, Oxford, Oxford University Press.

Fabbrini, S., 2015, Which European Union? Europe after the Euro Crisis, Cambridge, Cambridge University Press.

Ferrera, M., 2005, *The Boundaries of Welfare*, Oxford, Oxford University Press.

Fichte, J.G., 1807, 'Reden an die deutsche Nation' in Fichte's *Schriften zur Gesellschaftphilosophie*, Jena, Fischer.

Fontana, J., 1994, Europa ante el espejo, Barcelona, Editorial Critica.

Fourastié, J., 1979, *Les Trente Glorieuses ou la révolution invisible de 1946 à 1975*, Paris, Fayard.

Frieden, J., E., Jones 1998, "The political economy of European Monetary Union: a conceptual overview" in J. Frieden, D. Gros, E. Jones, *The New Political Economy of EMU*, Oxford, Rowman and Littlefield.

Gallie, D., & S., Paugam, 2002, "Social precarity and social integration", *Eurobarometer*, 56, 1.

Gallino, L., 2013, Il colpo di stato di banche e governi, Torino, Einaudi.

Gaonkar, D.P., ed. 2001, *Alternative Modernities*, Durham, Duke University Press.

Garelli, F., Offi, M., 1996, *Fedi di fine secolo. Paesi occidentali e orientali a confronto*, Milano, F. Angeli.

Geddes, A., 2013, Britain and the European Union, London, Macmillan.

Geertz, C., 1993, The Interpretation of Cultures: Selected Essays, Princeton, Princeton University Press.

Gellner, E., 1983, *Nations and Nationalism*, Oxford, Blackwell.

George, S., 1991, *Politics and Policy in the European Community*, Oxford, Oxford University Press.

Giddens, A., 1990, *The Consequences of Modernity*. Cambridge: Polity Press.

Giesen, B., ed. 1991, Nationale undi culturelle Identitat, Frankfurt, Suhrkamp.

Giussani, don L., 2005, *La libertà di Dio*, Milano, Marietti.

Glienicker Gruppe, 2013, Towards a Euro Union-without more integration, further crises are looming, Bruegel.org, 18 ottobre 2013.

Goio, F., 2012, "Some Reflections on Martinelli's Comparison between Nationalism in the EU and in the US", Quaderni di Scienza politica, XIX, VI, 3, December 2012.

Golini A., 2009, *Il futuro della popolazione nel mondo*, Bologna, Il Mulino.

Gozi, S., 2001, *Il governo dell'Europa*, Bologna, Il Mulino.

Grahl, J., & P., Teague, 1997, "Is the European Social Model fragmenting?" *New Political Economy* 2(3).

Greenfeld, L., 1992, *Nationalism: Five Roads to Modernity*, Cambridge MA, Harvard University Press.

Greenwood, J., e J., Dreger 2013, "Transparecy register: a European vanguard of strong lobby regulation?" *Interest Groups and Advocacy advance online publications*, 23 April 2013, http://www.palgrave-journals.com/iga/journal/v2/n2/full/iga20133a.html.

Grosby, S., 2001,"Primordiality", in A. Leoussi ed. Encycopedia of Nationalism, London, Transactions Publishers.

Guerrieri, P.P.C., Padoan, 2009, *L'economia europea*, Bologna, Il Mulino.

Haas, E.B., 1958, *The Uniting of Europe:Political, Social and Economic Forces, 1950–57*, Stanford, Stanford University Press

Haas, E.B., 1997, Nationalism, Liberalism and Progress, 2 vol. Ithaca (NY), Cornell University Press.

Habermas, J., 1985, Der philosophische Diskurs der Moderne, Frankfurt, Suhrkamp.

Hall, P., e D., Soskice eds. 2001, Varieties of Capitalism. The Institutional Foundations of Compatititve Advantage, Oxford, Oxford University Press.

Hardeman, S., Dijkstra, L., 2014, *The EU Regional Human Development Index*, European Commission, Joint Research Centre, Econometrics and Applied Statistics Unit.

Hastings, A., 1997, The Construction of Nationhood: Ethnicity, Religion and Nationalism, Cambridge, Cambridge University Press.

Hemerijck, A., 2012, *Changing Welfare States*, Oxford, Oxford University Press.

Herder, J.G., 1791, Ideen zur Philosophie der Geschichte der Menschheit, Berlin, Aufbau Verlag, 1965.

Hermann, C., 2014 "Crisis, structural reform and the dismantling of the European Social Model(s)", *Economic and Industrial Democracy*, December 17, 2014.

Hervieu-Léger, D., 1999, *La réligion en mouvement. Le pélerein et le converti*, Paris, Flammarion.

Hix, S., A., Nouri and G., Roland 2007, *Democratic Politics in the European Parliament*, Cambridge, Cambridge University Press.

Hobolt, S.B., e J., Tilley 2014, *Blaming Europe?* Oxford, Oxford University Press.

Hobsbawm, E., 2005, "Comment on Steven Grosby: the Primordia,Kinship and Nationality", in A. Ichijo & G. Uzalac eds. What is the Nation?, Cambridge, Cambridge University Press.

Hobsbawm, E., and T., Ranger eds. 1983, *The Invention of Tradition*, Cambridge, Cambridge University Press.

Horowitz, D.L., 2002 "The Primordialists" in D. Conversi ed. Ethnonationalism in the Contemporary World:Walker Connor and the Study of Nationalism, London, Routledge.

Hroch, M., 1985, *Social Preconditions of National Revival in Europe: a Comparative Analysis of the Social Composition of Patriotic Groups among the Smaller European Nations*, Cambridge, Cambridge University Press.

Huntington, S.P., 2004, Who Are We? The Challenge of America's National Identity, New York, Simon & Schuster.

Hutchinson, J., 2005, Nations as Zones of Conflict, London, Sage.

Hyman, R., 2005, "*Economic and Industrial Democracy*", December 17, 2014.

Inglehart, R., 1997, *The Silent Revolution. Changing Values and Political Styles Among Western Publics*, Princeton, Princeton University Press.

Inglehart, R., Norris, P., 2004, *Sacred and Secular: Religion and Politics Worldwide*, Cambridge University Press, Cambridge Mass.

Inglot, T., 2008, *Welfare States in East Central Europe, 1919-1994*, Cambridge, Cambridge University Press.

International Monetary Fund (IMF), 2018, World Economic Outlook, October 2018

Jaspers, K., 1947 "Vom europaeischen Geist", in J. Benda et al. eds. L'esprit européen, Neuchatel, Editions de la Boconnière.

Juncker, J.C., 2017, State of the Union.

Kautto et al. eds. 2001, *Nordic Welfare States in the European Context*, London, Routledge.

Kazepov, Y., 2005, ed., *Cities of Europe. Changing Contexts, Local Arrangements and the Challenge to Urban Cohesion*, Oxford, Blackwell.

Kedourie, E., 1960, Nationalism, Oxford, Blackwell.

Keynes, J.M., 1936, The General Theory of Employment, Interest and Money, London, Palgrave Macmillan.

Kitschelt, H., with A.J. McGann, 1995, *The Radical Right in Western Europe*, Ann Arbor, University of Michigan Press.

Kohler-Koch, B., 2000, *Network Governance Within and Beyond an Enlarged European Union*, Quebec City, Canadian European Studies Association.

Kohn, H., 1944, *The Idea of Nationalism: a Study on its Origin and Background*, New York, The Macmillan Co.

Kornai, J., 1992, The Socialist System. The Political Economy of Communism, Oxford, Clarendon Press.

Koser, K., 2007, *International Migration*, Oxford-New York, Oxford UP.

Kunisch, S., Boehm, S.A., Boppel, M., 2011, a cura di, *From Grey to Silver: Managing the Demographic Change Successfully*, Berlin-Heidelberg, Springer.

Kvist, J., 2013, "The post-crisis European social model:Developing or dismantling social investments" *Journal of International and comparative Social Policy*, 29(2): 91–107.

Lawrence, P., 2005, Nationalism:History and Theory, Harlow, Pearson Longman.

Le Galès, P., 2002, *European Cities. Social conflicts and Governance*, Oxford-New York, Oxford UP.

Leibfried, S., 2000, Social Policy in H. Wallace & W. Wallace eds. Policy-making in the European Union, Oxford, Oxford University Press.

Lengler, F., 2013, *Metropole der Moderne. Eine europaeische Stadtgeschichte nach 1850*, München, C.H. Beck.

Lijphart, A., 1999, Patterns of Democracy: Governments Forms and Performance in Thirty-Six Countries, New Haven, Yale University Press.

Lipset, S.M., e Rokkan, S., (1967). *Party Systems and Voter Alignments: Cross-National Perspectives*. New York, The Free Press.

Livi-Bacci, M., 2010, *In cammino. Breve storia delle migrazioni*, Bologna, Il Mulino.
Luft, S., 2016, *Die Flüchtlingskriese, Ursachen, Konflikte, Folgen*, München, Verlag C.H. Beck.
Magnette, P., 2005, *What is the European Union? Nature and Prospects*, Basingstoke, Palgrave Macmillan.
Majocchi, A., 2015 Comment on the Juncker Plan http://gestione.csfederalismo.it/index.php/it/pubblicazioni/commenti.
Majone, G., 1996, *Regulating Europe*, London, Routledge.
Magara, H., ed. 2014, *Economic crises and policy regimes: the dynamics of policy innovation and paradigmatic change*, chapter by A. Martinelli "A political analysis of the global financial crisis: implications for crisis governance", London, Elgar.
Mancini, F., 2000, *Democracy and Constitutionalism in the European Union*, London, Hart.
Mann, M., 1995, 'A Political Theory of nationalism and its Excesses'in S. Periwal ed. *Notions of Nationalism*, Budapest, Central European University Press.
Marks, G., 1993, "Structural policy and multi-level governance in the EC" in A. Cafruny and G. Rosenthal eds. *The State of the European Community*, vol.2, *The Maastricht Debate and Beyond*, Boulder, Lynne-Rienner, pp. 391–410.
Marshall, T.H., 1950, Citizenship and Social Class: And Other Essays, Cambridge, Cambridge University Press.
Martinelli, A., 2001 "Entrepreneurship" and "Employers' Associations", in *The International Encyclopedia of the Social and Behavioral Sciences*, Elsevier, vol. VII: 4545–4552, 4485–4489.
Martinelli, A., 2005 Global Modernization. Rethinking the Project of Modernity, London, Sage.
Martinelli, A., 2007, *Transatlantic Divide: Comparing American and European Society*, Oxford, Oxford University Press.
Martinelli, A., 2008, *La democrazia globale*, Milano, Università Bocconi Editore.
Martinelli, A., 2012, "Nationalism in the 21st Century: a European and United States Comparison", *Quaderni di Scienza politica*, anno XIX, terza serie, VI-n.3, Dicembre 2012.
Martinelli, A., 2013, *Mal di nazione. Contro la deriva populista*, Milano, Università Bocconi editore.
Martinelli, A., 2016, "Populism and the crisis of representative democracy" in A. Martinelli ed. *Beyond Trump. Populism on the Rise,* Milan, Ispi.
Martinelli, A., 2018, "National Populism and the European Union", *Populism*, volume 1. No.1, 2018: 59–71.
Martinotti, G., 1993, *Metropoli. La nuova morfologia sociale della città*, Bologna, Il Mulino.
Marx, K., (1867). *Das Kapital: Kritik der politischen Oekonomie. Volume 1: Der Produktionsprozess des Kapitals (1 ed.).* Hamburg: Verlag von Otto Meissner. DOI: 10.3931/e-rara-25773.

Mayer, M., (2016), *Germany's Response to the Refugee Situation: Remarkable Leadership or Fait Accompli?*,Washington D.C., Bertelsmann Foundation.

Mazey, S., e J., Richardson, 1993, Lobbying in the European Community, Oxford, Oxford University Press.

Mazzini, G., 1846–47, Thoughts upon Democracy in Europe, London, People's Journal.

Mendras, H., 1997, *L'Europe des Européens*, Paris, Gallimard.

Meny, Y., e Y., Surel 2000, *Par le peuple, pour le peuple*, Paris, Fayard.

Michalowitz, I., 2002, "Beyond corporatism and pluralism: towards a new theoretical framework", in A, Warleigh & J. Fairbrass eds. *Influence and Interest in the European Union: the New Politics of Persuasion and Advocacy*, London, Europe publications.

Micossi, S., 2015, "La governance europea" in Ispi Report 2015, *In mezzo al guado. Scenari globali e l'Italia*, Milano, Ispi.

Millward, A., 2000, *European Rescue of the Nation State*, 2° ediz. London, Routledge.

Mongardini, C., ed. 2001, La nascita di una coscienza europea, Roma, Bulzoni.

Moravcsik, A., 1998, *The Choice for Europe: Social Purpose and State Power from Messina to Maastricht*, Ithaca, Cornell Univ. Press.

Mosse, G.L., 1973, The Nationalization of the Masses, New York, Howard Fertig.

Motyl, A.J., 2001, Encyclopedia of Nationalism, 2 vol. San Diego,Academic Press.

Mudde, C., 2007, Populist Radical Right Parties in Europe, Cambridge, Cambridge University Press.

Muller, J.W., 2016, *What is Populism*. Philadelphia:University of Pennsylvania Press.

Münkler, H., Münkler, M., 2016, *Die neuen Deutschen: Ein Land vor seiner Zukunft*, Hamburg, RohwoltVergag.

New Pact for Europe Project, 2013, *"Strategic Options for Europe's Future"*, 1st Report.

New Pact for Europe Project, 2014, *"Towards a New Pact for Europe"*, 2nd Report.

Nida-Rümelin, J., 2017, *Über Grenzen denken, Eine Ethik der Migration*, Hamburg, Körber Stiftung.

Nora, P., 1986, *Les lieux de la memoire*, II, 1–3, *La nation*, Paris, Gallimard.

Norris, P., Inglehart, R., 2004, Sacred and Secular. Religion and Politics Worldwide, Cambridge, Cambridge UP.

Nugent, N., 2001, The Government and Politics of the European Union, Basingstoke, Plagrave Macmillan.

OECD *Economic Outlook*, various years, Paris.

Offe, C., 2003, "The European model of 'social' capitalism: Can it survive European integration?" *Journal of Political Philosophy* 11(4)

Offe, C., 2014, *L'Europa in trappola. Riuscirà la UE a superare la crisi?*, Bologna, Il Mulino.

Offe, C., e U., Preuss 2006, 'The problem of legitimacy in the European polity. Is democratisation the answer?' in C. Crouch C. & W. Streeck eds. *The Diversity of Democracy. Corporatism, Social Order and Political Conflict*, Cheltenham, Edward Elgar.

Ong, W.J., 1982, *Orality and Literacy: The Technologizing of the Word* (2nd ed. New York: Routledge, 2002).

Oltmer, J., 2016, *Globale Migration, Geschichte und Gegenwart*, Muenchen, Verlag C.H. Beck, 2nd edit.

Ozkirimli, U., 2010, *Theories of Nationalism: a Critical Introduction*, London, Palgrave Macmillan, 2nd edition.

Pace, E., 2004, *L'Islam in Europa: modelli di integrazione*, Roma, Carocci.

Pace, E., 2010, *Le religioni pentecostali*, Roma, Carocci.

Padoa Schioppa, T., 1994, *The Road to Monetary Union in Europe: the Emperor, the Kings and the Genies*, Oxford, Clarendon Press.

Padoa Schioppa, T., 2001, Europa forza gentile, Bologna, Il Mulino.

Peterson, J., e E., Bomberg 1999, *Decision-making in the European Union*, NewYork, St. Martin's Press.

Pfeifer, G., 1995, Eurolobbysmus: organisierte Interessen in der Europaeischen Union, Frankfurt, Peter Lang.

Pierson, P., ed. 2001, The New Politics of the Welfare State, Oxford,Oxford University Press.

Piketty, T., et al. 2014, *Our Manifesto for Europe*, The Guardian, My 2, 2014.

Pirenne, H., 2014, *Medieval Cities*, Princeton, Princeton UP, (1st ed., 1927).

Polanyi, K., 1944, The Great Transformation, New York, Farrar & Rinehart.

Pollack, M.A., 2005, "Theorizing the European Union: international organization, domestic polity or experiment in new governance?" Annual Review of Political Science, vol. 8, p. 357–398, June, 2005

Popper, K., 1963, *Conjectures and Refutations: the Growth of Scientific Knowledge*, London, Routledge and Kegan Paul.

Prodi, P., 2012, *Cristianesimo e potere*, Bologna, Il Mulino.

Prodi, P., 2013, *Università e città nella storia europea*, in *Università, dentro e fuori*, Bologna, Il Mulino.

Radaelli, C.M., 2003, *The Open Coordinating Method.A new Governance Architecture for the European Union?*, Stockholm, Swedish Institute for European Politics.

Recchi, E., 2018, (editor, with Adrian Favell), *Everyday Europe: social transnationalism in an unsettled continent*, Bristol, Policy Press.

Regini, M., 2011, *European Universities and the Challenge of the Market. A Comparative Analysis*, Cheltenham UK, E. Elgar.

Reif, K., E.H., Schmitt, 1980, "Nine second-order national elections", *European Journal of Political Research*, 8, 1, pp.3–44.

Renan, E., 1887, « Qu'est-ce qu'une nation? » *Discours et conférences*, Paris, Calmann-Lévy.

Renfrew, C., 1973, *Before Civilisation, the Radiocarbon Revolution and Prehistoric Europe*, London, Pimlico.

Risse, T., 2011, "The Euro between National and European identity", *Journal of European Public Policy*, online: 4 February, 2011: 487–505.

Rodrigues, M.J. ed. 2002, The New Knowledge Economy in Europe, Cheltenham, Edward Elgar.

Rokkan, S., 1970, *Citizens, Elections, Parties*, Oslo, Universitetvorlaget.

Rokkan, S., 1975, 'Dimensions of state formation and nation-building: a possible paradigm for research on variations within Europe', in C. Tilly ed. The Formation of National States in Western Europe, Princeton, Princeton University Press.

Rose, D., & Harrison, E., 2014, *Social Class in Europe: An Introduction to the European socio-economic Classification*, Routledge.

Rosselli, C., 1929, *Socialismo liberale*, Torino, Einaudi, 1979.

Rumford, C., 2002, The European Union. A Political Sociology, London, Blackwell.

Saraceno, C., 2012, *Coppie e famiglia. Non è questione di natura*, Milano, Feltrinelli.

Sassen, S., 1991, *The Global City: New York, London, Tokyo*. Princeton University Press

Scharpf, F.W. 2011, Monetary Union, Fiscal Crisis and the Preemption of Democracy, Max-Planck-Institut für Gesellschaftsforschun (MPIfG) Discussion Paper 11/11.

Schiek, D., ed. 2013, *The EU Economic and Social Model in the Global Crisis: Interdisciplinary Perspectives*, Farnham, Ashgate.

Schmitter, P., 2000, How to democratize the European Union... and why bother?, Lanham, MD, Rowman & Littlefield.

Shils, E., 1957, "Primordial, Personal, Sacred and Civil Ties", British Journal of Sociology, 8(2): 130–145.

Schraad-Tischler, D., Schiller, C., 2017, *Social Justice in EU*, Berlin, Bertelsmann Stiftung.

Schumpeter, J., 1942, Capitalism, Socialism and Democracy, New York, Harper & Brothes.

Sciortino, G., 2017, *Rebus Immigrazione*, Bologna: Il Mulino

Sieyès, E.J., 1789, *Qu'est-ce-que le Tiers Etat?*, Genève, Librairie Droz, 1970.

Smith, A., 1776, *An Inquiry into the Nature and Causes of the Wealth of Nations*, 1 (1 ed.). London: W. Strahan.

Smith, A.D., 1991, *National Identity*, London, Penguin

Smith, A.D., 2005, "The Genealogy of Nations:an Ethnosymbolic Approach" in A. Ichijo & G. Uzelac eds. When is the Nation?, London, Routledge.

Sozzi, F., 2013, '*National parties, political processes and the EU democratic deficit: the problem of Europarties institutionalization*', Working Paper Robert Schumann Centre for Advanced Studies, San Domenico di Fiesole, European University Institute.

Spinelli, A., & E., Rossi 1943, *Il Manifesto di Ventotene / The Ventotene Manifesto*, with a preface by E. Colorni., Editrice Ultima spiaggia "Sand Grains" book series by Nicola Vallinoto, July 2016 [bilingual edition in Italian and English].

Stanley & Ucen, Stanley B., & P., Ucen, 2008, *The Thin Ideology of Populism in Central and Eastern Europe: Theory and Preliminary Mapping*, unpublished.

Stone Sweet, A., Sandholtz, N. Fligstein eds. 2001, *The Institutionalization of Europe*, Oxford, Oxford University Press.

Streeck, W., 2013, *Gekaufte Zeit: Die vertagte Krise des demokratischen Kapitalismus*, Berlin, Suhrkamp (English translation, *Buying Time: The Delayed Crisis of Democratic Capitalism*, London, Verso Books).

Streeck, W., 2017, 'European Social Policy':Progressive Regression, *Keynote Address* at the Social Policy Association, Durham University, July 10–12, 2017.

Talani, L.S., 2014, *European Political Economy. Issues and Theories*, 2nd edition, Farnham, Ashgate.

Theodoropoulou, S., & A., Watt, 2011, Withdrawal symptoms: An assessment of the austerity package in Europe, Brussels, ETUI Working Paper 2011.02.

Therborn, G., 1995, European Modernity and Beyond: the Trajectory of European Societies 1945–2000, London, Sage.

Timus, N., e S., Lightfoot 2014, "Europarties:between the processes of deepening and widening", *Acta politica*, 49, pp. 1–4.

Tocqueville, A., (de), 1835–1840, *De la democratie en Amerique*, English translation *Democracy in America*, New York, Library if America.

Trabant, J., 2006, *Europäisches Sprachdenken: von Platon bis Wittgenstein*. München, Beck.

Trabant, J., 2014, *Globalesisch, oder was?: Ein Plädoyer für Europas Sprachen*, München, Beck.

Treaty on the European Union (TEU), 2007, https://eur-lex.europa.eu›resource›DOC_1.

Treaty on the Functioning of the Euopean Union (TFEU), 2007, https://eur-lex.europa.eu›legal-content›TXT.

Triventi, M., 2012, *Sistemi universitari comparati*, 2012, Milano, Bruno Mondadori.

Trow, M., 1973, *Problems in the Transition fron Elite to Mass Higher Education*, Berkeley, Carnegie Commission on Higher Education.

Tullio-Altan, C., 1995, *Ethnos e civiltà*, Milano, Feltrinelli.

UNICEF, 2014, *Levels and Trends in Child Mortality*, Report 2014, New York, United Nations Children's Fund.

Urbinati, N., 1998. "Democracy and Populism", *Constellations*, 5, no. 1 (March): 110–124.

U.S. Congress, 2011, The Financial Crisis Inquiry Report, 2011, Washington, D.C.

Van Hecke, S., 2010, "Do transnational party federations matter?(...why should we care?)", *Journal of Contemporary European Research*, 6(3), pp. 395–411.

Vaughan-Whitehead, E., ed. 2017, *The European Social Model in Crisis Is Europe Losing its Soul?*, Geneva, ILO.

Viesti, G., 2014, paper for the journal Stato e mercato Conference, Bologna, il Mulino.

Visser, J., 2006, "Union membership statistics in 24 countries", *Monthly Labor Review*, January 2006: 1–12.

Von der Leyen, U., 2019a, *A More Ambitious Union. My Program for Europe*, speech in the European Parliament, 23 July 2019.

Von der Leyen, U., 2019b, Opening statement in the European Parliament plenary, 27 November 2019.

Wallace, W., 1983, "Less than a federation, more than a regime. The community as a political system", in H. Wallace, W. Wallace, C. Webb (a cura di), *Policy-Making in the European Community*, Chichester, Wiley, pp. 403–436.

Wallerstein, I., 1980, *The Modern World-System, vol. I: Capitalist Agriculture and the Origins of the European World-Economy in the Sixteenth Century*, New York, Academic Press.

Waltz, K.N., 1979, *Theory of Interrnational Politics*, Reading, Addison. Weskey.

Walzer, M., 1992, What it Means to Be an American. Essay on the American Experience, Venice, Marsilio Pub.

Weber, M., 1930, *The Protestant Ethic and the Spirit of Capitalism* (original 1904–1905).

Weber, M., 1986, *The City*, Glencoe Ill, Free Press, (original 1920)

Weber, M., 1920, *Gesammelte Aufsätze zur Religionssoziologie*, Tübingen, Mohr [Now in Weber M., *Gesamtausgabe*, Vol. 1/19].

Weber, M., *Wirtschaft und Gesellschaft*, Tübingen: Mohr, 1922, x, 840 S. (Grundriß der Sozialökonomik; Abt. 3).

Weil, S., 1943, *Enracinement*, tr.it. *La prima radice. Preludio a una dichiarazione dei doveri verso la creatura umana*, Milano, Comunità, 1973.

Weiler, J.H.H., 1999, *The Constitution of Europe: Do the New Clothes have an Emperor? and Other Essays on European Integration*, Cambridge, Cambridge University Press.

Wilson, B.R., 1982, *Religion in sociological perspective*, Oxford-New York, Oxford University Press.

Windolf, P., *Die Expansion der Universitäten 1870–1985: Ein internationaler Vergleich*, Stuttgart: Enke Verlag, 2nd ed., 2004.

Wittrock, B., 2000, "Modernity: One, None or Many? European Origins of Modernity as a Global Condition", *Daedalus*, winter 2000.

Yuval-Davis, N., 1997, Gender and Nation, London, Sage.

Zeitlin, J., & P., Pochet eds. 2005, The Open Method of Coordination in Action. The European Employment and Social Inclusion Strategies, Bruxelles, PIE-Peter Lang.

Index

abolition of borders   39
abortion   93, 100
Academie Royale des Sciences   109
Accademia dei Lincei   109, 119
Accademia delle Scienze di Torino   110
Acceleration   130, 206, 309, 312
accountability   39, 122, 288–9, 325
ageing index   157
ageing process   157
agnosticism   91
Akademie der Wissenschaften   110
Amsterdam Treaty (1997)   215, 223, 229–30, 233, 265, 277, 288
Anabaptists   89
Anglican Churches   100
anti-colonial independence movements   53
anti-Semitism   88
army   4–5, 26, 42, 45, 342, 346, 348
assimilation   177
asylum seekers   59–61, 63, 135, 171–173, 336
atheism   91–92
austerity, fiscal   227, 240, 275–8
Authority on European Political Parties and European Political Foundations   236
automated processes   131

Baltic, languages   68
Banking Union   5, 313, 322, 325, 327, 336, 348
Basque, language   68
Berlin-Brandenburgische Akademie der Wissenschaften   110
Bertelsmann Stiftung   203
Bildung   112
Bioethics   100
birth rates   142, 146
blame shifting   65
Blut und Boden   45
Bologna Process   120
bourgeosie and working class   239
Brexit   1, 79, 135, 168, 209, 223, 240, 245–6, 249–53, 256, 261, 295, 335–6, 339, 344, 350
Buddhism   99, 103

Calvinism   89
Carbon border tax   248, 256, 354
Catharism   90
Catholic Church   27–8, 95, 102, 106, 150
Catholicism   94, 100–1
Celtic, languages   68
centre and periphery   21, 239
CERN   118
charismatic   59, 104
Charter of Fundamental Rights of EU (Nice, 2001)   31–2, 39, 215, 265
Childcare   160
children outside marriage   151–152
Christian religion   27–8
Christianity   27, 28, 88–90, 99–100, 104
Church and State   92
Cities, ancient   124–126
City-state   108, 127
civic, genealogical and cultural nationalism   46
class struggle   129
cleavage(s)   20–1, 36–7, 58, 60–2, 186, 191, 239–41, 243–4, 265, 296–7, 307, 330, 334–5, 352–3
CNR   118
CNRS   118
cohesion policy   61, 214, 231–2, 260, 297
cold war   3, 6, 37, 53, 60, 214–6, 239, 309
collegial presidency   218, 340–1
colonial expansion   77, 164
commitment   19, 39–40, 55, 58, 285, 352
Committee of European Regions   214
Common Foreign and Security Policy (CFSP, second pillar)   213–4, 228–9, 319
Communion and Liberation   100
compound democracy   217
consensual democracy   56
conspiratorial mindset   59, 64
constitutional guarantees   66
Constitutional Treaty   4, 5, 27, 212, 215–7, 232
constitutionalization of community law   209, 224
contradictions of European integration   54–5

INDEX 371

convergence between political unity and national unity   41
Coreper   219, 228
corporate governance   268, 274, 294, 316
cosmopolitanism   104, 180
Council (or Council of Ministers or Council of the Union)   218, 228
Council of General Affairs and External Relations   219
Council of Trent   109
Counter-Reformation   28, 89, 109
Creolization   69
critical mind   22, 64
Crusades   88, 90
culture industry   80, 85
Cyrillic alphabets   71

Declaratation des droits de l'homme et du citoyen   46
decolonization   165
deindustrialization   132, 265, 278, 330
Delor's Commission   221, 276, 288, 291, 308–10, 321, 349
democratic deficit   55, 62, 210, 212, 216, 241, 264, 322
demographic (asymmetries, cycle, growth, shifts, transition, trends)   13, 128, 141–2, 155–6, 164–5, 181, 212, 271–2, 281, 291
demos   16, 34, 39–40, 59, 83
dependency ratio   158
dialects   70, 74
digital communication, media   63–4, 75, 102
digital revolution, digitalization   60, 80–6, 256, 258, 303, 310, 333
diplomacy   26, 42
divorce rate   150
double matrix of European nationalism   44
dropout rate   115
dualism   189–92, 227
Dublin regulation   171, 174

early school leavers   196
East-West divide   153, 156, 194, 202
Ecofin   214, 219, 224–6, 264, 290, 314, 320–3, 354
Ecole Normale Superieure   111
Ecole Normale d'Administration   111
educational inequality   195–199

education, expenditure for   197
elderly, care for   161
Electoral Act (1976)   234
Elite universities   113
Empire   21, 26, 42, 69, 124
Employers' associations   264, 275, 286, 299
English, lingua franca   77
enlargement   4, 32, 209, 215, 220, 227–9, 243, 260, 271, 335
Enlightenment   16, 91, 95, 111
EP and Council co-decision   214–5, 222–3, 227–8, 230–3, 238, 242–3, 327, 339–40
EP prerogatives and responsibilities   223
Epidemics   129
equalty of rights and equality of opportunities   42
Erasmus Programme   13, 120, 180
Estonian, language   68
Ethics of responsibility   65
ethnicity   43, 46, 48–50, 52
ethno-symbolic   42, 50
ethnos   34, 49
ethos and epos   38, 39, 49
Eurobarometer   5, 35–6, 78
Eurobonds (union bonds)   57, 309, 332, 347, 353–4
Europe 2020   277, 288–9, 330
european army   3, 5, 342, 346, 348
European Atomic Energy Community (Euratom)   3, 213, 299
european budget   77, 233, 241, 248, 291, 326, 331–2, 344, 354
European Capitals of Culture   85
European Central Bank   57, 209, 249, 272, 306, 319327, 342
European Citizenship   3, 38–9, 76, 163, 179, 341
European citizenship   1, 3, 38–9, 76, 164, 168, 180, 341, 349
European civil society   12–13, 228
European civil wars   3, 18, 29, 54
European civilization   20, 28, 30, 38
European Coal and Steel Community (ECSC)   3, 213, 299
European Commission 2019–2024 composition   258–60
European Commission Investment Plan for Europe ('Juncker Plan')   330–1

European Commission's president   225, 238, 248–9, 296, 326
European Commission's president von der Leyen   245, 248–9, 256–8, 261, 292, 333, 342
European Council and Commission   218
European Council and Parliament co-decision   214–5, 22–3, 227–8, 230–3, 238, 242–3, 327, 329, 340
European Court of Justice   183, 208, 263, 273, 321, 341, 383
European Credit Transfer System   120
European Defence Community (EDC or CED)   3
European Economic Community (EEC)   3, 216, 297, 299, 321
European Free Trade Association (EFTA)   216, 300, 309
European Fund for Regional Development   309
European Fund for Strategic Investments (EFSI)   31
European identity   7, 15–16, 19, 40
European Investment Bank   256, 261, 331
european lieux de memoire   38
European model of Integration   10, 11, 13, 135
European Monetary Union (EMU)   214, 216, 220, 230, 232, 275–8, 280, 283, 290–3, 309, 313–5, 321, 325
European nationalism   7, 10
European Parliament   5, 88, 135, 184, 207, 223, 313
European Round Table   263
European Science Foundation   71
European Social Survey   201
European Stability Mechanism (ESM)   216, 279, 314, 322, 336, 338, 348, 353
European Trade Union Confederation (ETUC)   264
European Treasury   332, 346–7
European University Institute   121
European Value Survey   96, 98
European Youth Guarantee   292
eurosceptic parties   74, 236, 266, 249–50, 337
Euthanasia   93
Evaluation   121–122
excessive deficit procedure   321

family structures   143
family, social policies   151, 159
federal state, federalism   5, 7, 10, 33, 47, 56, 118, 135, 137, 165, 2017, 210, 220, 229, 293, 306, 317, 345–6
female roles   148
feminization   61, 272
feudal power   126
financial market   132
financial stability   259, 323, 327, 333
Finnish, language   68
fiscal austerity   227, 240, 275–8
Fiscal Compact Treaty   216, 314, 318, 321–5, 327, 329
fiscal consolidation   279, 281–2, 293, 325
fiscal crisis   137
Five Presidents Report   248, 342, 344
flexicurity   268, 277–8, 280–1, 284, 286
Fordian model   131
Foreign and Security Policy   213, 218, 227–9, 238, 249, 319, 340, 346
Foreign Policy   133
foreign workers   165
Four Presidents Report   248, 322, 325, 342
Framework Program for Research and Technological Development   16
Fraunhofer Gesellschaft   118
freedom (political)   2, 11, 22–4, 31–3, 46, 66, 126, 172, 257, 273
freedom, dignity, equality, solidarity and justice   31, 337, 350
freedom (religious)   46, 95, 103, 257
freedom of movement   40, 166, 168, 182, 213, 268
French Revolution   111
Frontex   183
future of the EU   35, 241, 2443–44

gastarbeiter   165
gender and social mobility   201–202
gender equality   203, 256–7, 269, 277
gender, division of labour   160
General Court (earlier Court of First Instance)   214, 223–5
generations and social mobility   201–202
Geneva Convention   171
German reunification   214, 284, 311
Germanic, languages   68

Global Cities Index   133
global economic interdependence   57, 61, 209, 306, 332
global finance   59, 306, 310, 318, 338
global governance   10, 217, 317–8
global modern condition   17
globalization   17, 132–133, 139
glocalism   139
Greek, language   69
Green New Deal for Europe   256, 334, 354
Gregorian University   109
ground rent   136

Habsburgs   91
harmonization   211, 264, 273–4, 276, 289, 308
healthcare   135, 157–8, 193–4, 203–4, 354
Helmholtz Gemeinschaft   118
Hindi, language   74
Hinduism   99
Hohenzollern   91
homo oeconomicus   22
household unit   142
Humboldtian Model   117
Hungarian, language   68, 72

ideal types   268, 302
identity and identification   15
IEA (International Association for the Evaluation of Educational Achievement)   196
imagined community   48
inclusion, exclusion   59, 161
Income distribution   189
Index of Social Inequality   203
India   67, 74
individualism   18, 21–5, 27–31
Indo-European, languages   68, 71
industrial relations   267, 270–1, 274, 276, 285–6
industrial revolution   26, 84, 113, 128, 239–40
industrialization   128
inequality (economic, health, housing, wealth)   185–89, 193, 195
infant mortality   155–158
infra-communitarian trade   301
infringement procedures   225, 257
inheritance taxation   189

integration (negative and positive)   57, 276, 289, 308
integration, migrants   176–178
intergovernmental method   208, 214–5, 227–9, 238, 319, 26338–9
International Monetary Fund (IMF)   187, 279, 287, 305
international relations   13, 19, 52–4, 78, 208
invented tradition   44
investiture struggle   106
Islamic religion and culture   88, 103
Islamism   105
Israel   88

Jehovah's Witnesses   98
Jesuit Order   109
Jewish culture   88, 90
Judaism   87
Juncker Commission   35, 248, 257, 258, 342

Kaiserliche Akademie der Wissenschaften   110
Keynes at home, Smith abroad   275, 299
Knowledge economy   32, 115, 278, 288, 330

labour market   132, 265
Language academies   69
languages, central and peripheral   67, 70
Latin, language   68, 69
Les trentes glorieuses   317
Liberal market economies and coordinated market economies   301–3
liberalization   189, 228, 275, 300, 305–6, 308, 344
life expectancy   193
lifelong learning   117, 197
lingua franca   77
linguistic contamination   72
linguistic policies   74–75
Lisbon strategy   4, 32, 230, 273, 275, 277–8, 284, 289, 330
Lisbon Treaty   4, 215–218, 223, 227, 230, 233, 274, 290, 319, 322, 324
loyalty   7–8, 15, 19, 39–40, 44, 46, 48–9, 55, 88, 107, 222, 01, 351, 362
Lutheranism   89

Maastricht parameters   214, 276, 280, 321, 323, 327
Maastricht Treaty (1992)   4, 33, 163, 166, 179, 213, 216, 225, 229–31, 233, 264, 266, 276, 309, 311, 319, 321
Maltese, language   68
market capitalism   25–6, 29–30
marriage institution   148
mass communication   44, 49, 70
mass literacy   69
mass universities   113, 120
maternity leave   159
Max Plank Gesellschaft   118
medieval cities   106, 124–127
medieval university   106
melting pot   9
mergers and acquisitions   302, 309
Methodism   89
metropolitan area   139
migrants integration   176–180
migration chains   176
migration movements   143
migrations and religion   102
migrations (economic, internal, political)   163, 170–1
migrations, selectivity   169
minority languages   82
mitopoiesis   15
mixed marriage   150
modern city   127
modernity   17–8, 21–6, 30–1, 41–4, 52, 99–101
modernization   16–17, 42, 91, 93, 97, 99, 155, 164, 202, 265, 276, 292–3
monotheism   87, 90
Mormonism   98
mortality rates   142, 155
multi-agency   207, 210
multi-stakeholders   55, 210–1, 232
multiculturalism   177, 182
multilevel governance   56, 212–3, 216, 227
multilingualism   72, 77
multinational corporation   132–133, 167, 180, 250, 265
multinational public space   12
multinational society   11, 182
multiple modernities   17, 25, 50
Muslims   103

nation building   6, 20, 41–3, 47, 52, 54, 239
nation plebiscite quotidien   45
Nation state   135
national populism (populist)   54, 60–3, 66, 181, 236, 240–4, 249–50, 287, 293, 313, 318, 333, 349
national sovereignty   24, 38, 48, 55–66, 299, 313, 352
nationalism and democracy   44
nationalist ideology's claims   45
nationhood   32, 42, 49
natural Law   24
NEET (Not in Employment, Education, or Training)   151, 196, 202
neo-corporatism   262
Neo-latin, languages   68
North-South divide   194, 202, 336
nursery school   160

OECD, Organisation for Economic Co-operation and Development   147, 282, 296, 305
open method of coordination   57, 211, 218, 274, 277, 287, 291
Opus Dei   101
Orthodox Churches   89, 94
Oxfam Report   185

pagan religions   87
pandemics Covid19 (Coronavirus)   353–4
parental leave   159
passions tristes de l'Europe   55
patriotism   32, 46, 57
peace   2, 4, 6, 38, 124
Pentecostalism   104
performing democracy   62
pidginization   69
Pillar of Social Rights   257, 292, 334, 344
PIRLS (Progress in International Reading Literacy Study)   196
PISA (Program for International Student Assessment)   196–197
Plurilingualism(multilingualism)   38–9, 69, 72, 75–77
Police and Judicial Cooperation in Criminal Matters (PJCC, third pillar)   213–4, 228–9, 319
political fragmentation   61, 111, 306, 317

political pluralism   36, 65, 262
polytechnic schools/universities   112, 122
polytheism   87
populism   37, 54–5, 58, 63, 66, 272, 287
post truths   64
post-democracy   212
post-Fordism   129
post-industrial age   131
pre-schooling   161
primordial ties   27, 52
privatization   304–5, 317
pro-EU parties   243, 245, 248, 258, 261, 349
Prometheus Unbound   22
promotion of science   31
Protestant Churches   100
Protestant Reformation   69, 89, 108
Protestantism   92, 94, 96, 104
publishing industry   81
Puritans   103

quadrivium   107
qualified majority   214, 218, 221, 229–31, 243, 256, 308, 321, 340

RAE (Research Assessment Exercise)   122
rankings of universities   118
rationalization   91–3
reading habits   80, 82
Recovery Fund 'Next Generation EU'   354
Referendum   4, 89
refugees   1, 24, 36–7, 40, 135, 174–6, 183–4, 245, 257, 336
regime change   60, 271, 303–4
regulation rather than rule   56, 211
regulations, directives, decisions and recommendations   217–8
regulatory agencies   211, 317
reinforced (enhanced) cooperation   4, 215, 227–8, 231–2
religion and science   92
religious education   95
religious fundamentalism   90, 99, 105
religious organization   92, 94
religious pluralism   94, 102, 104
Renaissance   19, 22, 26, 91, 125, 130
renationalization of conflict   55

representative democracy, liberal democracy   18, 27, 30, 54, 61–2, 66, 210, 212, 267–8, 271–2, 306, 313, 333
reproductive decisions   148
research and development (R&D)   290, 296, 307
research universities   18, 25, 117, 118
risk society   97
robot   131
Roma and Sinti   180
Romanticism   45–6
Royal Society   110
rule of law   19

scapegoat   59, 63–5, 212, 233
Schengen Agreement (Treaty)   4, 75, 135, 166, 182, 215
science and technology   25, 33
science (modern)   91, 93
scientific rationality   19
scientific research   25, 78, 264
Scientific Societies   109
Scientology   98
secularization   61, 91, 93–95, 97, 99
self government   126
separation of powers, division of powers   30, 66, 217, 225
serfdom   126
Shiites   103
Single European Act (SEA, 1986)   4, 213, 223, 230, 243, 276, 308
single household   143
Single market (First Pillar)   213, 228–9, 232
Single monetary policy   57, 297
Slavic, languages   72
social classes and religion   95
social dialogue   260, 264, 274, 277, 281–2, 292
Social Europe   36, 260, 264, 290–1, 320, 343
social mobility   20, 116, 177, 199–203
Social Policy Protocol (of the Maastricht Treaty)   214, 265, 277
solidarity   15, 24, 31–8, 41–2, 45, 49, 53, 88, 101, 181, 268, 270, 277, 285
sovereign debt crisis   279, 282, 319
sovereign, sovereign state(s)   20, 37, 53, 65, 207, 209–10, 239, 250, 285, 293, 320–2
Soviet Academy   110
spillover functional and political   56

Spitzen Kandidaten 248, 253
Stability and Growth Pact 256, 275, 319, 321, 353
Standard Average European (SAE) 71–72
state authority 42
structural funds 206
structural reforms 279, 283–4, 312, 332, 334, 343
student movement 120
Studium Generale 106
subjectivity 18, 21, 23–25, 27, 31
subsidiarity 214, 237, 270, 340, 345
Sunnis 103
supranational, communty method 214–5, 227–8, 230, 319, 322–3, 326, 339
sustainable development 31, 248, 304, 348

tax evasion 138
taxation systems 137
teaching universities 118
technological innovation 25, 26, 30, 300, 303, 304
temporary migrations 170
territorial imbalances 189–192
terrorism 19, 36–7, 40, 177–8, 343
thin and thick ideologies 59
Third mission of university 117
towns and country 239
trade unions 209, 262, 265–6, 268–9, 275, 299, 302
traditional media 63
translation 73–74, 81–82
transparency 57, 234–5, 237, 259, 262–3, 288, 316, 340, 345
Treaty of Rome (1957) 15, 32, 213, 222–225, 308, 343
Treaty on the European Union (TEU) 215, 338
Treaty on the Functioning of the European Union (TFEU) 215, 217, 274, 331, 338
trivium 107
Turkey 68, 132, 161, 184, 335
Turkish-Ottoman Empire 88

UNDP (United Nations Development Programme) 192
Unemployment and underemployment 62, 279, 281, 318, 330
UNESCO 74
UNICEF 155
Union of Industrial and Employers Confederations of Europe (UNICE) 263–4
United States (USA) 2, 7–8, 17, 27, 46, 78, 93, 114, 130, 141, 165, 183, 217, 240, 267, 294, 316, 335
unity through diversity 19
University Third Mission 117
Ural, languages 72
urban (development, governance, renewal) 129–30, 136–7
urbanization 128, 139
US Congress Final Report on the Financial Crisis 316
USSR 37, 141, 156–7
USSR implosion 53, 60, 309, 335

varieties of capitalism 26, 30, 240, 301, 303
Vatican Council 100
veto power(s) 222, 227, 310, 339
Visegrad group 1, 60, 64–5, 183, 349–50
Volunteering 181

Wealth distribution 189
Welfare and religion 96
welfare chauvinism 63
welfare shopping 276, 290
Welfare state model 160, 206, 267–93
Western Schism 108
White Paper on the Future of Europe and the Way Forward 248, 342, 344
world politics 47, 52, 54, 207
writing systems 71
WTO, World Trade Organization (previously GATT, General Agreement on Tariffs and Trade) 305

Xenophobic movements 180–181

Printed in the United States
By Bookmasters